INTERSECTIONS BETWEEN CORPORATE AND ANTITRUST LAW

Recent public debate on common ownership by institutional investors has brought awareness to one of the many intersections between the corporate and antitrust worlds. But the interplay between these two fields dates back to the dawn of US antitrust. This volume shines a light on the often underplayed and misunderstood connections between antitrust and corporate law and finance. It offers a multi-disciplinary perspective on highly trending issues, such as parallel equity holdings, interlocking directorships, the anticompetitive effects of certain corporate governance arrangements, and the relationships between ESG and not-for profit activities with antitrust law. This edited collection brings together leading experts from across the US, Europe, and Asia and provides a cross-border perspective on alternative policy approaches for the field. This title is also available as Open Access on Cambridge Core.

Marco Corradi is Assistant Professor at ESSEC Business School in Paris and Singapore.

Julian Nowag is Associate Professor at Lund University and Associate Researcher at the Oxford Centre for Competition Law and Policy.

GLOBAL COMPETITION LAW AND ECONOMICS POLICY

This series publishes monographs highlighting the interdisciplinary and multijurisdictional nature of competition law, economics, and policy. Global in coverage, the series should appeal to competition and antitrust specialists working as scholars, practitioners, and judges.

Intersections Between Corporate and Antitrust Law

Edited by

MARCO CORRADI

ESSEC Business School

JULIAN NOWAG

Lund University

CAMBRIDGE
UNIVERSITY PRESS

CAMBRIDGE
UNIVERSITY PRESS

Shaftesbury Road, Cambridge CB2 8EA, United Kingdom

One Liberty Plaza, 20th Floor, New York, NY 10006, USA

477 Williamstown Road, Port Melbourne, VIC 3207, Australia

314–321, 3rd Floor, Plot 3, Splendor Forum, Jasola District Centre, New Delhi – 110025, India

103 Penang Road, #05–06/07, Visioncrest Commercial, Singapore 238467

Cambridge University Press is part of Cambridge University Press & Assessment, a department of the University of Cambridge.

We share the University's mission to contribute to society through the pursuit of education, learning and research at the highest international levels of excellence.

www.cambridge.org
Information on this title: www.cambridge.org/9781108841870

DOI: 10.1017/9781108899956

First published 2023

A catalogue record for this publication is available from the British Library

Library of Congress Cataloging-in-Publication Data
NAMES: Corradi, Marco, 1977– editor. | Nowag, Julian, 1981– editor.
TITLE: Intersections between corporate and antitrust law / edited by Marco Corradi, ESSEC Business School; Julian Nowag, Lund University.
DESCRIPTION: Cambridge, United Kingdom ; New York, NY : Cambridge University Press, 2023. | Series: Global competition law and economics policy | Includes bibliographical references and index.
IDENTIFIERS: LCCN 2022032093 | ISBN 9781108841870 (hardback) | ISBN 9781108899956 (ebook)
SUBJECTS: LCSH: Antitrust law. | Corporation law.
CLASSIFICATION: LCC K3850 .I587 2023 | DDC 343.07/21–dc23/eng/20221201
LC record available at https://lccn.loc.gov/2022032093

ISBN 978-1-108-84187-0 Hardback

To all our Oxford professors, with infinite gratitude for their mentoring.

Contents

Figures

Tables

Contributors

Marco Corradi ESSEC Business School Paris and Singapore

Federico Ghezzi Bocconi University (School of Law)

Myungsu Hong College of Law, Myongji University

Carsten König University of Cologne

Ioannis Lianos President of the Hellenic Competition Commission; Chair of Global Competition, Law, and Public Policy at the UCL Faculty of Laws

Andrew P. McLean UCL Faculty of Laws

Michelle Meagher University College London – Centre for Law, Economics and Society

Yaron Nili University of Wisconsin–Madison Law School

Julian Nowag Faculty of Law, Lund University

Okeoghene Odudu Faculty of Law, Fellow in Law, Emmanuel College, University of Cambridge

Chiara Picciau Department of Law, University of Brescia

Edward B. Rock NYU Law School

Daniel L. Rubinfeld NYU Law School; UC Berkeley

Martin C. Schmalz Saïd Business School, University of Oxford

Martin Schunke Senior Associate, Hogan Lovells, Munich

Florence Thépot University of Strasbourg

Anna Tzanaki Department of Law, Lund University

Mareike Walter Attorney at Law and Former Associate of Hogan Lovells, Munich

Ramsi A. Woodcock University of Kentucky Rosenberg College of Law; University of Kentucky Gatton College of Business and Economics

Acknowledgements

The University of Oxford is the place where we met and without which our discussions about the interactions between antitrust and corporate law would never have happened. We are grateful to all those who generously supported our research: professors, librarians, university and college staff and last but not least all our friends.

We would like to thank Rica Papa for her excellent editing and research support.

We are also grateful to the Ragnar Söderbergs Stiftelse whose support helped both of us at different times to reduce our teaching load and focus on this research.

Introduction

This book is the fruit of longstanding conversations between the two editors. These conversations prompted them to organise a conference in Lund in 2018 and then to edit this publication. This book collects part of the proceedings of the conference; it equally includes some additional research.

Although the idea of this publication emerged from the interplay between two *legal* fields, company/corporate[1] and competition/antitrust[2] law, such interaction is extremely complex and encompasses vast areas of research that lay well beyond classical legal hermeneutics. Historical, economic, and political variables shape the understanding of the intersection between corporate and competition law: an intersection which academics have just started to explore and which this book aims to foster.

In fact, this edited collection of contributions by leading academics in the field is motivated by the presence of a gap in the academic literature. On the one hand, in major corporate restructurings such as M&A and spin-offs, competition and corporate law practitioners often work shoulder-to-shoulder. On the other hand, they tend to operate within separate spheres of knowledge. Such separation is often clear also within the same law firm, as distinct advisory teams are formed, being well-identifiable by their sectorial competence. It is therefore not surprising that the actual interaction between such advisory teams is often limited to little more than ensuring that relevant information is passed on. There are also other corporate operations which may carry antitrust implications – such as acquisitions of minority equity holdings and certain forms of earnout mergers – where the interplay between corporate law and competition law is not always perceived as relevant from a practical perspective and is scarcely analysed in legal research.

1 The terms corporate and company law are normally used interchangeably, while the first is normally employed in the US and the second in the UK and in the Commonwealth.

2 The terms competition and antitrust law are used interchangeably. Although there might be specific connotation when using one or the other, here they mean the rules governing the interaction between companies by means of corporation, unilateral conduct or their activities in form or mergers and acquisitions.

The organisation of both the professional and research activities dealing with corporate and antitrust law often results in the illusion of a well-defined separation between them.

Such separation between different spheres of legal knowledge contradicts the very dawn of antitrust law. During the late nineteenth century, vast areas of the US economy experienced a time of consolidation with the view of creating larger and better organised businesses – which in turn were able to better control the prices charged on the market. A wave of what we would today call mergers and acquisitions helped corporations in this regard. The attorney Samuel Dodd created the sophisticated structure of financial engineering renowned as the Standard Oil investment trust.[3] In the Standard Oil saga, the investment trust was employed to pool equity of different corporations with different denominations – hence apparently independent corporations – under the same control. At that time, the consolidation in particular sectors such as oil, steel, and railroads diminished competition and consequently increased prices. The Sherman Act was adopted as a reaction to counter the competitive harm of such forms of a corporate reorganisation. It prohibited monopolization and conspiracy in restraint of trade. Regardless, of the historical significance of the Sherman Act and the subsequent Standard Oil case (1911), the dawn of antitrust law was marked by the intensive employment of organisational law – in the form of corporate law and finance – for anticompetitive purposes.

When EU competition law was adopted, it benefited from the achievements of the earlier and longstanding US antitrust tradition. Nonetheless, it followed a well-distinct developmental path. In particular, the first EUMR applied a sophisticated and detailed test based on turnover thresholds and descriptions of specific forms of changes in control. But before the entry into force of the first European Merger Regulation in 1989, the Commission had already tried to use the EU rules on abuse of dominant positions (now Article 102 TFEU) to target mergers.[4] At those earlier times, it was clear that the relationship between corporate law arrangements and EU competition law did not necessarily have to be binary (i.e. control versus no-control) as in the first and second EU merger regulations. In the *Philip Morris* case,[5] the Court of Justice of the European Union had adopted the concept of influence for describing the effects of a company-holding equity in another company, hence leaving space for qualification of such influence in a rather nuanced way (i.e. potentially including also the chance that there could be equity holdings conveying 'some influence' without control).

The EU's legal framework left a gap between proper mergers and anticompetitive agreements as it did not fully account for the wider set of implications brought

3 By contrast, a couple of decades later, the dominant instrument for achieving concentration had become the holding company, as recognized by the Clayton Antitrust Act of 1914, section 7

4 See Case 6-72 *Europemballage Corporation and Continental Can v Commission* EU:C:1973:22.

5 Joined cases 142 and 156/84 *BAT and Reynolds v Commission* EU:C:1987:490.

by the evolution of economics. Neoclassical economists viewed economic actors as market-power-deprived actors engaging in arm's length transactions. In such a theoretical framework, firms could be seen as a black box unworthy of opening. Therefore, the governance dimension could be considered as being of little relevance if not totally irrelevant. But Ronald Coase's insights prompted new ways to explore the organisational role of the firm within a given economic system – highlighting the trade-off between internal coordination and external transaction costs. What Ronald Coase depicted as 'hierarchy' is visible in the organigram of any traditional corporation. Similarly, a trade-off between coordination and transaction costs can also be seen in the wider context of groups of companies and perhaps also in contexts such as common ownership. Hence, such attempts by institutional economics to understand the content of the above-mentioned black box may constitute a way to conceptualise the different topics in this book from an economic perspective.

Yet, the political perspective is also present in the analysis of the interaction between corporate and competition law – if, for example, we look at the interaction between corporate and competition law under the lenses of the Varieties of Capitalism literature.[6]

While nowadays the private, for-profit, corporation is the traditional model, it may not be the endpoint of the quest for understanding the organisational reality underlying modern business organisation. For example, public (i.e. listed) companies have only recently become the dominant world model. Before the 1980s and 1990s privatisation era, first inaugurated by Mrs Thatcher in the UK, state-owned or mixed-ownership corporations were dominant in Europe. And, they still are the dominant model in one of the fastest growing economy of the world, the People's Republic of China. Hence, under the same 'corporate' label, a multitude of business organisations, with different scopes and *raisons d'être*, are active around the globe. In this era of constant political and institutional change, we may witness the emersion of previously unknown models, involving not only changes in form but also in function. This may mean that even the 'classic' comparative functional perspective may face limits in analysing and explaining the different realities existing around the world. For example, one may wonder whether a Chinese and a US company carry out the same economic function.

The persisting and emerging cross-border diversity leaves us with a Socratic awareness of standing in front of the unknown. Without any ambition to formulate any theory or to come to systematisation of the relationships between corporate and competition law, we offer a few leitmotifs that can help with the kaleidoscopic reality of the everchanging dynamics inherent to such relationship. We have

[6] See e.g., B Hancké, M Rhodes and M Thatcher (eds), *Beyond Varieties of Capitalism: Conflict, Contradictions and Complementarities in the European Economy* (Oxford University Press, 2007); B Hancké (ed), *Debating Varieties of Capitalism* (Oxford University Press, 2009); W Friedman and G Jones, *Business History and Varieties of Capitalism* (Cambridge University Press, 2010).

identified – among the many – four leitmotifs inspired by the current debate on the interaction between corporate and competition law:

- The object and purpose of the corporation
- The boundaries of the corporation
- The governance of the corporation
- Beyond the boundaries of the corporation

The first part of the book explores the object and purpose of corporations and its interaction with competition law. It is in this context, Meagher explores the origins of modern corporations and the emergence of antitrust with a focus on shifting the balance between private and public power. Her chapter shows the complementary roles of corporate and antitrust law in their early interaction and argues that these seem too often forgotten nowadays. These historical and contemporary insights set the scene for an extremely promising area where the interaction between antitrust and corporate law is exponentially increasing: the corporate interest and the corporate *raisons d'être*. The corporation has often been employed as an empty shell for multiple purposes, but traditionally it is business corporations that have been at the core of antitrust interventions. Odudu shows that there is no real reason to subtract no-profit organisations from the application of competition law either. He highlights that the competition law model may apply to a diversified set of scopes while aiming to push economic and social actors to do their best in their respective fields. Nonetheless, shareholder value maximisation conceived as the core of Western corporations throughout the last decades is now heavily under attack, while the debate about the necessity to pursue ESG values in the corporate world is transitioning from the status of wishful thinking to the one of policy-making. Depending on how ESG penetrates the corporate law and governance agenda, this might translate into the inclusion of stakeholders in corporate law-making – including consumers, which represent the category traditionally protected by competition law. Corradi and Nowag claim that the interaction between corporate and competition law within ESG policy-making is only destined to increase here, given the fact that there is an ongoing discussion at multiple levels over the necessity to pursue ESG policies both through private and public policy tools. They also highlight that the most important area of urgent intervention may be innovation, given the crucial nature of dynamic efficiency to solve environmental and social issues.

The second part of the book explores the boundaries of the corporation. The antitrust and competition narrative subsumes economic operators under the term 'firm'. It would be too quick to equate the 'firm' with the 'corporation'; instead, antitrust and competition law understand the firm as organised economic activity. At times, the same term refers to a lower organisational dimension known as 'plant', i.e. a production facility. Yet, if we lift the 'firm' veil, it is indeed true that we often find a corporation behind or a group of companies made up of a parent company and its subsidiaries. From an economics perspective, Hansmann and Kraakman[7] describe the corporation as a legal invention directed to offer to investors the benefit of asset-partitioning through legal personality and limited liability. Such asset-partitioning allows for optimal financial investment diversification to develop. But asset-partitioning can also be employed to shield a group of companies from antitrust liability. Hence, the relationships of the corporation vis-à-vis third parties such as the antitrust enforcer may actually require modulation of such asset-partitioning. In Chapter 4, Koenig describes the intertwining between the principle of a single legal entity and the principle of separation within corporate groups, while highlighting the persistent tension between limited liability and responsibility for competition law infringements. Acknowledging the rationale of the derogations to asset partitioning imposed by competition law, Koenig also warns that an automatic vertical or horizontal liability within the corporate group disregards fundamental principles of corporate and civil law potentially leading to unreasonable results. In the subsequent chapter, Walter and Schunke explore this issue in more detail with a case study. In Germany, it has for some time been possible to restructure antitrust liability away by means of the so-called 'sausage gap'. The chapter explains the implications of the deployment of such a strategy and how EU competition law provided concepts that informed reforms of the German system. In Chapter 6, Hong explores the unique regulation around the chaebol in Korea and how it has evolved over time. Chaebol is a Korean phenomenon of large company groups which are connected primarily by family ties with formal legal links existing only occasionally. This corporate model, while specific to Korea, provides valuable insights for other economies on how to deal with informal ways of control in competition and corporate law.

The third part of the book explores the governance level, thereby entering into the very essence of organisational law and dealing with corporate constituencies and their conflicts of interest. In this part of the book, Woodcock proposes a new model of a corporation which represents a wider set of constituencies, which he calls 'counterparties'. He supports the idea of creating a balance of power in firm governance, whereby counterparties have the right to elect board members, therefore eliminating the internal forces that induce firms to exercise monopoly power. Moving the focus to directors' duties, Corradi and Nowag explain that corporate law and governance may occasionally restrict competition which can create problems which may be extremely difficult to solve by reverting to competition law. This seems to be the case with corporate opportunity rules, which may prevent directors from competing with the companies for which they serve as directors. While such a rule is an expression of a company's directors' duty of loyalty, in certain cases it may stifle dynamic competition.

7 Henry Hansmann and Reinier Kraakman, *The Essential Role of Organizational Law*, (2000) 110 Yale LJ 387. See also Henry Hansmann, Reinier Kraakman, and Richard Squire, *Law and the Rise of the Firm*, (2006) 119 Harv Law Rev 1333.

The fourth and final part of the book addresses the interaction between corporate and competition law beyond the boundaries of the corporation. This area is the most debated one in law and finance literature; it addresses some of the most contentious issues in competition law today. Within this area, two connected subthemes can be identified: questions of interlocking directors, that is to say, directors that are on the board of different companies, and questions of common ownership. Chapters 10 and 11, by Nili and Thépot, respectively, deal with interlocking directorships in the US and in Europe, respectively. They both highlight the potential connection between interlocking directorships and common ownership and the necessity to approach such potential restrictions of competition jointly. While Nili shows that it may be possible to target interlocking directorships under US competition law, he cautions against such an approach. Thépot shows that this area may represent a challenge in the present state of EU competition law. What remains to be explained is whether interlocking directorships may represent a tool through which common owners attempt restrictions on competition or if interlocking directorships may represent an independent explanation for restrictions of competition in markets where there is a significant presence of parallel holdings. Ghezzi and Picciau provide us with a more optimistic perspective on interlocking directorships, presenting the very peculiar case of the Italian ban on interlocking directorships in the banking sector. Their empirical analysis provides evidence of the disappearance of such a practice in the Italian banking sector. The ban and disappearance of interlocks were accompanied by an increase in competition in product markets. Ghezzi and Picciau show us that effective solutions to antitrust harm may come from banking law and thus legislation external to competition law.

This part of the book also features the debate about common ownership. In Chapter 12, Schmalz provides an overview of the debate on common ownership and evaluates the different policy proposals that have been advanced so far by US lawyers. He highlights the necessity of acting urgently for addressing the anticompetitive effects deriving from parallel holdings, without waiting for more economic research; he points to the damages that the present inaction causes to consumers. Rock and Rubinfeld in contrast, doubt that the overall increase in prices in the US is connected to common ownership, pointing instead at alternative explanations, such as the exponentially increased product market concentration – which has created 'superstar' firms with exorbitant market power. In Chapter 14, Corradi focuses on EU competition policies for common ownership suggesting that, regardless of the econometric findings on the issue of parallel holdings, sound policy-making should inspire the application of the counterfactual and should take into consideration wider implications such as the geopolitical ones. Finally, Tzanaki addresses the relationships between common ownership and present competition policies by reframing them into the wider picture of the intersection between corporate law and antitrust law. The final chapter by Lianos and McLean zooms in a specific area: digital value chains and the importance of Google, Apple, Facebook, Amazon, and

Microsoft. The chapter explores the ownership structures in digital value chains and how these might explain competitive strategies and broader economic models of behaviour, considering the conglomerate analogy frequently invoked. Moreover, they highlight distributional effects resulting from the ownership structure – in particular, when such effects are observed in the context of the broader concerns around these digital giants.

As human beings, we are living in very exciting and challenging times. Changes are occurring worldwide at an accelerated pace, which makes predictions on the evolution of the future business, financial, and overall social environment hardly reliable. Humanistic aspirations to better our world still collide with the most destructive instincts of human beings, as the war in Ukraine remind us. But the attempts to foster change, and hopefully a change for the best, are still living in the heart and actions of many. For sure, both corporations and the State have been and still are vessels and forces contributing in a substantial way to shape the world in which we live. We hope that this excursus on the intersection between corporate and antitrust law lights a candle – no matter how small – to the complex, tangled, and often unfathomable dynamics that animate the intersection between the corporate and the antitrust world. We want to express our heartfelt thanks to all our contributors for rowing together with us on unchartered waters!

PART I

The Object and Purpose of Corporations

1

Corporate Law, Antitrust, and the History of Democratic Control of the Balance of Power

Michelle Meagher

Grown to tremendous proportions, there may be said to have evolved a "corporate system"—as there was once a feudal system—which has attracted to itself a combination of attributes and powers, and has attained a degree of prominence entitling it to be dealt with as a major social institution.[1]

Adolf A. Berle and Gardiner C. Means, The Modern Corporation & Private Property (1932)

1.1 INTRODUCTION

Since their creation, corporations have proven to be vehicles for incredible aggregate wealth creation. Indeed, this was part of the intended design: the resource-strapped state sought a catalyst for public investment and so constituted the legal entity of the company, attaching to this artificial construct the rights and privileges that would allow it to successfully corral private capital.[2] From the creation of the Bank of England to the empire-building of the East India Company, the company form was harnessed as a tool for the expansion of public life.

It was, however, recognised at the outset that in creating a unique set of legal features that would make the company so attractive for private investment – in particular the later ability to own property, via the company, with limited liability – the state was not only creating its own co-investor in public wealth but there was also the possibility that the company would pose a threat to the state itself through its ability

Michelle Meagher is Senior Policy Fellow at the UCL Centre for Law, Economics and Society, and co-founder of the Inclusive Competition Forum and the Balanced Economy Project. This work builds on a previous article by the author, Michelle Meagher, 'Powerless Antitrust' (2019) 2(1) Competition Policy International Antitrust Chronicle. The author would like to thank the editors for their helpful substantive input. All errors remain the author's own.

1 Adolf A Berle and Gardiner C Means, *The Modern Corporation & Private Property* (Macmillan Company 1932) 3.

2 WG Roy, *Socializing Capital* (Princeton University Press 1997) 41, 48.

to channel and multiply the accumulation of private power.[3] The public's salvation, therefore, came with an inherent threat of its undoing.

As such, since its inception, the corporation has been involved in a delicate dance with the state both to route its productive capacity towards socially desirable ends and to control the corporation's power.[4] Today, as technological development and the mobilisation of international financial capital allow the power of the corporation to transcend that of the democratic state in both scale and scope, the tools of the past that were used with varying degrees of vigour to constrain the corporation are increasingly relevant. Corporate law and antitrust were once used to maintain the balance between the power of the corporation and the power of the state. Today, this vital role has been all but forgotten.

We have many regulatory tools that are used to proscribe the bounds of operation of the company, corporate law, and antitrust being two of them. Both disciplines are currently engaged in an active debate as to their core purpose in the modern context. Within antitrust, this has involved revisiting the 'consumer welfare standard' as the accepted litmus test of permitted competitive conduct; within corporate law, it manifests as a collective reflection on the shareholder primacy principle of corporate governance and the stakeholder capitalist model proposed as its alternative. Each debate would benefit from a more nuanced understanding of the origins of antitrust in corporate law (and vice versa) and the historical attempts to constrain the corporation as an entity with the built-in capability of challenging the state's governmental power.

What we see from looking at the history of corporate law and antitrust is that each discipline historically played a complementary role in maintaining the *balance of power* between private, economic concentrations and the demos. The now-separate conversations about corporate responsibility in the corporate governance sphere and about corporate power within competition policy circles have always, in fact, been fundamentally connected and targeted at the same set of risks.

This chapter will start in Section 1.2 by exploring the concept of the *balance of power*, which will then form the framework for our historical exploration of corporate and antitrust law. We will then consider two manifestations of private power that the state must regulate: its own public grants of monopoly power, considered in Section 1.3, and what we will designate as 'constructed monopolies', discussed in Section 1.4. Constructed monopolies differ from publicly granted monopolies in that they are generated within the market, and it is in reaction to the development of such monopoly market positions that modern antitrust law comes into being. It is tempting to consider such monopolies to be 'self-generating' and as such the

[3] JW Hurst, *The Legitimacy of the Business Corporation* (University of Virginia 1970) 43.

[4] For a useful 'potted history' of the corporation, particularly in America, see N Lamoreaux and W Novak, 'Introduction' in Lamoreaux and Novak (eds), *Corporations and American Democracy* (Harvard University Press 2017) 1–33.

mirror-image of the public grant of monopoly. But as we shall see the state is continually involved in co-creating the market and the conditions for monopoly – or competition – and thus 'constructed' is a more accurate framing for the modern monopoly than 'self-generating'.

Whereas modern antitrust forged its path in the regulation of constructed monopolies, corporate law marched into the territory of corporate responsibility, in particular, a responsibility towards investors. Corporate responsibility will be the focus of Section 1.5. Although at face value corporate responsibility seems to operate according to a different logic to the control of corporate and market power – focused instead on investor protections – we shall see that this is, or at least could have been, an aspect of the balance of power. Finally, this chapter will conclude in Section 1.6 by considering the relevance today of the concept of the balance of power to the operation of antitrust and corporate law.

1.2 BALANCE OF POWER

The challenge of maintaining the balance of power between the demos and industry stems from the phenomenon of economies of scale. As Ellis Hawley observes:

> One of the central problems of twentieth-century America has revolved about the difficulty of reconciling a modern industrial order, necessarily based upon a high degree of collective organization, with democratic postulates, competitive ideals, and liberal individualistic traditions inherited from the nineteenth century. This industrial order has created in America a vision of material abundance, a dream of abolishing poverty and achieving economic security for all; and the great majority of Americans have not been willing to destroy it lest that dream be lost. Yet at the same time it has involved, probably necessarily, a concentration of economic power, a development of monopolistic arrangements, and a loss of individual freedom and initiative, all of which run counter to inherited traditions and ideals.[5]

As Hawley describes, the industrial economy is prone to the agglomeration of production capacity, and with that concentration of economic resources comes a threat to individual freedom. Whether the industry is centralised within the state or centralised within private entities, the balance between the autonomy of society and the power of whoever commands the industry must be maintained. The allocation of property rights is thus central to society's response to economies of scale. After identifying the 'corporate system' in the quote with which this chapter began, Berle and Means emphasise that the '*Organization of property has played a constant part in the balance of powers which go to make up the life of any era*'.[6] For Berle and Means, the 'corporate system' not only channels resources towards corporations but the impact of the overall system is so great that '*it may even determine a large part of*

5 Ellis Hawley, *The New Deal and the Problem of Monopoly* (Princeton University Press 1966) vii.

6 Berle and Means (n 2) 3.

the behaviour of most men living under it'.[7] The corporation, as a tool for infrastructural and economic development, became the vessel into which increasing returns have been channelled, giving rise to an entity with equivalent powers to the state.

Although economies of scale may be part and parcel of technological development, it is important to note that the dominance of the corporation as an institution was not an inevitable consequence;[8] the corporation is a creature of the state.[9] Alternative modes of an economic organisation include partnerships, associations, municipal corporations, charities, and cooperatives. But it is the corporation that has really thrived, and it has done so with the explicit endorsement of the state. Historically, as we shall see in Section 1.3, the corporation was a positive creation of the state.[10] Today, the corporation exists at the pleasure of the state – anyone can start a corporation for any legal purpose and hardly any effort or bureaucracy is involved in the process. Yet still, the corporation relies on the passive acceptance of the state; the privilege of incorporation could be removed at any time.

The balance of power with which this chapter is concerned refers to the relationship between the power of the corporation and the power of the state. Given the mode of creation of corporate power, the balance of power is inherently reflexive. In a literal sense, the corporation's power does not – cannot – exist independent of the state that creates it,[11] and at the same time, the capacity of the state has become dependent on the economic contributions of corporations as the chosen vehicle for harnessing economies of scale. Being creatures of the state, corporations are tied up in conference with the state, continually negotiating their very existence. This allows the state to push the corporation in directions that benefit society but also gives rise to the opportunity, and leverage, for the corporation to push back.

The balance of power does not start with the desirability or otherwise of increasing returns to scale in economic terms. Concentrated centres of power can be corrosive to public life and are automatically suspect as such. As K. Sabeel Rahman reminds us:

> the biggest moral threats in a democratic society are those practices and arrangements that undermine the capacities and powers of citizens to be active political agents: the concentrated private power of firms that can dominate individuals in the economy; the diffused system of the market that can narrow one's life opportunities and prospects; the spectre of an unresponsive and unaccountable state itself.[12]

7 Ibid. 3.
8 Roy (n 3).
9 Ibid. 12.
10 Ibid.
11 Sandeep Vaheesan, 'The Profound Nonsense of Consumer Welfare Antitrust' (2019) 64 Antitrust Bull 479; Roy (n 3) 190.
12 KS Rahman, *Democracy against Domination* (Oxford University Press 2016) 13.

We can relate this notion of balance of power to Polanyi's concept of the 'double movement'.[13] As Polanyi explores in his seminal book *The Great Transformation*, the market is propelled to continuous expansion as it attempts to pull away from society and render the demos subservient to its logic. But this movement is met by a countermovement of society as society seeks to protect itself from the market's destructive capacity. This manifests as a concerted effort to protect society from the market.[14] Touching on the reflexive nature of the relationship between Berle and Means' 'corporate system' and the state, Polanyi developed the concept of 'embeddedness' which proposes that the market is embedded within society and the state.[15] This embeddedness ensures that the market's attempts to pull away from society will always be met by a corresponding countermovement, tethered as the market is to the society that generates it.

This indeed is just what happened in relation to the corporation. As Naomi Lamoureaux and William Novak describe, as the' *persistent growth in the scale and scope of the largest business corporations frequently challenged extant regulatory rubrics – most famously with the development of interstate trusts and holding companies'* society has proven to be '*surprisingly creative and versatile in generating new legal, administrative, and regulatory tools to bring even the most powerful corporations under a modicum of democratic control*'.[16]

Corporate law and antitrust have both played a role in this democratic countermovement. Corporate law constrains the scope of action of the entity that is the corporation. It thus can act as a check on the power of the corporation on the market and in society, not dissimilar to the remit of antitrust law. Meanwhile, antitrust looks to the external business arrangements of corporations, as well as other business organisations, and determines which configurations of capital are to be permitted the licence to wield collective power and which are to be forced to compete.[17] Antitrust was also once used to govern the corporation at an existential level, as a type of corporate law. Understanding the reactive, contingent, and ever-evolving nature of developments in each of these legal disciplines sheds light on the present-day efforts to respond to corporate domination.

1.3 GRANT OF MONOPOLY

The original model of the corporate 'licence to operate' was the corporate charter. In order to come into existence, a corporation required an affirmative act of the state – a decree of the sovereign or, later, an act of Parliament (in the United Kingdom),

[13] Karl Polanyi, *Great Transformation* (2nd ed Beacon Press 2001) 136.

[14] Fred Block, 'Introduction' in Karl Polanyi, *The Great Transformation* (Farrar & Reinhart 1944) xxii.

[15] Polanyi (n14) 60.

[16] Lamoreaux and Novak (n 5) 4.

[17] Sanjukta Paul, 'Antitrust as Allocator of Coordination Rights' (2020) 67(2) UCLA L Rev 380.

state legislatures, or Congress (in the United States).[18] Some of the first corporate charters were granted in England by a state eager to take advantage of private investment for the completion of public projects. By granting these artificial legal entities protection from liability and by guaranteeing a financial return, the corporate form was utilised as an engine for economic growth.[19]

Corporate charters were a rare privilege. Very few were granted before the turn of the nineteenth century.[20] Before the rise of manufacturing, charters were generally granted to provide transportation infrastructure, water utilities, to create banks and insurance companies.[21] Many of these early corporations, including the East India Company in England[22] and the Bank of New York in the United States,[23] were, as Eric Hilt describes, '*the largest business enterprises that had ever been created …, and were endowed with valuable legal priveleges that were not accessible to other firms*'.[24]

A corporation was a way for private citizens to pool together their resources, and although public benefit was initially a feature of charter grants, private gain was also part of the bargain. The presence of economies of scale and the public interest in seeing the relevant project completed were the justifications of a monopoly grant: it was felt that the underlying enterprise – the construction of a bridge or canal or road – would be unremunerative without some exclusive licence providing a barrier to entry.[25] Not all charters related to industries with substantial economies of scale, but the balance of power was most imperilled in relation to enterprises either with a tendency to grow in size or influence or where the monopoly related to some critical infrastructure or bottleneck in the economy.

Today, we think of monopoly in a narrow sense as the market position that allows a firm to raise price above cost and restrict output. Under the model of corporate chartering though, the grant of a monopoly licence – understood to be an exclusive right to engage in a particular enterprise – was one of several kinds of inducements that could be negotiated as part of a charter grant, all giving some kind of monopolistic privilege. For example, the Society for Establishing Useful Manufactures, which was a textile company chartered in New Jersey in 1791, secured permission to raise funds through a public lottery as well as obtaining exemptions for the company's employees from taxes and military service.[26] There was an inevitable reciprocity that simultaneously reinforced and delimited the role of the state as grantor of the

[18] Roy (n 3) 48–50; Hurst (n 4) 16.
[19] This was also the case in nineteenth century America. Roy (n 3)41.
[20] Hurst (n 4) 15–18; Joseph S Davis, *Essays in the Earlier History of Corporations* (Harvard University Press 1917)
[21] Eric Hilt, 'Early American Corporations and the State' in Lamoreaux and Novak (eds), *Corporations and American Democracy* (Harvard University Press 2017) 40; Roy (n 3) 52.
[22] William Dalrymple, *The Anarchy* (Bloomsbury Publishing 2019).
[23] Hilt (n 22) 41.
[24] Ibid.
[25] Ibid.
[26] Lamoreaux and Novak (n 5) 8.

privileges and the corporation as grantee: charters were granted at the behest of the state but a business would not seek a charter for an enterprise that did not require public support – for this, there was no need to incorporate.

With the grant of monopoly came corresponding power. Such power was not granted without protections. The countermovement to constrain the power of corporations to keep them embedded within society took several forms, which will be explored in this section: (a) restrictions on the ability to grant special privileges; (b) restrictions on the scope of the grant; (c) reservations of the power to revoke the charter; and (d) the introduction of general incorporation.

1.3.1 *Restrictions on the Ability to Grant Special Privileges*

The scope for nepotistic favouritism within the power of the state to grant special privileges has always been keenly felt. In the Tudor Royal Court, privileges – in the form of 'letters patent' – were dispensed liberally as quid pro quo for supporting the sovereign either politically or financially, or even simply given as favours to the sovereign's servants and courtiers.[27] The case of *Darcy v. Allen*,[28] known commonly as the *Case of Monopolies*, demonstrates both the profligacy of the grants and the public intolerance for sovereign power to be so abused. In that case, Queen Elizabeth I had granted an exclusive licence for the production of playing cards to her groom, which the court rendered invalid on the basis that it created a monopoly contrary to common law restraint of trade. In terms of the balance of power, we can understand the perversity of this particular special privilege – the grant of an exclusive licence to produce playing cards is not in fulfilment of some public need and yet it interferes with the right of others to earn their daily bread through an otherwise legally permitted enterprise and does so through the co-option of the state. The focus of the court was on the economic costs of monopoly but also, as Barry Hawk has described, on '*political constitutional objections to royal authority*'.[29]

Eventually, Parliament enacted the Statute of Monopolies in 1624 which prohibited the sovereign from making outright grants of monopoly except as a temporary reward for technological innovation – from which the modern patent is derived. Corporate charters, as opposed to other grants of monopoly privilege, which came with various restrictions attached, did however continue.

In the United States, the distaste for the abuse of public power for private gain found expression in the East India Company tea thrown into Boston harbour in 1773, and this sentiment continued after independence. Several states had antimonopoly provisions in their constitutions,[30] and there was even a proposal to include

27 Barry E Hawk, 'English Competition Law Before 1900' (2018) 63 Antitrust Bull 42.
28 *Edward Darcy Esquire v Thomas Allen of London Haberdasher* [1602] 77 ER 1260.
29 Hawk (n 28).
30 David Millon, 'The Sherman Act and the Balance of Power' (1988) 61 S Cal L Rev 1219, 1249.

an antimonopoly provision in the US Constitution or Bill of Rights.[31] Although states retained the ability to grant corporate charters, courts were reticent to embellish the grant of a charter with implied privileges. In *Charles River Bridge*,[32] when a new bridge was chartered to be built right next to the already-existing Charles River Bridge, the courts refused to interpret the grant of the earlier corporate charter as an implicit grant of monopoly to collect bridge tolls. Interpretation of corporate privileges was to err on the side of limitation, not expansion.

The US context before and after independence usefully illustrates the dual role of the corporation as a threat to the balance of power but also as a safeguard against the state. At the same time that the American colonists rejected English corporations like the East India Company as vehicles of oppression, they also embraced their own corporate organisations as protection against the British monarch.[33] Many of the early colonies had been formed as chartered companies and they governed themselves according to those charters as a way to ensure due process as between the colonists, with the governance provisions of the corporate charter serving as a model for the governance of public life.[34] Adhering strictly to the terms of the charter also served as a shield against interference by the granting power – the King in England. Individual state constitutions were eventually modelled on these charters.[35]

It also emerged as a legal principle that benefits conveyed by the state should not be capriciously withdrawn. The Contracts Clause in the US Constitution was instituted to protect contracts with the state from arbitrary abuse of state power. In the watershed *Dartmouth College* case,[36] the Supreme Court held that the state of New Hampshire could not unilaterally amend a previously granted charter. In that case, the charter for Dartmouth College had been granted by King George III, before the state of New Hampshire had even been formed. The court found that since the corporate charter constitutes a contract, it could not be unilaterally altered. It could only be changed through mutual consent.

Dartmouth College had the potential to permanently alter the balance of power in favour of corporations, and indeed the decision was hotly contested on these grounds by those who saw it as paving the way for arbitrary *private* power. As one commentator remarked: '*Sure I am that, if the American people acquiesce in the principles laid down in this case, the Supreme Court will have affected what the whole power of the British Empire, after eight years of bloody conflict, failed to achieve*

31 Ibid.

32 *Charles River Bridge v Proprietors of the Warren Bridge*, 36 US (11 Pet) 496 (1837).

33 Nikolas Bowie, 'Why the Constitution Was Written Down' (2019) 71 Stan L Rev 1397; Lamoreaux and Novak (n 5) 7.

34 Nikolas Bowie, 'Why the Constitution Was Written Down' (2019) 71 Stan L Rev 1397, 1407; Hurst (n 4).

35 Bowie (n 35) 1477.

36 *Trustees of Dartmouth College v Woodward*, 17 US (4 Wheat) 518 (1819).

against our fathers'.[37] States responded by enacting legislation that allowed them to insert 'reservation clauses' into corporate charters, maintaining the ability to alter and revoke grants going forward. Nevertheless, the principle of protection against state power, alongside the protections against corporate power built-in to the corporate charters themselves, continued as a theme in the regulation of the corporation.

1.3.2 *Restrictions on the Scope of the Grant*

Beyond limiting the ability of the sovereign or the state to grant monopolies, individual corporate charters tended to contain a whole host of provisions designed to constrain the size of the corporation and the extent of its power.[38] Charters would limit the industries and sectors in which a company could engage. They might contain limits on the amount of capital a corporation could accumulate and limits on the amount of debt. And, they would generally fix the lifespan of the corporation at the outset – sometimes to just a couple of decades or less.[39] Common law also restricted the right of corporations to own stock in other firms.[40] Each of these provisions was intended to circumscribe the corporation and thus limit its ability to expand beyond the granted scope and beyond the balance of power.

1.3.3 *Charter Revocation*

A crisis of the balance of power occurred when corporations outgrew the states that granted them the possibility of existence. The privilege of incorporation, which initially required an act of the state to create, came with not just restrictions in scope but also obligations to perform certain public duties, often including a commitment to complete the public venture for which the company was incorporated. For this reason, the sovereign or the state also retained the right to revoke the charter for either non-use or abuse.[41] This was a meaningful mechanism of public accountability and an existential threat to any company that abused its privilege or reneged on its commitment. But if the corporation no longer relied upon any individual state for its licence, then the balance of power would shift in favour of the corporation.

The procedure by which the corporate charter was initially challenged was known as a *quo warranto* proceeding. A *quo warranto* action is a demand made by the state on some individual or corporation to show 'by what warrant' or right they may exercise a particular franchise or privilege. The burden of proof was on

37 Henshaw quoted in R L Grossman, F T Adams, and C Levenstein, 'Taking Care of Business: Citizenship and the Charter of Incorporation (1993)' 3 New Solutions a Journal of Environmental and Occupational Health Policy 7–18.

38 Lamoreaux and Novak (n 5) 12.

39 Roy (n 3) 54.

40 Ibid. at 148, 149.

41 Herbert Hovenkamp, *Enterprise and American Law, 1836–1937* (Harvard University Press 1991) 56–9.

the respondent to show that they had the adequate right to enjoy the privilege in question. The procedure stemmed from an ancient legal writ in use in England since the twelfth or thirteenth century.[42] On Edward I's return to England in 1274, he ordered a general inquiry to be held throughout the land into the reported misconduct of the feudal lords in his absence.[43] The quo warranto writs were issued to challenge the privileges that the lords had taken the liberty of enjoying. The basis for adjudication was merely whether it could be factually established that the privilege had been validly granted by the King or his predecessors. If there was no valid basis for the grant, or no proof of the grant, then an ad hoc court convened for this purpose could order the privilege to be revoked.[44] In later cases against corporations, this would mean that the courts had the power to revoke the corporate charter.

Abuse of the charter usually meant a breach of one of the terms of the charter itself, – for example, the restrictions on scope.[45] But with the rise of the infamous 'trusts' in the second half of the nineteenth century, *quo warranto* proceedings and charter revocation were also used by state attorneys general as what Daniel Crane has described as a '*form of crude antitrust law*'.[46] This was how states, with limited tools available at the time, sought to return the balance of power in face of the epochal challenge of the new conglomerate business organisations.

Towards the end of the nineteenth century, *quo warranto* proceedings were brought frequently to challenge what we would now construe as anticompetitive conduct, first against vertical integration, and then against horizontal combinations.[47] These cases were not primarily about competition though, certainly not about the protection of 'consumer welfare'. They were instead motivated by a desire to protect society from the threat of economic concentrations – or in other words to correct the balance of power. Nevertheless, as a matter of form, state attorneys general often found it easier to rely on the argument that the corporation had strayed *ultra vires* from its charter rather than argue the public policy point of public detriment or economic harm, and they were quite successful as a result of this technical focus on the bounds of the charter – which the courts

42 Technically the particular procedure in use was the 'information in the nature of quo warranto' which had less onerous requirements. James L. High, A Treatise on Extraordinary Legal Remedies: Embracing Mandamus, Quo Warranto, and Prohibition (1874). I will refer simply to 'quo warranto' for ease of exposition.

43 Helen M Cam, 'Historical Revisions XXXVIII – The Quo Warranto Proceedings under Edward I' (1926) 11 History 143–148.

44 Few privileges were in fact revoked. The process was rather used as a form of revenue generation through the collection of fines. See Cam (n 44).

45 Discussed at Section 1.3.2.

46 Daniel Crane, 'The Dissociation of Incorporation and Regulation in the Progressive Era and the New Deal', in Lamoreaux and Novak (eds), *Corporations and American Democracy* (Harvard University Press 2017) 112.

47 Herbert Hovenkamp, 'The Classical Corporation in American Legal Thought', 76 Geo LJ 1593, 1669–72.

were accustomed to adjudicating and which the state had clear power to enforce via the courts.[48]

The question at the heart of these *quo warranto* cases was whether the trusts, comprised of trustees representing multiple individual enterprises, would be permitted the privilege of coordinating their economic assets in an analogous manner to the grant of licence given to all monolithic corporations and whether such a privilege would be read into the individual charter grants of the constituent companies. The trust mechanism was used to circumvent the restrictions in corporate charters that prevented companies from vertically integrating or owning stock in other corporations.[49] The term 'robber baron' which came to be synonymous with the tycoons of the Gilded Age such as John D. Rockefeller and Andrew Carnegie was perfectly apt: the trusts were attempting to assert baronial privileges akin to those of feudal times, and the state, just as Edward I in the thirteenth century sought to challenge the warrant by which those privileges were being asserted.

One of the key features of the second industrial revolution of the 1860s and 1870s, during which time the phenomenon of increasing returns to scale really comes to the fore in America, is the development for the first time of a national market across the United States.[50] Prior to that time, companies would typically seek a charter in the state in which their business was going to be predominantly operating because they would tend to need some state support, such as permission to print bank notes or the power to annex land, in order to operate the business at all – otherwise, there would be no need to incorporate.[51] When the trusts thrust themselves across state lines this co-dependence between corporation and state shifted and states founds themselves wooing these national conglomerates to incorporate in their jurisdiction. Unsurprisingly, *quo warranto* cases suing companies for bold expansion were hardly brought at all.[52]

1.3.4 *General Incorporation*

The original process of granting incorporation through an act of Parliament or Congress was bureaucratically burdensome. It was also open to lobbying and rife with exactly the nepotism that the Statute of Monopolies had attempted to remove from the Royal Courts.[53] The idea of allowing for general incorporation, through laws that would permit anybody to form a company for any legal purpose, was to

48 Martin Sklar, *The Corporate Reconstruction of American Capitalism, 1890–1916: The Market, the Law, and Politics* (Cambridge University Press 1988) 99; Naomi Lamoreaux and Laura Philips Sawyer, 'Voting Trusts and Antitrust: Rethinking the Role of Shareholder Litigation in Public Regulation, 1880s to 1930s' (2021) *Law Hist Rev*, 39(3), 569–600; Crane (n 47) 113.

49 Roy (n 3) 176–220.

50 Roy (n 3) 179.

51 Lamoreaux and Novak (n 5) 13; Roy (n 3) 145.

52 Lamoreaux and Sawyer (n 49).

53 Hilt (n 22) 41.

democratise the corporate vehicle and remove elitism from incorporation.[54] It was a move to restore the balance of power, but it contained within it a destabilising force that would again act to untether the corporation from society: with anybody able to form a company, the public perception shifted from incorporation as a privilege, granted at the sufferance of the state, to incorporation as a right.[55] The authority of the state to constrain the theoretically democratised corporation was thus compromised.

It was still recognised that the corporation was a vehicle through which private wealth would naturally multiply and thus general incorporation laws alone would not be sufficient to level the playing field across prospective incorporators. Hence, individual general incorporation statutes across the US states initially contained many of the same restrictions as had characterised individual corporate charters.[56]

This defence against corporate expansion was not to last. The pressure on states to accommodate the needs of the burgeoning corporations mounted at the end of the nineteenth century and a few states led the way in relaxing their corporate laws. Their target was the boon of registration fees and tax revenues that came with incorporation.[57] This phenomenon, as it played out across a few key states, has been termed the 'race to the bottom' – as states competed to attract corporations into their jurisdictions.[58] Today, Delaware is the preferred state of incorporation for publicly traded companies, but initially it was New Jersey that was victorious after loosening its law with successive amendments from the 1870s onwards, by which time the legacy restrictions of scope, limited cross-ownership and size of the corporation, had been replaced with a regime amenable to the now-common holding company structure.[59] This transformed the power of the corporation to control economic resources at an increasing scale and represented a fundamental shift in the balance of power.

As will be discussed in Section 1.4, contemporaneous to this relaxation of state incorporation laws, the 'democratic counterreaction' of state and federal antitrust

[54] Crane (n 47) 111; Laura Philips Sawyer, American Fair Trade: *Proprietary Capitalism, Corporatism, and the 'New Competition', 1890–1940* (Cambridge University Press 2018); Gerald Berk, 'Neither Markets nor Administration: Brandeis and the Antitrust Reforms of 1914' (1994) 8 Studies in American Political Development 24, 28; Millon (n 31) 1255; Hovenkamp, 'The Classical Corporation in American Legal Thought' (n 48) 34; Hovenkamp, *Enterprise and American Law* (n 42) 37–8.

[55] Robert Lowe, Vice President of the Board of Trade, who was the mastermind behind the Joint Stock Companies Act of 1856, declared: 'From then to now [incorporation] was a privilege. We hope to make it a right', quoted in John Micklethwait and Adrian Wooldridge, *The Company* (Modern Library 2005) 58. See also Thomas Linzey, 'Awakening the Sleeping Giant: Creating a Quasi-Private Cause of Action for Revoking Corporate Charters in Response to Environmental Violations' (1995) 13 Pace Envtl L Rev 219, 222 (noting that general incorporation elicited a 'shift in public opinion towards routine acceptance of a corporation's right to exist.'); Roy (n 3) 17.

[56] As discussed in Section 1.3.2. Lamoreaux and Novak (n 5) 3.

[57] Crane (n 47) 113–114.

[58] William Cary, 'Federalism and Corporate Law: Reflections upon Delaware' (1974) 83 Yale LJ Number 666.

[59] Lamoreaux and Novak (n 5) 13.

law, in its modern and less 'crude' form, was just taking shape.[60] The net effect was mixed and, as some commentators remarked at the time, somewhat confused: states were weakening corporate law, which had served as a powerful brake on corporate power, just as federal antitrust laws were being strengthened, in part to achieve the same aim.[61]

This context is critical to understanding the evolution of the trusts and the origins of modern corporate and antitrust law. It is clear that the balance of power has not been static; it is in constant, reactive flux. Initially, companies like Standard Oil opted to adopt the trust structure to implement their conglomerate concentrations precisely in order to avoid the corporate law prohibitions against cross-ownership in state incorporation laws.[62] Standard Oil and others rolled-up whole industries and granted what was essentially corporate control to a board of trustees, thus achieving by contract and trust deed what was prohibited by a merger under the terms of the charters.[63] Undeterred, state attorneys general used the *quo warranto* procedure to successfully challenge the trust arrangements as *ultra vires* the charters of the constituent corporations of the trusts.[64] It was by such a procedure that Standard Oil was forced to exit its initial trust.[65] The trusts then used their growing economic might and strategic leverage to lobby for the weakening of corporate law, and the states eventually obliged.[66] This then paved the way for the formation of giant single corporations, which tended still to be referred to as 'trusts', without the need to disguise their intentions behind the trust arrangement.[67] Corporate law thus granted, by default, greater ability to coordinate, and a relief from the necessity of competition (or the risks and instability of cartelisation of the constituent companies), to the expanded, conglomerate corporation – immunising, from antitrust scrutiny, to a certain extent, the underlying economic cooperation within the corporation. State and federal antitrust law was then used to attempt to reign in those newly emboldened corporations, but without the same powers to challenge monopoly power at an existential level or to act against abuse of corporate privilege per se.

1.4 CONSTRUCTED MONOPOLY

With general incorporation and the loosening of incorporation laws, the ability of the state to control the corporation through existential challenge was much diminished. The state was no longer the grantor of monopoly privilege, and yet monopolistic

60 Lamoreaux and Novak (n 5) 14.
61 Hovenkamp (n 42) 266.
62 Roy (n 3) 176–220.
63 Ibid. at 18
64 Ibid. at 210; Sklar (n 49) 99.
65 *State v Standard Oil Co*, 49 Ohio St 137, 184 (1892).
66 Hovenkamp (n 48) 1669; Roy (n 3) 15–16.
67 Roy (n 3) 279.

companies were arising anyway, taking advantage of technological advances, the growing national market, and the benefits of the corporate form itself – all of which, in different ways, gave rise to economies of scale.[68] The immediate need was therefore to identify other tools to constrain the increasingly problematic concentrations of power or, in other words, to address the tilting balance of power in favour of monopolies. This is where the joint origins of antitrust and corporate law rupture, spawning a fragmented approach to corporate regulation.[69] Within antitrust, there were two overlapping streams: (a) the use of common law to challenge coercive practices and (b) the passage of the Sherman Act in 1890. We shall consider the separate path of corporate law in Section 1.5.

1.4.1 *Common Law Restraint of Trade and Monopolisation*

The common law notions of 'restraint of trade' and 'monopoly', which had developed under English law and were transported across to the United States with colonisation, were both focused on conduct that sought to prevent others from entering a market and/or attempts to control prices and supply.[70] The concern was with coercion or the limitation of another party's freedom to trade.[71] It was a protection against abuse of imbalance of power but did not prevent or prohibit imbalance itself. Monopolisation, at common law, was effectively a special case of unlawful restraint of trade concerned again with exclusion from the market.

There was one sense in which the common law did act to promote balance of power. Common law restraint of trade applied not to corporations but also to other organisations. Unlike modern statutory antitrust, this common law tradition was permissive of coordination between a wide range of actors which may have served as a countervailing force to balance private corporate power with collective action on the part of workers, farmers, and others.[72] It has also been argued that the tolerance in the common law restraint of trade doctrine for cooperation between business competitors was in part due to the phenomenon of worker unionisation, creating both a model for cooperation among firms and a counterweight to cartels of producers.[73] Although economic power as such was not the primary focus of common law restraint of trade, there was at least this aspect of maintaining the balance and protecting not just competition but a person's right

[68] Hurst (n 4) 74.

[69] Crane (n 47) 110. See also KS Rahman, 'The New Utilities: Private Power, Social Infrastructure, and the Revival of the Public Utility Concept' (2018) 39 Cardozo L Rev 1628–34 (tracing the 'common genealogical roots' of corporate governance, antitrust and the public utility concept as responses to the problem of private power and the need to ensure accountability).

[70] Sklar (n 49) 103; Hawk (n 28).

[71] Hovenkamp (n 42) 274.

[72] Sanjukta Paul, 'Reconsidering Judicial Supremacy in Antitrust' (2020) 31 Yale LJ. See also Sanjukta Paul, 'Antitrust as an Allocator of Coordination Rights' (n 18).

[73] Hawk (n 28) 40.

to earn their daily bread.[74] Cooperation and coordination of economic resources were not unlawful per se under the restraint of trade doctrine.[75]

The common law did not however have experience responding to the nature of the conglomerate corporation that emerged at the turn of the twentieth century. The focus of the law had been relatively small-scale restraints of trade: interferences with the market, non-competes, and questionable business practices. The perspective was somewhat different from today: what we might deem to be anticompetitive conduct was often categorised as the essence of vigorous competition. As one example, in the seminal *Mogul Steamship* case, a cartel of shipowners engaged in trading tea in China responded to a new entrant by declaring that they would refuse cargo from any exporter who used the competitor's vessels and also put on extra sailings to match those of the entrant at below cost.[76] When the case reached the House of Lords, Lord Halsbury articulated the prevailing view that the very essence of competition was to '*compete for a time as to render trade unprofitable to your rival in order that when you have got rid of him you may appropriate the profits of the entire trade to yourself*'.[77]

Other than as observed above, common law restraint of trade did not concern itself in any meaningful way with the relative power of private firms and the state. After an earlier decision in the *Mogul Steamship* case, at the Court of Appeal, The Times newspaper commented that the case '*forces us to realise that we are left with no defence against the monopoly or "trust" except such as the Legislature chooses to give us*'.[78] As we have seen, 'defence against monopoly' was the purview of the statutes on monopoly and incorporation, but the focus there was on public grants of monopoly not on private power.

The remedies at common law for a successful claim of restraint of trade or monopolisation were to render the contract or conduct void. An unlawful restraint of trade was unenforceable. This was a private action. There was no scope for enforcement by the state.[79] Hence the reliance by state attorneys general on the less targeted *quo warranto* proceedings as 'crude antitrust'. State antitrust laws and the federal Sherman Act were enacted to allow for governmental enforcement, but the overlap with corporate law continued: some state antitrust laws contained provisions

74 Sanjukta Paul, 'Reconsidering Judicial Supremacy in Antitrust' (2020) 31 Yale LJ.

75 Ibid.

76 *Mogul Steamship Company, Ltd. V. McGregor, Gow & Company*, 21 Q.B.D. 544 (1889).

77 Sir Peter Roth QC, 'The Continual Evolution of Competition Law' (Speech at the 36th Blackstone Lecture, Oxford, 9 November 2018) www.catribunal.org.uk/sites/default/files/2018-12/The%20Continual%20Evolution%20of%20Competition%20Law.pdf accessed on 9 September 2021.

78 As quoted in Sir Peter Roth QC, 'The Continual Evolution of Competition Law' (Speech at the 36th Blackstone Lecture, Oxford, 9 November 2018) www.catribunal.org.uk/sites/default/files/2018-12/The%20Continual%20Evolution%20of%20Competition%20Law.pdf accessed on 9 September 2021.

79 By the late 1800s, at least 21 states had put common law restraint of trade onto a statutory and/or constitutional footing. But these laws were not vigorously enforced. Sklar (n 49) 93.

familiar from incorporation laws, making participation in trusts ultra vires or instituting a remedy of charter forfeiture for breach of the antitrust law.[80] Meanwhile, some interest groups continued to argue that the federal Sherman Act should contain or be complemented by a federal incorporation framework.[81]

1.4.2 *Sherman Act*

The Sherman Act was historic in giving the federal government, not just state governments, the power to address the balance of power. As William Novak explains, the progressive movement at the end of the nineteenth century explicitly identified the risks of concentrated power.[82] There were known risks in terms of political influence and potential corruption of government. But it was also understood that there was a risk to the 'balance of power' itself; not just an economic or political problem but also a constitutional one.

As it played out, the Sherman Act built on the restraint of trade model at common law, and not the more powerful tool of federal chartering which was a live alternative at the time and immediately after the law's passage.[83] Herbert Hovenkamp has noted that by preserving the common law position, with its tolerance for 'reasonable' monopoly power, the potential of the Sherman Act was considerably emasculated.[84] Meanwhile, David Millon argues that the reliance on the supposedly equalising force of competition to maintain the balance of power turned the Sherman Act into '*the dying words of a tradition that aimed to control political power through decentralization of economic power, which in turn was to be achieved through protection of competitive opportunity*'.[85] The theory was that disparate economic interests, dispersed through competition, would not be able to co-opt the state for private political gain. According to Millon,' *The Senate's conservative approach to the concentration crisis failed to appreciate the magnitude and complexity of the problem. The Sherman Act thus had little impact on the rapidly accelerating consolidation of big business*'.[86]

Instead, coordination among labour and small producers, often permitted at common law, became the occupying focus of antitrust enforcers, with the previously central concern with corporate power fading into the background.[87] Today, the

[80] Hovenkamp, *Enterprise and American Law* (n 42) 266; Roy (n 3) 191.

[81] Hutchison, 'Progressive Era Conceptions of the Corporation' (2017) 2017(3) Colum Bus L Rev 1017.

[82] William Novak, 'Law and the Social Control of American Capitalism' (2010) 60 Emory LJ 377, 393–4.

[83] Crane (n 47) 116; Hutchison (n 82) 1022; Sklar (n 49); Melvin Urofsky, 'Proposed Federal Incorporation in the Progressive Era' (1982) 26(2) Am J Legal Hist 160–183.

[84] Hovenkamp, *Enterprise and American Law* (n 42) 247.

[85] Millon (n 31)

[86] Ibid. See also Roy (n 3) 197 ('The limp legislation was as much an admission that the changes [in American industry] were irreversible as it was a futile gesture to restore a competitive world that had never existed.').

[87] Sandeep Vaheesan, 'Accommodating Capital and Policing Labor: Antitrust in the Two Gilded Ages' (2019) 78 Md L Rev 766.

influence of the Chicago School since the mid-twentieth century on antitrust law can be seen in the inconsistent treatment of cartels – treated as an ultimate evil with no redeeming 'efficiencies' – and mergers, which are often construed as presumptively 'efficient',[88] as well as the preoccupation with specific economic concepts of 'efficiency' and 'consumer welfare' as opposed to the broader concepts of democracy, both economic and political, and the balance of power.

1.5 CORPORATE RESPONSIBILITY

While the aspects of corporate regulation that we today recognise as antitrust forked away from corporate chartering in the direction of restraint of trade and monopoly, corporate law was forged in the model of the reciprocal obligations and commitments embodied by the original charters. Under this model, the balance of power would be maintained not primarily by the state but by empowering corporate stakeholders. This section will explore these mechanisms, in particular: a) shareholder protections and b) shareholder democracy.

1.5.1 *Shareholder Protections*

Alongside the restrictions to the scope of grant of any privilege which served to constrain corporate power,[89] corporate charters contained provisions expressly designed to protect investors. These rules have changed little to the present day: requirements to publish annual financial statements, rules on dividend payments, rules on electing directors – including protections for minority shareholders.[90] Equally, after the passage of the general incorporation laws, most corporate laws contained some mechanisms to protect shareholders: rules prescribing the number of directors – sometimes requiring them to be shareholders and/or citizens of the incorporating state; rules stipulating one share, one vote; limits on the total proportion of votes to be exercised by a single shareholder.[91] Underlying these provisions was the democratic concern that the special privilege of incorporation would be abused to the detriment of weaker shareholders and the public at large, a parallel line of thinking to that which precipitated the Sherman Act. Part of the purpose of these rules in corporate law was to maintain the balance of power.

There was also a direct way in which shareholder protections reinforced antitrust enforcement. As state attorneys general found their ability to bring *quo warranto* proceedings hampered by weakened corporate law, some minority shareholders challenged the anticompetitive use of the trust structure in state court through derivative

88 Ramsi A. Woodcock, 'Inconsistency in Antitrust'(2013) 68 U Miami L Rev 105.
89 Discussed in Section 1.3.2.
90 Hilt (n 22) 51–52.
91 Lamoreaux and Novak (n 5) 12.

suits.[92] This would generally involve the minority shareholders of an acquired entity, that was about to be rolled-up into a trust and shut down, bringing a suit to challenge the effective merger. In these cases, the complaining shareholders would launch derivative suits against the majority shareholders, reinforcing their case with allegations of illegal conduct under the antitrust laws, claims to which the state courts were on the whole sympathetic.[93] Shareholder protections thus had a role in challenging the power of the corporate entity.

1.5.2 *Shareholder Democracy*

Although the principle of shareholder primacy is widely accepted today,[94] the legacy of corporate chartering was initially the notion of public responsibility that came with the early charters. This assumption – that corporations were meant to act to the public benefit, continued, at least in the public imagination, into the early twentieth century.[95] Then in 1919, the Michigan Supreme Court decided the landmark case prioritising the primacy of the shareholders within the corporate structure, *Dodge v. Ford*, holding that '*A business corporation is organized and carried on primarily for the profit of the stockholders*'.[96] *Dodge* heralded a new era of corporate governance, equating corporate responsibility not with the public interest but with shareholder interests.

Among corporate legal scholars, it is often thought that Adolf Berle and Gardiner Means' seminal book *The Modern Corporation* cemented the shareholder primacy principle by demonstrating that the separation of ownership and control alienated shareholders from their property and left managers free to pursue their own interests. This then was the justification for giving shareholders primacy in corporate decision-making. But the context of the time lends a different reading. Despite *Dodge*, it was not business practice of the day to only consider the interests of shareholders in corporate governance.[97] The debate on the role of the corporation was between more or less managerial discretion, with the goal of public benefit taken as a given.[98] The animating purpose of *The Modern Corporation* was to explore the troubling phenomenon of rising corporate concentration in the US economy in the Gilded Age of the 1920s, which left a few 'princes of property' – the corporate managers – with unprecedented power over the whole economy and society.

92 Lamoreaux and Philips Sawyer (n 49).

93 Ibid.

94 See for an exception, eg, Lynn Stout, 'The Shareholder Value Myth' (2013) Cornell Law Faculty Publications Paper 771 http://scholarship.law.cornell.edu/facpub/771 accessed on 9 September 2021.

95 JN Gordon, 'The Rise of Independent Directors in the United States, 1950–2005: Of Shareholder Value and Stock Market Prices (2006) 59 Stan L Rev 1465.

96 *Dodge v Ford Motor Company*, 204 MI 459, 170 NW 668 (MI 1919).

97 William Bratton and Michael Wachter, 'Shareholder Primacy's Corporatist Origins' (2008) 34 J Corp L 99, 102.

98 Ibid. at 99.

Thus, Berle and Means' prescription of shareholder empowerment was intended as a democratising, counterbalancing force, rendering management, and therefore the corporation, accountable to the shareholding public and thereby society at large.[99] This was not to be an active democratic participation on the part of the masses, but rather a mechanism to collectivise capital interests and recreate reciprocal public responsibility on the part of the corporation. In terms of balance of power, this democratisation would constrain the power of the corporate entity in a more flexible way than a corporate charter – instead of fixing a list of public responsibilities at the outset, the corporation would be liable for meeting evolving shareholder – and therefore public – needs, on an ongoing basis.

What Berle and Means did not give sufficient weight to in their analysis was that it was not shareholders per se that had been alienated by the separation of ownership and control. Rather, particular segments of financial capital were able to push aside the needs of the general stockholding public, and with the development of the holding company, by then permitted under corporate and antitrust law, they were able to do so with even relatively small shareholdings.[100] This situation was made worse by the move towards further shareholder empowerment within corporate law. Certain shareholder classes were able to maintain control of corporate resources and thus effectively recreate the elitist special privileges of the chartering era.[101]

As a matter of theory, corporate law in the latter half of the twentieth century departed from the 'concession theory' of the corporation as a creature of the state. Building on Ronald Coase's *Theory of the Firm*, the 'nexus of contracts' theory framed the corporation as existing not in relation to the state but in relation to those involved in its creation – labour, input suppliers and capital, with the last having primacy within the nexus.[102] In harmony with neoclassical price theory and the transaction cost economics of the Chicago School, the nexus of contracts replaces the balance of power as the organising principle of corporate regulation, just as the Chicago School interpretation of 'consumer welfare' and 'efficiency' have come to displace the concept of 'corporate power' within antitrust. The shareholders' 'contract' is construed as one that guarantees the maximum possible return on investment – and any resulting imbalance of power is therefore irrelevant as all stakeholders must refer to the terms of their contracts at the nexus.

The democratising thrust of Berle and Means' prescriptions are all but forgotten to history, with Milton Friedman's succinct edict in 1970 operating in its place: 'The Social Responsibility of Business is to Increase Its Profits'.[103] Although over the

99 Ibid. at 121–2, 148–9.

100 Roy (n 3) 172–74.

101 Paul (n 73).

102 Frank H. Easterbrook and Daniel R. Fischel, The Economic Structure of Corporate Law (Harvard University Press 1991).

103 Milton Friedman, 'A Friedman Doctrine – the Social Responsibility of Business Is to Increase Its Profits' *The New York Times* (New York, 13 September 1970).

decades debates have still raged in legal scholarly circles over whether shareholder primacy is cogent, whether it is feasible, whether it is the law, and whether it exists as a concept, as of 2001, Henry Hansmann and Rainier Kraakman had declared 'The End of History for Corporate Law', with a resounding victory for shareholder primacy.[104] The emphasis in corporate law has narrowed considerably towards a focus on investor protection as such and not as part of the counterbalancing of corporate power within society. The power of the modern corporation of the twenty-first century must be viewed in this context.

1.6 THE BALANCE OF POWER TODAY

Where does the balance of power stand today? The forking paths of antitrust and corporate law away from the charter model and towards restraint of trade and shareholder primacy do not leave the state well-equipped to implement any countermovement against concentrations of economic power. Meanwhile, such concentrations are ascendant yet again, as the contributions to this book show: the evidence, again, of rising industrial concentration almost 100 years after Berle and Means' investigation; the inequality of share ownership, skewed towards the wealthy; the web of corporate ownership, enabled by the holding company structure, concentrating power among a few entities; the incidence of common ownership, particularly through asset managers. The dual concentrating impacts of financialisation and digitalisation, explored in more detail in the contribution from Ioannis Lianos and Andrew P. McLean, *Financialisation of the digital value chains and competition law*, in Chapter 16, leave us with a sense that the technologically and financially constructed monopoly will not bend to the balancing force of competition alone, nor to any imposition of corporate responsibility. Again, economies of scale, to the extent that they are an economic and technological reality, need not be a corporate inevitability – the power that comes with scale must be actively managed. When the economy, and society, is shaped by 'platform power' – the power to control the infrastructure of digital capitalism, the power to self-preference, the power to predict and influence consumer behaviour, the power to instrumentalise the generation and harvesting of personal data – the balance of power is gravely threatened. It may be argued that this is not the remit of antitrust or corporate law. But without antitrust to constrain the exercise of corporate power on the market and corporate law to constrain the power of the corporate entity as a corporation, other efforts by the state to regulate corporate conduct face unenviable hurdles to success.[105] The political,

[104] Henry Hansmann and Rainier Kraakman, 'The End of History for Corporate Law' (2001) 89 Geo LJ 439, 439 ('There is no longer any serious competitor to the view that corporate law should principally strive to increase long-term shareholder value.')

[105] Luigi Zingales, 'Towards a Political Theory of the Firm' (2017) 31 J Econ Perspect 113–130.

economic, and constitutional power of the corporation must be addressed at a foundational level, and it is the role of antitrust law and corporate law to do so.[106]

We will need to go further than the early, crude attempts at creating and simultaneously constraining the corporation if we are to meet this challenge. In this vein, Elizabeth Warren's Accountable Capitalism Act[107] revives the notion of federal chartering. States continue to have the power to revoke charters – the *quo warranto* procedure was codified into statute in most US states – although the power is little used. The procedure was actually abolished under English law in 1938,[108] but an equivalent power exists under section 124A of the Insolvency Act 1986 which allows the Secretary of State for Business to petition the courts for the winding up of a company 'in the public interest'. Ewan McGaughey has argued for the application of this provision against oil and gas companies in an attempt to combat climate change[109] – perhaps the ultimate example of the consequences of a persistent imbalance of power between the demos and corporations.

Again and again, however, the courts emphasise that winding up a company is a serious step,[110] as compared to the ease with which a company can be formed under a general incorporation framework. Without some longstop beyond which the corporation's existence will no longer be tolerated, the threat to corporate power posed by the state cannot be fully credible. Modern antitrust, hamstrung by the concepts of 'efficiency' and 'consumer welfare', can be no match for corporate domination and does not, as it stands, provide a sufficient counterweight. So too with corporate law that empowers insider groups of shareholders. The balance of power will continue to swing in favour of the corporation unless there is a mechanism for counterbalance. The roles of antitrust law and corporate law in embedding the corporation in society must be re-established.

106 Michelle Meagher, 'Powerless Antitrust' (2019) 2(1) Competition Policy International Antitrust Chronicle.

107 Accountable Capitalism Act, 115th Congress (2017–18) S. 3348.

108 Administration of Justice Act 1938, s 9.

109 Ewan McGaughey and Mathew Lawrence, *The Green Recovery Act* (Common Wealth 2020) section 21 www.common-wealth.co.uk/interactive-digital-projects/green-recovery-act#1 accessed 9 September 2021.

110 *Walter Jacobs* at 252, as cited in Keay, 'Public Interest Petitions' (1999) 20 Company Lawyer 296.

2

ESG Policies at the Intersection between Competition and Corporate Law

Marco Corradi and Julian Nowag

2.1 INTRODUCTION

The last decade has witnessed a radical shift in both the corporate governance and competition law debate: while profit maximisation was core and centre, its interaction with other objectives has come into focus.

Starting from the end of the 1970s,[1] and until just after the ENRON scandal, corporate governance was heavily focused on agency costs.[2] Nowadays, the leitmotiv inspiring the academic debate and catalysing the attention of the policy-makers is 'environmental, social and corporate governance' (ESG).[3] Obviously, this does not mean that the ESG debate was previously absent in the corporate law and governance debate.[4] The debate was simply not mainstream and had developed at the margin, as fuelled especially by management literature.[5] Beyond academia, the legal practice had already started adopting corporate social responsibility (CSR) codes in the early 1990s.[6] 'By the beginning of the twenty-first century, most large companies in the U.S. and Western Europe [had] formed their own policies CSR'.[7] As a matter of fact, the main tenets of CSR may be as ancient as civilisation.[8] And this is due to the fact that any human action is likely to produce externalities both on other human beings and on the environment. Nonetheless, the novelty that the recent preponderance of the ESG debate may bring is the degree to which logics not based

[1] M Jensen and W Meckling, 'Theory of the Firm: Managerial Behaviour, Agency Costs and Ownership Structure' (1976) 3 J Financ Econ 305.

[2] J Armour and J McCahery (eds) *After Enron: Improving Corporate Law and Modernising Securities Regulation in Europe and the US* (Hart Publishing, 2006).

[3] See for instance the vast set of papers collected on the European Corporate Governance Institute official website https://ecgi.global/content/sustainable-corporate-governance.

[4] See Section 2.3.

[5] See Section 2.3.

[6] F Madrakhimova, 'History of Development of Corporate Social Responsibility' (2013) 4 J Bus Econ 509, 515.

[7] *Ibid.*

[8] K Aggarwal, The Origins of CSR, https://medium.com/@krishaggarwaldosco/the-origins-of-csr-c1fd65102147.

on profit maximisation need to coordinate from a practical perspective and in day-to-day corporate strategy with the profit maximisation rationale, which has become mainstream in corporate finance.

In competition law, a similar shift in focus can be observed. The last decade(s) were marked by a focus on economics and competition law.[9] While the debate about ESG and competition law started in the EU back in the 2000s,[10] it seems that in the last years[11] the debate is becoming more mainstream. Overall, it might still be said that the discussion has been a very European discussion. Yet, more recently, the debate takes place more globally[12] with discussions and work at international fora such as the OECD and the International Competition Network.[13] In terms of agencies, the European focus is characterised by the Dutch and the Greek authorities taking the lead[14] and the European Commission aiming to update its horizontal guidelines.[15] With ESG becoming more mainstream both in corporate and competition law, the sustainability debate is also colouring other previously 'orthodox' areas of research, at the intersection of competition and corporate law. For instance, this is the case with regard to questions on how to deal with mergers negatively affecting sustainability;[16]

9 See eg A Witt, *The More Economic Approach to EU Antitrust Law* (Hart 2016); J Blockx, 'The Limits of the "More Economic" Approach to Antitrust' (2019), 42(4) World Compet 475–496.

10 See CECED (IV.F.1/ 36.718) Commission Decision 2000/ 475/ EC [2000] OJ L187/47; H Vedder, Competition Law and Environmental Protection in Europe: Towards Sustainability? (Europa Law Publishing 2003).

11 See eg S Kingston, Greening EU Competition Law and Policy (Cambridge University Press 2012), J Nowag, Environmental Integration in Competition and Free-Movement Laws (Oxford University Press 2017); OECD (2020), Sustainability and Competition, OECD Competition Committee Discussion Paper, www.oecd.org/daf/competition/sustainability-and-competition-2020.pdf (accessed 16 Feb 2022); European Commission, Directorate-General for Competition, Competition policy brief 2021-01 in September 2021, European Commission, 2021, https://data.europa.eu/doi/10.2763/962262 (accessed 16 Feb 2022); OECD (2021), Environmental Considerations in Competition Enforcement, OECD Competition Committee Discussion Paper, www.oecd.org/daf/competition/environmental-considerations-in-competition-enforcement.htm (accessed 16 Feb 2022), and the near exponential growth of literature since 2020.

12 See, for example, A Miazad, 'Prosocial Antitrust' (March 11, 2021) *Hastings Law Journal* (forthcoming, 2021), available at SSRN: https://ssrn.com/abstract=3802194 (accessed 16 Feb 2022).

13 See OCED papers in (n 11); Hungarian Competition Authority, 'Sustainable Development and Competition Law – Survey Report: Special Project for the 2021 ICN Annual Conference' (30.09.2022) www.gvh.hu/en/gvh/Conference/icn-2021-annual-conference/special-project-for-the-2021-icn-annual-conference-sustainable-development-and-competition-law (accessed 16 Feb 2022).

14 ACM, 2nd Draft Guidelines Sustainability Agreements: Opportunities Within Competition Law (2021) www.acm.nl/sites/default/files/documents/second-draft-version-guidelines-on-sustainability-agreements-oppurtunities-within-competition-law.pdf (accessed 16 Feb 2022); HCC, 'Staff Discussion Paper on Sustainability Issues and Competition Law' www.epant.gr/en/enimerosi/competition-law-sustainability/item/download/1896_9b05dc293adbae88a7bb6cce37d1ea60.html (accessed 16. Feb 2022); R Inderst, E Sartzetakis, and A Xepapadeas, Joint Technical Report on Sustainability and Competition for the HCC and the ACM (Jan 2021) www.epant.gr/en/enimerosi/competition-law-sustainability/item/download/2165_f998b905c20c0426f068e512186c6ec4.html (accessed 16 Feb 2022).

15 See European Commission (n 11).

16 See I Lianos with D Katalevsky, 'Merger Activity in the Factors of Production Segments of the Food Value Chain: – A Critical Assessment of the Bayer/Monsanto merger' CLES Policy Paper Series 2017/1 www.ucl.ac.uk/cles/sites/cles/files/cles-policy-paper-1-2017.pdf (accessed 16 Feb 2022).

or the anticompetitive effects of common ownership, a theory that was originally developed exclusively based on finance,[17] and which is now heavily affected by the ESG debate.[18]

Although much has been written about ESG until now, little (if anything at all) has been said about the interaction between competition and corporate governance policies in the area of ESG. In this chapter, we explore the intersection between competition policy and corporate policies in the area of ESG. We focus on ESG, sustainability, and innovation and highlight core research areas that require thorough academic enquiry in the sustainability/growth conundrum. We suggest that well-suited ESG policies for companies must take into consideration the possibility to operate through a multiplicity of policy tools, in particular corporate law, corporate governance, and competition policy tools. This chapter first provides a basic overview of the ESG debate and corporate behaviour. It then focuses on the interaction between ESG and corporate law and governance, as well as ESG and competition law. The final section explores the interaction of competition law and corporate law in the area of ESG policies. We highlight the necessity of coordinated policies, especially in the field of research and development (R&D) and innovation – that is dynamic efficiency.

2.2 THE ESG DEBATE AND CORPORATE STRATEGY

The post-WW2 demographic explosion and the unparalleled economic and industrial development are leading our world towards an uncertain future. The ecosystem is highly endangered, which in turn also puts the survival of the human species in question. Big corporations, regardless of who their owners are, put under strain planet Earth and the life that populates it, not only by extracting raw materials up to the level of exhaustion but also by rendering the condition of air, soil, and water less and less suitable for life.

If richer countries have benefited from such overexploitation of the world resources by their economic empires and corporations – raising their living standards at unprecedented levels – poorer countries seem to be paying the price of such reckless entrepreneurial conduct.

The NGOs and international institutions such as the UN have been at the forefront at asking for more sustainable and responsible behaviours by the State, companies, and more generally by every single individual in the face of the present crisis.[19] This is particularly true for those who consume the biggest slices of the world's

[17] J Azar, M Schmalz and I Tecu, 'Anticompetitive Effects of Common Ownership' (2018) 73 J Fin 1513.

[18] J Azar et al., 'The Big Three and Corporate Carbon Emissions around the World' (2021) J Fin Econ; see also Chapter 14, in this book.

[19] See, for example, World Commission on Environment and Development, Our Common Future (Oxford University Press 1987).

cake.[20] While States have been stepping up their game, progress has been slow and the focus has also shifted towards private actors, corporations in particular. However, competition lawyers and economists often seem to express a preference for regulation to achieve sustainability.[21]

For competition lawyers and competition economists, regulation has obvious advantages. Most of the time, regulation is seen as being able to address sustainability more directly with a more uniform (or competitively neutral) effect on market participants than private action. This competition-policy centric view may not be agreed upon by other governmental agencies. The desirability, effectiveness, and efficiency of regulation in specific situations seem to be questionable. For example, regulation, in particular traditional command and control regulation, is often considered inefficient.[22] And, even where regulation might be efficient, other questions around its feasibility and effectiveness might be encountered. These can result, for example, from the political compromises that need to be found at the national or international level, with the effect of favouring the lowest common denominator. Similarly, the most efficient regulation on paper may, in many cases, fall victim to insufficient implementation, jurisdictional/geographical limitations, or other administrative burdens.[23]

In the absence of regulation, private-sector voluntary initiatives have gained importance and are also frequently encouraged by States. Another reason for this shift to private sector initiatives might purely be the scale that such initiatives may achieve. Corporate actions and strategic market choices can have larger effects than State interventions. For example, the environmental improvement derived by Amazon going CO_2-neutral would be slightly bigger than if the whole of Sweden went CO_2-neutral.[24] Thus, it is not surprising that the UN's sustainable development goals directly address private business and their activities.

20 See, for example, D Schlosberg and L Collins, 'From Environmental to Climate Justice: Climate Change and the Discourse of Environmental Justice' (2014) 5(3) WIREs Clim Change, 359–374; H Shue, *Climate Justice: Vulnerability and Protection* (Oxford University Press 2014); D Schlosberg, J Dryzek, and R Norgaard, *The Oxford Handbook of Climate Change and Society* (Oxford University Press 2011); L Meyer & D Roser, 'Climate Justice and Historical Emissions', (2010) 13(1) Crit Rev Int Soc Polit Phil, 229–253.

21 Instead of many see, for example, Maarten Pieter Schinkel and Yossi Spiegel, 'Can Collusion Promote Sustainable Consumption and Production?' (2017) Int J Ind Org 371–398.

22 For an overview on see: D Cole and P Grossman 'When Is Command-and-Control Efficient? Institutions, Technology, and the Comparative Efficiency of Alternative Regulatory Regimes for Environmental Protection' (1999) Wisconsin Law Rev 887–938.

23 Pacheco et al., 'Governing Sustainable Palm Oil Supply: Disconnects, Complementarities, and Antagonisms between State Regulations and Private Standards' (2020) 14:3 Regulat Govern 568–598.

24 Amazon emitted 2020 around 60.64 million tons of CO_2 in 2020 see, https://fortune.com/2021/06/30/amazon-carbon-footprint-pollution-grew/ (accessed 15 Feb. 2022), Sweden emitted around 45.5 million tons of CO_2 in 2020, see www.statista.com/statistics/449823/co2-emissions-sweden/ (accessed 15 Feb. 2022).

For private business, the ESG debate is nothing new. In fact, the corporate debate[25] – especially as enriched by managerial sciences –[26] has focused for a long time on corporate social responsibility (CSR), that is, a way to embed in management strategy and soft law ESG objectives at large (which at the time were not as precisely detailed as in the modern debate). The older CSR debate was revived several times, decade after decade,[27] until the recent explosion of the ESG-connected literature.[28] But if non-corporate literature may have seen CSR as a promising ally towards a greener and more just future, corporate literature often denounced its limited reach in pursuing such objectives – especially in a transnational context.[29] As a reaction to the often generic and blurred content of CSR codes, corporate governance recently witnessed the emersion of a goal-oriented movement, organised around sustainable development goals (SDG)[30] – once again strongly inspired by management literature.[31] As goals are characterised by benchmarking, CSR objectives can finally be given proper tracks and verifiable milestones to reach.[32]

The shifting focus of the ESG policy discourse to companies and to their strategic interaction on the market entails that both competition and corporate law are relevant to the ESG debate. These two areas of law are crucially shaping the behaviour of companies by setting the inner and outer limits of their action; by being teleologically connected, their paths are inevitably destined to be intertwined.

2.3 ESG POLICIES, CORPORATE LAW AND GOVERNANCE

The ESG debate has touched upon topics that are not new in the corporate law and in corporate governance fields of research. Examples of such popular topics are as follows: short versus long-termism (together with their connection to the corporate

[25] W Katz, 'Responsibility and the Modern Corporation' (1960) 3 J Law Econ 75–85.

[26] R Eells, 'The Traditional Corporation', in *The Meaning of Modern Business* (Columbia University Press, 1960) 38–49.

[27] J Hetherington, 'Fact and Legal Theory: Shareholders, Managers, and Corporate Social Responsibility' (1968) 21 Stan L Rev 248; A Carroll, 'A Three-Dimensional Conceptual Model of Corporate Performance' (1979) 4 Acad Manag Rev 497–505; E Epstein, 'The Corporate Social Policy Process: Beyond Business Ethics, Corporate Social Responsibility, and Corporate Social Responsiveness' (1987) 29 Calif Manage Rev 99–114.

[28] A Carroll and J Brown, 'Corporate Social Responsibility: A Review of Current Concepts, Research, and Issues' (2018) Corp Soc Responsib.

[29] G Frynas, 'The False Developmental Promise of Corporate Social Responsibility: Evidence from Multinational Oil Companies' (2005) 81 Int Aff 581–598.

[30] H Grove and M Clouse, 'Focusing on Sustainability to Strengthen Corporate Governance' (2018) 2 Corp Govern Sustain Rev 38–47.

[31] T Tsalis et al., 'New Challenges for Corporate Sustainability Reporting: United Nations' 2030 Agenda for Sustainable Development and the Sustainable Development Goals' (2020) 27 Corp Soc Responsib Environ Manag 1617–1629.

[32] See a practical 'mise en oeuvre' of the relationship between CSR and SDG in the KPMG report titled: 'Sustainable Development Goals (SDGs): Leveraging CSR to Achieve SDGs' https://assets.kpmg/content/dam/kpmg/in/pdf/2017/12/SDG_New_Final_Web.pdf

ownership structure and to the nature and incentives of corporate owners)[33] and the shareholder versus stakeholder theories of the corporate purpose.[34] Ultimately, such topics have been approached in the light of the environmental and social challenges of the twenty-first century. But not only old themes have been revisited and re-coloured. New themes, such as specific ESG-oriented shareholder and bondholder stewardship, now represent a significant share in the corporate governance literature.[35]

Research questioning the desirability of long-termism dates back to the second decade of the twenty-first century; it has represented a prominent voice in the United States[36] and in the UK corporate governance debate.[37] Such debate has crossed the Anglo-American cultural border, reaching the European Union policy-makers[38] and also EU Member States' policy-makers – for instance, the French one, which introduced the Florange Law.[39] Nobel prize Joseph Stiglitz has identified short-termism as one of the adversaries of sustainable policies and widely advocated for the pursuance of long-term oriented policies.[40] Stiglitz notices that

> [i]nequality has increased markedly in the last third of a century, partially because neoliberal doctrines, reflected in the Washington Consensus led to rewriting the rules of the economy in ways which led to more inequality and slower growth (as a result of excessive focus on financialization and the associated short-termism).[41]

Soon a cascade of corporate governance studies analysing short- versus long-termism from an ESG perspective followed. The relationship between short- versus long-termism and corporate governance can be tackled from different angles. Short-termism has been traditionally seen as a consequence of the pressure exercised on corporate directors by shareholders (especially investment funds) which are supposed to pursue a short-term maximisation of their investments – although such an

33 See infra text corresponding to n 37 ff.

34 See infra text corresponding to n 56 ff.

35 Ibid.

36 M Roe, 'Corporate Short-Termism – in the Boardroom and in the Courtroom' (2013) Bus Lawyer 977.

37 C Mayer, *Firm Commitment: Why the Corporation Is Failing Us and How To Restore Trust In It* (Oxford University Press 2013).

38 Directive (EU) 2017/828 of the European Parliament and of the Council of 17 May 2017 amending Directive 2007/36/EC as regards to the encouragement of long-term shareholder engagement, OJ L 132, 20.5.2017, *pp.* 1–25.

39 LOI no. 2014-384 du 29 mars 2014 *Visant à Reconquérir l'Economie Réelle*, JORF n 0077 du 1 avril 2014, Texte no. 3. See the Florange Act in comparative perspective in F Alogna, et al., 'The Shareholder in France and the United States: A Comparative Analysis of Corporate Legal Priorities', *Business & Law Review, Business & Law Association (Association Droit & Affaires (AD&A)) Paris* (2020).

40 J Stiglitz, *Rewriting the Rules of the American Economy: An Agenda for Growth and Shared Prosperity* (WW Norton & Company, 2015).

41 J Stiglitz, 'An Agenda for Sustainable and Inclusive Growth for Emerging Markets' (2016) 38 J of Policy Model 693, 702.

assumption is clearly questionable as there is no homogeneity among institutional investors from this point of view.[42]

Correctives to such short-termism orientation have been proposed. For instance, Bolton and Samama have proposed the introduction of the 'loyalty share', to reward shareholder that engage in long-term commitment to the company.[43] It has also been argued that directors who are more insulated from shareholders are more likely to adopt long-term strategies.[44] Or, that more long-termism would set a remedy to the disempowerment of stakeholders.[45] By contrast, other research has shown that empowering stakeholders in some cases can worsen the effects of short-term strategies.[46] And, evidence has emerged that shareholders' short-termism could actually be seen as a correction to the dark sides of managerial long-termism, that is, over-optimism regarding the success of long-term plans.[47]

The general contrast to short-termism as a potential remedy to unsustainable policies has been embraced in research commissioned by the EU Commission: the Ernst & Young's 'Study on Directors' duties sustainable corporate governance'.[48] But what corporate governance literature has questioned is the very relationship between long-termism and the pursuance of ESG policies. A prominent dissenting opinion against the original identification of short-termism with unsustainable policies has been Mark Roe's one. Based on Roe's previous studies, Roe, Spamann, Fried and Wang have also heavily criticised the Ernst and Young's proposal, not only showing the inappropriate conflation of short-termism with sustainability but also the absence of empirical evidence of such relationship.[49] Roe and Shapira have also explained that the purported connection between short-termism, pro-shareholder policies and unsustainable strategies has found its way into the general discourse on ESG, thanks to the strong narrative inherent to the terminology adopted in the debate. Good, reliable, long-term commitment versus bad, unreliable, short-term strategies[50] prompts policy-makers to adopt the first triad.

42 And note that the same kind of fund may also adopt differentiated strategies. See K Greenfield, 'The Puzzle of Short-Termism' (2011) 46 Wake Forest L Rev 627, 638–639.

43 P Bolton and F Samama, 'Loyalty-Shares: Rewarding Long-Term Investors' (2013) 25 J Appl Corp Finance 86.

44 See the seminal statement by M Lipton, 'Takeover Bids in the Target's Boardroom' (1979) 35 Bus Lawyer 101.

45 See the literature cited by M Roe, 'Stock Market Short-Termism's Impact' (2018) 167 U Pa L Rev 71, 109.

46 H Almeida et al., 'Do Short-Term Incentives Affect Long-Term Productivity?', European Corporate Governance Institute–Finance Working Paper 662 (2020).

47 M Barzuza and E Talley, 'Long-Term Bias' (2020) Colum Bus L Rev 104.

48 Ernst & Young's 'Study on Directors' Duties Sustainable Corporate Governance' (April 2020), available at https://op.europa.eu/en/publication-detail/-/publication/e47928a2-d20b-11ea-adf7-01aa75ed71a1/language-en, 9–31.

49 M Roe et al., 'The European Commission's Sustainable Corporate Governance Report: A Critique', available at *SSRN* (2020).

50 M Roe, and R Shapira. 'The Power of the Narrative in Corporate Lawmaking', available at *SSRN* 3703882 (2020).

Mark Roe has challenged not only the conventional view on the detrimental effects of short-termism for sustainability. He has also demystified another common belief, that is, that short-termism has determined a fall in research and development and consequently in innovation.[51] Roe's position is clearly based largely on the fact that the US hosts the largest number of high-tech companies in the world, which clearly invest large sums in research and development and are leading innovators. Jesse Fried has added another important piece to the short-termism puzzle: he has shown that long-term shareholders may well demand even worse value destruction than short-term ones.[52] This again makes us doubt of the suitability of the promotion of long-term equity holdings for sorting out positive effects on structural investment and innovation.

Fried and Wang have also calculated that the effective distribution of companies' net income to investors (often held responsible for fund depletion and consequent incapability to invest in innovation) is not as significant as it is often claimed.[53] Similar results have been found with reference to EU companies, once taking into account new equity issuances.[54] Short-horizon investors have also been considered as a stimulus to competitiveness, especially with reference to innovation parameters.[55]

Roe's and Freed & Wang's observations are extremely useful when it comes to assess the innovation deriving from R&D. But it is worth remembering that disruptive innovation does not necessarily require significant investments in research and development. And corporate law mechanisms underlying disruptive innovation may require taking into consideration corporate law rules different than the ones mentioned by the mainstream literature that focuses on research and development.[56] Being innovation based upon recombinational dynamics of blocks of knowledge, rules such as the corporate opportunity doctrine, the directors' duty not to compete and other contractual arrangements such as no-compete clauses may become prominent.[57] And we have already highlighted that such rules may escape the EU's competition radar.[58]

Instead of relying on the long-termism argument, part of the ESG debate has invested directly in the shareholder versus stakeholder conundrum – especially tackling the relationship between company and a vast range of stakeholders, among

51 Roe (n 45).

52 J Fried, 'The Uneasy Case for Favoring Long-Term Shareholders' (2014) 124 Yale LJ 1554.

53 J Fried and C Wang, 'Short-Termism and Capital Flows' (2019) 8 Rev Corp Finance Stud 207.

54 J Fried and C Wang, 'Short-Termism, Shareholder Payouts and Investment in the EU' (2021) 27 Eur Financ Manag 389.

55 M Giannetti and X Yu, 'Adapting to Radical Change: The Benefits of Short-Horizon Investors' (2021) 67 Manag Sci 4032.

56 M Corradi, *Corporate Opportunities, A Law and Economics Analysis* (Hart, 2021) Ch 5.

57 Ibid.

58 See Chapter 8 in this book and also M Corradi and J Nowag, 'Enforcing Corporate Opportunity Rules: Antitrust Risks and Antitrust Failures', forthcoming on *European Business Law Review*.

which consumers – hence impinging deliberately on an area (consumers) that has traditionally been competence of competition policies.[59]

During the age of privatisation, European private companies have taken up the role previously carried out by the state in granting the provision of public goods and services,[60] often achieving questionable results in terms of pricing and efficiency.[61] In the context of privatisation, the Milton Friedman's 'maximising shareholder value' rationale may not provide a correct representation of the corporate positioning vis-à-vis consumers.[62] Colin Mayer has advocated for the acknowledgement that 'a corporation is an employer, investor, consumer, producer and supplier all rolled into one'[63] and that '[t]he repositioning of corporations, capital and control' is 'fundamental implications for business, economics and public policy as the Copernican revolution had for astronomy'.[64] Colin Mayer asserts that companies actually work for solving people's problems, hence viewing consumers as the recipient of a service more than the target of lucrative business activity.[65] It goes without saying that among collective problems, we can easily mention the necessity to build up a sustainable future.

As we have shown, the ESG debate in the field of corporate law and governance is very animated, full of controversies, and overall in its nascent phase – even to the extent to which scholars are still debating about the efficiency of corporate law and governance tools for addressing ESG concerns.

As highlighted in the previous section, public intervention in the ESG arena seems to rely heavily upon private initiative. But given the fact that private initiative is still surrounded by a high degree of uncertainty, it is inevitable that private

59 On consumer welfare, H Hovenkamp, 'Distributive Justice and the Antitrust Laws' (1982) 51 Geo Wash L Rev 1; B Orbach, 'The Antitrust Consumer Welfare Paradox' (2001) 7 J Compet Law and Econ 133.

60 D Bös, 'Privatization in Europe: A Comparison of Approaches' (1993) 9 Oxford Rev Econ Policy 95.

61 K Schmidt, 'The Costs and Benefits of Privatization: An Incomplete Contracts Approach' (1996) 12 J Law, Econ, and Organ 1; For the distributional consequences of privatizations, see N Birdsall and J Nellis, 'Winners and Losers: Assessing the Distributional Impact of Privatization' (2003) 31 World Development 1617.

62 C Mayer, *Prosperity: Better Business Makes the Greater Good* (Oxford University Press, 2018) 2. Mayer's theses were criticized by L Bebchuk and R Tallarita, 'The Illusory Promise of Stakeholder Governance', available at SSRN 3544978 (2020), to whom Mayer reacted with a further paper: C Mayer, 'Shareholderism Versus Stakeholderism – A Misconceived Contradiction. A Comment on 'The Illusory Promise of Stakeholder Governance' by Lucian Bebchuk and Roberto Tallarita', *European Corporate Governance Institute-Law Working Paper* 522 (2020).

63 *Ibid.* at 4.

64 *Ibid.* at 5.

65 C Mayer, 'The Future of the Corporation and the Economics of Purpose', ECGI Finance Working Paper 710/2020. These principles have been adopted by a recent policy document by the British Academy, 'Principles for Purposeful Business', that sets general principles and supports the idea that '[r]egulation should expect particularly high duties of engagement, loyalty and care on the part of directors of companies to public interests where they perform important public functions'; The British Academy, 'Principles for Purposeful Business' (2019) www.thebritishacademy.ac.uk/publications/future-of-the-corporation-principles-for-purposeful-business/.

and public powers will keep on passing each other the torch. While competition law is often placed among the private law area, it often uses traditional command and control mechanisms known traditionally in the area of public intervention. In contrast, corporate law is more clearly in the realm of private law – although some of its rules – especially those pertaining to securities – can be described as public too. With both fields affecting corporate behaviour substantially, these two fields need increasing dialogue. In certain cases, such a dialogue will end with exacting from each other a degree of intervention that the other area is not able to offer. In other cases, the same dialogue may well end up requiring a common and coordinated intervention in the same field. These two potential kinds of interaction are, respectively, the subject of the two following sections. We will start by highlighting the progress of competition law with reference to the pursuance of ESG objectives, and we will finally highlight the necessity of joint competition and corporate law intervention in the area of technological innovation.

2.4 ESG POLICIES AND COMPETITION POLICY

In the competition field, ESG is not frequently discussed. But a similar debate develops under the heading of competition and sustainability or the more concrete UN implementation of SDGs. Yet, while the exact boundaries between ESG and SDG are sometimes difficult to draw, a certain overlap between SDGs and ESG cannot be denied. One may see SDGs and ESG as overlapping but different in the way they are pursued. And while we have seen some attempts to allow reporting of companies on SDG,[66] the ESG debate has a different origin. To simplify, one may say that SDGs set out goals, while ESG is more about methods and processes within companies and their reporting on a range of environmental and social matters. Given that this area of research is rather new, we also acknowledge that the semantic fields of such new terms may be rather blurred at times, as such terms are given more and more detailed meaning by their contextual application.

The above-mentioned difference in meaning also explains the different focus of the debates in corporate and competition law. The corporate debate and its focus on long-term versus short-termism can be understood if one takes into account the process orientation of ESG. As such, this debate has much less prominence in competition law. In competition law, the debate is more focused on sustainability broadly and only lightly touches upon the SDGs as points of orientation to gain a better understanding of what sustainability actually is.

However, certain elements about the long- versus short-term focus can also be observed in the context of the sustainability debate in competition law. For example, the time horizon for the expected benefit is sometimes a matter of discussion,

[66] See KPMG, 'How to Report On the SDGs: What Good Looks Like and Why It Matters (Feb 2018), https://assets.kpmg/content/dam/kpmg/xx/pdf/2018/02/how-to-report-on-sdgs.pdf

especially with regard to what time horizon should be employed when measuring sustainability benefits such as a reduction in CO_2 emissions. While the time frame, for example, in merger cases is usually short to medium (up to five years), the full benefits of CO_2 reductions now may only be experienced in 50 years. Here, the debate is normative as well as technical. On the normative side, one might question whether the importance of, for example, CO_2 reduction and the delayed nature of benefits derived from action today justify a different approach.[67] From a more technical point of view, the question of the time horizon presents itself as a question of proof rather than policy.[68] Crucial is here the discount rate applied to such future benefit,[69] an argument can be made about 'discounted away' sustainability benefits because future costs might be grossly underappreciated as the example of climate change shows.[70] Recently, the Dutch Competition Authority's draft guidelines address this matter and suggest the use of the standard social-cost-benefit tools of Dutch government agencies. The draft guidelines also suggest that avoided environmental damage should be monetised by means of environmental or 'shadow' prices.[71]

While this area shows the tension between an approach that takes a long-term perspective from short-term ones, the debate in competition law is more outcome-focused. The questions are to what extent the enforcement of competition law can support or hinder the achievement of sustainability.[72] In other words, to what extent competition law can be a sword in the fight for more sustainability or to what extent sustainability outcomes might serve as a shield against prohibitions against certain actions by competition law.[73] The possibly closest link to the debates in corporate governance is stakeholders, that is, constituencies whose interests are affected by corporate action can also be heavily affected by the above-mentioned sword and shield perspective on competition law. The calculation of gains and losses born by different stakeholders can form a bridge between the debates in competition law

[67] It can, for example, be compared to innovation questions where similar questions can arise. Yet, the benefits of CO2 reductions might be their very nature be felt even later. On the comparison to innovation questions see Hellenic Competition Commission, Staff Discussion Paper on Sustainability Issues and Competition Law (2020), available www.epant.gr/en/enimerosi/competition-law-sustainability/item/download/1896_9b05dc293adbae88a7bb6cce37d1ea60.html (accessed 05 Oct 2020) para 25.

[68] K Coates & D Middelschulte, 'Getting Consumer Welfare Right: The Competition Law Implications of Market-Driven Sustainability Initiatives' (2019) 15:2–3 Eur Compet J 321.

[69] In general, see also R Inderst, E Sartzetakis, and A Xepapadeas, Joint Technical Report on Sustainability and Competition for the HCC and the ACM (Jan 2021) www.epant.gr/en/enimerosi/competition-law-sustainability/item/download/2165_f998b905c20c0426f068e512186c6ec4.html (accessed 16 Feb 2022).

[70] Hellenic Competition Commission, Staff Discussion Paper on Sustainability Issues and Competition Law (2020), available at www.epant.gr/en/enimerosi/competition-law-sustainability/item/download/1896_9b05dc293adbae88a7bb6cce37d1ea60.html (accessed 05 Oct 2020) para 111.

[71] *Ibid.* at para 50.

[72] This framework is developed in Julian Nowag, Environmental Integration in Competition and Free-Movement Laws (Oxford University Press 2017) 1–12.

[73] See Simon Holms, 'Climate Change, Sustainability and Competition Law' 8:2 (2020) *J Antitrust Enforc* 355.

and corporate law, where the sustainability impact on such stakeholders may come under scrutiny. In fact, an analysis of the stakeholder interests can provide grounding for the theoretical debates and help quantifying the overall welfare effects of the combination of competition and corporate law policy on each stakeholder.

The interaction between competition and sustainability as the first point of reference might be provided by economics. Sustainability and competition economics both highlight resource efficiency, innovation, and the role of the private sector. Moreover, economics is the most important tool to understand the market forces at play and this is crucial to determine the dynamics harming or supporting sustainability.

Foundational on the interaction between sustainability and competition is Elinor Ostrom's work on the sustainable management of common pool resources.[74] Her Nobel prize-winning work explored the tragedy of the commons. It showed that rational profit maximisers in unfettered competition lead to disastrous outcomes for that commons. It moreover showed that in reality co-operation rather than competition can be expected.[75] Ostrom's foundational work focuses on real-world cases where cooperation takes place. Yet micro-economists do not frequently study sustainability initiatives by private parties. There are theoretical micro-economic studies by even fewer authors[76] which apply the standard assumptions and models used in competition economics, including the rational profit maximiser assumption for firms. These suggest that, in general, competition will lead to greater sustainability gains where consumers value sustainability. These papers highlight that there are only a few situations where cooperation has positive outcomes on sustainability. Instead, they suggest that government regulation is a more efficient solution. This literature attributes such findings mainly to the fact that profit-maximising firms have limited incentives to invest in sustainability. It is here where the first points of interaction with the corporate law and governance become apparent. Where corporate law and governance prescribe profit maximisation, the theories about the relationship between competition and sustainability have the most explanatory force. However, the further corporate law and governance move away from the profit maximisation maxim, the harder it becomes to apply these theories.

74 See E Ostrom, Governing the Commons: The Evolution of Institutions for Collective Action (Cambridge University Press 1990).

75 Picking up on theme of competition leading to suboptimal outcomes, see Maurice Stucke and Ariel Ezrachi, *Competition Overdose* (Harper Business 2020).

76 See, for example, M P Schinkel and Y Spiegel, 'Can Collusion Promote Sustainable Consumption and Production?' (2017) Int J Ind Organ 371–398. L Treuren and M P Schinkel, 'Can Collusion Promote Sustainable Consumption and Production? Not Beneficially Beyond Duopoly' (March 1, 2018) Amsterdam Law School Research Paper No. 2018-02, Amsterdam Center for Law & Economics Working Paper No. 2018-01; F Martinez, S Onderstal and M P Schinkel, 'Can Collusion Promote Corporate Social Responsibility? Evidence from the Lab' (Nov 2019) Tinbergen Institute Discussion Paper TI 2019-034/VII; M P Schinkel and L Tóth, 'Compensatory Public Good Provision by a Private Cartel' (January 2020) Tinbergen Institute Discussion Papers 19-086/VII.

A second important avenue in the sustainability competition debate is the question of sustainable innovation as both sustainability and competition law and policy recognise the importance of companies in driving innovation. Where sustainability is explored as a dynamic parameter of competition – that is, one that consumers value as a non-price quality variable –[77] a dynamic innovation-focused assessment seems adequate. In this context, one may ask whether more competition or more cooperation will foster sustainability innovation. General models from the study of the interaction between competition and innovation suggest that a more nuanced assessment is required: one that takes into account practices and specific situations. In other words, the answer to the Schumpeter-Arrow debate over innovation in a competitive or monopolistic setting is best answered on a case-by-case basis, by examining the concrete situation.[78] Similarly, innovation in sustainability needs to be assessed in a concrete situation.

Equipped with these insights, it becomes clear that competition law needs to take a flexible approach. On the one hand, competition leading to innovation in terms of sustainability needs to be protected; and on the other hand, cooperation needs to be possible where it fosters innovation that leads to sustainability. We will explore the two different scenarios that can, as highlighted before,[79] also be compared to competition law as a sword to protect sustainable innovation and sustainable innovation as a shield.

2.5 ESG POLICIES, COMPETITION LAW, AND CORPORATE LAW: ANOTHER MISSING CONNECTION?

As already stressed, some of the EU research on corporate policy strategies and ESG objectives have been highly criticised for the absence of their consistency and lack of empirical analysis.[80] More thorough research in the field is needed. Given that such research, as well as the research on sustainability and competition law, are *in fieri*, it might not be surprising that there has been no research on the interaction between corporate and competition law. In fact, both policy areas are still heavily occupied with themselves. Nonetheless, we firmly believe that sustainability and ESG objectives are crucial in the long run and that corporate and competition policies will inevitably interact in the ESG area. Hence, it is necessary to anticipate and facilitate such encounters, by foreseeing potential conflicts and by softening sharp edges.

77 See, for example, C Volpin, 'Sustainability as a Quality Dimension of Competition: Protecting Our Future (Selves)' (July 2020) CPI Antitrust Chronicle 9–18.

78 For a good overview of the Schumpter-Arrow debate and questions regarding specific market conditions in Pharma, see Michael A. Carrier, 'Two Puzzles Resolved: Of the Schumpeter–Arrow Stalemate and Pharmaceutical Innovation Markets' (2007) Iowa L Rev 393.

79 See text to n 73.

80 See Section 2.3.

At the most basic level, the competition law and sustainability debate is a debate about outcomes with a focus on the extent to which competition law is a useful and viable tool. The ESG and SDG debate in corporate law and governance seems more process-focused, aimed at identifying means that allow for measurement and reporting, but academics are also studying contractual tools for forcing the pursuance of such objectives.[81]

Chapter 14 already deals with the potential ESG clash in competition and corporate law policies in the fields of common ownership. Nonetheless, we do not believe that this will necessarily represent the ESG's main stumbling block. We have highlighted and believed in the importance of the special role of dynamic innovation for more sustainable growth. What is essential is that EU policy-makers avoid treating corporate law and governance and competition law in isolation in the pursuance of such a goal. Instead, it needs to be ensured that both legal regimes are streamlined and that potential stumbling blocks presented by their interaction are addressed.

The 2020 COVID-19 crisis illustrates the importance of swift innovation as the necessity of finding a vaccine in a very short time. In such catastrophic events, even a small acceleration towards new inventions can be hugely important and can have beneficial effects on a global scale. Dynamic efficiency is crucial for the future of our planet, for the environment and for increasing productive efficiency – hence producing less waste.[82]

The attention to innovation also brings into focus other questions on border between corporate and competition law. For example, as we have explained in Chapter 8, corporate opportunity rules and the directors' duty not to compete with the company may have a direct effects on innovation. A large incumbent company, often with a corporate venture capital division, is able to purchase a vast array of innovative start-ups and develop or shutdown at its discretion a whole range of different innovations.[83] In these situations, the competition among such different innovative solutions is withdrawn from market mechanisms and market forces. Instead, innovation becomes subject to a balance of interests within the incumbent corporation where the best innovations might not be developed for instance because it does not fit with the incumbent industrial strategy.

The debates around the tech companies and their corporate venture capital divisions have highlighted the problem: and both corporate law and competition law may find themselves unable to sufficiently address any such obstacle to innovation.

[81] J Armour, L Enriques, T Wetzer, 'Green Pills: Making Corporate Carbon Commitments Credible' (November, 2021).

[82] OECD, *Towards a Green Growth* (2011); www.oecd.org/greengrowth/48012345.pdf. But some do not see in innovation a solution to environmental issues. See M Cohen, 'Ecological Modernization and Its Discontents: The American Environmental Movement's Resistance to an Innovation-driven Future' (2006) 38 *Futures* 528. Amore balanced approach in. A Grunwald, 'Diverging Pathways to Overcoming the Environmental Crisis: A critique of Eco-modernism from a Technology Assessment Perspective' (2018) 197 J of Clean Prod 1854.

[83] Corradi, Corporate Opportunities (n 56) Chapter 6.

And as we have highlighted elsewhere[84] corporate opportunity rules may facilitate the exercise of such power by the incumbent company and competition law authorities and courts may find that such arrangements are not subject to competition law as they occur within the corporation. Similar concerns are raised by an alternative version of the same corporate strategy adopted by incumbent corporations. In the case of killer mergers, the incumbent has the intention of shutting down the potential competitor. While in these cases competition law may apply, the tools are not well adjusted to such problems.[85] The potential restriction of competition is carried out through corporate means and seems to be hard to control through the traditional competition law analysis, which may be ill suited for tackling dynamic competition issues at large.

While these specific examples highlight some of the interactions between corporate law and competition law in the in context of innovation for sustainability, we can also take a broader perspective. And if we widen our perspective, we may well see that the interaction between corporate strategy – as affected by corporate law and governance – and competition law is only destined to increase in quality and in dimension. If the core objective of corporate strategy is increasingly found in the reconciliation between profit-maximising strategies and ESG objectives, corporate strategy may more and more depart from the dualistic idea of either competing or colluding on prices. The overall paradigm shifts in the business world that is highlighted by corporations adopting ESG or SDG polices – cannot be without effects on fundamental paradigms of competition law. This is so in particular because competition law risk losing touch with the business reality that is affected by corporate law and governance changes. This risk of a disconnect might occur where competition theory still conceives the corporation as pure profit maximiser – and does not ponder the ESG variables and the way they might modify the conception of the corporate interest in the future.

2.6 CONCLUSIONS

The theoretical challenge represented by the encounter of corporate and competition policies in the ESG area seems considerable – as well as very exciting – given the vast number of issues that must be solved. In this chapter, we have only attempted to sketch out some interesting aspects of a future discussion likely to occupy vast areas of the corporate and competition literature in the coming years. Anecdotally, it is often said that both doctrine and jurisprudence strive to bring within their competence areas of the law that traditionally belong to other fields. But this is not the case for ESG, especially when it comes to find practical real-world solutions. The

[84] See Corradi Nowag (n 58).

[85] M Corradi and J Nowag, 'Enforcing Corporate Opportunity Rules: Antitrust Risks and Antitrust Failures' Eur Bus Law Rev 2022 (forthcoming).

challenge is so that the hope rests upon corporate action. Yet, corporate and competition lawyers seem critical of corporate action and easily denounce them as insufficient and ineffective when it comes to pursuing ESG objectives.[86] Such an attitude, demanding that someone else provides viable and effective solutions, seems a common psychological reaction: when challenges are tough, we may perceive them as insurmountable and are tempted to stand by and look for an external rescuer. But it is equally true that such external rescue is unlikely to come. Therefore, action is needed.

In this paper, we propose that enquiring about the interaction between competition and corporate ESG policies is a good starting point, and that we may need to focus especially on dynamic innovation. This may represent the first step for tackling the wider debate. While it may look like a small step, it is crucial in fact. If the environmental and social challenges are so hard, the best human talents have to be employed. And only well-suited and well-coordinated competition and corporate policies can grant that financial resources and incentives for innovative projects along their path of a more sustainable future.

[86] R. Tallarita, Portfolio Primacy and Climate Change *available at SSRN* 3912977 (2021).

3

Not-for-Profit Organisations and Competition Law

Okeoghene Odudu

3.1 INTRODUCTION

A not-for-profit organisation is one that is barred from distributing net earnings to individuals who exercise control over the organisation, such as members, officers, directors, or trustees.[1] The organisation may be funded by donors (philanthropists), government, service users, or a combination of all three and may benefit from charitable status, special tax advantages, or a special institutional status (e.g. be public body).[2] It is common for professional associations, healthcare service providers, and educational establishments to operate on a not-for-profit basis.[3] There are often claims that competition law *does not* or *should not* apply to entities that operate on a not-for-profit basis.[4] This chapter considers how competition law assesses the actions of entities operating on a not-for-profit basis. Implicit in this presentation is an assumption that similar concerns arise in all competition law jurisdictions. While the points made are thus of general application, they are illustrated with examples from the United States, EU, and United Kingdom. Section 3.2 explains why operating on a not-for-profit basis is not accepted as a reason to exclude an entities activities from the scope of competition law. Section 3.3 considers situations in which competition law is applied to non-profit providers and in which it is generally accepted that no modification is required. Section 3.4 considers situations in which competition law is applied to not-for-profit providers, but it is not applied

Professor of Competition Law, Faculty of Law; Director of the Centre for European Legal Studies; Fellow in Law, Emmanuel College, University of Cambridge.

1 H Hansmann, 'The Role of Nonprofit Enterprise' (1980) 89 Yale LJ 835–901.

2 S Rose-Ackerman, 'Altruism, Nonprofits, and Economic Theory' (1996) 34 J Econ Lit 701, 723–725.

3 Ibid. at 701–728. Although both public (government) and private not for profit organisations are treated as equivalents in this chapter, there is some evidence that they may behave differently and thus warrant different treatment: D Almond, J Currie, and ESimeonova, 'Public vs Private Provision of Charity Care? Evidence from the Expiration of Hill-Burton Requirements in Florida' (2011) 30 J Health Econ 189–99

4 C Capps, D Carlton, and G David, 'Antitrust Treatment of Nonprofits: Should Hospitals Receive Special Care?' (2020) 58 Economic Inquiry 1183–1199; F Entin, T Fletcher, and J Teske, 'Hospital Collaboration: The Need for an Appropriate Antitrust Policy' (1994) 29 Wake Forest L Rev 107–68.

in the same way as it is applied to for-profit providers – competition law is modified. The modification manifests itself as a heightened threshold for intervention; a reluctance to apply standard presumptions of harm and enhanced need for evidence to establish an infringement; an increased willingness to accept and a broader menu of acceptable justifications; and finally, a reluctance to impose sanctions on not-for-profit providers. Section 3.5 concludes by considering when and why competition law ought to be modified on account of the entity engaged in contested conduct operating on a not-for-profit basis.

3.2 THE RELEVANCE OF COMPETITION LAW IN MARKETS SERVED BY NON-PROFITS

Markets are relied on to produce sufficient quantities of desirable goods and services. The market is at is best when it is responsive to *voice*, *voice* involving patrons communicating their concerns to the provider of goods or services.[5] Providers of goods and services are most responsive to *voice* when it is possible for those exercising voice to *exit*, i.e. obtain goods or services from an alternative provider. Exit is important for two reasons. First, the possibility of *exit* reduces the cost of exercising voice. *Voice* is costly if patrons have no option but to continue receiving goods or services from the supplier after exercising voice, even if the patrons concerns are not addressed.[6] Secondly, the possibility of exit motivates suppliers to take the *voice* of patrons seriously.[7] When the possibility of exit exists, firms have incentives to continually improve the quality of their goods and services; provide new types of goods and services; and to minimise the resources consumed in the production of their goods and services.[8] In the absence of a possibility of exit, firms need not be responsive to voice and instead can be said to possess market power. Those with market power face a reduction in the incentives to improve, or to provide new offerings, or to minimise the resources being consumed.[9]

Competition law plays a central role in ensuring the effectiveness of voice in relation to entities operating on a for-profit basis. To what extent is competition law's role in ensuring that voice is effective, relevant to non-profit entities? Theories of the not-for-profit form suggest that such entities exist because the for-profit market will fail to provide the relevant goods and services[10]; because

5 AO Hirschman, *Exit, Voice, and Loyalty; Responses to Decline in Firms, Organizations, and States* (Harvard UP 1970) 34. Voice is broader than complaints and is defined at page 30 as 'any attempt at all to change, rather than to escape from, an objectionable state of affairs.'

6 *Ibid.* at 39.

7 *Ibid.* at 82.

8 Capps, Carlton, and David (n 4) 1183–99.

9 F M Scherer, 'Schumpeter and Plausible Capitalism' (1992) 30 *J Econ Lit* 1416, 1425–30.

10 B Weisbrod, *The Nonprofit Economy* (Harvard UP 1988); and R Steinberg, 'Economic Theories of Nonprofit Organizations' in W Powell and R Steinberg (eds), *The Nonprofit Sector: A Research Handbook* (2nd ed, Yale UP 2006) 117–39.

they can be trusted to provide higher quality goods and services in situations of high information asymmetry between buyers and sellers[11]; or because they are trusted where contracts are difficult to monitor and enforce.[12] What is important is that not-for-profit entities are argued to exist for reasons that differ from the reasons for profit entities exist. This then gives rise to claims for different treatments under competition law on three distinct grounds. Firstly, on the idea that an inability to distribute profits removes the incentive (though crucially, not the ability) to restrict competition.[13] Second, there is an idea that not-for-profit organisations ought to be trusted not to act in a manner determinantal to their patrons.[14] A third basis for the claim of special treatment is that the specific regulatory oversight to which the not-for-profit entity is subject will either satisfy the concerns that competition law is designed to address or trump any obligation competition law would seek to impose.[15]

Philipson and Posner formalise a model in which not-for-profit providers are not responsive to voice, i.e. they not only exercise market power, but also do so in a manner that is harmful to patrons.[16] The empirical literature also supports the view of there being nothing inherent in the not-for-profit organisational form that would render the concerns of competition law otiose.[17] Since not-for-profit entities ***do*** exercise market power and the exercise of market power by not-for-profit entities does have at least the potential to be harmful, legislatures, competition authorities, and courts have concluded that operating on a not-for-profit basis is insufficient to

[11] HB Hansmann, 'The Role of Nonprofit Enterprise' (1980) 89 Yale LJ 835–901.

[12] M Jegers, *Managerial Economics of Non-Profit Organizations* (Routledge 2008) 16–21.

[13] JP Newhouse, 'Toward a Theory of Nonprofit Institutions – Economic Model of a Hospital' (1970) 60 Am Econ Rev 64–74; W Lynk, 'Nonprofit Hospital Mergers and the Exercise of Market Power' (1995) 38 J Law and Econ 437–61. Lynk's article was then criticised in D Dranove and R Ludwick, 'Competition and Pricing by Nonprofit Hospitals: A Reassessment of Lynk's Analysis' (1995) 18 *J Health Econ* 87–98.

[14] P Francois, 'Not For Profit Provision of Public Services' (2003) 113 Economic Journal C53-C61. It is clear that such trust can be mis-placed: see R Herzlinger, 'Can Public Trust in Nonprofits Governments Be Restored?' (1996) 74 Harv Bus Rev 97–107.

[15] See Herzlinger and W Krasker, 'Who Profits from Nonprofits' (1987) 65 Harv Bus Rev 93–106 (summarizing and challenging the exceptionalism claimed by not for profit organizations); S Srikanth, 'College Financial Aid and Antitrust: Applying the Sherman Act to Collaborative Nonprofit Activity' (1994) 46 Stan L Rev 919, 936 (arguing that a restriction of competition may advance overall social welfare), and M Schlesinger, T Marmor, and R Smithey, 'Nonprofit and for-Profit Medical Care: Shifting Roles and Implications for Health Policy' (1987) 12 J Health Pol Pol'y L 427–457 (arguing for regulation based on type of organization)

[16] T Philipson and R Posner, 'Antitrust and the Not For Profit Sector' (2009) 52 JLE 1–18.

[17] D Haas-Wilson and C Garmon, 'Hospital Mergers and Competitive Effects: Two Retrospective Analyses' 2011 18 Int'l J Econ Bus 17–32; F Sloan, et al., 'Hospital Ownership and Cost and Quality of Care: Is There a Dime's Worth of Difference?' (2001) 20 J Health Econ 1–21 (finding not for profits may produce at lower cost, but do not offer greater quality); P Born and C Simon, 'Patients and Profits: The Relationship between Hmo Financial Performance and Quality of Care' (2001) 20 *Health Affairs* 167–174 (finding that for profit providers do not provide a higher nor lesser quality of care); Capps, Carlton, and David (n 4) 1183–1199 (find the mere fact that an entity operates on a not for profit basis does induce it to provide higher levels of public benefit)

warrant exclusion from competition law scrutiny.[18] Rather than the nature of the organisations operating in the market, focus is instead placed on the nature of the activities being performed – competition law being applied to all activities that can be described as economic or commercial in character.[19] After all, like all organisations, the not-for-profit organisation must decide whether to compete or cooperate with other organisations in the pursuit of its aims.[20]

3.3 COMPETITION LAW UNMODIFIED

What has been the experience of applying competition rules to entities operating on a not-for-profit basis? The most obvious examples arise in relation to self-regulatory bodies of the liberal professions.[21] Professional associations operating on a non-profit basis have been condemned for creating barriers that prevent non-members of the association from offering services competing with those offered by their members;[22] attempting to fix the price or other terms on which their members might

18 Under US antitrust law see: *Goldfarb v Virginia State Bar*, 421 US 773, 786–787 (1975); *US v Brown University*, 5 F3d 658, 666 (3d Cir 1993). Under EU and UK competition law, see Case C-244/94 *Fédération Française des Sociétés d'assurance v Ministère de L'agriculture et de la Pêche* ECLI:EU:C:1995:392, para 21; Case CE/2890-03 *Exchange of Information on Future Fees by Certain Independent Fee–Paying Schools* [20 November 2006] Decision of the Office of Fair Trading, paras 1312–1316.

19 Under US antitrust law, see: *Goldfarb v Virginia State Bar*, 421 US 773, 786–787 (1975). Under EU competition law see: Case 155/73 *Giuseppe Sacchi* ECLI:EU:C:1974:40, para 14; *Case C-41/1990 Klaus Höfner and Fritz Elser v Macrotron Gmbh* ECLI:EU:C:1991:161, para 19.

20 Note the general paradox that competition is designed to enhance cooperation: P Rubin 'Emporiophobia (Fear of Markets): Cooperation or Competition?' (2014) 80 South Econ J 876–889.

21 See Commission, 'Report on Competition in Professional Services' (Communication) COM (2004) 83 final https://eur-lex.europa.eu/legal-content/EN/TXT/?uri=celex%3A52004DC0083; Commission, 'Professional Services – Scope for more reform: Follow-up to the Report on Competition in Professional Services (Communication) COM (2004) 83' COM (2005) 405 final https://eur-lex.europa.eu/legal-content/EN/AUTO/?uri=celex:52005DC0405; OECD, 'Competition In Professional Services' DAFFE/CLP(2000)2; Monopolies Commission (UK), *Professional Services: a report on the general effect on the public interest of certain restrictive practices so far as they prevail in relation to the supply of professional services* (Cmnd 4463, 1970); L Terry, 'The European Commission Project Regarding Competition in Professional Services' (2009) 29 Nw J Int'l L & Bus 1

22 Office of Fair Trading, The control of entry regulations and retail pharmacy services in the UK para. 2.20–2.22, 3.8–3.12, 3.18–3.22; NMa Press Release, 'Pharmacies in Assen and Tilburg Must Lift Restrictions on Competition' (22 June 2004) www.acm.nl/en/publications/publication/5859/NMa-Pharmacies-in-Assen-and-Tilburg-Must-Lift-Restrictions-on-Competition; NMa Press Release, 'Suspects Pharmacies in Assen of Restricting Competition' (2 April 2003) www.acm.nl/en/publications/publication/5994/NMa-Suspects-Pharmacies-in-Assen-of-Restricting-Competition; NMa Press Release, 'NMa Suspects Pharmacies in Breda of Restricting Competition' (6 June 2003) www.acm.nl/en/publications/publication/5862/NMa-Suspects-Pharmacies-in-Breda-of-Restricting-Competition; NMa Press Release, 'NMa fines Dutch National Association of General Practitioners for Illegal Establishment Recommendations' (9 January 2012) www.acm.nl/en/publications/publication/6719/NMa-fines-Dutch-National-Association-of-General-Practitioners-for-illegal-establishment-recommendations; The Competition Authority (Ireland), 'Competition in Professional Services: general medical practitioners' (2010) paras 2.59, 3.3, 6.17–6.31, 7.1–7.20, 8.8–8.13

do business;[23] and for limiting the ability of members to promote their services as against other members.[24] Trade association's not representing professions, but operating on a not-for-profit basis, are also condemned if they play a role in fixing terms and conditions (including price and profit margins) on which their members will supply goods or services – matters which should be settled by competitive forces.[25]

Many examples can be found of competition law being applied to cooperatives and mutual organisations providing, for example, insurance and pensions.[26] Other prominent examples of not-for-profit entities being scrutinised under competition law involve state-owned enterprises operating on a not-for-profit basis being condemned for excluding others from the market or reserving the market to themselves.[27] Equally important is the role merger control has played in ensuring that the option for exit (and the role exit plays in strengthening voice) is preserved even when all in the market operate on a not-for-profit basis. So, for example, the *Bundeskartellamt* has prevented mergers between public hospitals operating on a not-for-profit basis.[28] In the UK, the competition authority reviewed a merger between two charities, which, though operating on a not-for-profit basis and primarily as a grant making body raising funds and distributing them to independent scientists, obtain intellectual property rights that result from the research it funds. The risk that the licensing of IPRs might not occur in a way beneficial to society was the focus of the competition authority's concern.

[23] Finnish Competition Authority, 'Finnish Competition Authority Yearbook 2003' www.kkv.fi/globalassets/kkv-suomi/julkaisut/vuosikirjat/kilpailuvirasto/2003/kivi-vuosikirja-2003-en.pdf accessed 24 November 2019; and respectively, see Co-operation & Competition Panel (UK), 'North Yorkshire and York PCT and York Hospitals NHS Foundation Trust Conduct Complaint' (22 March 2012) http://webarchive.nationalarchives.gov.uk/20130513202829/http://www.ccpanel.org.uk/content/cases/North_Yorkshire_and_York_PCT_and_York_Hospitals_NHS_Foundation_Trust_Conduct_Complaint/120322_York_PCT_Assura_conduct_complaint_PUBLISHED.pdf

[24] Monopolies and Mergers Commission (UK), *Services of Medical Practitioners: A report on the supply of the services of registered medical practitioners in relation to restrictions on advertising* (Cm 582, 1989) paras 7.6, 7.21, and 8.5 (action taken under section 7(1)(c) and (2) of the Fair Trading Act 1973). Consider also The Competition Authority (Ireland) (n 22) para 5.1–5.16; the Commission's approach: 'Professional Services: overview' (*European Commission*, 14 December 2012) https://ec.europa.eu/competition/sectors/professional_services/overview_en.html accessed 24 November 2019; F Miller, 'Competition Law and Anticompetitive Professional Behaviour Affecting Health Care' (1992) 55 *MLR* 453, 479; Monopolies Commission (n 21) para 214, 251–52 and 272.

[25] Joined Cases 209 to 215 and 218/78 *Heintz van Landewyck SARL v Commission* ECLI:EU:C:1980:248, para 85–89; Office of Fair Trading, 'Trade associations, professions and self-regulating bodies' (2004) OFT 408.

[26] Case C-244/94 *Fédération Française des Sociétés d'Assurance* ECLI:EU:C:1995:392, para 21; Case C-67/96 *Albany International BV v SBT* ECLI:EU:C:1999:430, para 85; See also Case C-250/92 *Gøttrup-Klim Grovvareforening v Dansk Landbrugs Growareselskab AmbA (DLG)* ECLI:EU:C:1994:413.

[27] Commission Decision 90/456/EEC of 1 August 1990 concerning the provision in Spain of international express courier services [1990] OJ L233/19; Case C-41/90 *Höfner and Elser v Macrotron* GmbH ECLI:EU:C:1991:161; Case C-475/99 Ambulanz Glöckner ECLI:EU:C:2001:577.

[28] 'Bundeskartellamt prohibits for the first time merger between public hospitals' (*Bundeskartellamt*, 13 December 2006) www.bundeskartellamt.de/SharedDocs/Meldung/EN/Pressemitteilungen/2006/13_12_2006_Krankenhausuntersagung_eng.html (last accessed 10 Nov 2021).

As with the for-profit sector, price-fixing, market sharing, and market foreclosure have been the main issues addressed. Harmful conduct has been found, notwithstanding the fact that the entities involved operate on a not-for-profit basis. And the need to ensure an environment in which the incentive to improve are maintained has remained paramount. Competition concerns are therefore to be addressed in the normal way, notwithstanding the fact that some entities to be scrutinised operate on a not-for-profit basis. What is also true is that not-for-profit entities have continued to operate, notwithstanding the need to comply with competition law and that competition law has been sufficiently flexible to take account of the not-for-profit form within the existing framework of the law.

3.4 COMPETITION LAW MODIFIED

Although it is the case that the standard competition law framework is applicable and applied to not-for-profit entities, it is not the case that operating on a not-for-profit basis does not matter. Competition law can be seen to be modified in four ways when courts and competition authorities are called on to assess the compatibility of a not-for-profit providers' conduct with the law. First, the court or authority may operate a heightened threshold for intervention. Second, the authority may modify the mode of assessment that it applies when it scrutinises not-for-profit entities. Third, the authority may admit or be amenable to a greater range of justifications than is otherwise the case. Finally, the authority may be influenced by the not-for-profit nature of the organisation when it comes to imposing sanctions.

3.4.1 *Threshold of Intervention*

One way in which not-for-profit providers are treated differently is that a higher threshold may be required to trigger intervention by a competition authority. A good example of this is the examination of the higher education market, in which the UK government has sought to harness the power of choice and competition.[29] To better understand how the market for undergraduate education in England functions, in October 2013, the competition authority launched a call for information.[30]

[29] Para 14 of Schedule 1 of The Restrictive Trade Practices Act 1976 had previously placed the provision of primary, secondary or further education, and university or other higher education beyond the reach of competition law. These exclusions are not carried over into the Competition Act 1998.

[30] Office of Fair Trading, 'Call for information on the undergraduate higher education sector in England' (October 2013) https://assets.publishing.service.gov.uk/media/533559bd40f0b62e99000015/HE-CFIs.pdf. The competition authority's interest in examining this market was motivated by 'changes to the financing of undergraduate courses (with an increase in the funding resulting from student fees and a decrease in direct funding from government)'; Office of Fair Trading, 'Higher Education in England: An OFT Call for Information' (March 2014) OFT 1529, para 1.3, note 5, para 2.4; para 3.11–3.14).

One question raised in the call for information was whether all institutions charging a uniform fee for all undergraduate courses resulted from either express or tacit collusion.[31] Is it is plausible for multi-product firms, in a non-concentrated market, to arrive at identical prices for undergraduate courses, when their cost structures differ and particularly when in relation to graduate courses there is wide price variation? This pattern of pricing would seem to provide reasonable grounds for suspecting an infringement.[32] In *Dyestuffs*, considering price increases applied by 10 firms to a small range of dyes, when each firm produced between 1,500 and 3,500 of some 6,000 dyes, the European Commission felt that:

> [i]t is not conceivable that without detailed prior agreement the principle producers … should several times increase by identical percentages the prices.[33]

Considering not-for-profit providers of higher education, however, the UK competition authority declined to take further action on the basis that it 'has received no complaints or evidence of either explicit or tacit collusion between higher education institutions with respect to fee setting'.[34] The competition authority seems to set a high threshold for intervention, suggesting that in order to launch an investigation into collusion by not-for-profit entities, it would require 'evidence that would amount to *a compelling case of anti-competitive behaviour*'.[35]

A further example of the reluctance to intervene can be seen in the UK competition authorities open letter to the head teachers of almost 30,000 State schools. The letter draws attention to the high price of school uniforms, caused in part by 74% of schools requiring parents to purchase uniforms from a single, named retailer or from the school itself. This created a captive market for chosen suppliers, allowing them to charge an additional £52 million per year. The letter advises schools either to cease specifying from whom uniforms may be obtained, or to award the right to supply on a basis that takes into account the cost to parents. Further, the letter urges parents to complain to school governors if they are dissatisfied with the schools' decision to use an exclusive supplier. The letter does not however warn, as it could and arguably should, that the school's licencing of their logo, crest, or uniform design to a supplier or retailer is clearly subject to competition law and all the consequences that this entails.

[31] Office of Fair Trading, 'Higher Education in England: An OFT Call for Information' (n 30) para. 6.4

[32] The threshold for investigation set out in section 25 of the Competition Act 1998. The 'reasonable suspicion' threshold is not a high bar (see, by analogy, para 7 of the Competition Appeal Tribunal judgment in ACS v OFT).

[33] Re Cartel in Aniline Dyes, para 7; and Case 48/69 *Imperial Chemical Industries Ltd v Commission of the European Communities (Dyestuffs)* ECLI:EU:C:1972:70, para 1–6, 54, and 83–87.

[34] Office of Fair Trading, 'Higher Education in England: An OFT Call for Information' (n 30) paras 1.17, 6.5, and 6.7.

[35] *Ibid.* at paras 6.10 and 6.14 (emphasis added).

3.4.2 *Mode of Assessment*

One of the most celebrated illustrations of the mode of assessment being modified arose when a number of universities operating on a not-for-profit basis, including eight Ivy league schools, adopted a common policy on how to award financial aid.[36] The aim was to enable able students to access the best available education regardless of their ability to pay and to create a more diverse student body by making education available to the economically disadvantaged.[37] It was first agreed among the schools that each would cease to provide merit based aid.[38] Additionally, it was agreed that no student would be awarded more aid than was justified by financial need (determined by a common formula). By ensuring that aid was granted only to the extent that a student was needy, a greater number of needy students would benefit from financial aid.[39] To what extent is the granting of this eleemosynary support subject to antitrust scrutiny?

The US Department of Justice's essential objection was that the schools were effectively setting a maximum discount or a minimum price.[40] Such price restraints are among the more serious violations of competition law. Such conduct is ordinarily subject to a *per se* prohibition. Antitrust scrutiny is warranted notwithstanding that the entities operate on a not-for-profit basis.[41] Is a *per se* assessment warranted in relation to entities operating on a not-for-profit basis? As the presumption of harm underpinning the *per se* approach has developed in the context of ***for-profit*** firms, the argument has been made that the *per se* approach should not be invoked or relied on in relation to ***not-for-profit*** firms.[42] Consequently, there was great reluctance to

36 An account and analysis is given in S Salop and L White, 'Policy Watch: Antitrust Goes to College' (1991) 5 J Econ Perspect 193–202; D Carlton, G Bamberger, and R Epstein 'Antitrust and Higher Education: Was There a Conspiracy to Restrict Finiancial Aid' (1995) 26 Rand J Econ 131–147.

37 *US v Brown University*, 805 F Supp 288 (ED Pa 1992) 292; *US v Brown University*, 5 F3d at 664. Schools were concerned that hitherto admission had been determined by ability to pay rather than on merit-based criteria: *US v Brown University*, 805 F Supp 288 (ED Pa 1992) 304–305.

38 *US v Brown University*, 805 F Supp at 293.

39 Carlton, Bamberger, and Epstein (n 36) 142–144; Compare with the situation in the United Kingdom, in which the regulator sought to discourage Universities from offering discounts: Donald MacLeod, 'Universities warned against offering cash for places' (*Guardian*, 25 May 2006) www.theguardian.com/education/2006/may/25/highereducation.choosingadegree

40 S Salop and L White, 'Policy Watch: Antitrust Goes to College' (1991) 5 J Econ Perspect 193, 194–195; Carlton, Bamberger, and Epstein (n 36) 132–133. A key element in the characterisation of the financial aid package is offered before the applicant accepts an offer of a place at the school. This may be distinguished from support that institutions offer to students that have already accepted offers or already commenced study at the school. This latter type of support is not available to prospective customers (students) but is limited to those already in receipt of the education service, cf Office of Fair Trading, 'Assessment of Market Power' (OFT 415, September 1999) 6.

41 *US v Brown University*, 5 F3d at 667–668.

42 See *Arizona v Maricopa County* 457 US 322 (1982) and *California Dental Association v FTC*, 526 US 756, 771 (1999) n 10; *Goss v Memorial Hosp System*, 789 F2d 353 (5th Cir 1986); *Northwest Wholesale*

subject the arrangement to the *per se* mode of analysis and instead the court wished for a more in-depth examination to be conducted and harm to be more specifically articulated and demonstrated.[43]

3.4.3 *Range of Justifications*

The fact that the entities operate on a not-for-profit basis can encourage courts and agencies to accept a broader range of justifications than is generally available.[44] In relation to not-for-profit providers, there is much sympathetic commentary advocating the inclusion of a broader range of considerations in the competition law assessment than is typically admitted.[45] In the Ivy league financial aid case, it was not unarguable that promoting economic diversity and educational access on a not-for-profit basis may justify any harm arising from a restriction of competition.[46] This reflects a general tendency to at least listen to arguments that harm arising from a restriction imposed by not-for-profit providers are necessary to achieve a greater good. Accepting this argument forces competition law to confront a number of issues. What types of benefit or value are acceptable for a not-for-profit organisation to pursue when those benefits or values conflict with those promoted by competition law?[47] Who must be the beneficiary of the conduct and what justifies those harmed by the anti-competitive conduct being compelled to pay for that benefit?[48]

An opportunity to confront these issues arose when the competition authority in the United Kingdom considered whether the centralised system used to apply for places at higher education institutions could harm competition between institutions, to the detriment of students.[49] Both the limit on the number of courses a

Stationers, Inc v Pac Stationery & Printing Co, 472 US 284, 105 S Ct 2613, 86 L Ed 2d 202 (1985); *Wright v Southern Mono Hosp Dist*, 631 F Supp 1294 (ED Cal 1986); *Everhart v Jane C Stormont Hosp*, 1982-1 Trade Cas (CCH) 64703, 1982 WL 1833 (D Kan 1982); Srikanth (n 15) 938–39; Notes 'Antitrust and Nonprofit Entities' (1981) 94 *Harv L Rev* 802–820, 808–814.; Carlton, Bamberger, and Epstein (n 36) 144–46; P Kolovos 'Antitrust Law and Nonprofit Organizations: The Law School Accreditation Case' 71 NYU L Rev (1996) 689–731; 'Notes: United Charities and the Sherman Act' (1982) 91 Yale LJ 1593, 1597 fn 25; and T Greaney, 'Antitrust and Hospital Mergers: Does the Nonprofit Form Affect Competitive Substance?' (2006) 31 J Health Pol Pol'y L 511, 521–25. Improving Healthcare: A Dose of Competition A Report by The Federal Trade Commission and Department of Justice (July, 2004), chapter 4: www.ftc.gov/sites/default/files/documents/reports/improving-health-care-dose-competition-report-federal-trade-commission-and-department-justice/040723healthcarerpt.pdf

43 US v Brown University, 805 F Supp 288, 300–301 (ED Pa 1992); *US v Brown University*, 5 F3d at 672.

44 *US v Brown University*, 5 F3d at 675–678.

45 Srikanth (n 15) 940–43.

46 *US v Brown University*, 805 F Supp at 678. The Ivy league schools entered settlement agreements so there is no final judgment.

47 See 'Notes: United Charities and the Sherman Act' (n 42) 1603–1611.

48 C Cicoria, 'European Competition Law and Nonprofit Organizations: A Law and Economics Analysis' (2006) 6 Global Jurist Topics 1, 40–42.

49 Office of Fair Trading, 'Higher Education in England: An OFT Call for Information' (n 30) para 6.24–6.30.

student may apply for and the inability to apply to both the University of Oxford and the University of Cambridge can be described as restrictions of choice.[50] Yet, if these restrictions could be cognised as restrictions of competition, the competition authority seemed willing to accept that the restriction could be justified on the ground that it enabled 'a more in-depth assessment of each candidate'.[51] Such a justification was put forward in a letter published in the Times Higher Education Supplement to justify the prohibition on applying to both Oxford and Cambridge, claiming:

> If a significant proportion of the applicants to whom [Oxford] offered places were liable to go instead to Cambridge, then to avoid lots of places going to waste, we would have to treat admissions as a central university process, playing the statistics of large numbers rather than selecting the students for our own colleges.[52]

The competition authority seemingly accepts that 'since each additional choice that an applicant makes puts a cost on the institution, it may be efficient to restrict the number of choices that each applicant can make'.[53] What is unusual about such an approach is that the identified benefits would appear to accrue to the institutions rather than to the students and so there appears to be an acceptance that benefits to not-for-profit institutions may offset harm to the users such institutions are intended to serve.[54]

3.4.4 *Sanctions*

Even when an unjustified restriction of competition is identified, competition authorities might be reluctant to impose sanctions on entities operating on a not-for-profit basis. The not-for-profit organisation may thus be said to benefit from what might be described as 'soft' enforcement. Two examples can be offered. In England and Wales, an infringement of competition law was committed when six State-owned health care providers exchanged information about the price each would charge for privately funded health care services.[55] No sanction was imposed notwithstanding the fact that information exchange relating to price ranks among the most egregious of competition law infringements. Instead, the competition authority was

50 The importance of choice has also been emphasised by the UK Competition Appeal Tribunal: see, for example, Genzyme v OFT [2004] CAT 4, paras 255, 468 and 585.

51 Office of Fair Trading, 'Higher Education in England: An OFT Call for Information' (n 30) para 6.29.

52 Letters, Dangerous combination, September 5, 2013

53 Office of Fair Trading, 'Higher Education in England: An OFT Call for Information' (n 30) para 6.35.

54 This contradicts the identified limitation that even, in public service markets, any restriction must be 'to the benefit of students' or users: Office of Fair Trading, 'Higher Education in England: An OFT Call for Information' (n 30) para 6.35.

55 See Letter to NHS Trusts with Private Patient Units enclosing competition law compliance guidance http://webarchive.nationalarchives.gov.uk/20140402161850/http://www.oft.gov.uk/shared_oft/public-markets/PPUs.pdf and Press release: NHS Trusts with Private Patient Units provide assurances to OFT to ensure competition compliance (16 August 2012) https://webarchive.nationalarchives.gov.uk/ukgwa/20121003141315/http://www.oft.gov.uk/news-and-updates/press/2012/71-12.

satisfied by assurances that the information exchange had ceased and that the parties would provide their staff with training on competition law compliance.

An even more striking example is the investigation into the operation of 50 schools that operate on a not-for-profit basis.[56] The schools had exchange detailed information about the fees that they intended to charge for their education services. The information exchange was organised by the bursar of Sevenoaks School, to whom the participant schools submitted details of their current fee levels, proposed fee increases (expressed as a percentage), and the resulting intended fee levels. The Sevenoaks bursar subsequently circulated this information among the Participant schools in tabular form. The information exchanges resulted in higher fees being charged than would otherwise have been the case and the procedure in force at the time meant that it was not possible to consider whether the arrangement was justifiable.[57] Although the regular and systematic exchange among competitors of each other's pricing intentions is a serious infringement, the competition authority decided to limit the penalties to £10,000. Such lenient treatment of such a serious violation was based in part in recognition that 'the Participant schools are all non-profit making charitable bodies'.[58]

3.5 WHY MODIFY?

Although not-for-profit entities may enter the market with a sense of or commitment to public service, there is nothing inherent in the organisational form to ensure this outcome. Do effective alternatives to voice, reinforced by the possibility of exit exist in relation to not-for-profit providers? Is competition law the best mechanism to ensure the effectiveness of voice and exit in the non-profit context and are competition authorities best placed to ensure compliance by not-for-profit entities? In a market occupied exclusively by not-for-profit entities, it may be that a regulatory regime exits in which the concerns of competition law are already accounted for or in which the concerns can be decentralised by granting concurrent powers. An important consideration, however, is that not-for-profit entities operate in markets that are also served by for-profit entities – the so-called, mixed markets. Some of the claims of non-profit exceptionalism apply only when a market is served exclusively by not-for-profit entities.[59] Exit and voice therefore remain important mechanisms through which patrons maximise the benefit they obtain from service provision by non-profit entities. It is for this reason that the actions of not-for-profit entities remain within the scope of competition law. Though competition law applies and has been applied to the activities

56 Office of Fair Trading Press Release, 'OFT issues statement of objections against 50 independent schools' (9 November 2005) https://webarchive.nationalarchives.gov.uk/20080908111732/http://www.oft.gov.uk/news/press/2005/214-05.

57 *Exchange of Information on Future Fees by Certain Independent Fee–Paying Schools* (n 18) paras 1359–1375, 1381–1383 [See SI 2004/1261 of UK Competition Act 1998].

58 *Ibid.* at para 1427.

59 E Searing, 'Charitable (Anti)Trust: The Role of Antitrust Regulation in the Nonprofit Sector' (2014) 5 Nonprofit Policy Forum 261, 262; Srikanth (n 15) 948, 955.

of not-for-profit providers, a reluctance to apply competition law full bloodied can be observed. What explains the reluctance to apply and tendency to modify the law?

A first point is that the extent to which *activities* of not-for-profit organisations, as distinct from the organisations themselves, fall within the scope of competition law can at times be difficult to determine. A case in point is the raising of funds to finance activities that each organisation will separately provide free at point of use. Can it be argued that fundraisers are selling something tangible to donors (separate from the services offered free at point of use) such that fundraising itself warrants competition law scrutiny?[60] There is undoubtedly competition for donations, since there are more organisations and causes seeking funds than there are funds.[61] The economic literature shows that competition for donations increases the cost of raising funds (and by a greater amount than the increase in total funds raised).[62] Suppressing competition can therefore reduce the cost of fundraising and leave more resources available to promote the organisations mission.[63] Is it objectionable for competition to be suppressed?[64]

In *Dedication & Everlasting Love to Animal v. Humane Society of the United States*, in which it was alleged that the Humane Society of the United States monopolised the market for donations to support of animal welfare, fundraising by not-for-profit organisations was not considered to be an antitrust issue.[65] At the same time, it has been recognised that collective fundraising or a fundraising monopoly may make it more difficult for those not part of the collective effort to raise funds and it may be difficult for them to gain an allocation of the funds raised – the ability of new organisations to raise funds for new causes may be impacted.[66] Can it be right that no antitrust scrutiny is possible when the impact on competition is not necessarily beneficial or benign?

[60] S Rose-Ackerman, 'Charitable Giving and "Excessive" Fundraising' (1982) 97 Q J Econ 193–212; S Rose-Ackerman, 'Altruism, Nonprofits, and Economic Theory' (n 2) 710–15; T Norgard, 'How Charitable Is the Sherman Act?' (1999) 83 Minn L Rev 1515, 1533–34, 1543–45; 'Notes: United Charities and the Sherman Act' (n 42) 1598–1600.

[61] J Saxton and M Guild, 'It's Competition, but Not as We Know It' (*nfpSynergy*, October 2010) 4–6, 10–11, 25–28.

[62] See for example Rose-Ackerman, 'Charitable Giving and Excessive Fundraising' (n 60) 193–212.

[63] Philipson and Posner, 'Antitrust and the Not For profit Sector' (n 16) 7–9.

[64] See 'Notes: United Charities and the Sherman Act' (n 42); Office of Fair Trading, 'Assessment of Market Power' (n 40) 8.

[65] 50 F3d 710 (9th Cir 1995). See also Charitable Donation Antitrust Immunity Act of 1997, Pub L No 105-26, 111 Stat 241 (1997). The decision is often contrasted with that of *Virginia Vermiculite v WR Grace Co* 156 F 3d 535 (4th Cir 1998). However in this later case it is the conduct or the donor rather than the not for profit recipient that is being challenged. In the UK, see ME/1074/02 Completed merger between the Imperial Cancer Research Fund and the Cancer Research Campaign (https://webarchive.nationalarchives.gov.uk/ukgwa/20090903210627/http://www.oft.gov.uk/advice_and_resources/resource_base/Mergers_home/mergers_fta/2002/imperial-cancer); ME/4034/09 Seniorlink Eldercare/ Aid Call resulting from the completed merger between Help the Aged and Age Concern, para 10 (https://webarchive.nationalarchives.gov.uk/ukgwa/20161129204513/https://assets.publishing.service.gov.uk/media/555de35440f0b669c4000091/Seniorlink.pdf)

[66] 'Notes: United Charities and the Sherman Act' (n 42) 1603–1605.

A second point is that the modifying tendencies are not always triggered. This then makes it clear that something other than non-for-profit status is at work. Operating on a not-for-profit basis could function as a proxy for trustworthiness or selflessness and so it remains the case that 'those who stand to profit financially from restraints of trade cannot be trusted to determine which restraints are in the public interest and which are not'.[67] If the non-distribution constraint does not exclude the possibility of an entity acting in the interests of the organisation or its members rather than the consumer, it would seem that competition law is applied unmodified. This would account for the sustained scrutiny applied to self-regulatory bodies and cooperatives, notwithstanding that they operate on a not-for-profit basis.

A third point is that there remains a lingering sense that competition law does not provide an appropriate frame of reference with which to view the activities of not-for-profit entities.[68] The sense that competition law is somehow trespassing motivates the imposition of high evidential burdens, not only to establish violations but also to even launch an investigation. Recognising that being subject to a competition law investigation is not costless, even in relation to compliant behaviour, justifies the increased thresholds, particularly when bearing such cost necessarily results in reduced resources being available for activities in the general interest.[69] The same may be true of the modified approach to sanctions. The modifying tendencies are to be understood as simple recognition that it is not in the public interest to enforce competition laws against all conduct falling within the literal scope of the prohibition.

3.6 CONCLUSION

While there will always be claims that competition law <u>does not</u> or <u>should not</u> apply, there is nothing inherent in the not-for-profit form to justify this claim. Particularly, there is nothing to indicate that applying competition law has been harmful to the causes served by non-profit providers; there are clear indications that competition law has been applied in a way that addresses real harm to patrons; and modifications are made, when appropriate, to ensure that the mission served by not-for-profit entities is not harmed by the application of competition law. All this should leave us confident that competition law can pierce the veil of the not-for-profit form and examine (in its own small way) whether the public interest is genuinely being served.

[67] E Elhauge, 'The Scope of Antitrust Process' (1991) 104 Harv L Rev 667, 672.

[68] Office of Fair Trading, 'Higher Education in England: An OFT Call for Information' (n 30) paras 1.15, 6.15–6.23; Department for Business, Innovation and Skills, 'Competition Issues in the Further Education Sector' (October 2013) BIS Research Paper Number 141, 5 https://assets.publishing.service.gov.uk/government/uploads/system/uploads/attachment_data/file/248707/bis-13-1235-competition-issues-in-the-further-education-sector.pdf, noting that 'The strong focus on social obligations means that many providers need to work closely with other local stakeholders and providers to develop a comprehensive skills offer that meets the needs of their community. While there can be important efficiency gains from working together, cooperation can provide an opportunity for anti-competitive agreements to be made.'

[69] *Exchange of Information on Future Fees by Certain Independent Fee–Paying Schools* (n 18) para 36

PART II

The Boundaries of the Corporation

4

The Boundaries of the Firm and the Reach of Competition Law

Corporate Group Liability and Sanctioning in the EU and the US

Carsten König

4.1 INTRODUCTION

It is an essential feature of modern company law that the shareholders are not personally liable for the debts of the company. This form of asset partitioning, often referred to as 'limited liability', fulfils a number of important functions.[1] Any exception to the rule is therefore controversially discussed. In recent times, however, the number of exceptions seems to be increasing. An important example can be found in EU competition law. Under the so-called 'single economic entity doctrine', parent companies can be held liable for competition law infringements by their subsidiaries. The doctrine only applies to controlling shareholders or, in the words of the EU Courts, to shareholders who exercised a decisive influence over the conduct of a subsidiary at the time when the subsidiary infringed the competition rules.[2] The application of the doctrine, which is generally considered to have no equivalent

Postdoctoral Researcher, University of Cologne, Germany, Email: carsten.koenig@uni-koeln.de. The author sincerely thanks the editors for valuable comments on the original draft. The chapter was completed in August 2021. It was therefore not possible to include Case C-882/19 *Sumal* ECLI:EU:C:2021:800, in which the ECJ held that a subsidiary may be liable for damages if its parent company has infringed Article 101 TFEU. As indicated below in Section 4.4.1, such liability cannot be justified with the functions of the single economic entity doctrine discussed in this chapter. This means that subsidiary liability either serves another function that would still need to be worked out in more detail (e.g. facilitating the enforcement of claims by allowing them against a company based in the same country as the injured party) or that the decision is not convincing.

1 J Armour and others, 'What Is Corporate Law?' in R Kraakman and others (eds), *The Anatomy of Corporate Law: A Comparative and Functional Approach* (3rd edn, Oxford University Press 2017) 8–9; H Hansmann and R Kraakman, 'The Essential Role of Organizational Law' (2000) 110 Yale LJ 387, 395–396, 423–428; F Easterbrook and D Fischel, 'Limited Liability and the Corporation' (1985) 52 The U Chicago L Rev 89; F Easterbrook and D Fischel, *The Economic Structure of Corporate Law* (Harvard University Press 1991) 41–47; S Bainbridge and T Henderson, *Limited Liability: A Legal and Economic Analysis* (Edward Elgar Publishing 2016) 44–85.

2 The leading judgment is still Case C-97/08 *Akzo Nobel and Others v Commission* ECLI:EU:C:2009:536, paras 58–60. For further case law see below, Section 4.2 at n 8–10, 14, 16–18.

in US antitrust law, does not presuppose that the parent company itself has done anything wrong. It does not matter whether the parent company knew about the subsidiary's infringement and tolerated it. Nor does it matter whether the parent could have prevented the infringement. The liability of the parent company is based on structure, not behaviour, and is justified above all by the possibility of control.

There is of course no doubt that European company law – like all advanced commercial law systems – recognises the corporate law principle of limited shareholder liability. The European Court of Justice (ECJ) has even ruled that shareholder liability may, under certain conditions, infringe Article 63 of the Treaty on the Functioning of the European Union (TFEU).[3] That provision governs the free movement of capital, a central element of the European internal market, itself the economic backbone of the European Union. However, the ruling of the Court related primarily to non-controlling shareholders. Moreover, the ECJ has explained that, while limited shareholder liability seems to be accepted as the general rule,[4] 'it cannot be concluded therefrom that this is a general principle of company law applicable in all circumstances and without exception'.[5] It seems that the liability of parent companies for antitrust fines is precisely one of these exceptions. In any event, the ECJ has clearly rejected all attempts to challenge the antitrust liability of parent companies by invoking the principle of limited shareholder liability.[6] Although the Court's arguments in this context often sound very formalistic, it seems obvious that the main reason for rejecting such attacks on parent company liability simply is that the judges give greater weight to the objectives of the single economic entity doctrine than to the principle of limited liability, at least in the specific setting of competition law offences.

It is therefore regrettable that the various functions of the single economic entity doctrine are still not properly appreciated. Although the liability of parent companies for infringements by subsidiaries has been recognised in European competition law for decades, much of the literature continues to lose itself in fundamental criticism.[7]

[3] Case C-81/09 *Idryma Typou* ECLI:EU:C:2010:622, paras 47–70. The case concerned a Greek law establishing the liability of persons holding more than 2.5% of the shares of press or television companies for payment of administrative fines imposed on such companies for violating rules of professional conduct.

[4] See also *Idryma Typou* (n 3), Opinion of AG Trstenjak, paras 33–34; Council Regulation (EC) 2157/2001 of 8 October 2001 on the Statute for a European company (SE) [2001] OJ L294/1, art 1(2); Directive 2009/102/EC of the European Parliament and of the Council of 16 September 2009 in the area of company law on single-member private limited liability companies [2009] OJ L258/20, art 2(1).

[5] *Idryma Typou* (n 3), para 42. See also para 44.

[6] See eg Case C-508/11 *Eni v Commission* ECLI:EU:C:2013:289, paras 78–83; Case C-501/11 P *Schindler Holding and Others v Commission* ECLI:EU:C:2013:522, paras 101–104; Case T-389/10 *SLM v Commission* ECLI:EU:T:2015:513, paras 388–389; Case T-39/07 *Eni v Commission* ECLI:EU:T:2011:356, paras 113–118; Case T-138/07 *Schindler Holding and Others v Commission* ECLI:EU:T:2011:362, para 83.

[7] See eg M Leddy and A van Melkebeke, 'Parental liability in EU competition law' (2019) 40 ECLR 407; A Kalintiri, 'Revisiting Parental liability in EU competition law' (2018) 43 EL Rev 145; B Wardhaugh, 'Punishing parents for the sins of their child: extending EU competition liability in groups and to subcontractors' (2017) 5(1) JAE 22; B Leupold, 'Effective enforcement of EU competition law gone too far? Recent case law on the presumption of parental liability' (2013) 34 ECLR 570.

As a result, a thorough examination of the functions of the doctrine and its essential components is still lacking. Against this background, the purpose of this chapter is to examine in more detail the contexts in which the European Commission and the EU Courts invoke the single economic entity doctrine. As we shall see, the use of the doctrine is more nuanced than is generally thought. In particular, the doctrine is not only used to establish the liability of parent companies but also serves important functions in the calculation of fines and their enforcement. Only when these functions as well are appreciated is it possible to make informed statements about the proper reach of the doctrine. It is important to emphasise this because various extensions of the doctrine are currently being discussed. Unfortunately, it often remains unclear what purposes they would actually serve.

Section 4.2 starts with a brief look at the conceptual background of the single economic entity doctrine, which will allow us to better understand the approach of the courts. Section 4.3 then explores three distinct functions of the doctrine: to induce parent companies to control the conduct of their subsidiaries, to ensure the correct calculation of fines and to ensure that fines are actually paid. All three purposes will be analysed in detail and it will become clear that it is important to distinguish the different functions, as they each have their own implications. Section 4.4 discusses borderline questions of group liability: whether companies other than parent companies should also be liable for infringements committed by affiliated companies and whether it can be justified to hold parent companies liable not only for fines but also for damages, i.e. claims brought by private actions. Section 4.5 then broadens the view and asks how the problems solved in the EU by the single economic entity doctrine are addressed in US antitrust law. It will become clear that while on paper there is indeed no liability of parent companies for antitrust infringements by their subsidiaries in the US, the reality is more complex. Section 4.6 concludes.

4.2 LEGAL AND ECONOMIC ENTITIES

The starting point for all discussions on parental liability in the case law of the EU Courts is the concept of an undertaking. According to a widely used formulation, that notion 'must be understood as designating an economic entity, even if, from a legal perspective, that unit is made up of a number of natural or legal persons'.[8] That phrase was first used by the ECJ in *Hydrotherm* (1985) to explain that competition is 'impossible' between a legal person and its sole owner, as they necessarily have identical interests and act jointly on the market.[9] The variety of forms offered

[8] Case C-597/13 *Total v Commission* ECLI:EU:C:2015:613, para 33; Case C-231/11 *Commission v Siemens Österreich and Others* ECLI:EU:C:2014:256, para 43; Case C-628/10 P *Alliance One International and Standard Commercial Tobacco v Commission* ECLI:EU:C:2012:479, para 42.

[9] Case C-170/83 *Hydrotherm* ECLI:EU:C:1984:271, para 11.

by company law is simply not relevant for competition law purposes and the same applies to the exact distinction and delineation of legal entities. The EU Courts have held since *ICI* (1972) that the formal separation between two companies with different legal identities is not decisive for applying the competition rules.[10] If one company controls the other and they therefore behave uniformly in the market, liability may be attributed to the controlling company.[11] For the purposes of applying the competition rules, it is the unity of those companies' conduct on the market that matters, and not their separate legal personality. Similarly, the Courts have always rejected the idea – repeatedly put forward by companies and their lawyers[12] – that the corporate law principle of limited shareholder liability could have any meaning in this context. Instead, insisting on different legal personalities and separate assets is seen as a misplaced form-based approach that ignores economic realities and does not meet the needs of competition law enforcement.[13]

The Courts have even gone so far as to describe the joint and several liabilities of multiple legal entities constituting a single economic unit as 'merely the manifestation of an *ipso jure* legal effect of the concept of an "undertaking"'.[14] However, it has rightly been pointed out that the Courts do not automatically hold liable all entities that act jointly in the market as an economic unit.[15] At least so far, the focus has been on the liability of parent companies. This liability is not primarily justified by the uniform market behaviour of the undertaking, but by the parent company's control over the subsidiary. According to the case law, the conduct of a subsidiary may be imputed to the parent company 'where, although having a separate legal personality, that subsidiary does not decide independently upon its own conduct on the market, but carries out, in all material respects, the instructions given to it by the parent company'.[16] A parent company will only be liable for offences committed by its subsidiary if the parent is in a position to exercise a decisive influence over the commercial policy of

[10] Case C-48/69 *ICI v Commission* ECLI:EU:C:1972:70, para 140. See also Case C-73/95 P *Viho v Commission* ECLI:EU:C:1996:405, para 50.

[11] Another important consequence is that two members of the same economic unit cannot collude with each other in terms of Article 101 TFEU, see *Viho v Commission* (n 10), para 51; Guidelines on the applicability of Article 101 of the Treaty on the Functioning of the European Union to horizontal co-operation agreements [2011] OJ C11/1, para 11. This view is shared by US antitrust law, as the US Supreme Court has made clear in the landmark decision *Copperweld v Independence Tube*, 467 US 752 (1984).

[12] See above, n 6.

[13] cf O Odudu and D Bailey, 'The Single Economic Entity Doctrine in EU Competition Law' (2014) 51 CML Rev 1721, 1745.

[14] Case C-625/13 P *Villeroy & Boch v Commission* ECLI:EU:C:2017:52, para 150; Case C-247/11 P *Areva v Commission* ECLI:EU:C:2014:257, para 122; *Commission v Siemens Österreich and Others* (n 8), para 57.

[15] Kalintiri (n 7) 156; Odudu and Bailey (n 13) 1746–1747.

[16] Case C-155/14 *Evonik Degussa and AlzChem v Commission* ECLI:EU:C:2016:446, para 27; *Villeroy & Boch v Commission* (n 14), para 146; Case C-293/13 *Fresh Del Monte Produce v Commission* ECLI:EU:C:2015:416, para 75; Case C-179/12 P *The Dow Chemical Company v Commission* ECLI:EU:C:2013:605, para 52.

the subsidiary and does in fact exercise that influence.[17] This is presumed, however, for the specific case that the parent company holds all or almost all shares in the subsidiary.[18] It is then up to the parent company to rebut the presumption of control by adducing sufficient evidence to show that the subsidiary acted independently on the market at the time it committed the competition law infringement.

Ironically, in recent years, an almost form-based use of the concept of an undertaking has emerged. While initially the instrumental approach was strongly emphasised, in recent years, the Courts have sometimes tried to find meaning in words instead of exploring the relevant problem. In particular, the substantive examination has occasionally been replaced by a reference to established definitions and (alleged) precedents.[19] Moreover, the Courts have begun to treat the economic unit as akin to a legal entity, sometimes even seeming to endow it with legal personality. The apparent *de facto* personification of the economic unit seems to be linked to the growing number of arguments before the Courts based on fundamental procedural rights. For example, the Courts have countered the argument that parental liability infringes the principle of personal responsibility with the claim that this principle only applies to the economic unit, and they have made the same argument for the principle that the penalty must be specific to the offender and the offence. The ECJ held in *Siemens Österreich* (2014) that these principles 'relate only to the undertaking per se, not the natural or legal persons forming part of the undertaking'.[20] Similarly, the General Court (GC) explained in *Nynäs* (2012) that parental liability 'does not in any way constitute an exception to the principle of personal responsibility, but is the expression of that very principle', as the parent company and its subsidiaries form a single undertaking and are thus collectively responsible.[21] This reasoning has been rightly criticised in the literature.[22] The undertaking is not a legal entity and therefore cannot be a bearer of rights

[17] Case C-172/12 *EI du Pont de Nemours v Commission* ECLI:EU:C:2013:601, paras 44–45; *The Dow Chemical Company v Commission* (n 16), para 55–56; Case C-107/82 *AEG v Commission* ECLI:EU:C:1983:293, para 50; *Akzo Nobel and Others v Commission* (n 2), Opinion of GA Kokott, paras 47–50.

[18] Case C-516/15 *Akzo Nobel and Others v Commission* ECLI:EU:C:2017:314, para 54; Case C-58/12 P *Groupe Gascogne v Commission* ECLI:EU:C:2013:770, para 38; *Alliance One International and Standard Commercial Tobacco v Commission* (n 8), para 46; *Akzo Nobel and Others v Commission* (n 2).

[19] For examples, see below Section 4.4.1.

[20] *Commission v Siemens Österreich and Others* (n 8), para 56. See also Case T-827/14 *Deutsche Telekom v Commission*, ECLI:EU:T:2018:930, para 503; Case T-470/13 *Merck v Commission* ECLI:EU:T:2016:452, para 530.

[21] Case T-347/06 *Nynäs Petroleum and Nynas Belgium v Commission* ECLI:EU:T:2012:480, para 40. See also Case T-419/14 *The Goldman Sachs Group v Commission* ECLI:EU:T:2018:445, para 188.

[22] Leddy and van Melkebeke (n 7) 414; Kalintiri (n 7) 158–159; Leupold (n 7) 579; S Thomas, 'Guilty of a Fault that one has not Committed. The Limits of the Group-Based Sanction Policy Carried out by the Commission and the EU Courts in EU-Antitrust Law' (2012) 3(1) J ECL & Pract 11, 15–16; A Winckler, 'Parent's Liability: New case extending the presumption of liability of a parent company for the conduct of its wholly owned subsidiary' (2011) 2(3) J ECL & Pract 231, 233.

and duties, let alone of fundamental rights.[23] To equip the undertaking with legal personality would confuse the economic and the legal level and would inevitably lead to misconceptions. The notion of undertaking is merely a legal mechanism by which certain objectives can be achieved – attribution, parental liability – and the concept of a single economic unit helps to explain why these objectives are appropriate. But a simple reference to the economic unit can never replace substantive arguments and it should not be used to disguise the solution of legal problems.

Even if the approach of personifying the undertaking *de facto* is not convincing, it is understandable that the EU Courts try to counter the often fundamental, uncompromising criticism by companies and their lawyers of the single economic entity doctrine with similarly heavy artillery. And apparently, the Courts believe that it would be more difficult to justify parental liability as a form of vicarious liability. Ultimately, however, the concept of the Courts will only gain acceptance if it goes beyond a mere interpretation of words. If the Courts really want to convince, and maybe even provide an example for other jurisdictions, they must show that their approach is good policy. This is actually not that difficult. As I will show in the following section, most of what the Courts do on the basis of the single economic entity doctrine, is justified by good reasons. However, it will also become obvious that it is important to clearly distinguish between the different purposes that the unitary perspective on corporate groups is intended to serve.

4.3 THREE DISTINCT FUNCTIONS

Much has been written about the concept of undertaking and its implications for the liability of corporate groups, but the exact functions of the single economic entity doctrine continue to be underexplored. Most of the debate still is concerned with the legitimacy of the doctrine, often ignoring that legitimacy cannot be separated from purpose. A good starting point for the question what purpose parental liability serves is provided by Advocate General (AG) Kokott in her opinion in *Akzo Nobel* (2009).[24] She relied on four main arguments:

> Where [...] a parent company exercises decisive influence over its subsidiaries [...] it accords with [1.] the *principle of personal responsibility* and with [2.] the *objective*

[23] The EU Charter of Fundamental Rights only refers to natural and legal persons (cf eg Articles 42–44). This finding is not altered by the fact that Articles 47–50 on fundamental procedural rights use a broader wording ('everyone', 'anyone', 'no one'), as it is a fundamental principle of Western legal thought that the ability to have rights and duties is inextricably linked with legal personality, see eg Armour and others (n 1) 5–8; S Worthington, *Sealy and Worthington's Text, Cases, and Materials in Company Law* (11th edn, Oxford University Press 2016) 42–62; D Goddard, 'Corporate Personality – Limited Recourse and Its Limits' in C Rickett and R Grantham (eds), *Corporate Personality in the 20th Century* (Hart 1998) 11–12; M Dan-Cohen, *Rights, Persons, and Organizations: A Legal Theory for Bureaucreatic Society* (University of Califonia Press 1986) 14–15.

[24] The recognition of the 100%-shareholding presumption and its extension to cases in which the parent company holds almost all of the shares in the subsidiary have led to a sharp increase in parental liability cases.

> *of effective enforcement of the competition rules* to hold all the companies of the group [...] jointly and severally liable [...]. Only in that way can it also be ensured that, when assessing the amount of a fine to be imposed, [3.] the *true economic strength of the whole undertaking is correctly taken into account* and that [4.] the *successful enforcement of the fine is not jeopardised by any transfers of assets* between the parent company and its subsidiaries (enumeration and emphasis added).[25]

In Section 4.2, above, I have already explained that I do not consider it appropriate to apply the principle of personal responsibility to economic units. The other three points, however, are as correct as they are important and they certainly deserve more attention – both by the courts and in the literature. They are discussed in more detail below.

4.3.1 *Controlling the Conduct of the Subsidiary*

Promoting the effective enforcement of competition law is probably the most important objective of the single economic unit theory. But how exactly does the liability of parent companies contribute to this objective? The clearest statement by one of the EU Courts on this point is to be found in the GC's judgment in *Dow Chemical* (2012). In that decision, the GC stated that 'as a result of the parent company's power of supervision, the parent company has a responsibility to ensure that its subsidiary complies with the competition rules'. The Court further explained that '[a]n undertaking which has the possibility of exercising decisive influence over the business strategy of its subsidiary' may be presumed 'to have the possibility of establishing a policy aimed at compliance with competition law and to take all necessary and appropriate measures to supervise the subsidiary's commercial management'.[26] Unfortunately, the GC made these statements in a case in which the parent company's control was not self-evident – the case concerned a 50/50 joint venture. On appeal, the ECJ did not support the GC's view, but instead maintained that the latter had pondered about the parent's responsibility 'purely for the sake of completeness' and that the statement was therefore not contestable by legal means.[27] Regrettably, the GC did not see this as an encouragement for any further reflection of this kind.

But the GC was right. As I have explained elsewhere in more detail,[28] holding parent companies liable for competition law infringements by their subsidiaries serves a number of important objectives. Three reasons should be highlighted here.

[25] *Akzo Nobel and Others v Commission* (n 2), Opinion of AG Kokott, para 43.

[26] Case T-77/08 *Dow Chemical v Commission* ECLI:EU:T:2012:47, para 101.

[27] *The Dow Chemical Company v Commission* (n 16), para 62–63.

[28] C König, 'An Economic Analysis of the Single Economic Entity Doctrine in EU Competition Law' (2017) 13 J CL & E 281; see also C König, 'Comparing Parent Company Liability in EU and US Competition Law' (2018) 41 World Competition 69, 88–93.

First, parental liability restores effective deterrence where subsidiaries are underdeterred, for example, because they lack sufficient assets to pay a fine or because they misjudge the situation on the basis of insufficient information.[29] From a deterrence perspective, it can make sense to involve the parent company in compliance efforts, if the subsidiary does not respond to the threat of monetary sanctions. However, two conditions should be met: First, it must be likely that the parent company will respond better to incentives than the subsidiary, for example, because the parent has more assets or better information. Second, the parent company must be able to influence the behaviour of the subsidiary and deter it from infringing the law. Typically, both will be the case. Parent companies often possess more assets and better information, and they are in a good position to steer their subsidiaries in the right direction. They can select and replace their subsidiaries' management, they can establish group-wide compliance mechanisms, and they can set up compensation and promotion schemes that reward compliance and discourage any form of illegal behaviour. In this respect, holding parent companies liable for their subsidiaries' offences serves a similar function to other forms of vicarious liability, such as the liability of employers for wrongs committed by their employees or the liability of parents for the behaviour of their children.

A second reason for parental liability is that it prevents parent companies from opportunistically exploiting limited liability to separate their assets from their risks.[30] It is well known from corporate law and economics research that limited liability may induce shareholders to externalise risks to third parties, in particular to involuntary creditors who cannot insist on contractual protections.[31] A strategic use of limited liability allows shareholders to fully benefit from the opportunities for profit, but to disassociate themselves from the company in the event of losses. Such incentives may also exist with regard to infringements of competition law. For example, companies could be tempted to bundle their sales activities in markets particularly susceptible to cartels in weakly financed subsidiaries. If an infringement of competition law were to occur, the damage could then be contained to the subsidiary, while the parent company would remain unaffected. Extending liability to the parent company undermines such strategies. It eliminates the incentive for opportunistically exploiting limited liability and re-internalises all competition law risks to the corporate group and its ultimate shareholders.

29 König, 'Economic Analysis' (n 28) 299–311; König, 'Comparing' (n 28) 89–92.

30 König, 'Economic Analysis' (n 28) 311–319; König, 'Comparing' (n 28) 92–93.

31 N Mendelson, 'A Control-Based Approach to Shareholder Liability for Corporate Torts' (2002) 102 Colum L R 1203; H Hansmann and R Kraakman, 'Toward Unlimited Shareholder Liability for Corporate Torts' (1991) 100 Yale LJ 1879; D Leebron, 'Limited Liability, Tort Victims, and Creditors' (1991) 91 Colum L Rev 1565; C Stone, 'The Place for Enterprise Liability in the Control of Corporate Conduct' (1980) 90 Yale LJ 1, 65–76; P Halpern, M Trebilcock and S Turnbull, 'An Economic Analysis of Limited Liability in Corporation Law' (1980) 30 UTLJ 117, 145–150.

The third reason for parental liability is that enforcement is expensive and that parent companies often have a comparative cost advantage over the state.[32] Many of the most serious competition infringements take place in secret. They are difficult to detect and investigate. As a result, competition authorities have to devote considerable resources to ensure that infringements are established in a way that withstands judicial review. High costs of enforcement are an important reason why competition law relies heavily on cooperative measures such as leniency programmes and settlements. The liability of parent companies can also be seen as a means to save enforcement costs. Parent companies are in a good position to take over part of the investigation work that would otherwise have to be carried out by authorities. They can obtain reports from their subsidiaries, examine contracts and accounts and, if necessary, conduct internal investigations. As internal control mechanisms usually already exist for the purpose of group management, parent companies can typically implement investigative measures at a lower cost than the state. Given the greater cost-effectiveness of internal reviews, this not only turns public costs into private costs but saves administrative costs overall.

Occasionally, it is claimed that the actual design of the single economic entity doctrine does not fit these policy objectives. For example, it is argued that the doctrine does not reward compliance efforts but punishes them because the parent company is liable even if it does everything in its power to prevent the subsidiary from committing competition law violations.[33] Moreover, it has been questioned why the parent company is also liable if the subsidiary is solvent[34] and why the application of the doctrine does not depend on whether the parent could actually have prevented the infringement.[35] However, the strongest incentive to commit to compliance comes from the possibility of avoiding liability altogether. The parent company is rewarded for its compliance efforts by not being liable if no infringement occurs. If the parent company succeeds in deterring the subsidiary from committing infringements, the question of liability does not arise at all – neither for the parent nor for the subsidiary. Furthermore, the same questions could be asked about the liability of employers under the doctrine of *respondeat superior*. Both concepts cannot be reduced to a single objective and they are based on fairly general conditions to cope with a large number of different cases. The fact that efficient deterrence can be achieved in individual cases even without vicarious liability does not mean that

32 König, 'Economic Analysis' (n 28) 308–309.

33 Leddy and van Melkebeke (n 7) 415–416; Kalintiri (n 7) 162; S Mobley, D Mourkas and G Murray, 'Parent Liability for Joint Venture Parents: The Courts' 'EI du Pont' and 'Dow Chemical' Judgments in Conflict with Optimal Compliance Incentives' (2014) 35 ECLR 499, 503–505; A Pera and G Pisanelli, 'Prevention of Antitrust Violations: Which Role for Compliance Programs?' (2013) 34 ECLR 267, 271; Thomas (n 22) 17; K Hofstetter and M Ludescher, 'Fines against Parent Companies in EU Antitrust Law: Setting Incentives for "Best Practice Compliance"' (2010) 33 W Comp 55.

34 Kalintiri (n 7) 158.

35 Thomas (n 22) 17.

vicarious liability as a whole is not important for deterrence. Hardly any doctrine does justice to every individual case. It would be possible to differentiate the conditions for the liability of parent companies to a greater extent, but legal certainty would suffer as well. Given this trade-off, it seems justifiable that the doctrine is based on rather general conditions. Moreover, in accordance with the case law of the EU Courts, the Commission has discretion as to whether or not to invoke the parent company's liability.[36] Where the application of the doctrine does not contribute to general or specific deterrence, it can therefore remain unapplied.

4.3.2 *Ensuring the Correct Calculation of the Fine*

Another objective of the single economic entity doctrine is to enable a proper calculation of fines. As we shall see, it is very important to distinguish this function from the one discussed in the previous section. In case law, however, both functions are sometimes confused. The starting point for all consideration is that the benchmark for the calculation of fines is the objective of deterrence. The Courts have repeatedly stressed that the Commission must ensure that the fine has the necessary deterrent effect.[37] They have also explained that, as far as the specific deterrence of the infringing undertaking is concerned, the deterrent effect must be assessed in relation to the size and the economic power of the undertaking, for which it is necessary to take into account its global resources.[38] As pointed out by AG Kokott in her statement quoted above, in this context, it is important to correctly assess the 'true economic strength of the whole undertaking', i.e. the corporate group. The Courts, therefore, assume that – in so far as turnover is relevant for the calculation of the fine – it is the consolidated turnover of the group as a whole that must be taken into account. In *Group Gascogne* (2013),[39] the ECJ explicitly referred to Article 1(1) of Directive 83/349[40] for the purpose of determining the 10% turnover cap according to Article 23(2) of Regulation 1/2003[41] and paragraph 32 of the 2006

[36] Case C-125/07 P *Erste Group Bank and Others v Commission* ECLI:EU:C:2009:576, paras 81–82; Case T-543/08 *RWE and RWE Dea v Commission* ECLI:EU:T:2014:627, para 136; Case T-259/02 *Raiffeisen Zentralbank Österreich v Commission* ECLI:EU:T:2006:396, paras 331–332.

[37] Case C-100/80 *Musique Diffusion française v Commission* ECLI:EU:C:1983:158, para 106; Case T-42/07 *Dow Chemicals and Others v Commission* ECLI:EU:T:2011:357, para 148; Case T-31/99 *ABB Asea Brown Boveri v Commission* ECLI:EU:T:2002:77, para 166. Cf also paragraph 4 of the 2006 Fining Guidelines (n 42).

[38] Case C-286/13 *Dole Food and Dole Fresh Fruit Europe v Commission* ECLI:EU:C:2015:184, para 142; *Groupe Gascogne v Commission* (n 18), para 49–50; Case C-413/08 *Lafarge v Commission* ECLI:EU:C:2010:346, paras 102, 104.

[39] *Groupe Gascogne v Commission* (n 18), para 43. See also Case T-72/06 *Groupe Gascogne v Commission* ECLI:EU:T:2011:671, paras 106–117.

[40] Seventh Council Directive 83/349/EEC of 13 June 1983 based on the Article 54 (3) (g) of the Treaty on consolidated accounts [1983] OJ L193/1 (Seventh Company Law Directive).

[41] Council Regulation (EC) No 1/2003 of 16 December 2002 on the implementation of the rules on competition laid down in Articles 81 and 82 of the Treaty, [2003] OJ L1/1.

Fining Guidelines.[42] Today, the relevant provision is to be found in Article 22(1) of the Accounting Directive 2013/34,[43] which, like its predecessor, obliges parent companies and subsidiaries to prepare consolidated financial statements. The aim is to provide 'a true and fair view of assets and liabilities, the financial position and the profit and loss' of the whole group of companies.[44] It should be noted, however, that the conditions for determining 'parent undertakings' and 'subsidiary undertakings' within the meaning of Article 22(1) of the Accounting Directive are set out exclusively in that provision. The criteria listed there are similar to those used in EU competition law to determine economic units – but they are not identical. It is therefore not necessarily the competition law concept of an undertaking that decides on the attribution of turnover.

The conclusion that only consolidated group turnover can be decisive in so far as turnover is relevant for the calculation of the fine is already apparent from the fact that turnover can easily be reallocated within the group. Competition law investigations take a long time, so companies usually know that a fine will be imposed well in advance of the actual imposition of the fine. If the managers of a corporate group could be sure that only the turnover of the subsidiary will be taken into account, they could adapt to this and shift the turnover to other companies in the group. This is particularly true where the Commission does not normally take into account the turnover during the cartel infringement but, as in the case of the 10% turnover cap, the turnover in the year preceding the prohibition decision. At this stage, the company is usually aware that a fine will soon be imposed. Against this background, it is surprising that the ECJ apparently wants to limit the relevance of consolidated group turnover to cases in which liability is attributed to the parent company. In the *Groupe Gascogne* judgment, at least, the Court held that the Commission is entitled to rely on group turnover where it 'has established to a sufficient legal standard that an infringement may be attributed to a company which heads a group'.[45] If that was meant as a condition, the Court would be wrong. For the reasons set out above, it must *always* be the consolidated group turnover that is taken into account, even if only a single subsidiary is liable. Interestingly, the ECJ recognises that the Commission cannot be required to demonstrate the decisive influence of the parent company for each subsidiary whose turnover it wishes to include in the calculation of the fine, as these are 'two separate issues serving different purposes'.[46] This

42 Guidelines on the method of setting fines imposed pursuant to Article 23(2)(a) of Regulation No 1/2003 [2006] OJ C210/2 (2006 Fining Guidelines or simply Fining Guidelines).

43 Directive 2013/34/EU of the European Parliament and the Council of 26 June 2013 on the annual financial statements, consolidated financial statements and related reports of certain types of undertakings [2013] OJ L182/19 (Accounting Directive).

44 Article 4(3) and recital 9 of the Accounting Directive (n 43); Recital 5 of the Seventh Company Law Directive (n 40).

45 *Groupe Gascogne v Commission* (n 18), para 55.

46 *Groupe Gascogne v Commission* (n 18), para 57.

observation is correct and the conclusion must ultimately be that the calculation of the fine should not depend at all on the economic unit as developed for the attribution of liability. Instead, the Commission should simply always be allowed to rely on consolidated accounts as defined in Chapter 6 of the Accounting Directive.

There is an important difference between the liability function of the single economic entity doctrine and its use for the correct calculation of fines, and that is the point in time that is decisive. The liability function is linked to the parent company's control and its ability to prevent competition law infringement. Liability based on this ground should therefore apply only to corporate entities which were able to exercise a decisive influence during the infringement. For the calculation of the fine, however, the relevant point in time should in principle be the date of the prohibition decision. The reason is that fines serve primarily as a deterrent and thus have a forward-looking purpose. In particular, the objective of specific deterrence, i.e. ensuring compliance with the undertaking addressed by the prohibition decision, requires the fine to be set in such a way as to anticipate the undertaking's future behaviour. This is an important finding because the undertaking at the time of the decision may be quite different from the one at the time of the infringement.[47] The objective of setting the fine in such a way as to prevent future infringements may even justify taking into account the economic strength of entities which were not part of the undertaking at the time of the infringement. In contrast to the liability function, it is irrelevant for the calculation of the fine whether other members of the group could have prevented the competition law infringement. Instead, it is simply a matter of correctly taking into account the actual economic strength of the group when calculating the fine.

4.3.3 *Ensuring the Payment of the Fine*

Another important objective of the single economic entity doctrine, derived from the case law of the EU Courts, is to ensure that fines are actually paid. Even though the Courts adopt an approach which comes close to personifying the economic unit formed by a group of companies,[48] they accept that the Commission can only address its decisions to natural and legal persons.[49] This is the only way to ensure that decisions imposing fines are enforceable under Article 299 TFEU. In this context, the ECJ has described the joint and several liabilities of parent companies and their subsidiaries as 'an additional legal device available to the Commission to strengthen the effectiveness of the action taken by it for the recovery of fines imposed

[47] See eg Case C-637/13 P *Laufen Austria v Commission* ECLI:EU:C:2017:51, paras 44–51; Case C-408/12 *YKK and Others v Commission* ECLI:EU:C:2014:2153, paras 55–68, 95–99; Case C-50/12 *Kendrion v Commission* ECLI:EU:C:2013:771, paras 55–58.

[48] See above, Section 4.2 at n 19–23.

[49] *Commission v Siemens Österreich and Others* (n 8), para 55. See also Case C-823/18 *Commission v GEA Group* ECLI:EU:C:2020:426, Opinion of GA Pitruzzella, para 43.

for infringement of the competition rules'.[50] Moreover, the Court has explained that extending liability to the parent company 'reduces for the Commission, as creditor of the debt represented by such fines, the risk of insolvency [...]'.[51] On other occasions, the ECJ has emphasised that joint and several liability 'cannot be reduced to a type of security provided by the parent company in order to guarantee payment of the fine imposed on the subsidiary'.[52] Thus, the Court has clarified that securing the enforcement of the fine is one purpose of parental liability, albeit not the only one.

Since fines for competition offences are often very high, it is not surprising that companies go to great lengths to avoid them. Past experience has shown that this sometimes includes corporate restructuring. A fairly well-known example that happened in Germany is discussed in detail in Chapter 5 of this book.[53] In this case, the *Bundeskartellamt* had to close its proceedings because a restructuring had made it impossible to enforce the fines. This case was one of the reasons why the German legislator decided to introduce parental liability based on the European model as part of the Ninth Amendment to the German Competition Act.[54] As far as the particular function of ensuring the enforcement of fines is concerned, parent company liability competes with other approaches, such as the liability of legal and economic successors or simply faster enforcement of fines. However, it is clear that it becomes more difficult and therefore less attractive to avoid fines through restructuring if liability is also extended to the parent company.

The Courts have in the past linked the problem of collecting the fine with the objective of deterrence.[55] Such a connection does indeed exist since a fine which is not collected cannot contribute to deterrence. According to this logic, if the subsidiary defaults on payment, liability should be extended only to those who could have prevented the infringement, i.e. the parent company at the time of the infringement (or several successive parent companies if there has been a change of control during the period of the infringement). However, as illustrated by successor liability,[56] deterrence is not the only possible objective of such a form of contingent liability. It could also be seen as an attempt to ensure that a large financial claim by the Commission

50 *Villeroy & Boch v Commission* (n 14), para 152; *Commission v Siemens Österreich and Others* (n 8), para 59; See also Case T-475/14 *Prysmian and Prysmian cavi e sistemi v Commission* ECLI:EU:T:2018:448, para 153; *The Goldman Sachs Group v Commission* (n 21), para 201.

51 *Villeroy & Boch v Commission* (n 14), para 152; *Commission v Siemens Österreich and Others* (n 8), para 59. See also *Areva and Others v Commission* (n 14), para 132.

52 *Kendrion v Commission* (n 47), para 56; Case C-243/12 *FLS Plast v Commission* ECLI:EU:C:2014:2006, para 107.

53 See Chapter 5, M Walter and M Schunke: 'Piercing the Corporate Veil: The German Sausage Saga'.

54 C König, 'Digital Economy, Antitrust Damages, and More: The 9th Amendment to the German Competition Act' (2017) 1 CoRe 261, 264.

55 Eg *Commission v Siemens Österreich and Others* (n 8), para 59; *Areva v Commission* (n 14), para 132.

56 Legal or economic successors do not control the infringing undertaking during the time of the infringement and therefore could not have prevented the infringement. It is therefore difficult to justify successor liability with deterrence.

is met in order to protect the EU budget and ultimately European taxpayers. Seen in this light, there would not even need to be a link between the party liable and the competition law infringement. Instead, the substitute debtor could be anyone who held a significant stake in the subsidiary at some point between the beginning of the infringement (when the debt was first incurred) and the payment of the fine (when it is fulfilled). If the main objective is to avoid subsequent restructuring, it makes sense to focus on a point in time before the investigations become known.

To be clear, such liability, which is not linked to the control during the infringement, has not yet been established under EU competition law.[57] Yet, that does not mean that it could not exist.[58] First steps in this direction can be found at the Member State level. Germany has created a form of substitute liability in 2017, as part of its strategy to close loopholes in its former liability law. Under Section 81a of the German Competition Act,[59] a sum equal to the fine can now be demanded from parent companies as well as legal and economic successors if the fine cannot be enforced against a subsidiary or predecessor responsible for an infringement.[60] This type of liability has the advantage that it does not contain any accusation regarding the infringement – the substitute debtor need not have been affiliated with the subsidiary at the time of the infringement – so that the procedural guarantees of the law on fines need not be applied. For this reason, the German legislator suggests, for example, that the provision can also be applied retroactively, even though the law on fines is characterised by the principle that acts can only be punished if they were prohibited before they were committed.[61] In fact, the same approach could be used for other high liabilities, such as tax debts – without it being relevant whether any of the companies have infringed the law. Such liability would not be a sanction but would be justified solely by the need to prevent evasive conduct aimed at circumventing high payment obligations.

57 It is settled case law that it falls, in principle, to the legal or natural person managing the undertaking in question when the infringement was committed to answer for that infringement, even though, at the time of the decision finding the infringement, the operation of the undertaking was no longer its responsibility. See Case C-352/09 P *ThyssenKrupp Nirosta v Commission* ECLI:EU:C:2011:191, para 143; Case C-248/98 P *KNP BT v Commission* ECLI:EU:C:2000:625, para 71; Case C-279/98 P *Cascades v Commission* ECLI:EU:C:2000:626, paras 78–79; Case C-286/98 P *Stora Kopparbergs Bergslags v Commission* ECLI:EU:C:2000:630, para 37.

58 The ECJ has so far only held that joint and several liability created by the single economic entity doctrine cannot be used 'to force one company to bear the risk of the insolvency of another company where those companies have *never* formed part of the same undertaking' (emphasis added), *Areva v Commission* (n 14), para 132.

59 An English version of the German Competition Act ('Gesetz gegen Wettbewerbsbeschränkungen' or simply 'GWB') can be found at www.gesetze-im-internet.de/englisch_gwb/ accessed on 30 December 2020.

60 The relevant point in time for determining whether a company is responsible as parent company or legal or economic successor under s 81a GWB is the time when the investigation becomes known. This is to avoid companies reacting to the notification of the investigation with restructuring.

61 Draft by the Federal Government, Bundestag paper No 18/10207 (in German) 94–95 http://dipbt.bundestag.de/dip21.web/bt accessed on 30 December 2020.

4.4 BORDERLINE ISSUES OF LIABILITY

After these remarks on the distinct functions that the single economic entity doctrine fulfils in EU competition law, it is now time to reflect on the recent debates on extensions of the doctrine. As we have seen, it is important to distinguish between the question of the calculation of fines and that of liability. The fact that, for example, the turnover of another company should be taken into account in the calculation of the fine does not mean that this company should also be liable. While the calculation of fines depends on a correct assessment of the economic strength of all affiliated companies at the time of the prohibition decision, attribution of liability should be concerned with the question of who could have prevented the competition law infringement at the time when it occurred. This difference must also be kept in mind in the following considerations. It means, in particular, that, at least as a general rule, a much narrower approach is required with regard to liability than with regard to the calculation of fines.

4.4.1 *Sibling Liability*

The first issue to be looked at is the liability of sister companies. It has been claimed in the literature that the liability of sister companies already follows from the concept of the single economic unit.[62] Since sister companies form an economic unit with the parent company and with each other, they shall, according to this view, be mutually liable for their respective competition law infringements. This position is closely linked to the view that it is the economic unit as such which commits the infringement and that the infringement can therefore be attributed to all the legal entities constituting the economic unit, i.e. essentially all members of the corporate group.

The Courts have so far acknowledged the liability of a sister company only in the rare case where one sister company exercises a decisive influence over the other.[63] For other constellations, the case law is not yet clear. The ECJ has held in *Aristrain* (2003), that it is not possible 'to impute to a company all of the acts of a group even though that company has not been identified as the legal person at the head of that group with responsibility for coordinating the group's activities'.[64] The GC has apparently understood this to mean that liability can only be attributed bottom-up in the direction of (direct and indirect) parent companies, but not top-down in the

62 C Kersting, 'Liability of Sister Companies and Subsidiaries in European Competition Law' (2020) 41(3) ECLR 125, 128, 133, 135–136.

63 Case T-43/02 *Jungbunzlauer v Commission* ECLI:EU:T:2006:270, paras 101–105, 123–133.

64 Case C-196/99 P *Aristrain v Commission* ECLI:EU:C:2003:529, para 98. The ECJ went on to explain in para 99 that 'the simple fact that the share capital of two separate commercial companies is held by the same person or the same family is insufficient, in itself, to establish that those two companies are an economic unit with the result that […] the actions of one company can be attributed to the other and that one can be held liable to pay a fine for the other'.

direction of subsidiaries or even horizontally in the direction of sister companies. For example, it held in *Parker ITR* (2013) that the Commission cannot attribute to a subsidiary the responsibility of its parent company for the unlawful conduct of another subsidiary, which ultimately also means that the subsidiary is not liable for the infringement of the other subsidiary.[65] In other decisions, the GC has indicated that it interprets *Aristrain* as meaning that liability can only be attributed to the parent company.[66] Christian Kersting, on the other hand, has claimed that the real problem in *Aristrain* was that the existence of a single economic unit had not been proven, because there was already no 'parent company' which would have managed the companies of the group in a uniform manner.[67] That is correct, but it is unclear whether this was a decisive point for the ECJ.

Other judgments, such as the GC's *Michelin* decision[68] and both Courts' judgments in the *Versalis* litigation,[69] are less significant, as they do not concern the question of liability but the calculation of fines – in particular, the relevant turnover to be taken into account and the question of recidivism. As has been repeatedly stressed in this chapter, these are distinct issues that have little to do with the establishment of liability. Nor does it seem sensible to look for the solution in the notion of the undertaking or the concept of the single economic unit.[70]

The decisive factor must ultimately be the purpose of declaring a particular legal entity liable. It has been argued that the liability of sister companies is necessary to properly capture the economic strength of the group.[71] But that is not correct. As already shown,[72] it is true that the calculation of fines should be based on the group as a whole. This does not mean, however, that all members must also be individually liable. Remember that the ECJ has made it clear in *Group Gascogne* (2013) that, where the liability of the ultimate parent company is established, the Commission 'is entitled, for the purposes of assessing the financial capacity of that company, to take into consideration the latter's consolidated accounts inasmuch as they may be regarded as constituting a relevant factor of assessment'.[73] The consolidated accounts, however, automatically include the assets, liabilities, financial positions, profits, and losses of all subsidiaries in terms of Chapter 6 of the EU Accounting Directive 2013/34.[74] Furthermore, the ECJ has pointed out that it is, in this context,

65 Case T-146/09 *Parker ITR and Parker-Hannifin v Commission* ECLI:EU:T:2013:258, para 124.

66 *Groupe Gascogne v Commission* (n 39), paras 112, 114; *Deutsche Telekom v Commission* (n 20), paras 511–513.

67 Kersting (n 62) 131.

68 Case T-203/01 *Michelin v Commission* ECLI:EU:T:2003:250.

69 Case C-93/13 P *Commission and Others v Versalis and Others* ECLI:EU:C:2015:150; Case T-103/08 *Versalis and Eni v Commission* ECLI:EU:T:2012:686.

70 See above, Section 4.2.

71 Kersting (n 62) 132–133.

72 Section 4.3.2 at n 45–47.

73 *Groupe Gascogne v Commission* (n 18), para 55.

74 See, in particular, Article 22(1) and 24(7) of the Accounting Directive (n 43).

not necessary for the Commission to show that each subsidiary was controlled by the parent company.[75] Thus, the Court has clearly separated the question of liability from that of attribution of turnover – and that was the right thing to do.

As explained in detail above,[76] extending liability to legal entities that were not directly involved in the infringement serves to induce them to influence the conduct of the real perpetrator. If this is understood, it is obvious that the mutual liability of sister companies for their respective infringements makes little sense. The same applies to holding subsidiaries liable for infringements committed by their parent companies.[77] Instead, liability should depend strictly on the possibility of control. In corporate groups, however, control is typically exercised from top to bottom. A parent company can take steps to ensure that its subsidiaries do not commit any infringements and holding the parent liable can therefore contribute to deterrence. But sister companies cannot control each other any more than subsidiaries can control their parent companies. The approach of extending liability to companies which are at the same or lower level in the corporate hierarchy than the actual perpetrator is therefore misguided.

4.4.2 *Actions for Damages*

Another issue is whether parent company liability is also justified in actions for damages. This has been the subject of much debate since the entry into force of the EU Directive on Antitrust Damages Actions in 2014. The issue has gained further attention since the ECJ recently held in *Skanska* (2019) that the concept of 'undertaking' within the meaning of Article 101 TFEU constitutes an autonomous concept of EU law and cannot have a different scope with regard to the imposition of fines on the one hand and actions for damages on the other.[78] However, the answer to the question of parental liability for damages cannot be found in terms and definitions, but only in a purposeful interpretation of the relevant provisions. If one assumes, as seems reasonable, that liability for damages does not only serve the purpose of compensation but is also supposed to contribute to deterrence, there is little reason not to apply the principles of parental liability also in actions for damages. This is particularly true if one further assumes that damages actions concern, at least in part, harm that is not adequately taken into account in fine proceedings. A rule of holding parent companies liable for damage caused by their subsidiaries then ensures that the necessary incentives for compliance are also set in relation to these positions.

[75] *Groupe Gascogne v Commission* (n 18), para 57.

[76] Section 4.3.1.

[77] See eg Case T-677/14 *Biogaran v Commission* ECLI:EU:T:2018:910, paras 206–234. This case is difficult to assess because the reasoning is not entirely clear. However, it appears that the GC was strongly influenced by the fact that both the parent company and the subsidiary were directly involved in the infringement; see e.g. paras 218–219.

[78] Case C-724/17 *Skanska Industrial Solutions and Others* ECLI:EU:C:2019:204, para 47.

4.5 THE EU–US DIVIDE

Finally, given the comparative perspective of this book, it will now briefly be discussed how the issues of this chapter are treated in US antitrust law. It is often stressed that there is a strong contrast between the EU and the US system with regard to the liability of parent companies.[79] Indeed, in the US law on antitrust sanctions, there is no general rule of parent company liability for the antitrust infringements of their subsidiaries. Sections 1 and 2 of the Sherman Act both address 'persons', defined in Section 7 of the same Act as including 'corporations and associations'. These terms are based on a rather narrow legal understanding, which in no way resembles the functional approach developed by the ECJ with regard to the term 'undertaking' in Articles 101 and 102 TFEU and Article 23 of Regulation 1/2003. As a result, in US antitrust law, the focus with regard to the establishment of liability is very much on the specific legal entity whose employees committed the violation. However, the requirements of the Sherman Act are not so strict that it would not have been possible to develop a different approach. The reasons for the striking US–EU divide must therefore lie elsewhere. Apparently, up to now, there has simply been no need in US antitrust practice for holding parent companies liable. I have tried elsewhere to help answer the question of what might be the reasons for this phenomenon.[80] Besides the fact that complex group structures are simply much rarer in the US than in Europe (which makes the advantages of parental liability less obvious),[81] the greater significance of other liability mechanisms is likely to play a major role. In particular, the higher relevance of individual liability of managers and employees can be expected to fill some of the deterrent gaps, to which the EU is responding by extending liability to other legal entities.

However, I would like to use this opportunity to draw attention to two other important points. First, it is clear, in this context as well, that the question of liability should not be confused with that of the calculation of fines. While it is true that US antitrust law does not generally recognise parent companies' liability for fines, it is equally true that the rules on the calculation of fines do make a difference according to whether a company is part of a larger group or not.[82] This can be seen, for example, in the

[79] Leddy and van Melkebeke (n 7) 412–413; König, 'Comparing' (n 28) 76–82. Undertakings have even attacked the single economic entity doctrine on the grounds that it is not recognised in US antitrust law, but without any success. See *Eni v Commission [C-508/11]* (n 6), para 78–86; *Eni v Commission [T-39/07]* (n 6), paras 106–118.

[80] König, 'Comparing' (n 28) 82–100.

[81] M Becht and C Mayer, 'Introduction' in F Barca and M Becht (eds), *The Control of Corporate Europe* (Oxford University Press 2001); M Faccio and L Lang, 'The Ultimate Ownership of Western European Corporations' (2002) 65 J Fin Econ 365; R La Porta, F Lopez-De-Silanes and A Shleifer, 'Corporate Ownership Around the World' (1999) 54 J Fin 471.

[82] Chapter 8 of the US Sentencing Guidelines (n 84) refers to 'organisations' which are defined in 18 U.S.C. § 18 as 'a person other than an individual', and include, according to the official commentary to USSG §8A1.1. 'corporations, partnerships, associations, joint-stock companies, unions, trusts, pension funds, unincorporated organizations, governments and political subdivisions thereof, and

rules on recidivism.[83] According to §8C2.5(c)(1)(A) of the US Sentencing Guidelines (USSG),[84] an organisation's culpability score is to be increased by one point if the organisation committed any part of the offence less than ten years after a criminal adjudication based on similar misconduct.[85] This is comparable to the European Commission's approach under paragraph 28 of the 2006 Fining Guidelines, except that these do not provide for a maximum period. In our context, it is important that the official comment to §8C2.5(c), published by the US Sentencing Commission, explains that in determining the prior history of an organisation 'the conduct of the underlying economic entity shall be considered without regard to its legal structure or ownership'.[86] This shows an openness to approaches that would be comparable with the broad European concept of 'undertaking'. However, the approach under §8C2.5(c) appears to be more nuanced and not primarily aimed at including other legal entities in the analysis. On the contrary, the Guidelines make it clear that even within one legal unit, there can be several economic units, each of which may or may not be classified as a repeat offender. This is already hinted at in §8C2.5(c), which not only mentions the 'organisation' as a reference point for recidivism but also a 'separately managed line of business'. The official comment explains that, where separately managed lines of business exist, 'only the prior conduct or criminal record of the separately managed line of business involved in the instant offense is to be used'.[87] Furthermore, the comment gives the example of two companies merging and becoming separate divisions and separately managed lines of business within the merged company. In such a case, 'each division would retain the prior history of its predecessor company'.[88] As this makes clear, the focus is still on the divisions and not simply on the new company as a whole (as it would be under EU competition law).

An expansive approach can be found in §8C2.5(b), which concerns the involvement or tolerance by high-ranking managers. The provision refers to the size of the workforce for qualifying how much the culpability score is to be increased.

non-profit organizations'. Although the term seems very open, it is not clear from the wording of § 8A1.1. or the official comment whether a group of companies could, for the purposes of the Sentencing Guidelines, be regarded as one single 'organisation'.

83 On the significance of recidivism in US antitrust enforcement see J Connor, 'Recidivism Revealed: Private International Cartels 1990–2009' (September 2010) https://ssrn.com/abstract=1688508 accessed on 30 December 2020; D Ginsburg and J Wright, 'Antitrust Sanctions' (November 2010) https://ssrn.com/abstract=1705701 accessed on 30 December 2020; G Werden, S Hammond and B Barnett, 'Recidivism Eliminated: Cartel Enforcement in the United States Since 1999' (September 2011) https://ssrn.com/abstract=1927864 accessed on 30 December 2020.

84 2018 Guidelines Manual Annotated (United States Sentencing Commission 2018) www.ussc.gov/guidelines/2018-guidelines-manual-annotated accessed on 30 December 2020.

85 If the criminal adjudication was less than five years ago, the culpability score will be increased by two points, USSG §8C2.5(c)(2)(A). Alternatively, the increase can also be justified with civil or administrative adjudication(s) based on two or more separate instances of similar conducts, see §8C2.5(c)(1)(B) and §8C2.5(c)(2)(B).

86 2018 Guidelines Manual Annotated (n 84) USSG §8C2.5, Comment 6.

87 *Ibid.* at USSG §8C2.5, Comment 5.

88 *Ibid.* at USSG §8C2.5, Comment 6.

However, it does not only focus on the 'organisation' but also on the 'unit of the organisation', which is defined in the comment as meaning 'any reasonably distinct operational component of the organisation'.[89] It is further explained that, if a large organisation has several large units such as divisions or subsidiaries, 'all these types of units are encompassed within the term "unit of the organisation"'.[90]

In other contexts, it is less clear whether the entire group can be considered or whether the focus is strictly on legal entities. This is the case, for example, with regard to the inability to pay. According to §8C3.3(a) of the US Sentencing Guidelines, courts shall reduce the fine below that otherwise required to the extent that imposition of such fine would impair the organisation's ability to make restitution to victims. Furthermore, §8C3.3(b) allows for the same reduction if a court finds that the organisation is not able and, even with the use of a reasonable instalment schedule, is not likely to become able to pay the minimum fine under the Guidelines. It is further stated that the reduction under any of the two provisions shall not be more than necessary to avoid substantially jeopardising the continued viability of the organisation. However, neither the Sentencing Guidelines nor a recently published memorandum makes it clear whether the economic situation of affiliated companies should also be considered.[91] As a matter of policy, this is essential, as companies might otherwise try to influence their liability by shifting assets to other members of the corporate group.

Other important parameters, which are strongly influenced by the single economic unit doctrine in EU competition law, have no equivalents in US fining practice. This applies, for example, to the 10% turnover limit and the deterrence multiplier. All in all, however, it can be said that the unitary perspective on corporate groups plays a role under Chapter 8 of the US Sentencing Guidelines.

The second important qualification to be made here is that, when it comes to the US American fining practice, there is a big difference between the law on the books and the law in action. For the 20 years from 2000 to 2019, the Corporate Prosecution Registry created by Brandon Garrett lists 293 antitrust decisions.[92] Only three of these cases were resolved with a conviction. In contrast, 278 cases (almost 95%) were resolved by non-prosecution agreements (12), deferred prosecution agreements (2), or plea agreements (264). The fact that by far most cases are resolved by negotiated settlements gives prosecutors considerable leeway, also with regard to the sanctioning of groups of companies. This can be seen, for example, by looking at some of the international cartel cases that, in the EU, have led to the application of the single

[89] *Ibid.* at USSG §8C2.5, Comment 2.

[90] *Ibid.*

[91] US Department of Justice, 'Evaluating a Business Organization's Inability to Pay a Criminal Fine or Criminal Monetary Penalty' (Memorandum 8 October 2019) www.justice.gov/opa/speech/file/1207576/download, accessed on 30 December 2020.

[92] Corporate Prosecution Registry (University of Virginia & Duke University) https://corporate-prosecution-registry.com/ accessed on 30 December 2020.

economic entity doctrine. In *Hydrogen peroxide* (2006), for example, the European Commission imposed a fine of 25.2 million euros on Akzo Nobel NV, Akzo Nobel Chemicals Holding AB and EKA Chemicals AB.[93] The latter was considered the actual perpetrator, whereas the other two companies were held liable as parent companies.[94] With regard to the US American part of the hydrogen peroxide cartel, a plea agreement was concluded between the US Department of Justice and Akzo Nobel Chemicals International BV,[95] at the time a wholly owned subsidiary of Akzo Nobel NV and the parent company of Akzo Nobel Chemicals Holding AB, i.e. two of the three companies addressed in the European decision. Interestingly, the plea agreement refers to 'the defendant, including its subsidiaries' as a producer and seller of hydrogen peroxide.[96] Furthermore, even though the agreement was only signed in the name of Akzo Nobel Chemicals International BV, full and truthful cooperation is promised by '[t]he defendant and its parents and subsidiaries that are engaged in the sale or production of hydrogen peroxide'.[97] This should probably include EKA Chemicals AB (or its successors), which are, however, not mentioned in the agreement.

Similar broad language can also be found in other plea agreements.[98] It seems that although a specific legal entity is always singled out as the contracting party, in reality, the agreement is effectively concluded with the whole group. There is no indication that the US Department of Justice would relieve parts of a unified group of companies of their responsibility simply because they are organised in separate legal entities. This applies, in particular, to cooperation obligations. The relevant passages in plea agreements typically also refer to parent companies, subsidiaries, and successors collectively referred to as 'related entities'.[99] They all need to provide documents and make their employees available if so requested by the Department of Justice, and they all benefit from preferential treatment as long as they comply with the plea agreement. It is therefore obvious that the use of plea agreements avoids some of the problems that need to be solved in the EU with complex attribution mechanisms. Prosecutors in the US use the threat of conviction as leverage to secure the voluntary cooperation of the whole group. Since appeal procedures do

93 *Hydrogen peroxide (and perborate)* (Case COMP/38.620) Commission Decision 2006/903/EC of 3 May 2006 [2006] OJ L353/54, para 530.

94 *Hydrogen peroxide (and perborate)* (n 93), paras 381–382.

95 *US v Akzo Nobel Chemicals International*, Plea Agreement of 17 May 2006, US District Court N.D. California, www.justice.gov/atr/case/us-v-akzo-nobel-chemicals-international-bv accessed on 30 December 2020.

96 *Ibid.* at para 4.

97 *Ibid.* at para 13.

98 See e.g. *US v DuPont Dow Elastomers*, Plea Agreement of 29 March 2005, US District Court N.D. California, www.justice.gov/atr/case/us-v-dupont-dow-elastomers-llc accessed on 30 December 2020, para 13; *US v Elf Atochem*, Plea Agreement of 12 April 2002, US District Court N.D. California www.justice.gov/atr/case-document/plea-agreement-111 accessed on 30 December 2020, para 14.

99 *US v Akzo Nobel Chemicals International* (n 95), para 13; *US v DuPont Dow Elastomers* (n 98), para 13; *US v Elf Atochem* (n 98), para 14.

not play a role where cases are resolved by negotiated settlements, judicial review of antitrust decisions is much less important in the US than in the EU. Enforcers can therefore take the liberty of differentiating somewhat less carefully between distinct legal entities and it is usually not important to prove specific contributions by individual members of the group.[100]

In conclusion, the assertion that there is no liability of parent companies under US antitrust law must therefore be refined in two important ways. On the one hand, the US Sentencing Guidelines allow the particularities of corporate groups to be taken into account at least in some respects. While this cannot solve the problem of liability gaps, it will ensure that the calculation of fines does not ignore the economic reality. On the other hand, and this is even more important, the use of plea agreements gives the US authorities considerable leeway, which they can also use to prevent evasive behaviour by groups of companies. This is a very effective way – albeit less transparent than the European Commission's much more formalistic approach – to ensure that all responsible actors are actually addressed.

4.6 CONCLUSION

The findings of this chapter can be summarised as follows:

1. In a clear departure from fundamental principles of company law, EU competition law emphasises the common responsibility of corporate groups regardless of separate corporate personalities and limited shareholder liability. This is because competition law is about assessing the actual effects of corporate behaviour, for which company law formalities play no role.
2. The challenges posed by corporate groups cannot be solved by metaphysical considerations of the undertaking or the single economic unit. The *de facto* personification of the undertaking by the EU Courts is also mistaken. The undertaking is not a person, but merely a legal concept that is supposed to be open to economic realities. As such, it can be used to answer questions of attribution and liability, but it does not answer these questions by itself.
3. The single economic entity doctrine serves three important objectives: (A) to induce parent companies to control the conduct of their subsidiaries, (B) to ensure the correct calculation of fines, and (C) to ensure that fines are actually paid. It is important to clearly distinguish between these functions, as they each have different implications.

[100] A similar tendency can be found in recent EU decisions based on settlements, see eg *Spark plugs* (Case AT.40113) Commission Decision of 21 February 2018 [2018] OJ C111/26, para 79; *Lighting systems* (Case AT.40013) Commission Decision of 21 June 2017 [2017] OJ C333/4, paras 63, 66; *Car battery recycling* (Case AT.40018) Commission Decision of 8 February 2017 [2017] OJ C396/17, paras 274, 278, 282, 286; *Trucks* (Case AT.39824) Commission Decision of 27 September 2017 [2020] OJ C216/9, paras 95, 97–100.

4. The threat of liability can be used to encourage parent companies to prevent infringements by their subsidiaries. But that presupposes two things: (A) the parent company must respond better to incentives than the subsidiary and (B) the parent company must be able to deter the subsidiary from infringing the law. It is therefore correct to make the parent company's liability dependent on its control over the subsidiary at the time of the infringement.
5. Fines will only have a deterrent effect on groups of companies if the calculation takes into account the economic strength of the whole group at the time of the prohibition decision. When the Commission imposes a fine on a company which is part of a group, it should therefore be entitled to rely on consolidated accounts as defined in Chapter 6 of the Accounting Directive. This should not depend on whether it also holds other members of the group liable.
6. In order to ensure the payment of fines, other entities within a group may be held liable as substitute debtors. In theory, this type of liability could be completely independent of any link to the infringement. The absence of such a connection could even mean that the procedural guarantees of the law of fines do not have to be applied.
7. Holding sister companies mutually liable for each other's competition law infringements or holding subsidiaries liable for infringements by parent companies does not contribute to the objective of deterrence. The reason is that control in groups of companies is typically exercised only from top to bottom, but not the other way round or horizontally.
8. Extending the rule of parental liability from the law of fines to the law of damages can contribute to deterrence as it ensures that the necessary incentives for compliance are also set in relation to harm that is not adequately taken into account in the calculation of fines.
9. While it is true that parent company liability does not exist as a general rule in US antitrust law, it must also be recognised that in the vast majority of cases this is not decisive because they are resolved by negotiated settlements. This practice provides the US authorities with the necessary flexibility to take due account of the specificities of corporate groups.

5

Piercing the Corporate Veil

The German Sausage Saga

Martin Schunke and Mareike Walter

5.1 INTRODUCTION: CORPORATE RESPONSIBILITY AND COMPETITION LAW

The question under which circumstances an undertaking is liable for its own competition law infringement – not to mention the liability for infringements committed by an affiliated undertaking – is of invaluable practical importance. From the early days of European competition law, there has been an interesting legal relationship between the 'single economic entity' as the addressee of EU competition law and the respective entities under national corporate laws. Legend has it, businesses in some European jurisdictions can avoid fines by way of corporate restructuring, while in other jurisdictions, this is not an option.[1] The present contribution traces the developments in the EU and in Germany during recent years with special regard to the so-called German 'sausage gap' – a once well-known and much-exploited lacuna that helped shelter companies from liability through specific corporate restructuring.

Section 5.2 of this chapter discusses underlying principles of corporate and competition law, providing the relevant context for an in-depth analysis of the German 'sausage gap'. Section 5.3 addresses the evolution of German law and jurisdiction with regard to restructuring efforts aimed at avoiding cartel fines. Section 5.4 then focuses on the European competition law developments with regard to liability for cartel damages claims and, in particular, assesses the interplay of the European concept of the 'single economic entity' with underlying principles of law. Finally, Section 5.5 offers some concluding remarks and an anticipated outlook on these issues moving forward.

Martin Schunke is Senior Associate with Hogan Lovells, Munich; Dr. Mareike Walter is Attorney-at-law in Munich and former Associate with Hogan Lovells, Munich. The views expressed in this contribution are solely those of the authors and do not necessarily reflect the views of Hogan Lovells or its clients.

[1] R Klotz, 'ECN+ Ante Portas Editorial' (2018) 2 CoRe 71, 72.

5.2 ENTITY PRINCIPLE AND ENTERPRISE PRINCIPLE – A COMPARATIVE PERSPECTIVE

Corporate law, both nationally and internationally, is based on the premise of the individual corporation – the legal entity. This stems from the fundamental defining characteristic of the corporation constituting a separate legal person with rights and obligations distinct from those of its owners.[2] The logical consequence of this perception is the 'corporate veil', the concept of limited corporate liability under which the shareholders of a corporate entity are not (personally) liable for the entity's debts. This understanding is largely determined by the traditional concept of a single corporate entity. The emergence of corporate groups in modern economies, where shareholders or creditors often are corporations themselves, has not fundamentally changed this standard conception of the corporation in case law or relevant literature.

However, the nature of a corporate group will not be fully appreciated where too much emphasis is placed to the separate legal entity within a group, the 'entity view' only. So on the other hand, the enterprise view would focus on all of the legal entities that form the corporate group as part of a single economic operation.[3] Historically, 'enterprise view' and 'entity views' have therefore provided for competing theories of liability within tort law and various statutory regimes. Tension between the enterprise and the entity approach, as well as the courts' general hesitation to impose enterprise liability, can be explained in part by the factually complex nature of the corporate group itself as well as by the complicated exercise for uniformly defining the 'corporate group'.[4]

So whereas the principle of limited liability is provided for in many company law systems, the exception of abolishing the rules of limited liability to the benefits of creditors of the corporation is often referred to as 'veil-piercing' and is mostly shaped by courts.[5] However, situations that call for a piercing of the corporate veil are recognised in virtually all jurisdictions.[6] There are rather different situations in which corporations of a group are held liable, but most of which do not presuppose the existence of a group. Such are internal liability of the shareholders towards the

2 Generally, a company consists of five basic elements: legal person, limitation of liability, transferable shares, delegated management in a board structure and investor ownership, R Kraakman and others, *The Anatomy of Corporate Law: A Comparative and Functional Approach* (3rd edn, OUP 2017) 5ff; C Windbichler, 'Konzernrecht: Gibt es das?' (2018) NZG 1241, 1244; for a comprehensive overview with further references from a US American perspective see for example V Harper Ho, 'Theories of Corporate Groups: Corporate Identity Reconceived' (2012) 42 Seton Hall L Rev 879, 884ff.

3 Harper Ho (n 2) 898.

4 Harper Ho (n 2) 898ff.

5 For a US-focused analysis of veil-piercing jurisprudence see Harper Ho (n 2) 898.

6 M Venturuzzo and others, *Comparative Corporate Law* (1st edn, West Academic Press 2015) 151ff.

company, external liability towards third parties, fiduciary duties, contract and tort, attribution of risk, knowledge and fault as well as contractual responsibility, etc.[7]

In contrast, abstracting to the level of the corporate group, a real enterprise perspective implies that the group as a whole bears rights and obligations that either derive from those of one or more members of the group or may also be independent. For the sake of preserving the limited liability within the group, derivative liability of the group (or one entity within the group) based on wrongful conduct by another affiliate has generally been rejected within veil-piercing doctrine.[8] From a comparative perspective, US courts have determined that 'piercing the corporate veil' vertically or extending enterprise-wide liability horizontally (when the separation between the corporation and its shareholders produces anomalous or inequitable results) might occur only in exceptional circumstances.[9]

Interestingly, from an empirical perspective, veil-piercing is common with regard to statutory provisions such as environmental and antitrust law. However, it does not arise as often as one would expect, even less with regard to tort law cases, and it is more likely to occur when the shareholder behind the veil is an individual rather than another corporation.[10] Imposing obligations and potential for liability on the corporate group – or on a parent corporation as a proxy for the group as a whole – is always problematic because it compels the courts to disregard the formal legal identity of the individual companies comprising the group. If applied broadly or unpredictably, this approach could threaten the very existence of corporate groups as it threatens the risk assessment of shareholders as investors.

5.3 THE GERMAN SAUSAGE SAGA: HIDING BEHIND THE CORPORATE VEIL

5.3.1 *The 'Sausage Gap' – Background*

In 2014, the German Federal Cartel Office ('FCO') imposed fines totalling €338 million on 21 sausage manufacturers for illegal price-fixing agreements between 1997 and 2009, which sought to implement industry-wide price increases for the

7 Harper Ho (n 2) 946. In German law, for example, liability for a withdrawal destroying the economic basis (*existenzvernichtender Eingriff*) and the immoral damage to the company (*sittenwidrige Schädigung*).

8 Harper Ho (n 2) 918.

9 Harper Ho (n 2) 900.

10 T Cheng, 'The Corporate Veil Doctrine Revisited: A Comparative Study of the English and the U.S. Corporate Veil Doctrines' (2011) University of Hong Kong Faculty of Law Research Paper https://ssrn.com/abstract=1790610 or http://dx.doi.org/10.2139/ssrn.1790610 accessed 17 August 2017; J Matheson, 'The Modern Law of Corporate Groups: An Empirical Study of Piercing the Corporate Veil in the Parent-Subsidiary Context' (2009) 87 NCL Rev 1091; for a survey of veil-piercing doctrine and practice, see K Strasser, 'Piercing the Veil in Corporate Groups' (2005) 37 Conn L Rev 637, 637 n 1; R Thompson, 'Piercing the Corporate Veil: An Empirical Study' (1991) 76 Cornell L Rev 1036, 1038; R Thompson, 'Piercing the Veil Within Corporate Groups: Corporate Shareholders as Mere Investors' (1999) 13 Conn J Int'l L 379.

sale of sausage products to the retail trade. Two of the alleged conspirators, partnerships with limited liability (*GmbH & Co. KG*) that were initially fined €128 million, belonged to the largest German sausage manufacturer – a holding company ultimately held by an entrepreneurial family.[11]

After lodging appeals against the fines, the two partnerships' major assets were transferred for the benefit of other entities within the group. The partnerships were subsequently subject to formal liquidation proceedings and ultimately dissolved. As a consequence of internal restructuring measures of this sort, the addressees of the fines had literally ceased to exist. According to the FCO, the proceedings therefore had to be closed.[12]

Whenever talking about the 'sausage gap' (*Wurstlücke*), it must be kept in mind that this was no isolated incident – it was merely the most noteworthy due to the level of fines imposed. In the course of these proceedings, the FCO's president publicly expressed his dismay as the FCO grudgingly had to drop fines imposed on three other accused companies on account of similar internal restructuring measures. This led to a failure to collect a significant portion of imposed fines (i.e. €238 million).[13]

But why was the chain of liability cut in these – and previous – cases without legislative interference? Context can be provided when looking at the principles that follow and the provisions under German law.

5.3.1.1 Competition Law Infringements as Administrative Offences

German competition law is based on the tenet that competition law violations are administrative offences (*Ordnungswidrigkeiten*) which are considered sub-level of crime punished by fines under Sec. 81 (1)–(3) German Act on Regulatory Offences ('ARO'). The ARO is historically conceived in the way that fines require subjective accountability of the distinct addressee on whom they are imposed. Although fines can also be imposed on a legal entity (Sec. 30 ARO), German competition law like the ARO would in principle require a specific legal person to be such an addressee. This idea is based on the ARO's principle of liability which is – disregarding terminological subtleties for this purpose – nothing more than the principle of fault (Sec. 12 ARO).[14] In short, since responsibility stems from the (legal)

[11] FCO Case Report [2017] B12-13/09; FCO, 'Bundeskartellamt imposes fines on sausage manufacturers' (Press release 15 July 2014) www.bundeskartellamt.de/SharedDocs/Meldung/EN/Pressemitteilungen/2014/15_07_2014_Wurst.html;jsessionid=nn=3591568, accessed 6 June 2020.

[12] FCO, 'Proceedings against companies of ClemensTönnies group concluded – fines of 128 million euros cancelled due to restructuring measures' (Press release 19 October 2016) www.bundeskartellamt.de/SharedDocs/Meldung/EN/Pressemitteilungen/2016/19_10_2016_Wurst.html accessed 6 June 2020.

[13] FCO, '"Wurstlücke" – Weitere Bußgelder in Höhe von rund 110 Mio. Euro entfallen in Folge von unternehmensinternen Umstrukturierungen' (Press release 26 June 2017) www.bundeskartellamt.de/SharedDocs/Publikation/DE/Pressemitteilungen/2017/26_06_2017_Bell_Wurstl%C3%BCcke.pdf?__blob=publicationFile&v=3 accessed 6 June 2020.

[14] M Löbbe, 'Konzernverantwortung und Umwandlungsrecht' (2013) 177 ZHR 518, 524.

person's behaviour, it cannot be attached to an entity's assets and, as such, cannot be transferred nor subject to legal succession.

5.3.1.2 Legal Entity Principle and Principle of Separation

In order to hold a legal entity accountable under German law, it is required that a specific natural person or corporate body has acted on behalf of the legal entity – the legal entity principle (*Rechtsträgerprinzip*).[15] According to the Act against Restraints of Competition ('ARC') applicable at the time of activities of the 'sausage cartel', a fine could only therefore be imposed on a legal person if the administrative offence had been committed by a corporate body or an employee working for the company in a managerial capacity. The imposition of a fine required (and still requires) a direct relationship between the acting perpetrator and the legal entity on whose behalf it has acted.[16] This relationship ceases to exist in the case of universal succession due to a merger or as a result of a company's de-registration after liquidation proceedings. Since the perpetrator did not act on behalf of the absorbing legal entity but, rather, on behalf of the merged entity, the chain of liability is cut where assets are transferred to such a succeeding legal entity. Even if the natural person involved in a cartel continues to conduct business within the succeeding company, there would be no subrogated liability for the newly founded (or respectively surviving) company.

German corporate law is further based on the premise of legal independence of the individual group companies. Although these companies are economically and legally linked within the group in a variety of ways, corporate law does not create a collective legal entity. According to this principle of separation (*Trennungsprinzip*),[17] a legal entity is only liable for its own activities, even within a group of companies. In general, there is no accessory liability to the detriment of the parent company for the liabilities of a subsidiary. This is a fundamental principle also under tort law. Of course, the parent company may be liable for any of its own infringements of management obligations (Sec. 31 German Civil Code) but only where the parent company was directly involved by action or omission – a condition not often met.

5.3.1.3 Application of These Principles in German Case Law and Legislative Attempts to Establish Liability in Cases of Succession

Long before the renowned 'sausage gap', companies had taken advantage of the provisions on legal succession in order to avoid fines. The German Federal Court

[15] BGH, KRB 55/10 *Versicherungsfusion* [2011]; BGH, KRB 47/13 *Silostellgebühren III* [2014]; BGH, KRB 2/10 *Transportbeton;* MLöbbe (n 14) 520ff, 541.

[16] BGH, KRB 8/85 *Bußgeldhaftung* [1986] para 11; *Silostellgebühren III* (n 15); T Mäger and F von Schreitter, 'Die kartellrechtliche Bußgeldhaftung nach der 9. GWB Novelle – Überblick und Kritik' (2017) NZKart 264, 265.

[17] Windbichler (n 2) 1244ff; Löbbe (n 14) 539ff.

('Federal Court') had already addressed the problem of corporate legal succession in 1986. Bound by the concepts of the legal entity and the separation principle, the Federal Court developed the so-called concept of 'near-identity'.[18] According to this concept, the successor is only liable for fines in cases of legal succession where the succeeding company is, from an economic perspective, still the same. This concept required that (i) the assumed (acquired) assets continued to be separated from the assets of the actual person or entity responsible for the infringement; (ii) such assets were used in the same or similar manner as before; and (iii) constitute a significant part of the successor's assets. In other words, they have retained an economically independent position, characterising the succeeding legal entity (the new legal entity merely forming a new legal and economic shell).

These conditions derived from the specific circumstances of the case such that subsequent case law was dealt with on a case-by-case basis. As such, a comprehensive framework to address legal succession with regard to liability for antitrust fines could not be established. For instance, sticking to the criteria that the assets of the responsible company remain essentially undiminished within the assets of the succeeding company, the Federal Court denied any legal succession in a case of a 'merger between equals' in which both the assets of the succeeding company and assets of the merged company had been operationally unified.[19]

However, the Federal Court was not oblivious to the opportunities for circumventing an imminent fine by companies employing targeted arrangements under company law.[20] Specifically, the Federal Court pointed out that an extension of the legal succession in liability for fines in cases of this kind would lead to 'group liability'. But in light of the principle of separation, the adoption of such group liability was reserved for the legislator which is obliged to determine its nature and limits.[21]

This reasoning is further underpinned by another essential aspect of administrative offences: the law of administrative offences is traditionally seen as the 'little brother' of criminal law. With regard to the criminal law character, the constitutional prohibition of analogy in criminal cases forbids any application beyond the limits of literal interpretation.[22] Thus, as long as it is not provided for de lege lata, responsibility for fines cannot be transferred on the basis of universal succession.

In 2014, the Federal Court in *Silostellgebühren III* considered the implications of EU law, namely of the effet utile.[23] In this case, the FCO claimed that liability for fines of the legal successor could be justified on the basis of the direct application

[18] *Bußgeldhaftung* (n 16) para 13; later affirmed and refined in BGH, KRB 55/10 *Versicherungsfusion* [2011]; BGH, KRB 2/10 *Höhe der Verbandsgeldbuße* [2011]; *Silostellgebühren III* (n 16) para 12; BGH, KRB 39/14 *Melitta* [2015] para 3.

[19] BGH, KRB 55/10 *Versicherungsfusion* [2011] para 19.

[20] Speaking of 'unfortunate consequences': *ibid.* at para 25.

[21] *Ibid.* at para 25.

[22] *Ibid.* at para 12; derived from art 103 para 2, Basic Law for the Federal Republic of Germany.

[23] *Silostellgebühren III* (n 16) paras 18, 33.

of Article 5 (1) Regulation (EC) No 1/2003 – in other words, confirming the EU concept of the 'single economic entity'.

The Federal Court confirmed its concept of so-called 'near identity' and explicitly rejected the claim that EU standards could be directly applied to determine the undertaking as the economic unit under German law. The Federal Court recognised that the Member States' courts had to make full use of the interpretative range of German legal provisions with regard to the effet utile. However, EU legislation would empower only the European Commission to take decisions against a single economic entity, not the national competition authorities and courts.[24]

The Federal Court drew a clear line between the obligation to interpret national law in conformity with EU law and the obligation to obey general principles of national law in such an interpretation. The Federal Court emphasised the limits of literal interpretation as well as the principle of legal certainty, which prohibited interpretation contra legem in this case.[25] According to constitutional principles also found in EU primary law (e.g. Article 49 (1) Charter of Fundamental Rights; Article 7 Human Rights Convention), criminal liability could not simply be inferred by interpreting national law which does not provide for such liability. Such an interpretation would not be compatible with EU law.[26] Interestingly, the Federal Court saw no need to refer the matter to the Court of Justice of the European Union ('CJEU') since 'the correct application of Union law was so obvious as to leave no room for reasonable doubt'.[27]

Meanwhile, the legislator attempted to bridge some of the 'gaps' that had become obvious in the practice of the Federal Court. In 2013, statutory liability was introduced in constellations of universal succession and partial universal succession by split-up, where the fine could accordingly be imposed on the legal successor.[28] However, the legislator did not include all cases of legal succession – not covered were certain cases of partial legal succession such as spin-off (*Abspaltung*) and carve-out and cases of singular succession (*Einzelrechtsnachfolge*, e.g. asset deals).[29] Hence, legal succession with regard to liability for fines still required that the perpetrator company ceased to exist. Therefore, 'co-liability' – for example of the parent company following the model of EU law – was still not provided for under German law.[30]

As it happens, and despite sausages being a German speciality, the sausage 'gap' was not peculiar to Germany. In 2017, for example, the Lisbon Appeal Court found that a parent company could not be held liable for an antitrust infringement by omission under general Portuguese rules, leading to a reduction of the total fines

[24] *Ibid* at para 24.
[25] *Ibid* at para 19.
[26] *Ibid* at para 20.
[27] *Ibid* at para 32.
[28] s 30 (2a) ARO, implemented in 2013 in the course of the 8th amendment of the ARC.
[29] Other restructuring measures such as transformation of form were also not included.
[30] Mäger and von Schreitter (n 16) 265.

that were imposed on the group by the Portuguese Competition Court.[31] The Competition Authority did not test this ruling subsequently – leading to speculation that this might also result in a Portuguese 'sausage gap'.[32]

5.3.2 *The End of the Sausage: German Reform of the ARC*

Ultimately, it was not until 2017 that the legislator closed the infamous 'sausage gap' in the course of the 9th amendment of the ARC[33]. On the occasion of the implementation of the EU Damages Directive[34], the 9th amendment significantly extended the liability for fines imposed in cartel fine proceedings in three regards.

Firstly, it introduced the liability of the economic unit (former § 81 (3a) ARC, now § 81a (1) ARC)[35]. If a 'person in a leading position' commits an administrative offence by which the competition law duties of the 'undertaking' have been infringed, fines can also be imposed on other legal persons that 'made up' (formed) the undertaking at the time of the infringement and that exercised direct or indirect decisive influence over the management of the entity which infringed competition law.

Secondly, the liability of the legal successor was tightened by introducing unlimited[36] liability for the legal successor (former § 81 (3b) ARC, now § 81a (2) ARC) and stipulating the liability of the economic successor (former § 81 (3c) ARC, now § 81a (3) ARC). This means that the universal legal successor is liable in cases where the legal entity responsible under competition law no longer exists. In addition, a singular legal successor (e.g. acquirer of assets) can be liable, even where the legal entity continues to exist but has become economically irrelevant. Thus, every transfer of a business unit that was involved in a competition law infringement can cause liability for fines in respect of the successor.

Finally, these changes were accompanied by the introduction of a contingent liability during the transition period to also cover restructuring measures until the new regulations became fully effective.[37]

31 Michael Sousa Ferro, 'The Portuguese "Sausage Gap": Parent Company Liability for Antitrust Infringements Not Yet Assured in Portugal' (2017) 1 CoRe 266.

32 *Ibid.*

33 Federal Law Gazette I 1416 'Neuntes Gesetz zur Änderung des Gesetzes gegen Wettbewerbsbeschränkungen' (2017).

34 Directive 2014/104/EU of the European Parliament and of the Council of 26 November 2014 on certain rules governing actions for damages under national law for infringements of the competition law provisions of the Member States and of the European Union [2014] OJ L349/2 (EU Damages Directive).

35 § 81 (3a) to (3e) ARC have been transferred identical in wording into § 81a ARC (1) through (5) by Federal Law Gazette I 2 'Gesetz zur Änderung des Gesetzes gegen Wettbewerbsbeschränkungen für ein fokussiertes, proaktives und digitales Wettbewerbsrecht 4.0 und anderer Bestimmungen' (2021).

36 Contrasting the usual regime of s 30 (2a) ARO, § 81a (2) ARC does not limit the liability to the value of the acquired assets if a competition infringement under European or German law is concerned.

37 Separate contingent liability section (which now is obsolete due of lapse of time frame) in former § 81a ARC Federal Law Gazette I 1416 'Neuntes Gesetz zur Änderung des Gesetzes gegen Wettbewerbsbeschränkungen' (2017).

These above-described measures went beyond simply closing the so-called 'sausage gap'. The intent was to fully harmonise German law with EU practice concerning liability for cartel fines. Introducing liability of the economic unit provoked significant criticism insofar as it violated the principle of legal certainty, the principle of fault, and the principle of in dubio pro reo.[38] Putting aside constitutional concerns for a moment, from an enforcer's perspective, the provisions extended liability to the successors of restructured companies and their parent companies with the aim of preventing cartel members from escaping fines by means of internal restructuring. In other words: one would expect German law should have been prepared for the 'wurst' case, right? However, the tension between entity liability versus enterprise responsibility in relation to antitrust infringements committed by other legal entities (under justifying circumstances) was thereby only solved with regard to fines.

5.3.3 *Developments with Regard to Cartel Damages Claims*

The persisting divergence in the treatment of the single economic entity versus the legal entity becomes more obvious when looking at the flip side of the coin: the capacity to be sued. The Member States' courts have been reluctant to employ the single economic entity principle also in civil damages situations. For example, in 2018, the French Supreme Court ruled that the notion of an economic entity is not applicable to damages claims deriving from anti-competitive conduct. According to the court, competition law should not interfere with the principle of personal liability under French civil law.[39]

In Germany, in the course of implementing the EU Damages Directive, the 9th ARC amendment also adapted the rules on 'Damages and Disgorgement of Benefits' – establishing the framework for compensation for harm caused by a competition law infringement.[40] While the rules on fines have drawn a verbal connection to the concept of the single economic entity (§ 81 ARC, cf o), the rules on damages (§§ 33a (1)ff ARC) still revert to the 'infringer' as the addressee of claims without further description of the specific legal entity. This prompted a vibrant discussion among scholars as to whether the closing of the 'sausage gap' with regard to the collection of fines would also have an impact on civil law liability in cartel damages claims.[41]

38 O Mörsdorf, 'Nachfolger- und Konzernhaftung wegen Verstößen gegen das Unionskartellrecht' (2020) *ZIP* 489, 490; T Ackermann, 'Unternehmenssteuerung durch finanzielle Sanktionen' (2015) *ZHR* 179 538, 550, 551; M Habersack, 'Aktienkonzernrecht – Bestandsaufnahme und Perspektiven' (2016) AG 2016, 691, 696, 697; S Thomas, 'Die sogenannte wirtschaftliche Einheit: Auslegungsfragen zur neu eingeführten akzessorischen Konzernhaftung im deutschen Kartellbußgeldrecht' (2017) AG 637, 644ff.

39 Cour de cassation, Chambre commerciale, *Optical Center c/ Frères Lissac, Lissac enseigne, Gadol et Audioptic Trade Services* [2018] n° 16-24.619 17-11.909 ECLI:FR:CCASS:2018:CO00123.

40 Determined in s 2 Damages and Disgorgement of Benefits (§§ 33ff ARC).

41 S Wachs, 'Faktische Übernahme des wirtschaftlichen Unternehmensbegriffs für die Passivlegitimation bei Follow-on-Klagen?' (2017) *WuW* 2; H Schaper and P Stauber, 'Ausgewählte Themen des neuen Kartellschadensersatzrechts – Schadensersatz, Abwälzung, Gesamtschuld und Innenausgleich'

The EU concept of the single economic entity would not apply in this way – at least not until the German legislator introduced liability of the group or liability of the parent company for civil damages. The basic principles of German tort law, in particular, the legal entity principle, would continue to apply.[42] Since the EU Damages Directive[43] did not explicitly regulate the question of responsibility and the acquis communautaire had not yet specified the civil liability of group companies for cartel damages, the question of attribution was to be solved by national law.[44]

Yet, the opposite opinion emphasises that a provision in a Member State's civil law does not meet the requirements under the principle of effectiveness if it declares only part of the company liable for damages. This would be in contrast with the EU perspective where the whole company commits the underlying infringement.[45] The EU legislator only would have clarified such a point in the EU Damages Directive if it had wanted to deviate from the EU concept of the undertaking addressed in Article 1 (1) EU Damages Directive. The CJEU in *Kone* had already developed requirements for national tort law based on the principle of effectiveness and, at the same time, explicitly referred to the undertaking.[46] Thus, the undertaking could be sued under EU law.[47] Injured parties would bear far more than the normal risk of insolvency if only a small sub-unit of the group could

(2017) *NZKart* 279; R Bechtold and W Bosch, in R Bechtold and W Bosch (eds), *Gesetz gegen Wettbewerbsbeschränkungen: GWB* (9th edn, CH Beck 2018) § 33 para 7.

42 Bechtold and Bosch (n 41) § 33 para 7; J Bornkamm and J Tolkmitt in: Langen and Bunte (eds) Kartellrecht (13th edn, Luchterhand 2018) § 33a para 15; V Emmerich in: T Körber, H Schweitzer, D Zimmer (eds), *Immenga/Mestmäcker, Wettbewerbsrecht* (6th edn, CH Beck 2020) § 33 GWB para 22ff; Wachs (n 41) 2.

43 See EU Damages Directive (n 34) art 1 (1) and recitals 11ff.

44 Bechtold and Bosch (n 41) para 7; W Wurmnest in: Loewenheim/Meessen/Riesenkampff/Kersting/Meyer-Lindemann (eds), *Kartellrecht* (4th edn, CH Beck 2020) § 33a GWB para 30 (LMRKM); V Emmerich in *Immenga/Mestmäcker: Wettbewerbsrecht* (n 42) § 33a para 30ff; denying a corresponding derivation based on the principle of effectiveness: LG Berlin, 16 O 193/11 Kart, *Fahrtreppen* [2013]; LG Düsseldorf, 37 O 27/11 Kart – *Aufzugskartell* [2016] ECLI:DE:LGD:2016:0908.37O27.11KART.00 NZKart 490, 492; S Mäger and von Schreitter (n 16) 270ff; P von Hülsen and B Kasten, 'Passivlegitimation von Konzernen im Kartell-Schadensersatzprozess? – Gedanken zur Umsetzung der Richtlinie 2014/104/EU' (2015) *NZKart* 296, 299; R Harnos, 'Harmonisierung des Kartellbußgeldrechts qua effet utile?' (2016) *ZWeR* 284, 299ff; S Thomas and S Legner, 'Die wirtschaftliche Einheit im Kartellzivilrecht' (2016) *NZKart* 155, 157.

45 C Kersting in: Kersting/Podszun, Die 9. GWB-Novelle (1st edn, 2017) c 7 para 25ff with further references in connection with the European concept of undertaking, EU Damages Directive (n 34) art 1 (1) and an external civil-law partnership of the group (para 34ff); W Jaeger in: LMRKM (n 44) art 101 (2) AEUV, para 55ff, 59.

46 Case C-557/12 *Kone AG and Others v ÖBB-Infrastruktur AG* [2014] ECLI:EU:C:2014:1317, para 37.

47 C Kersting, 'Die neue Richtlinie zur privaten Rechtsdurchsetzung im Kartellrecht' (2014) WuW 564, 565; C Kersting, 'Kartellschadensersatzrecht nach der 9. GWB-Novelle' (2017) VersR 581, 584ff; W Jaeger in: LMRKM (n 44) art 101 (2) AEUV para 55; V Emmerich in *Immenga/Mestmäcker: Wettbewerbsrecht* (n 42) § 33 para 32; T Lettl, 'Kartellschadensersatz nach der Richtlinie 2014/104/EU und deutsches Kartellrecht' (2015) WRP 537, 538; T Makatsch and A Mir, 'Die neue EU-Richtlinie zu Kartellschadensersatzklagen – Angst vor der eigenen "Courage"?' (2015) *EuZW* 7, 8; A Petrasincu, 'Kartellschadensersatz nach dem Referentenentwurf der 9. GWB-Novelle' (2016) *WuW* 330;

be held liable. Assets could easily be reduced to the detriment of the injured party. Groups could transfer assets of subsidiaries which committed competition infringements to other group entities or even pool such competition risks in subsidiaries with low capitalisation.

However, even supporters of that view doubt that the far-reaching EU concept of liability as such takes sufficient account of the fundamental principles of legality, legal clarity, and fault. For example, it is often stated that the principle of personal responsibility on the EU level has become purely abstract and is overshadowed by practically irrebuttable presumptions.[48]

So how do the discussed concepts of the legal entity principle and the separation principle in the Member States' civil law systems relate to the EU concept of the single economic entity? Before addressing by reference to the CJEU's ruling in *Skanska* (Section 5.4), we will briefly recall the cornerstones of the concept of the single economic entity in EU competition law.

5.3.4 *The Concept of the Single Economic Entity in Contrast to Legal Entity Principle and Principle of Separation*

In EU competition law, an independent concept of enterprise prevails, namely the single economic entity. The addressee of competition law is the undertaking, which is to be understood as any entity or body engaged in economic activity, regardless of its legal status and the way in which it is financed.[49] This often involves a (whole?) group of companies.[50] Thus, the CJEU affirms both the possibility of imposing a fine on the legal or economic successor of the company committing the competition law violation in the event that this company ceases to exist[51] and the possibility

H Schweitzer, 'Die neue Richtlinie für wettbewerbsrechtliche Schadensersatzklagen' (2014) *NZKart* 335, 343 [on art 11 (1) of the EU Damages Directive]; A Weitbrecht, 'Die Umsetzung der EU-Schadensersatzrichtlinie' (2015) *WuW* 959, 964; Ministerial Counsellor A Jungbluth, as cited in K Pipoh, 'Umsetzung der Kartellschadensersatzrichtlinie (2014/104/EU) in das deutsche Recht' (2016) *NZKart* 226. Left open by H Stauber and P Schaper, 'Die Kartellschadensersatzrichtlinie–Handlungsbedarf für den deutschen Gesetzgeber?' (2014) *NZKart* 346, 347.

48 Meyer-Lindemann, in: Kersting/Podszun (n 45) c 17 para 42; M Kling, 'Die Haftung der Konzernmutter für Kartellverstöße ihrer Tochterunternehmen' (2010) *WRP* 506, 510ff; P Voet van Vormizeele, 'Die EG-kartellrechtliche Haftungszurechnung im Konzern im Widerstreit zu den nationalen Gesellschaftsrechtsordnungen' (2010) *WuW* 1008, 1018ff.

49 Settled case-law since Case C-41/90 *Höfner und Elser* [1991] ECLI:EU:C:1991:161, para 21; Case C-189/02 P *Dansk Rørindustri and Others* [2005] ECLI:EU:C:2005:408, para 112.

50 Case C-97/08 P *Akzo Nobel* [2009] ECLI:EU:C:2009:536, para 54ff; Case C-521/09 P *Elf Aquitaine* [2011] ECLI:EU:C:2011:620; Case C-516/15 P *Akzo Nobel and Others v Commission* [2017] ECLI:EU:C:2017:314, para 43ff; Case T-144/07 *ThyssenKrupp Liften Ascenseurs and Others* [2011] ECLI:EU:T:2011:364, para 92ff; Case C-170/83 *Hydrotherm* [1984] ECLI:EU:C:1984:271, para 11; see also § 81a 1) ARC.

51 Case C-49/92 *Anic* [1999] ECLI:EU:C:1999:356, para 145; Case C-125/07 P *Erste Bank Group and Others* [2009] ECLI:EU:C:2009:576, para 76; on the conditions for imposing a fine on the successor in the event of the survival of the old company: Case C-280/06 *ETI SpA and Others* [2007] ECLI:EU:C:2007:775, para 49ff.

of imposing a fine on the parent company for competition infringements committed by its subsidiary.[52] Inasmuch as an undertaking may consist of several legal entities,[53] the European Commission may also sanction other legal units for this infringement instead of or in addition to the legal entity responsible for the competition infringement. In the former case of sanctioning the successor instead of the responsible corporate entity that ceased to exist, the company continues to exist within the successor (economic continuity); in the latter case of sanctioning the parent company for competition infringements of its subsidiary, both legal entities are considered part of a single economic entity.[54]

The liability of a company's successor under EU law obviously intends to ensure the effectiveness of competition law by making it impossible to escape liability through restructuring, sale or liquidation of the legal entity responsible.[55] With regard to the attribution of liability within a corporate group, this objection is less convincing. The case law tends to indicate an efficiency-driven structural liability of the parent company so that a parent company is held liable as a guarantor for the compliant conduct of the group subsidiary on account of its factual possibilities to influence the subsidiary.[56] The prerequisite for the joint responsibility of legally independent companies, therefore, is that the parent company exercises (can exercise?) decisive influence on the subsidiary so that the subsidiary essentially follows instructions from the parent company.[57] In turn, this is presumed where the shareholding is almost complete (close to 100%).[58]

5.4 THE OTHER END OF A SAUSAGE – IS THERE A CORPORATE VEIL AFTER SKANSKA?

5.4.1 *The Setting and the CJEU's Decision in* Skanska

Against the backdrop of the tension between the EU concept of the single economic entity and the legal entity principle governing national civil laws and laws of civil procedure, the CJEU's 2019 ruling on national reference in *Skanska* was highly anticipated. In a nutshell, the CJEU was required to clarify whether determining who is liable for compensating victims of a cartel in breach of Article 101 TFEU is a

52 *Akzo Nobel* [2009] (n 50) para 58.

53 *Hydrotherm* (n 50) para 11; more recently: *Akzo Nobel* [2009] (n 50) para 55; *Akzo Nobel and Others v Commission* [2017] n 50) para 48.

54 N Pauer, '*The Single Economic Entity Doctrine and Corporate Group Responsibility in European Antitrust Law*' (1st edn, Wolters Kluwer 2017) 199, 201; J Biermann in *Immenga/Mestmäcker: Wettbewerbsrecht* (n 42) preface to art 23 of Regulation (EC) No 1/2003, para. 112.

55 *ETI SpA and Others* (n 51) para 41.

56 Reading the case-law in this way: Mörsdorf (n 38) 490 with further references.

57 Settled case-law since Case 48-69 *Imperial Chemical Industries Ltd* [1972] ECLI:EU:C:1972:70, paras 132, 135; *Akzo Nobel* [2009] (n 50) para 58.

58 *Akzo Nobel* [2009] (n 50) para 60.

matter of EU or national law.[59] In doing so, the CJEU shifted the rules for attribution of liability for cartel fines within the group (the single economic entity) to questions of civil liability for damages (i.e. who can be sued in damages cases).

The main proceedings concerned a follow-on damages claim brought by the City of Vantaa against a nationwide cartel in the asphalt market implemented in Finland between 1994 and 2002. The City of Vantaa brought a damages action against the defendants (jointly and severally), who had acquired 100% of the shares in each of the supposed cartelist companies (or their then parent companies) in the year 2000 and, later, dissolved and liquidated these companies. The defendants had taken over their respective assets and continued their respective operations. The Finnish Competition Authority had uncovered the asphalt cartel in March 2002 and proposed fines in 2004, whereupon the Finnish Supreme Administrative Court (on the basis of Article 81 EC old version) imposed these fines on the defendants in September 2009 using the economic continuity test.

The defendants argued, *inter alia*, that they were not liable for claims against independent legal entities (their former subsidiaries). Furthermore, the claims were said to no longer exist as they had not been included in the respective liquidation procedures. These arguments led to contradictory decisions from the district and appeal courts in Finland. Whereas the District Court held that the principle of economic continuity must be applied in the same way as in administrative fine proceedings (on account of the principle of effectiveness), the Helsinki Court of Appeal denied civil liability for lack of a legal basis in Finnish law. It was the Finnish Supreme Court that referred the case to the CJEU as it had to decide between, on the one hand, the assumption that only the legal entity that caused the damage is liable for this, and, on the other hand, EU case law permitting any person to claim compensation for damages resulting from an infringement of Article 101 TFEU. The Court asked whether the determination of the liable party with regard to damages caused by an infringement is a matter of EU or national law and, if a matter of EU law, whether the principle of economic continuity should be applicable like in cases concerning fines.

The CJEU held that it was a matter of EU law to determine the entity required to provide compensation for damages caused by an infringement of Article 101 TFEU. It confirmed that the effectiveness of Article 101 TFEU would be jeopardised if undertakings responsible for damages caused by an infringement of EU competition rules were able to escape liability simply by changing their identity.[60] The CJEU also vaguely addressed the methodological approach for determining the entity under EU law, suggesting that it should be the same as with regard to the imposition of fines under Article 23 (2) of Regulation No 1/2003.[61]

59 Case C-724/17 *Vantaan kaupunki v Skanska Industrial Solutions and Others (Skanska)* [2019] ECLI:EU:C:2019:204.

60 *Skanska* (n 59) para 28, 46.

61 *Ibid.* at para 47.

5.4.2 *Ratio of* Skanska *and Open Questions*

If not read as a mere individual ruling, the notion of the court was indeed groundbreaking and not compulsory as Article 101 TFEU does not determine particularities of civil liability. Nor did the EU Damages Directive clarify these topics in 2014. The Commission itself, referring to joint and several liability under the EU Damages Directive, had argued that the person liable to pay damages should be determined under national law.[62]

A variety of questions remains, deriving from the two pillars of the case. On the one hand, there is the CJEU's case law regarding fundamental principles of the private enforcement system developed since *Courage/Crehan*[63] and on the other, there is the very specific notion of undertaking in EU competition law.

5.4.2.1 Is There a European Claim for Damages?

Based on the panacea that is the principle of effectiveness, the CJEU elevates the private damages claim together with the determination of the opponent to the level of EU primary legislation. The Advocate General (in *Skanska*) claimed that this idea was not entirely new as Article 101 TFEU already has a direct effect and produces legal consequences in relations between individuals. It thus creates rights for the benefit of individuals which the national courts must safeguard.[64] However, recognising the principles of equivalence and effectiveness means acknowledging that

> in the absence of EU rules governing the matter, it is for the domestic legal system of each Member State to lay down the detailed rules governing the exercise of the right to claim compensation for the harm resulting from an agreement or practice prohibited under Article 101 TFEU.[65]

There are probably more open questions after *Skanska* than before. From a doctrinal point of view, for example, how does a claim for damages under EU law fit into the legal framework of the Member States when EU law demands the claim's existence and determines the liable persons while the other conditions are (probably) governed by national law? Will there be further prerequisites for damages claims to be derived directly from EU law in the future? Advocate General Wahl's opinion[66] could indicate that the substantive criteria of the right to damages, such as a causal link, were also governed by Article 101 TFEU and not by domestic law, which (only)

[62] European Commission, Proposal for a Directive of the European Parliament and of the Council (2013), COM:2013:0404:FIN; EU Damages Directive (n 34), recitals 11, 37.

[63] Case C-453/99 *Courage Ltd v Bernard Crehan and Bernard Crehan v Courage Ltd and Others* [2001] ECLI:EU:C:2001:465. For a list of the leading cases see *Kone* (n 46) paras 20–25.

[64] Opinion of AG Wahl in *Skanska* (n 59) paras 80, 81.

[65] *Skanska* (n 59) para 27, citing *Kone* (n 46) para 24 and the case-law cited therein.

[66] Opinion of AG Wahl *Skanska* (n 59) para 38ff.

had to be assessed by reference to the principle of effectiveness. This seems at least questionable in light of the *Kone* decision;[67] however, the CJEU did not address this issue in *Skanska*. In general, to define requirements of a national civil law claim under the influence of EU law leads to muddy waters. From a dogmatic perspective, it creates a strange impact on the unity of the legal system, both at the EU and the Member States' level. It should therefore be noted that competition law damages claims remain claims under the respective applicable national law and that only the existence of a claim for damages, the person of the obligated party (undertaking), and the person of the entitled party (everyone) are defined by EU primary law.[68] The same outcome could have been achieved without the ratio of *Skanska* by employing the principle of effectiveness when applying national law.

5.4.2.2 What Is 'the Undertaking' Anyway?

With the abovementioned, the EU notion of the undertaking is decisive. The CJEU in *Skanska* merely recalls that the undertaking is

> any entity engaged in an economic activity, irrespective of its legal status and the way in which it is financed [...] even if in law that economic unit consists of several persons, natural or legal.[69]

Transferring the concept of 'undertaking' to damages claims simplifies the matter, yet it misses the point. An analysis of the European Commission and the CJEU practice shows that the concept of a single economic entity that has been used to identify the undertaking is not at all a consistent concept.[70] In particular, the attribution of responsibility within the group derived from the concept of the single economic entity is controversial. While numerous authors try to fit such attribution into a conceptually coherent framework and consider it necessary for the effective enforcement of EU competition law,[71] the (arguably) greater part of the literature criticises sanctions against legal persons not responsible for the competition law infringement.[72]

[67] P Hauser, 'Der Ersatzpflichtige im Kartelldeliktsrecht: Anwendung des Grundsatzes wirtschaftlicher Kontinuität?' (2019) *WuW* 123, 125; A Weitbrecht, 'Kartellschadensersatz 2019' (2020) *NZKart* 106, 106; J Zöttl, notes to 'EuGH: Kartellrecht: Umbrella Pricing – Kone' (2014) *EuZW* 586, 589.

[68] Arguing for a continuum with regard to harmonization: M Hjartström and J Nowag, 'EU Competences and Damages Directive: The Continuum Between Minimum and Full Harmonisation' (2019) Lund University Legal Research Paper Series, LundLawCompWP 2/2019 May 2019 https://ssrn.com/abstract=3383613 accessed 17 August 2021.

[69] *Skanska* (n 59) para 36ff; citing judgment in *ETI SpA and Others* (n 51) para 38 and the case-law cited therein and citing judgment in Case C-516/15 P *Akzo Nobel and Others v Commission* [2017] EU:C:2017:314, para 48 and the case-law cited therein.

[70] Pauer (n 54) 9, 143ff pinpointing to special ambivalence of case-law with regard to joint ventures.

[71] Predominantly, C Kersting 'Liability of Sister Companies and Subsidiaries in European Competition Law' [2020] 41(3) *ECLR* 125, 130, with further references to earlier publications.

[72] Mörsdorf (n 38); W Bosch, 'Verantwortung der Konzernobergesellschaft im Kartellrecht' (2013) 177 *ZHR* 454, 461ff; R Bechtold and W Bosch, 'Der Zweck heiligt nicht alle Mittel' (2011) *ZWeR* 160, 160ff; M Kling,

5.4.2.2.1 GROUP LIABILITY? There are voices arguing that the CJEU wanted to establish what is discussed with the buzzword 'group liability'. In accordance with the case law, imputing a subsidiary's competition law infringement to the parent company would only be a symptom of imputation to the single economic entity. Hence, albeit not visible in case law yet, the economic unit can be held accountable for the infringement that is to say, subsidiaries are liable for parent and sister companies.

With regard to German civil law, the concept of the single economic entity could be mirrored by stipulating a legal capacity of the corporate group forming a civil law partnership (*Gesellschaft bürgerlichen Rechts or GbR*, Sections 705ff German Civil Code).[73] The GbR is the basic partnership type and most general form of partnership under German company law. Conveniently, a private partnership can be established without formal requirements for any purpose that could (and would typically) be something as small as two people jointly renting an automobile for a weekend trip. Infringements by parts of the economic unit could then be attributed to such partnership leading to a joint and several liabilities of the other constituent parts of the economic unit as a consequence. This opinion pinpoints that the liability of the economic unit must be understood as the liability of all legal entities constituting the economic unit.[74] From a comparative perspective, similar forms of partnerships might provide the same reasoning in other Member States.[75] In fact, the idea was already considered (but discarded) in the UK in the 1950s as a 'single economic unit theory'.[76]

However, every solution which ascribes the single economic entity to a partnership is contradictory: the single economic entity in EU case law is primarily found in constellations of control (parent/subsidiary). A group that might form a single economic entity can at the same time hardly constitute a partnership under civil law because of the typical relationship of superiority and subordination within the group, which is not consistent with the equal pursuit of objectives that characterises a partnership. Due to the complexity in dealing with corporate groups, a ubiquitous 'corporate group (liability) law' does not exist. Internationally, there is a persistent rumour, that some jurisdictions have implemented comprehensive regulations of the corporate group, thereby creating a distinct entity form governed by

'Wirtschaftliche Einheit und Gemeinschaftsunternehmen – Konzernprivileg und Haftungszurechnung' (2011) *ZWeR* 169, 177ff; A Riesenkampf and U Krauthausen, 'Liability of Parent Companies for Antitrust Violations of their Subsidiaries' (2010) 31 ECLR 38, 41; van Vormizeele (n 48) 1013ff.

73 Kersting (n 71) 128.

74 Kersting (n 71) 128: 'joint action on the market triggers joint liability'.

75 Gragdansko Druzestvo (Bulgaria); Société civile (France); Società semplice (Italy); Maatschap (Netherlands); Enkelt bolag (Sweden).

76 DHN, [1976] 1 WLR at 850. DHN notwithstanding, English judges have asserted that there is no presumption that group companies be treated as a single economic unit or an enterprise under English company law, see only Cheng (n 10) 60ff.

its own body of law.[77] However, despite many jurisdictions enacting rules for corporate groups,[78] it must be stated that there is no such thing as 'the corporate group law'.[79] Even EU law which contains a large number of laws relevant to groups does not maintain a comprehensive group law system.[80] Thus, to refer to them as cases of a corporate group, liability would be misleading.

Even proponents in favour of a group liability recognise that there might be cases where such a corporate group liability is not justifiable.[81] Neither the method nor the results of full-blown group liability within the single economic entity are therefore convincing.

5.4.2.2.2 THE SINGLE ECONOMIC ENTITY UNRAVELLED There lies a problem of dogmatic derivation at the heart of the single economic entity. Initially, the concept was developed for the application of the so-called 'group privilege'.[82] The single economic entity doctrine is unchallenged with regard to the origin of competition or the intensity of that competition in a market.[83] In other words, it is clear that in general rights of control define a single economic entity. However, it is unclear why and under which circumstances the existence of such right should be used to attribute liability. As highlighted before, the CJEU shifts the burden of determination to a presumption. Unlike a legal entity, an economic entity is not clearly defined but requires an ad hoc appreciation by a court based on several factual elements, ones which may be subject to changes over time. The use of presumptions here is tempting, but problematic with regard to legal certainty, the principle of culpability, and the presumption of innocence.

For a variety of reasons, scholars therefore argue that there is no unique single economic entity doctrine that can be used for both identifying the single economic entity with regard to a unified competitive force on the market and attributing liability for infringements of competition law.

77 Harper Ho (n 2) 885 with further references.

78 In Italy since the reform of the codice civile (2004); Turkey 2011; in France exist for example special rules in the law on the corporate duty of vigilance of parent companies and instructing companies in Code de Commerce L 225-102-4; text books on the continent also often hold chapters dealing with corporate group constellations; see for example Windbichler (n 2) 1242 with further detailed references.

79 Windbichler (n 2) 1241. Central legal aspects regulated with regard to corporate groups are eg profit and loss absorption and accounting integration and consolidation.

80 H Fleischer, 'Europäisches Konzernrecht: Eine akteurzentrierte Annäherung' (2017) *ZGR* 1, 8ff, 15.

81 In case changes in the single economic entity suggest that the new member of the single economic entity did not contribute to the infringement of the past, for example, disposing shares of 50 percent in a subsidiary and forming a joint venture with another company should not imply that the second mother of the joint venture is liable with regard to the subsidiaries' cartel infringements of the past; see C Kersting, 'Kartellrechtliche Haftung des Unternehmens nach Art. 101 AEUV' (2019) *WuW* 290, 297.

82 For a detailed discussion of the emergence and implications of the single economic entity doctrine in EU competition law, see O Odudu and D Bailey, 'The Single Economic Entity Doctrine in EU Competition Law' (2014) 51 CMLR 1721.

83 Odudu and Bailey (n 82) 1738; for Merger Regulation context see para 175 of the Commission's Jurisdictional Notice [2008] OJ C 95/1 and for the context of vertical agreements see art 1 (2) VBER 330/2010 [2010] OJ L 102/1.

The case law has been extensively analysed and differentiated numerous areas of application of the concept of the single economic entity.[84] In this light, one could even doubt the argumentative intrinsic value of the single economic entity with regard to the attribution of liability.[85]

Against the backdrop of the friction caused by the legal entity principle as a ubiquitous concept in all industrial states and in light of the CJEU's case law, it is argued that the concept of the single economic entity itself is only the consequence of applying the principle of effectiveness but not a condition for the effective enforcement of competition law. Case law concerned with the application of the principle of economic continuity and parental liability would usually employ both lines of argumentation in parallel without a strict dogmatic differentiation.[86]

The principle of effectiveness itself is the standard according to which any assessment of a single economic entity is to be made. That conclusion is supported by the fact that EU institutions can in no way avoid designating a legal entity as an addressee for the statement of objection in a second step. An 'economic entity' without a legal entity is not a suitable addressee for measures of the European Commission. To stay in line with the sausage picture: a kind of black pudding that can hardly be nailed to the wall.[87] EU institutions impose fines on parents and subsidiaries as joint and several debtors in a two-step approach. The European Commission firstly determines the undertaking and secondly identifies a legal person against which a fine is enforced.[88] This approach can be best explained by the principle of effectiveness.

In this respect, the judgment in the *Skanska* case could be seen as a confirmation of this context-dependent understanding of the single economic entity. Strikingly, the CJEU in *Skanska* justified the transfer of principles from the context of fines to the context of private actions for damages solely on the basis of the common root of both sanction regimes in the efficiency objective.[89] Yet, the CJEU does not comment on the prerequisites of the single economic entity which would have been expected in this context. Due to this contextual understanding of the single economic entity, parental liability appears to be appropriate and necessary in the absence of an equally effective means for the effective enforcement of EU law.[90]

84 For a comprehensive overview Odudu and Bailey (n 82) 1721.

85 Mörsdorf (n 56) 493.

86 *Ibid.*, with reference to *ETI SpA and Others* (n 51) paras 41, 42.

87 Providing the original metaphor: Windbichler (n 2) 1244.

88 Pauer (n 54) 9; see also art 299 TFEU.

89 Mörsdorf (n 38) 494; R Harms and P Kirst, 'Der kartellrechtliche Unternehmensbegriff' (2019) *EuZW* 374, 378.

90 Admittedly, the CJEU's case law, according to which the existence of a group-internal compliance system must be regarded as proof of the existence of an economic unit between parent company and subsidiary, seems to provide suboptimal incentives for preventing group-internal competition law infringements, see Mörsdorf (n 38) 495; Case C-501/11 P *Schindler Holding* [2013] ECLI:EU:C:2013:522, para 113ff.

On the other hand, liability of the subsidiary for competition law infringements by the parent or a sister company does not appear to provide incentives for avoiding such infringements. The single economic entity is conceptually characterised in a way that only one part (usually the parent company) exerts a decisive influence on the other parts and thus is in a position to control behaviour to a significant extent. Behavioural incentives, on the other hand, have no effect when there is no possibility for the subsidiary to influence the behaviour of the parent or sister company. Liability of the subsidiary or sister company is not even necessary to prevent the parent company from transferring assets to these companies. Transferred assets are accessible due to the liability of the (economic) successor and the liability of the parent company.[91]

5.4.2.2.3 IMPLICATIONS OF THE CJEU'S RULING IN *SKANSKA* FOR NATIONAL RULES ON FINES? *Skanska* found that acquiring companies may be held liable for the damage caused by the infringement and that in determining the liable entities the same principles (concept of undertaking) are to be applied as in cases concerning fines.[92] With that, one could argue that the ruling's implications are equally relevant to the law on the imposition of fines. It follows from the equal treatment of fines and damages regarding the notion of undertaking that the addressee of a fine is equally directly defined by Article 101 TFEU when national cartel authorities impose fines for an infringement of Article 101 TFEU.

According to this reading, the ECN Plus Directive[93] only has clarifying effect insofar as it requires Member States to ensure that fines can also be imposed on 'undertakings' and that the notion of undertaking applies for the purpose of parent and successor liability (cf Article 13 (1), (5), and recital 46).[94]

The introduced § 81a (1–5) of the German ARC would (probably) no longer be required as far as infringements of EU competition law are concerned and even for pure German cases. The CJEU's ruling in *Skanska* has no direct impact on matters of national competition law, where they do not affect trade between Member States. However, since the German legislator has amended the key provisions of German competition law by implementing the term 'undertaking' explicitly in order to align relevant legal provisions with EU law, the development of EU law is recreated by German law.[95]

[91] Mörsdorf (n 38) 495.

[92] *Skanska* (n 59) para 51.

[93] Directive (EU) 2019/1 of the European Parliament and of the Council of 11 December 2018 to empower the competition authorities of the Member States to be more effective enforcers and to ensure the proper functioning of the internal market [2019] OJ L11/3 (ECN Plus Directive).

[94] Hauser (n 67).

[95] Explanatory Memorandum to the draft Seventh Act amending the ARC, Bundestag publication of 12 August 2004, 15/3640, 22; J Biermann in: *Immenga/Mestmäcker, Wettbewerbsrecht* (n 42) preface to § 81 GWB, para 37.

More importantly, the CJEU has not limited the temporal effects of its ruling.[96] Since the CJEU in preliminary rulings clarifies only existing EU law, the finding that the determination of the undertaking is a matter of EU law, ironically, already applied in 2017. From this viewpoint, the German 'sausage gap' would not even have existed, but would have been a mere error of law. It did not take long after *Skanska* until it was hypothesised it could be possible to reopen and continue fine proceedings that were discontinued due to the lack of (solvent) addressees with the parent company or the economic successor.[97]

For mergers and acquisitions, the outcome of the *Skanska* ruling underscores the importance of due diligence. Broadened liability might trigger a higher demand for buyer-protective representations and warranties regimes in share deals and even asset deals. Particularly, compliance warranties of future transactions might include an explicit commitment by the seller's business with regard to competition law compliance. Once there are reasonable grounds to suspect that the acquirer will be an addressee of antitrust-related claims originating from the transferred business, a special indemnity might be granted by the seller holding the acquirer harmless from any claims in this regard, ideally backed up by a parent company guarantee in order to mitigate the risk that the selling entity ceases to exist. One crucial point of negotiation will be the corresponding limitation period for claims resulting from a breach of such warranty or indemnity. Since the CJEU in *Skanska* explicitly rejected limiting the temporal effects of the decision and since competition law infringements often remain in the dark for several years, acquirers might consider the usual limitation periods to be insufficient.

5.4.3 *Developments After* Skanska

The Member States' courts have so far taken different approaches towards questions that have arisen since *Skanska*.

The question of how the principle of economic continuity will be applied will certainly become even more pressing in the future as it impacts not only the 'given' group but a multitude of potential third-party purchasers. As regards the purchase of an undertaking, the CJEU does not seem to presuppose any fault on the part of the purchaser. Rather, the purchaser 'takes over its assets and liabilities, including its liability for breaches of EU law'.[98] By way of example, a German court's ruling regarding legal succession held that the company taking over a business unit of the alleged cartelist via spin-off was liable for cartel damages on the basis of a corporate law regulation in the Transformation Act (*Umwandlungsgesetz*).[99] The

96 *Skanska* (n 59) para 55ff.
97 Hauser (n 67).
98 *Skanska* (n 59) para 40, citing Case C-448/11 P *SNIA v Commission* [2013] EU:C:2013:801, para 25.
99 OLG Düsseldorf, U (Kart) 18/17 *Schienenkartell* [2019] ECLI:DE:OLGD:2019:0123.UKART.18.17.0A, para 31ff.

successor did not participate in the alleged infringement. However, the German court applied the existing liability scheme of the Transformation Act and affirmed joint and several liabilities of the cartelist and its successor for damages that arose up to the point in time when the spin-off took effect (i.e. by registration in the commercial register). Although the infringement putatively existed even until after this point in time, liability was not extended for the successor in this regard. In short, the court made use of an existing corporate liability regime, which is designed to protect creditors in general, not specifically creditors of cartel damages claims. Unlike in *Skanska*, the successor neither had been involved in the infringements itself nor did other aspects command an extension of the claimants' recoverable assets from a normative point of view.

With regard to the more general question of horizontal or vertical liability for competition law infringements of other group companies, a majority of German courts have rejected the possibility of being sued for cartel damages in civil court in relation to a parent's subsidiary or a sister company and thus, in principle, its civil liability for infringements committed by other members of the same economic unit.[100] Even while quoting *Skanska,* courts have referred to the EU principle of personal responsibility.[101] If there is a lack of decisive influence, national courts have not reflexively attributed liability to a subsidiary or sister company. Rather, they have focused on whether the subsidiary had control over the actions of the other group companies.

Against the backdrop of national rules which have incorporated parental liability through the transposition of the EU Damages Directive[102], commentators eagerly awaited the CJEU's findings in the case of *Sumal*. Divergent decisions[103] in Spain had caused a referral to the CJEU for a preliminary ruling on whether a subsidiary can be liable for its parent company's conduct.[104] The CJEU was asked to elaborate on the context of intra-group relationships and, in particular, whether the concept of the single economic entity is to be understood with regard to control or also with regard to other intra-group aspects (such as being a beneficiary of a parent or sister company). The opinion of the Advocate General, in this case, suggested that control alone is not a suitable criterion for assessing liability since subsidiaries do not

[100] LG Mannheim, 14 O 117/18 Kart *LKW-Kartell* [2019] ECLI:DE:LGMANNH:2019:0424.14O117.18KART.0A; LG München I, 37 O 6039/18 *Löschfahrzeug-Kartell* [2019] ECLI:DE:LGMUEN1:2019:0607.37O6039.18.0A; indicating a dissenting opinion, but without ultimate decision in this case LG Dortmund, 8 O 75/19 *Sanitärgroßhändler* [2020] ECLI:DE:LGDO:2020:0708.8O75.19KART.00 para 46, citing Case C-97/08 P *Akzo Nobel* [2009] ECLI:EU:C:2009:536, para 54.

[101] Case C-286/13 P *Dole Food* [2015] ECLI:EU:C:215:184, para 140; *Skanska* (n 59) para 32, 39.

[102] eg Portugal: art 3 (2) Lei n.º 23/2018; Spain: art 71.2 (b) Ley de Defensa de la Competencia.

[103] Case C-882/19 *Sumal SL* [2021] ECLI:EU:C:2021:800; eg Juzgado de lo Mercantíl No 3 de Valencia [2019] ECLI:ES:JMV:2019:34; Audiencia Provincial de Barcelona Sec. 15 [2019] Rollo núm. 775/2019-2ª, ECLI:ES:APB:2019:9370A, para 11.

[104] Request for a preliminary ruling from the Audiencia Provincial de Barcelona of 3 December 2019, Case C-882/19 *Sumal* [2019] OJ C87/7.

exert control over their parents. However, the Advocate General also highlighted the principle of personal liability.[105] A 'downward' liability would require that the subsidiary not only was controlled by the parent company but also was objectively necessary for the infringement of the parent company.[106] The market conduct of the subsidiary must have made it possible to concretise the effect of the infringement. Only then, the parent and subsidiary would be jointly and severally liable.[107] A consequent application of that reasoning means that there can be more than one single economic entity within a group of companies depending on the context of the respective case.

Eventually, the CJEU holds the subsidiary liable as part of the economic unit even if it is not the addressee of the imposed fines and thus once more pierces the corporate veil. Remarkably, the CJEU's ruling only partially adopts the Advocate General's proposed criteria for this veil-piercing. In *Sumal*, the CJEU first reiterates the established concepts of undertaking and economic unit and the element of control.[108] However, after acknowledging the fact that the same parent company may be part of several economic units depending on the respective activity of a conglomerate, the CJEU adopts broader requirements in order to establish joint and several liability in cartel damages cases. Liability shall not be construed to a subsidiary if the parent's infringements are committed in the context of economic activities entirely unconnected to the subsidiaries' own activity in which the subsidiary was in no way involved.[109] However, the damaged party has (only) to show that the subsidiary formed such an economic unit by proving (i) the economic, organisational and legal links between the defendant subsidiary and its parent and (ii) a specific link between the subsidiary's economic activity and the subject matter of the infringement of the parent (i.e. by proving that both entities distribute identical products).[110] So, the CJEU does not implement an automatism of vertical and horizontal liability. But it is just a matter of time before the CJEU will be asked to specify to what extent a product (range) must be identical.

Referring to the right to an effective remedy and to a fair trial, the CJEU cryptically emphasises that the subsidiary must dispose of all means necessary to defend itself. In particular, it must be able to dispute that it belongs to the same economic unit as its parent but as well defend itself with regard to the decision of the Commission arising from previous public enforcement.[111] Means with regard to the latter are

105 Case C-882/19 *Sumal SL* [2021] ECLI:EU:C:2021:800, para 42; opinion of the Advocate General Giovanni Pitruzella, C-882/19 *Sumal* [2021] ECLI:EU:C:2021:293, para 39, 64.

106 Opinion of the Advocate General Giovanni Pitruzella, C-882/19 *Sumal* [2021] ECLI:EU:C:2021:293, para 57.

107 *Ibid.* at para 57 ff.

108 Case C-882/19 *Sumal SL* [2021] ECLI:EU:C:2021:800, para 41–44 citing i.a. *Akzo Nobel*.

109 Case C-882/19 *Sumal SL* [2021] ECLI:EU:C:2021:800, para 47.

110 *Ibid.* at para 51 f.

111 *Ibid.* at para 53.

factually limited, however, since national courts cannot rule against the existence of an infringement already found by the European Commission.[112] The contradiction is obvious: the subsidiary is factually not able to exercise such rights, since the European Commission grants such rights of defence only to the entities involved in infringement proceedings, but not to affiliated 'third-parties', which according to *Sumal* can later be sued as part of an economic unit. The CJEU here considers it sufficient that during such infringement proceedings the economic unit exerted such rights of defence.

Supposedly, the CJEU's ruling opens the path to the liability of any of the sister companies, since any legal entity that is part of the economic unit which has committed an infringement can generally be the addressee of damage claims.[113] With that, a new form of forum shopping is possible where damaged parties will consider and weigh favourable conditions in different member states such as presumptions regarding the amount of damages or different statutes of limitation. It will be crucial for subsequent rulings that the CJEU finds suitable criteria that also consider aspects of property and investment protection if the parent company does not hold 100% of the shares.

5.5 CONCLUSIONS AND OUTLOOK

This chapter initially outlined the basic premises that corporate law is built on globally: the entity principle and the enterprise principle that, depending on the point of view and field of law, make the unity or multiplicity of the group of companies stand out. In this context, the chapter portrayed how the focus on the single corporation legal entity principle and the principle of separation has been utilised in some instances to avoid liability for cartel fines by restructuring in Germany. This infamous gap was eventually closed by wide-reaching reforms.

Highlighting the persistent tension between the issues of limited liability and responsibility for competition law infringements, the chapter then discussed how basic corporate law principles relate to the EU concept of the single economic entity, with particular regard to private damages claims. This chapter finally argues that the CJEU ruling in *Skanska* reaffirms that liability for fines and damages should follow a cautious assessment in relation to the principle of effectiveness, which is also the starting point for determining the single economic entity. This may lead to a more contextual and nuanced understanding of the single economic entity and, in turn, a more balanced approach with regard to the allocation of liability within corporate groups (i.e. to the extent required by the principle of effectiveness). In any case, the chapter emphasises that an automatic vertical or even horizontal liability within the corporate group disregards fundamental principles

[112] *Ibid.* at para 55.

[113] Compare Case C-882/19 *Sumal SL* [2021] ECLI:EU:C:2021:800, para 50.

of corporate and civil law and would lead to unreasonable results. Against the backdrop in which EU economic law is still a picture puzzle, it is important that EU courts post-*Skanska* and *Sumal* take the opportunity and focus on the general context of matters relating to multi-corporate enterprises. Such focus would avoid that excessive regulatory tendencies regarding group external law undermine general principles of civil law systems in the Member States which could produce equally conclusive results.

6

Korea's Chaebol Regulations and the Relationship between Competition and Company Law

Myungsu Hong

6.1 INTRODUCTION

Regulations on chaebol[1] in Korea are cited by comparative corporate lawyers as a rare example of attempts to regulate corporate groups. Most OECD countries do not have similar regulations;[2] in this regard, chaebol regulations are recognised as one of the unique regulations in Korea. A chaebol consists of a number of companies, and of course, corporate law will apply to corporate governance. In Korea, however, chaebol regulations under the competition law have replaced those that existed under corporate law to some extent. Therefore, the set of rules which I am going to analyse in this chapter is a very meaningful example of the interactions between corporate law and competition law. It is clear that the reason for such rules being found almost only in Korea is due to the presence of chaebol, of which there are few equivalent economic entities in other countries. Therefore, before looking into chaebol regulations, it is necessary to understand how chaebol came to exist in Korea and the position they hold in the national economy. This understanding, of course, has not always been consistent, but the minimal agreement reached in the process of reconciling these disagreements between ideas[3] has provided the basis for chaebol regulation and supported the legitimacy of regulation.

In Korea, chaebol regulations began in earnest in 1987. There have been several revisions to the law since then, but the basic framework of the regulation that was first introduced has continued without major changes. This means that the

Myongji University.

[1] In Korea, chaebol means family property in a dictionary sense. However, it is commonly used to refer to a large group of family-controlled companies. The important characteristics of chaebol will be discussed in detail in the next section.

[2] A similar example can only be found in Japan. After World War II, Japan dismantled zaibatsu, which were similar to chaebol. Perhaps in the West, the German Konzernrecht is an interesting similar example.

[3] In general, two positions can be distinguished. One position calls for strengthening of such regulations with a focus on the negative aspects of chaebol. The other position focuses on the positive functions, especially those that contribute to national economic growth and therefore call for regulations to be eased

basic understanding of chaebol is maintained, but several revisions to the regulations suggest that changes have occurred in the perception of chaebol problems and regulatory goals. Thus, the history of the current regulations must be considered in understanding them. This process will reveal issues that have been resolved or remain unresolved so far. These might be the drivers of future regulatory changes.

This article will proceed in the following order. First, the specific significance of chaebol, their impact on the Korean economy, and the practical background of the regulations will be reviewed. Then, a deductive review of regulations on chaebol and the significance and details of the current legal system will be conducted, and the significance of the various disputes that have arisen regarding the existence or content of these regulations will be examined. In addition, an assessment of a series of legal tools related to the improvement of governance will be carried out with regard to the strengthened corporate law. Based on these discussions, this article will conclude by making predictions on the significance of chaebol on the Korean economy in the future and reviewing the direction of the ongoing discussions on improving the relevant regulations.

6.2 SIGNIFICANCE AND EVALUATION OF CHAEBOL

6.2.1 *Economic Development and the Rise of the Chaebol*

The emergence of chaebol in Korea is in line with the rapid development of the economy. The formation of initial capital is important for economic development in underdeveloped countries, and this requires the establishment of an investment security and investment inducement system.[4] In Korea, this process was carried out in earnest by the government after the Korean War, where the Korean government fostered investment directly by direct government investments. In the process, the economic resources generated by foreign free or paid financial support were concentrated on a small number of companies actively engaged in the economic development program. This government support provided these companies with an opportunity to grow into chaebol.

The government's leading role in economic development was embodied in a five-year economic development plan that began in 1962. In particular, the five-year plan that was carried out from the first to fourth plan prioritised economic growth.[5] In accordance with this plan, the government carried out specific allocations of resources. For example, the first five-year plan contained a preferential allocation of funding for the light industry, the second plan for heavy industry, and

4 M Levy Jr, 'Some Social Obstacles to Capital Formation in Underdeveloped Areas' in *Capital Formation and Economic Growth* (Princeton University Press 1955) 469–479.

5 See T Park, *원형과 변용: 한국 경제개발계획의 기원 (Original Form and Transformation: Origin of the Korea Economic Development Program)* (SNU Press 2007).

the third plan for the chemical industry. In accordance with these plans, funding was given to specific operators in the field. In this process, Hirschman's unbalanced growth theory[6] became the theoretical basis for economic policy. The performance of leading industries, which had been subject to intensive support under this policy, expanded to related front and rear industries, just as the development of the chemical industry has led to the development of the textile industry ahead and the refinery industry behind. It eventually led to the growth of the entire national economy. In terms of economic development, these strategic choices and practices certainly had a positive effect. Yet, the focused allocation of resources to a small number of industry players also had negative effects such as introducing inequality in the economic system. The emergence of chaebol is a symbolic representation of negative effects. Chaebol has been a key driver of the government's development policy, and at the same time, the biggest beneficiary of growth. In this regard, the analysis that 'the Korean government has hardly put a brake on the accumulation of family property as long as it is reinvested in production activities deemed by planners to be high in priority',[7] provides a proper understanding of the relationship between the government and chaebol at this time. The family underlying the chaebol was an advantageous way of accumulating capital as it served as a powerful means to avoid capital leaks in a culture where it is hard to expect a member of the family to pursue his own interests at the expense of the interests of the whole family. Also, the government did not impose any real restrictions on the expansion of chaebol as long as they followed the government's development program, which resulted in the size of chaebols growing in lockstep with the rapid growth of the national economy.

There has been a fundamental change in the government's economic policies since the 1980s. By that time, the size of the economy had grown too much to be run by the government's programs. Similarly, the pursuit of other values such as resolving inequality problems in addition to economic development has emerged as an unavoidable social agenda, shifting the government-led economic management style to one based on private initiatives. Symbolising this change was the Monopoly Regulation Act that was enacted in 1980, which was the first legislation to institutionalise competition policies in Korea. In this new environment, where private sector autonomy is expanded and market functions strengthened, chaebol achieved explosive growth. This trend continued until the 1997 foreign exchange crisis. This crisis in late 1997 resulted in a fundamental change in the previous industrial structure. Above all, it was an opportunity to put the brakes on business behaviour and the chaebols' unconditional expansions; since then, there have been structural changes focused on high-value-added industries. But this change did not lead to a

6 The unbalanced growth theory that the Korean government followed was close to Hirschman's model. See A Hirschman, *The Strategy of Economic Development* (Yale University Press 1965) 62.

7 M Kim and others, *한국 경제 사회의 근대화 (Modernization of Korean Economy and Society)* (Korea Development Institute 1981) 44.

change in the industrial structure, where chaebol plays a central role in the entire industry. As such, the trend of chaebol leading the industry as a whole has been maintained. But the gap between chaebols is widening and the influence of the top chaebol is increasing. This development may continue depending on the changes in the industry and the extent to which the chaebols respond.[8]

6.2.2 *Characteristics and Definitions of Chaebol*

6.2.2.1 Characteristics in Finance

As mentioned earlier, in Korea, chaebol has grown as the biggest beneficiaries of state-led economic development. The government allocated limited resources to a small number of entities that responded to its economic development strategy, thereby pursuing efficient and sustained economic development. This specific allocation of resources carried out by the government was mainly done by means of financial support, The government also paid attention to the establishment of an institutional basis to ensure that the process was carried out efficiently. Under the Act on Temporary Measures for Financial Institutions enacted in June 1961 and the Act on the Handling of Illegal Property Accumulation enacted in October of the same year, the voting rights of bank shares held by major shareholders were restricted or recovered.[9] The government thereby strengthened its control over general banks, and the revision of the Korea Bank Act in 1962 strengthened the government's authority to intervene in the Bank of Korea.[10] On this institutional basis, the government took the initiative in implementing growth-oriented financial policies such as follows: 1) allocation of foreign loans, the main source of financing since the early 1960s; 2) financial support in the process of clearing up insolvent companies, which was implemented several times from the late 1960s to the mid to-late 1980s; 3) financial support to foster general trading companies for the purpose of expanding exports in the 1970s, and 4) financial support during the consolidation of the heavy and chemical industry in the late 1970s and early 1980s.[11] Through such financial support, the business sectors of chaebol expanded to include new industries and

[8] As of 2020, the Samsung Group (425 trillion Won), the largest among large business groups designated by the Fair Trade Commission, had 83 times the total assets of the smallest Samyang Group (5 trillion Won).

[9] Control over banks was represented by Samsung Group, which actively took over the sale of government-owned bank shares in 1957, after which the Samsung Group owned about 50 percent of the shares of four commercial banks. This resulted in the internalization of financial institutions. See H Lee, 한국 재벌형성사 *(History of the Formation of Korean Chaebol)* (Bibongchulpansa 1999) 84–85.

[10] D Oh, '통화금융제도의 발전 (Development of Monetary System)', in Byeongjik Ahn (ed), *한국경제성장사 (History of Korean Economic Growth)* (SNU Press 2001) 277.

[11] B So, '한국기업의 소유집중과 경제 효율성' (Concentration of Ownership and Economic Efficiency of Korean Companies), in *한국의 대기업: 누가 소유하며 어떻게 지배되는가 (Korea's Big Enterprise: Who Owns and How it Is Controlled)* (POSCO MRI 1995) 59.

markets. The support focused on light industries in the 1960s and heavy industries[12] in the 1970s served as a catalyst for chaebol entry into these fields. In other words, the government's economic development policy was implemented mainly by providing financial support to leading sectors, and the economic entities that received resources entered various industries and expanded the scope of their business, which resulted in the formation of an industrial structure based on chaebol.[13]

The government's financial support for the chaebol, which continued during the economic development process, also had an important impact on the chaebol's capital management style and ownership structure. The financial support for chaebol meant that chaebol financing was biased towards external borrowing rather than equality. There are numerous reasons for this bias. Some of these reasons include tax differences where interest payments on borrowing funds were treated as expenses, while dividends on shares are not,[14] low-interest financial support below-market interest rates, internal funds insufficient to allow for expansion into new industries, and an insufficiently developed capital market.[15] Due to these factors, a financial structure emerged in chaebol management that relied heavily on borrowing funds, resulting in the high debt-to-equity ratio of the companies, one of the main criticism during the 1997 financial crisis.[16] Furthermore, the practice of relying on borrowing funds is deeply related to the establishment of a generalised ownership structure for chaebol. The fact that borrowing funds have become the main source of funds for the expansion of chaebol means that the expansion process did not affect the existing ownership structure; rather, it increasingly strengthened the ownership structure, a structure dominated by the owners and their families during the chaebol formation period.[17]

12 Heavy industry is an industry that produces large and heavy products or uses large and heavy equipment and facilities, which usually requires a lot of capital. Light industry means an industry that does not have these characteristics.

13 See J Jeong, '한국전쟁과 전근대적 계급관계의 해체' (Korean War and Dismantling Pre-Modern Class Relations), in *한국의 대기업: 누가 소유하며 어떻게 지배되는가 (Korea's Big Enterprise: Who Owns and How it Is Controlled)* (POSCO MRI 1995) 59.

14 In particular, regarding the discussion focusing on the fact that interest payments on debts to others are treated as expenses while dividends on equity capital are not, see M Choi, *한국조세의 제문제 (Korea's Taxation Problems)* (Josetongramsa 1988) 377.

15 See So (n 12) 67.

16 The debt-to-equity ratios of major chaebol that went bankrupt in 1997 are as follows.

	Hanbo	Sammi	Jinro	Kia	Haetae	New Core
asset ranking	14	25	19	8	24	28
debt-to-equity	648%	3,333%	4,836%	522%	669%	1,253%

S, Cho, '경제위기 이후 재벌정책에 대한 평가' (Evaluation of Chaebol Policy After the Economic Crisis), in *21st Century Korean Enterprises' Competitiveness* (SNU's Corporate Competitiveness Research Center 2002) 10.

17 See O Kwon, *경제법 (Economic Law)* (Beopmunsa 2019) 239–240.

6.2.2.2 Characteristics in Ownership Governance

In general, chaebols are exclusively controlled by owners and their families. The fact that a chaebol's decision-making authority is wholly vested in the owner and that such control is inherited within the family is the basis for this understanding. It is worth noting, however, that this governance relationship was not built by direct ownership by the owner or his family. For example, the owner and his family owned only 3.3% of the 10 largest chaebols in 2002, and this figure has only changed to 2.5% in 2019.[18] In other words, 100% control is carried out with a small stake. This divergence creates an inconsistency between ownership and control.[19]

Given such small stakes, cross-shareholdings are extremely important as a means of enabling the exclusive control of affiliates by the chaebol owners. Although mutual investment is restricted under the Commercial Act and the Monopoly Regulation Act prohibits cross-shareholding[20] and circular ownership[21] by large enterprise groups, the practice of cross-shareholding between affiliates continues, and this structure provides for exclusive control by chaebol owners with small stakes.[22] The pyramid scheme, which culminates in holding companies or substantial holding companies, is also a factor that enables this dominance.[23]

Furthermore, this ownership structure continues through family succession. The succession itself should not be viewed negatively. It is important to note that the succession of control is not done by normal procedures for the transfer of rights, but in a way that utilises cross-affiliated investments to form a new governance relationship centred on the successor. The succession of Samsung Group, for example, took place in the 1990s in a manner whereby the immediate family of the owner of the group obtained new control over Samsung Everland (an unlisted company), which plays an important role in the group's equity structure.[24]

[18] KFTC, 'Status of Stock Ownership of Enterprise Groups Subject to Disclosure in 2019' (Press Release 5 September 2019) 4.

[19] See O Kwon (n 18) 240.

[20] In this chapter, cross-shareholding means that Company A and Company B own mutual shares.

[21] In this chapter, circular ownership refers to a circular structure in which Company A acquires Company B shares, Company B acquires Company C shares, and Company C acquires Company A shares.

[22] The ratio of shareholdings between affiliates in 59 large enterprise groups in 2019 was 46.7 percent. KFTC, 'Status of Stock Ownership of Enterprise Groups Subject to Disclosure in 2019' (n 19) 3.

[23] Under a pyramid structure built by a chain of shareholdings, in other words a practical holding company method, exclusive control of more than the equity ratio may be possible. See R Morck, D Strangeland, and B Yeung, '*Inherited Wealth, Corporate Control and Economic Growth: The Canadian Disease?*' (1998) National Bureau of Economic Research, Inc Working Paper 6814, 10–11 www.nber.org/papers/w6814 accessed on [24/06/2021].

[24] Lee Jaeyong, the only son of Chairman Lee Kunhee, became the largest shareholder by holding a 31.9 percent stake in Samsung Everland under the voluntary allocation of convertible bonds in 1996, while Samsung Everland held 20.56 percent of the company's shares, giving it substantial control together with Chairman Lee Kunhee, who holds 26 percent of the actual shares in Samsung Life Insurance. For a detailed explanation of this process, see D Lee, '재벌의 반봉건성과 자본주의적 옹호의 허구성' (The Half-Feudalism of Chaebol and The Laxity of Capitalist Advocacy) (2000) 18 Democratic Laws

6.2.2.3 Characteristics in Organisation and Operation

Given a structure in which the control of the chaebol is exclusively attributed to one head, the organisation and operation of chaebol are carried out in a corresponding manner. Chaebol involves a number of affiliates gathering together to form a group. Each affiliate has an independent decision-making structure as required by Commercial Act, but in practice, the final decision-making authority is vested in the head (owner), and the whole affiliate is operated as an integral part of the single decision-making structure led by the head. This aspect is evident when a chaebol is made up of a holding company system. But even when it is not, they are operated similarly as they operate around a company that is a *de facto* holding company. Of course, the chaebol themselves are making efforts to enhance management efficiency, and one of these efforts is to respect the autonomous management judgment of their affiliates.[25] However, as long as control is wholly attributable to one head (owner), the management independence of each affiliate will be limited.

It also needs to be considered that many chaebols are entering a number of industries and show aspects that can be characterised by the so-called non-relevant diversification. In particular, industries on which the government had focused during the relevant economic development period, such as export replacement industries in the 1960s, heavy and chemical industries in the 1970s, and information and communication industries since the 1990s, have become important milestones in the process of chaebol expansion. As a result of this process, most of the chaebols now make inroads into various industrial sectors, and this 'non-relevant diversification' phenomenon is understood as one of the important characteristics of chaebols.[26] Of course, It is also necessary to keep in mind that industrial diversification itself can be a corporate strategy.[27] However, it was hard to avoid problems such as a lack of expertise in a number of industries, excessive and overlapping investments, and

196–199. For a discussion on the unfairness of the purpose of issuance, the unfairness of the process of issuance, and the unfairness of the value of issuance as legal issues with this succession process, see N Kwak, '삼성계열사의 통모불공정 주식발행에 대한 소송적 대응: 현황과 과제' (Litigationary Response to Samsung affiliates' Unfair Stock Issue: Current Status and Tasks) (2000) 18 *Democratic Laws* 275ff.

25 Through the Frankfurt Declaration in 1993, the Samsung Group officially declared that it aims to establish an organizational culture of 'autonomy and creativity.' See Samsung, *삼성 60년사(Samsung 60 Years)* (Samsung 1998) 220ff.

26 See B Chung and Y Yang, *한국 재벌부문의 경제분석 (Economic Analysis of Korea's Chaebol Sector)* (Korea Development Institute 1992) 26. However, the degree of diversification varies from chaebol to chaebol. About this, see Lee (n 10) 156 and W Song and S Lee, *재벌의 사업구조와 경제력 집중 (The Concentration of Chaebol's Business Structure and Economic Power)* (Nanam 2005) 274 and below. In the end, the expansion of chaebol needs to be understood by combining horizontal and vertical perspectives, and typically, after entering a new industry, vertical expansion centered on the industry in question is organically integrated to complete the Chaebols overall structure.

27 See S Lee and S Han, '한국기업집단의 다변화와 이윤율' (Diversification and Profit Rate of Korean Enterprise Groups) (1998) 6 *Industrial Organization Research* 55.

worsening financial health of the chaebol due to the transfer of risks between affiliates.[28] Such concerns over excessive diversification have been embodied in policies to strengthen the expertise in industries since the late 1980s and inducing chaebol to engage in the large-scale specialised enterprises that accompanied restructuring after the 1997 financial crisis. Yet such policies are still far from realising their objectives, and the situation continues where affiliates of chaebol are distributed across various industries and also have a dominant position in many markets.[29]

With the affiliates that make up the chaebol distributed throughout various industries and the final decision-making power over them being concentrated in one person, an organisational response to carry out such decisions effectively may be inevitable. If a chaebol establishes a holding company system, the holding company functions as a headquarters and affects subsidiaries or their subsidiaries. On the other hand, if it is not a holding company system, an organisation that can assist the control of chaebol owners may be needed, and it is common for a large-scale secretariat to be set up or a special organisation, such as a restructuring headquarters, to act as a control organisation for all affiliates. Such a unified way of operating the group has created the problem of limiting room for affiliates to manage efficiently and flexibly. It created management inefficiencies that make it difficult for them to respond effectively in the face of intensifying competition. There are also concerns that such organisations generally exist as illegal organisations, with the result of reduced functions for the Board of Directors as the voting bodies of each affiliate based on corporate law.[30]

6.2.2.4 Significance of Chaebol

In light of the characteristics of the chaebol mentioned above, chaebol means a business group consisting of multiple affiliates owned by the owners and their families, and whose control is effectively vested in the owner. Being owned by the owner and his family means that the right to claim the distribution of the remaining property legally belongs to them, but as mentioned earlier, they do not have absolute equity rights in the affiliates, and investments between the affiliates play a decisive

28 S Cho, '외환위기 이후 재벌구조 변화에 대한 실증분석: 리스크 이전 및 주가수익률 동조화를 중심으로' (Empirical Analysis of Changes in the Structure of Chaebol After the Asian Financial Crisis: Focused on the Transfer of Risks and the Synchronization of Share Price Returns) (Korea Development Institute 2002) 33–34, shows that risk-transfer among chaebol affiliates has not decreased since the 1997 economic crisis. I Hwang, '재벌구조의 특징과 장점, 경영성과에 대한 실증연구' (Empirical Research on the Characteristics and Issues, Management Performance), in *재벌구조의 특징과 쟁점 (The Characteristics and Issues of the Chaebol Structure)* (Korea Economic Research Institute 2002) 51. In addition, the empirical analysis conducted in the late 90s concluded that related diversification in industry has a higher profit rate than non-relevant diversification, and that excessive diversification reduces gross margin. See Lee and Han (n 28) 67–68.

29 Cho (n 29) 34.

30 For chaebol, decision-making is actually decided at the owner's family meeting, not the board of directors of enterprises, and to understand it as the characteristics of Korean chaebol, which operate the modern corporate system in a feudal way, see D Lee (n 25) 192–193.

role in the attribution of total control. Also, the fact that a chaebol is a group of multiple companies, not a single company, that they enter various industries, and that they are dominant in most industries are commonalities shared by most chaebols. It is also important to note that the operation of business groups is carried out in a unified and single manner based on control wholly attributable to the head and that organisational arrangements arise for this purpose.

6.2.3 *The Assessment of Chaebol in the Korean Economy*

Chaebols are becoming economic entities that embody the concentration of economic power at each level of market concentration, general concentration, and ownership concentration. The degree of general concentration is understood as the share of a particular enterprise or enterprise group in the entire industry or entire national economy.[31] As an indicator of this share, the total amount of capital, total assets, employment, etc., from a stock perspective and sales, net income, output, and value added from a flow perspective are utilised. The ownership concentration, beyond the perspective of wealth inequality or equity, relates to the ownership structure of enterprises, the most important production organisation in a capitalist economy that recognises private ownership of means of production. In other words, the concentration of ownership as a concentration of economic power means that the enterprise's issued shares or remaining claims are concentrated in a small number of individuals or their families,[32] and this makes it a key issue for the allocation and utilisation of economic resources through the entity to individuals. Therefore, this problem is not separated from the problem in which the control of a company or a business group is wholly attributed to an individual.[33]

In Korea, chaebol exists as entities that embody the concentration of economic power that is understood from various perspectives. First of all, with regard to market concentration, according to a survey in 2015, the industry concentration was 49.2% when the affiliates of the conglomerate were included in the top three companies in accordance with the CR3 criteria.[34] If the affiliates were not in the industry, the industry concentration was 45.2%. And the figure was 28.9% when the affiliates are entering the industry but are not included in the top three.[35] The figures suggest that chaebol affiliates' entry into an industry and increased market share are correlated with industrial concentration. It is also worth noting that, when looking at the cases of abuse of a market-dominant status, most of the abuses are found to be caused by

[31] See I Hwang, *경제력집중, 한국적 인식의 문제점 (Concentration of Economic Power, Problems of Korean Recognition)* (Korea Economic Research Institute 1997) 25.

[32] *Ibid.* at 26.

[33] *Ibid.* at 27.

[34] This means the sum of the market shares of companies within the top three.

[35] See KFTC, 'Announcement of the Results of Market Structure Survey as of 2015' (Press release 27 April 2018) 11.

TABLE 6.1 *Change of total assets and GDP (2010–2019)*

	2010	2011	2012	2013	2014	2015	2016	2017	2018	2019
Total assets	703 (581)	816 (706)	940 (798)	1,018 (886)	1,074 (970)	1,122 (936)	1,166 (945)	1,213 (1,011)	1,298 (1,107)	1,352 (1,167)
GDP	1,323 (1,094)	1,389 (1,202)	1,440 (1,223)	1,501 (1,306)	1,563 (1,411)	1,658 (1,383)	1,741 (1,411)	1,836 (1,531)	1,898 (1,619)	1,919 (1,657)

Units: trillion Won(billion US$)

affiliates belonging to chaebol.[36] It is also noteworthy that the current Monopoly Regulation Act targets business groups with assets of more than 10 trillion won in affiliates for special regulations. In 2020, 27 business groups controlled by the owner that can be classified as chaebol have an average of 48.2 affiliates. This situation suggests that concentration in individual markets in Korea is closely related to chaebol. The general concentration by chaebol is also increasing in Korea. Table 6.1 shows how general concentration by the top 10 chaebols has been developing in Korea since 2010 through changes in total assets and GDP.

The total asset growth rate of the 10 largest chaebols during the period was 92.3%, well above the GDP growth rate of 45.0%. Also, compared with GDP, the total assets of the top 10 chaebols rose from 53.1% in 2010 to 70.5% in 2019. These figures indicate that chaebols account for a large portion of the national economy and that this trend is also deepening, increasing the general concentration of chaebol. It is hard to find a case in which chaebols have not shown complete control by their owners in terms of ownership concentration. However, as noted earlier, this control is not achieved by an absolute interest. As of 2019, only 0.9% of the top 10 chaebols hold stakes in affiliates held by their heads, while only 2.4% of them have such stakes held by family members. However, 54.3% of the shares are held between affiliates by cross or circular shareholdings. Such an equity relationship allows the owner to exercise 100% control over the entire group. Therefore, the issue of ownership concentration could be replaced by the issue of having full control of a chaebol with a small stake and whether there is a mechanism in place to check them internally and externally to ensure managerial efficiency.

To sum up the above analysis, chaebols are becoming economic entities that embody the concentration of economic power at each level of market concentration, general concentration, and ownership concentration. It is also important to note that these three types of economic concentration define the complex nature of chaebol. In other words, market concentration can be intensified by large business groups,[37]

36 Of the cases (69 cases) of abuse of market dominant position regulated by Korea Fair Trade Commission since 2000, more than 70% were cases (50 cases) of abuse by affiliates of chaebol.

37 The expansion of chaebol's general concentration may affect their affiliates' market concentration in individual markets by brand effects (image utilization effects), internal financial effects, and

general concentration can be increased by strengthening the dominant position maintained in a large number of markets, and problems can be aggravated by the fact that ownership concentration is used to control large business groups.[38] As a result of this complex nature, attempts of regulating to address one type of economic concentration will inevitably only have limited effect.

It is hard to deny that chaebol has made positive contributions to economic development in Korea.[39] However, chaebol has also had negative consequences, and in particular, the concentration of economic power within the chaebol. Chaebol's concentration of economic power accounts for a high portion of the national economy, and this concentration continues to grow, negatively affecting individual markets. In addition, the phenomenon of almost absolute control being concentrated on the owner creates centralisation. The overall characteristics of this pattern of economic concentration are also concerning. Chaebols are also seen negatively from non-economic perspectives. Economic power concentrated on chaebol is cited as one of the main factors of social instability, as it is a source of deepening wealth inequality and polarisation problems; furthermore, the concentration of economic resources on a small number of individuals could undermine the foundation of democracy.[40] While the importance of such problems and the discussion of these issues should not be denied, for the order and operation of the economy, the core of the problem of chaebol is the concentration of economic power leading to a disruption to the market economy, which should be maintained as mandated by the constitution.[41] The general concentration of chaebol can have a negative impact on competition in individual markets. In addition, the concentration of decision-making authority during the course of the chaebol's operations can lead to inefficient resource allocation, which is recognised as a concrete example of this problem.

6.3 REGULATION OF CHAEBOL

6.3.1 *Significance and Contents of the First Chaebol Regulation*

The first legislation aimed directly at regulating chaebols was made by the First Amendment of the Monopoly Regulation Act in 1986, and it is necessary to examine the meaning of the legislation itself. First of all, it is highly significant that the

aggregation of resources. See D Cho, 한국재벌 *(Korean Chaebol)* (Maeil Business Newspaper Publisher 1997) 18–28.

38 In this regard, the three types of economic concentration do not always evolve in the same direction, and the diversification of large enterprise groups increases general concentration but reduces market concentration, see Hwang (n 29) 26.

39 Initial capital accumulation, active performance of R&D, utilization of economic resources including human resources, and leading investment in high value-added industries promoted by competition between chaebols are mentioned.

40 Regarding the correlation between the expansion of political democracy and the strengthening of competition policies, see D Gerber, *Law and Competition in Twentieth Century Europe* (Oxford University Press 2001) 16.

41 N Seong, 헌법학 *(Constitutional Law)* (Beopmunsa 2013) 271–272.

legislation was made through a revision of the Monopoly Regulation Act, Korea's competition law. This demonstrated the legislative determination to deal with the chaebol issue from the perspective of competition policy. It is also important to note that while institutionalising chaebol regulations, the government proposed suppression of the concentration of economic power as the title of the regulation clause. This legislation reflects the perception that the essence of the chaebol problem is economic concentration. Finally, it should be noted that the Japanese Anti-Monopoly Act had a significant impact on legislation at that time. Japan's Anti-Monopoly Act was enacted as part of its economic democratisation policy after World War II and the intent to avoid an economic operation method centred on zaibatsu (chaebol),[42] which was the basis of the previous wartime economic operation.[43] The Allied Military Government dismantled the existing zaibatsu and later imposed a ban on holding companies in Anti-Monopoly Act enacted in 1947 to prevent the formation of new zaibatsu.[44] In addition, as companies belonging to disbanded zaibatsus gradually formed keiretsus(affiliates), reflecting concerns that such a keiretsu could lead to market rigidity, the Anti-Monopoly Act was amended in 1977 to introduce regulations limiting the total amount of shares that can be held in companies belonging to the same keiretsu.[45] In the Korean economy, chaebol held an important position similar to that of zaibatsu in Japan before World War II, and for this reason, the Japanese Anti-Monopoly Act became a strong legislative model for the revision of the Monopoly Regulation Act.

According to the original regulations, a regulation banning holding companies was introduced, and a system was enacted to regulate the equity investments of large enterprise groups, which organised chaebols under a legal conception. Specifically, Article 7–2 of the revised 1986 Act prohibited the establishment of holding companies, and Article 7–3 stipulated the prohibition of mutual investment, Article 7–4 limited the total amount of investment, and Article 7–5 restricted the voting rights of insurance and financial companies belonging to large enterprise groups.

The holding company was the method used to form a zaibatsu before World War II, and therefore the Japanese Anti-Monopoly Act limited the powerful means of forming a zaibatsu through regulations prohibiting such. Although chaebols were not utilising a holding company structure at that time, concerns that a holding company system could be an easy way to control a large number of companies

[42] While Japan's zaibatsu, which existed before World War II, had similar characteristics to Korea's chaebol in that they were composed of multiple affiliates run by the owner family, they were distinguished from Korea's chaebol in that they were composed of holding companies, had banks inside the group, and played a key role in the wartime economy.

[43] See E Hadley, *Antitrust in Japan* (Princeton University Press 1970) 496.

[44] See S Kisugi, '日本の競争政策の歴史的概観(1): 戰前から1977年改正まで' (A Historical Overview of Competition Policy in Japan: From Pre-War to Revision 1977) in Akira Gotou (ed), *Competition Policy in Japan* (Tokyo University Press 1998) 20–23.

[45] See A Gotou, '一般集中關聯およびその制定，制定後の經緯' (The Progress of General Concentration and Its Enactment and Post-Enactment), in A Gotou (ed), *Competition Policy in Japan* (Tokyo University Press 1998) 235.

with small capital, given Japan's regulatory cases, led to the introduction of a regulation banning holding companies in the Monopoly Regulation Act as a precautionary measure.

It is also noteworthy that legislation regarding existing chaebols regulated their equity investments instead of directly demanding structural changes such as dismantling enterprise groups. At that time, chaebols were generally forming enterprise groups through circular shareholding structures, so the regulation on investment limited the formation or maintenance of enterprise groups. In order to clarify the chaebol subject to regulation, a large group of enterprises was designated among chaebols when certain legal scale and structural requirements were met,[46] and a regulatory framework was established. First, cross(mutual)-shareholdings between affiliates were prohibited in principle. However, since these regulations had limits to regulating circular (not mutual)-shareholdings, to compensate for this regulation were introduced as a second prohibition that uniformly limited the total amount of investments made by affiliates[47] belonging to large enterprise groups. The regulation on the ceiling for total amount of investment was expected to be a regulation that could have a real impact on the structure of the enterprise group that involved such things as circular investment.[48] As a third prohibition, regulations were introduced to limit voting rights of shares of affiliates held by financial and insurance companies belonging to large enterprise groups, which were also aimed at preventing huge amounts of funds being raised from customers and used like private coffers to expand or strengthen their affiliates.

6.3.2 *Changes in Holding Company Regulations*

The change from a ban of a holding company to a system that allows them in principle stems from the revision of the Monopoly Regulation Act in February 1999. Originally, the ban was justified based on concerns that holding companies could be a means of forming a large enterprise group by controlling a large number of companies with very small capital. However, this perception changed and led to a fundamental shift in regulation.

In particular, the revision of the Japanese Anti-Monopoly Act in 1997, which became a legislative model, had a significant impact on changes to regulations on holding companies under the Monopoly Regulation Act. In Japan, it was considered that holding companies are no longer likely to function as a means of forming

[46] According to Art 21 (1) and (2) of the Enforcement Decree of the current Monopoly Regulation Act, large enterprise groups have been dualized into groups of companies subject to mutual investment restrictions or disclosures, and the former has total assets of at least 10 trillion Won, while the latter is based on at least 5 trillion Won.

[47] It means a company controlled by the owner.

[48] See KFTC, *시장경제 창달의 발자취 – 공정거래위원회 20년사 (The Footprint of Market Economy – 20 Years' History of Korea Fair Trade Commission)* (KFTC 2001) 86.

zaibatsu, and that companies need to be given a choice to take advantage of the positive functions of holding companies. The law as was thus changed prohibiting holding companies only when business control was excessively concentrated.[49] This change in Japan led to a reconsideration of holding companies with respect to the Monopoly Regulation Act in Korea. The functional advantages of holding companies due to the separation of ownership and management between companies, and the fact that the holding company system is relatively transparent compared to the existing chaebol structure based on circular investments, were highlighted in the debates around the changes in Korea. Yet, certain restrictions were imposed on holding companies and subsidiaries, reflecting the view that there was still concern that holding companies would become means of concentration of economic power. Article 8–2(1) of the 1999 Amendment prohibited holding liabilities exceeding the amount of net assets (No. 1), holding shares of subsidiaries less than 50/100 (No. 2 30/100 in the case of listed subsidiaries), holding shares for controlling purposes in domestic companies other than subsidiaries (No. 3) and general holding companies having financial and insurance subsidiaries and financial holding companies having general subsidiaries according to the principle of separation of financial and industrial capital (Nos. 4 and 5). In addition, it was in principle prohibited for a subsidiary of a holding company to have a grandchild company under Article 8–2(2). The above-mentioned regulations on holding companies, in particular those under paragraph 1 No. 2 and those on subsidiaries under paragraph 2, are deeply related to attempts to block the possibility of enterprise groups expanding horizontally or vertically.[50] This restriction reflects the legislative intention to address concentration of economic power.

After the changes to the law on holding companies, it was expected that a number of large enterprise groups would introduce a holding company system, and the Korea Fair Trade Commission (hereafter KFTC)'s policy reflected that change. Above all, the enhanced transparency and efficiency of corporate governance of holding companies as compared to the circular structure, typical of chaebol, have become a corner stone for policy formation.[51] Yet, since not many chaebols switched to holding company systems, measures have been sought to facilitate the transition to a holding company. As a result, the revisions to the law continued to ease the restrictions imposed on holding companies. The actions regulated under Article 8–2(1) of the current Monopoly Regulation Act include holding more than twice the total amount of capital, owning shares of a subsidiary less than 40/100 of the

49 See A Gotou, '一般集中の規制' (The Regulation of General Concentration) in A Gotou (ed), *Competition Policy in Japan* (Tokyo University Press 1998) 238. Meanwhile, with the revision of the Japan Anti-Monopoly Act in 2002, exceptional regulations on holding companies were replaced in a way that regulates excessive business controlling power regardless of company type.

50 See D Lee, *지주회사 (Holding Company)* (Sechang 2001) 24 and below.

51 See M Hong, *재벌의 경제력집중 규제 (Regulation of Economic Concentration of Chaebol)* (Kyunginmunwhasa 2006) 175–176.

total number of shares issued by that subsidiary, owning shares of a domestic company that is not an affiliate in excess of 5/100 of the total number of shares issued by that company, or owning shares of domestic affiliates other than subsidiaries. The actions regulated under Article 8–2 (1) of the current Monopoly Regulation Act include holding more than twice the total amount of capital, owning shares of a subsidiary less than 40/100 of the total number of shares issued by that subsidiary, owning shares of a domestic company that is not an affiliate in excess of 5/100 of the total number of shares issued by that company, or owning shares of domestic affiliates other than subsidiaries. These requirements are considerably less stringent than those when imposed when holding companies were first allowed. The number of holding companies increased gradually in response to these eased requirements. After holding companies was allowed in 1999, only seven companies switched to the holding company system by 2000. But this number increased gradually with the deregulation, rising to 173 in 2019. It also appears that 39% of the large business groups have transformed their structure into a holding company-oriented one.

6.3.3 *Changes in Cross or Circular Investment Regulations*

The core of the regulations for large business groups is investment regulation, which is also the most controversial part of the process of changing the regulations. The legal prohibition of cross-shareholding was circumvented through indirect(circular) investment. Thus, a regulation on indirect investment relations was made to supplement the ban on mutual investments.

The investment ceiling regulation introduced in the original legislation was aimed at limiting the total investment in affiliates belonging to large business groups to a certain percentage of their net assets. This regulation was criticised as excessive for limiting unconditionally the investment on a formal basis without distinguishing the purpose or content of the investment. Moreover, such strict investment regulations could be a real impediment to the active investment activities of the entity. In addition, the issue of the effectiveness of the system in actually suppressing cross-shareholding Was strongly raised.[52] In 2009, the total investment ceiling regulation was finally abolished.

However, after the abolition of the total investment ceiling regulation, the amount of investments between affiliates belonging to large enterprise groups soared significantly. Table 6.2 highlights changes to the equity ratios of the owner, family, and affiliates in the Top 10 large enterprise groups with owners since 2004.

Due to this situation, concerns over chaebol's concentration of economic power arose again, and it served as an opportunity to seek legislative countermeasures. As a result, a regulation banning new circular investments was introduced by the 2014 revision of the Act. While not prohibiting established curricular investments, Article

[52] See M Hong, *경제법론I(Theory of Economic Law I)* (Kyunginmunwhasa 2008) 177–178.

TABLE 6.2 *Equity ratio of owner, family, and affiliate*[53]

	2004 (%)	2006 (%)	2008 (%)	2010 (%)	2012 (%)	2014 (%)	2016 (%)	2018 (%)	2019 (%)
Owner	1.3	1.4	1.1	1.0	0.9	0.9	0.9	0.8	0.9
Family	3.1	3.7	3.2	3.1	2.7	2.8	2.6	2.5	2.4
Affiliate	43.3	46.0	45.6	44.0	52.8	49.5	54.9	55.2	54.3

9–2(2) of the Amended Act, prohibit a company belonging to a large enterprise group from forming or strengthening a new circular investment.

6.3.4 *Other Attempts of Regulation*

The first large enterprise group regulation was based on a ban on the establishment of holding companies and the regulation of investments between affiliates by existing large enterprise groups, but it was questionable whether such a system was sufficient to curb the concentration of economic power by chaebol. Thus, legislative supplementation continued; first was the regulation on debt guarantees, which was introduced by the revision to the law in 1992. The debt guarantees between affiliates could pose financial risks to the entire group and problems with the inefficient allocation of resources. The first inter-affiliates debt guarantee regulation was limited to 200% of capital but was lowered to 100% under the revision in 1996, and the regulation was strengthened by prohibiting debt guarantees entirely after the revision in 1998.

The thought that chaebol problems could be corrected by the market's ability to adjust autonomously also had an important impact on changes to the regulations on large enterprise groups. The legislation reflected the recognition that inefficient governance or management in the capital market or commodity market can be controlled, and that it is important for enterprise groups to provide key information so that these functions can be exercised effectively. Thus, obligations were imposed with regard to disclosure of prior resolutions and key details of the board of directors (as revised Monopoly Regulation Act in December 1999), disclosure of important matters of unlisted companies belonging to large enterprise groups (as revised in December 2004), and disclosure of the status of large business groups (as revised in March 2009).

As a type of unfair trade practices, regulations on unfair support practices also have important implications in relation to curbing the concentration of economic power by chaebol. In the course of running a group of companies, support for uncompetitive affiliates is not only a means of maintaining and expanding the economic

[53] KFTC, 'Status of Stock Ownership of Enterprise Groups Subject to Disclosure in 2019' (n 19)

concentration. At the same time, it can lead to a negative impact on the national economy through the inefficient allocation of resources as a result of such transactions with marginal enterprises. The regulation of unfair support practices introduced through the revision of the Monopoly Regulation Act 1996 was prescribed in a way that regulates unfair trade practices, but as discussed in the legislative process, the substance of the regulation focuses on the inter-affiliate transactions that take place within large enterprise groups.[54] From a competition policy point of view, the significance of regulating unfair support practices can be understood in two ways. First, it is noteworthy that it provided a basis for the control of chaebol's group operations from the perspective of individual markets. Regulating the specific actions of chaebol as unfair trading practices in individual markets may be in line with the structure of competition laws formed to protect competition in individual markets Second, this approach is meaningful in that it can contribute to curbing economic concentration in terms of general concentration. In addition, the regulation of unfair support practices was carried out by ex-post evaluation of transactions, unlike other economic concentration regulations based on the imposition of ex-ante obligations, which meant that they were outside of the uniform and formal regulatory framework. The regulation of unfair support acts can be said to be a unique type of regulation of the Korean Monopoly Regulation Act that is difficult to find in other countries, so there are difficulties in forming regulatory legal principles for unfair support practices. But to some extent, such principles have been established through the regulatory practices of KFTC and court rulings. The Supreme Court ruled, in relation to the unfairness of such support practices, that:

> It is based on whether fair trade is likely to be infringed upon due to the support practice that hinders competition in the relevant market or causes concentration of economic power.[55]

Thus, the Supreme Court presented the effects on competition in individual market and concentration of economic power as a double criterion for determining the unfairness of support practices.

The introduction of these regulations and the composition of legal principles were assessed to be appropriate, but there were certain limitations to the actual regulations. In particular, the law needed strengthening in the case of transactions conducted for the purpose of obtaining profits for individuals with special relationships with affiliates, where measures did not fall under support practices or not meeting the requirements of unfairness. Thus, in 2013, Article 23–2 was introduced under the Monopoly Regulation Act. This article prohibited certain transactions where

[54] According to a 2002 survey, internal transactions accounted for 38.1 percent of the total sales of the top five large enterprise groups. Wongeun Song and Sangho Lee (n 26) 148–149. The 2019 survey showed that the portion of internal transactions in the top 10 large enterprise groups owned was 13.8 percent. See KFTC, 'Status of internal transactions of enterprise groups subject to disclosure in 2019' (Press release 15 October 2019) 1.

[55] Supreme Court, 2001Du7220 12. 3. 2004 (S Kor).

the owner or his family obtains private profits through a transaction in particular by means of the attribution of interests.[56] The significance of the regulation can be viewed positively, but the difficulty of judging unfairness still remains and the question of whether the regulation will be effective has not been resolved.[57]

6.4 DIRECTION OF DISCUSSION ON IMPROVING CHAEBOL REGULATIONS

6.4.1 *Adequacy of Subject of Regulation*

Under the Monopoly Regulation Act, chaebol regulations were introduced with the aim of curbing them as the concentration of economic power by chaebols intensified. However, the chaebol themselves were not accepted as legal concepts, and as aforesaid, large enterprise groups of a certain size[58] and structure as a group of multiple affiliates were subject to regulation. At the time of legislation, no differentiation took place between the large enterprise groups and economic entities generally perceived as chaebols. Hence, there was no problem with the subjects of this regulation other than pointing out the inadequacy of intentionally avoiding the term chaebol that had negative implications for the public in Korea. Most of the large enterprise groups that were initially designated shared the characteristic elements of chaebol. Absolute control by the owners and their families. Thus, the concept of large enterprise groups of a particular size and the requirement of having multiple companies was not problematic in embracing chaebol as regulatory targets.

However, problems began to materialise when a group of state-owned enterprises or an enterprise group without governance by natural people was designated as a large enterprise group. There was no control by the owner as a natural person in this enterprise group, thus lacking the problem of ownership concentration that was traditionally perceived as a problem of chaebol. This raised the question of whether the regulations formed to target chaebol were not over-inclusive. Discussions on this

56 Motives for internal transactions, regardless of efficiency, are represented by tunneling and propping, and this regulation is meaningful as a regulation on internal transactions conducted for tunneling motives. See M Baek, 'An Empirical Study on Tunneling Using Internal Transaction Data among Affiliates of Large Enterprise Groups' (PhD thesis, Seoul National University 2019) 21–27.

57 In addition, efforts to improve the governance structure under the Commercial Act are also meaningful as regulations on chaebol. The outside directors and compliance support personnel as internal control systems were introduced in the commercial law, and the introduction of intensive voting, written voting, and electronic voting systems to protect minority shareholder interests can also be seen as part of improving governance structure. Such a system can be seen as a certain contribution to improving the governance structure of affiliates belonging to conglomerates. However, since the governance problems of chaebol have the dual nature of individual corporate governance and corporate group governance, attempts to improve governance will inevitably have certain limitations under the Commercial Act.

58 At the time of legislation, relative criteria were adopted by the gross asset ranking (30th), and the 2001 amendment to the Monopoly Regulation Act changed to absolute criteria.

issue led to the conclusion that even enterprise groups without an owner are subject to the regulation because enterprise groups without owners can also cause problems with regard to general concentration. In particular, since the 2000s, the increase in the number of affiliates belonging to enterprise groups without an owner, and the expansion of the total size, have served as a strong basis for supporting this approach.[59]

However, discussions continue regarding the need for differentiated regulation between enterprise groups that still have owners (traditional chaebol) and those that have flagship companies at the centre without personal control. Furthermore, the emergence of new types of large enterprise groups is drawing attention. As the digital economy develops, digital companies of such as Naver, Kakao, Netmarble, and Nexon Group are included in the regulation list because they meet the requirements of large enterprise groups. These enterprise groups, which follow the growth of the IT industry, are emerging as the new large enterprise groups. Yet, there are significant differences between such companies and traditional chaebols in terms of governance and distribution of industries. Specifically, the emerging enterprise groups are characterised by the fact that control over the enterprise group is largely not based on a circular ownership structure, that the business sectors are concentrated in the IT sector and do not show a tendency to diversify non-related sectors, and that their status as platform operators is being strengthened, suggesting the need for change to the regulatory system that was formed with consideration towards traditional chaebol.

6.4.2 *Approach by Type of Enterprise Groups*

The above discussion could be expanded to transform a single regulatory framework into a regulatory framework commensurate with the characterisation of enterprise groups. As mentioned, about 40% of large business groups are switching to holding company systems. Groups with holding company systems differ from groups that have not transitioned in terms of the way of control and structural transparency, and this difference will need to be reflected in regulations.

These discussions also relate to the government's policy of encouraging holding companies. The KFTC focused on transparency in the governance structures of holding company systems and continuously implemented policies to expand holding companies. In the process, a number of rules were eased that initially imposed limits on holding companies being used as means to concentrate economic power, resulting in an increase in the number of enterprise groups that switched to holding companies.[60] Whether such a policy is still valid needs to be discussed, and if it is

[59] Among the large enterprise groups designated for 2019, POSCO, Nonghyup and KT groups were included as ownerless enterprise groups.

[60] The number of holding companies increased from 25 in 2005 to 173 in 2019. In 2019, there were 173 holding companies, 915 subsidiaries, 973 grandchildren and 95 great-grandchildren. And 23 groups of the 59 large enterprise groups switched to holding company structure as of 2019. See KFTC, 'Analysis of Holding Company Status Under Monopoly Regulation Act in 2019' (2019) 2–8.

indeed recognised as valid, additional challenges will be placed on how to adjust the content and level of regulations for holding companies and circular investments.

6.4.3 *Strengthening the Market vis-a-vis Chaebol*

As we saw earlier, regulations on chaebols are aimed at holding companies or large business groups, mainly by demanding a ban on certain activities regarding equity investments. The legitimacy of these regulations arises from the intent to effectively cope with the economic concentration problems caused by chaebol. It is important to keep in mind that it is the task of the Monopoly Regulation Act to address competition problems caused by chaebol in individual markets.

Although one should not deny the importance of regulation on unfair support practices and profit-taking practices of related parties as stipulated in the Monopoly Regulation Act, the effectiveness of these regulations has been questioned. It can be pointed out that it is still not easy to find a reasonable regulatory basis theoretically and practically. The Supreme Court showed that 'unfairness' has two aspects, competition restrictions and economic concentration. But it is not clear what aspects or factors of economic concentration can be considered in the context of unfairness, especially in the case of profit-taking practices of related parties. It will need to be supplemented in the future. Such improvements to legal principles will not only have a positive effect on strengthening the enforcement of regulators but will also result in regulatory clarity for market participants. Furthermore, this will make a meaningful contribution to increasing the market's autonomous control functions.

It is also necessary to look at the issue from the perspective of the protection or promotion of small- and medium-sized enterprises or independent companies that are not affiliated with chaebol. In other words, the concentration of economic power may be addressed through the growth of small- and medium-sized/independent companies. The regulation of chaebol and the protection of small- and medium-sized/independent enterprises can contribute to the suppression of economic concentration and the realisation of free and fair competition. The promotion of small- and medium-sized/independent companies can also be meaningful as a supplement to one-sided regulatory policies. To this end, it is important to provide an opportunity for the growth of small- and medium-sized/independent enterprises in various aspects.

In this regard, there can be no question as to the importance of traditional competition laws in ensuring that opportunities for the growth of small- and medium-sized/independent enterprises. In general, small- and medium-sized/independent enterprises and affiliates belonging to chaebol are related vertically or horizontally. In the case of vertical relationships, it is important to ensure that the trade relationship between small- and medium-sized/independent enterprises and chaebol affiliates is carried out fairly throughout the production and distribution process. In the case of horizontal relationships, it will be important to prevent anti-competitive behaviour.

Furthermore, various economic resource support programmes, including financing, will be needed so that competition between small- and medium-sized/independent enterprises and the affiliates under the umbrella of a chaebol can be substantive.

6.5 CONCLUSION

With the revision of the Monopoly Regulation Act in 1986, regulations on chaebol began to take place. Lawmakers at the time thought that the concentration of chaebol's economic power had a negative impact on the market economy order. This idea has so far been basically maintained. Various measures have been devised and institutionalised to curb the concentration of economic power. Nonetheless, when comparing the situation at the time of the first legislation and the present one, the concentration of economic power by chaebol has actually increased. In this respect, the effectiveness of the regulation may be questioned, but if we assume that there is no such regulation, it may be understood that the present condition is based on the minimum deterrent function of the regulations. The question is whether chaebol-oriented economic management methods will be effective even in the face of future platform-based changes to industries and the fierce competition for innovation, and such recognition should be reflected in the maintenance or revision of the chaebol regulatory framework under the current Monopoly Regulation Act. Of course, chaebol themselves are seeking improvement on these issues. However, there is still a need for support to ensure that these chaebol's own efforts will be effective. From this perspective, efforts to improve corporate governance, such as strengthening shareholders' rights and interests and enhancing the power of the Board of Directors under the Commercial Act, could make meaningful contributions. At this point, however, it is difficult to completely dispel concerns about the concentration of economic power in terms of general concentration or ownership concentration only by improving governance structure, and the need to regulate the entire enterprise group that is composed of affiliates will inevitably be considered positively. On the other hand, in pursuing chaebol policies, caution is required when it comes to the issue of social costs incurred in the formation and operation of business groups. Of course, there will be expenses incurred in forming and operating an enterprise group, but chaebol will only take into account their own private costs. Therefore, it is difficult to expect chaebol to include social costs, such as hindering the growth of competitive independent companies or distorting the efficient allocation of resources, among the costs to be considered when they evaluate their profits and expenses in the process of setting their goals. Such inconsistencies between private and social costs provide justification for regulatory agencies' policy interventions, while also serving as a limitation to remain within the scope as much as possible.

PART III

The Governance of Corporations

7

Antitrust by Interior Means

Ramsi A. Woodcock

7.1 INTRODUCTION

Monopoly is fundamentally a problem of imbalance of power among a firm's counterparties: the suppliers, workers, managers, shareholders, and consumers who do business with the firm.[1] The archetypical monopoly oppresses a particular counterparty – consumers – by charging them high prices for the products they buy from the monopoly.[2] In this case, consumers suffer, and one or more of the firm's other counterparties benefits: shareholders if the additional profits are paid to them as dividends; workers if the additional profits are paid to them as higher wages; suppliers if the additional profits are paid to them as higher supply prices; and managers if the additional profits are paid to them as higher executive compensation. But a firm can monopolize any of the markets in which the firm does business, not just the consumer-facing markets into which the firm sells its products.[3] The firm can monopolize – technically, monopsonize[4] – supply markets,

Wyatt, Tarrant & Combs Associate Professor of Law, University of Kentucky Rosenberg College of Law, Secondary Appointment, University of Kentucky Gatton College of Business and Economics. Marco Claudio Corradi, Daniel J. H. Greenwood, and Julian Nowag provided helpful comments. This research was supported by a grant from the John S. and James L. Knight Foundation.

1 A synonym for 'counterparties,' as the term is used in this chapter, is the term 'patrons' employed by Henry Hansmann in his work. See H Hansmann, *The Ownership of Enterprise* (The Belknap Press of Harvard University Press 1996) 12. The category of firm 'stakeholders' is somewhat broader because it includes victims of a firm, such as community members affected by pollution, who do not voluntarily do business with the firm. See R Edward Freeman and others, *Stakeholder Theory: The State of the Art* (Cambridge University Press 2010) 40–42. Through damages awards, courts effectively set the price at which such 'involuntary' counterparties do business with the firm. Because courts can set the price fairly, the governance alternative to antitrust described in this chapter is not needed to address problems of monopoly pricing in such involuntary markets. See R Woodcock, 'The Antitrust Duty to Charge Low Prices' (2018) 39 Cardozo L Rev 1741, 1764–66.

2 See H Varian, *Intermediate Microeconomics: A Modern Approach* (7th edn, WW Norton & Company 2006) 423–24.

3 See *ibid.* at 471–77.

4 For the sake of brevity, the term 'monopoly' and its derivatives will be used here to refer to market power whether exercised on the sell-side or the buy side. In the case of exercise of buyside power, the proper term is, technically, 'monopsony'.

labour markets, management markets, and even the market for investments in which shareholders compete (though that is unlikely because capital markets are so large).[5]

Every market monopolized by a firm is an opportunity for the firm to oppress the particular counterparty that stands on the other side of the market from the firm by charging the counterparty monopoly prices. In the extreme case in which the firm monopolizes all of the markets in which the firm does business – supply markets, labour markets, management markets, investment markets, and product markets – the firm has the ability to oppress all of its counterparties. Which counterparties will the firm actually oppress or, more to the point, which counterparty will the firm not oppress and will thereby benefit from the oppression of the other counterparties? Some party must benefit, as the firm is just the sum of its counterparties, a nexus of contracts, and cannot oppress for its own independent benefit.

The counterparty that the firm will favour is the counterparty that dominates the governance of the firm. That controlling counterparty will be able to induce the firm to charge monopoly prices to other counterparties but not to itself, and indeed will induce the firm to transfer the firm's monopoly profits to it. Therefore, not one but two sorts of power determine whether a firm will exercise monopoly power. First, the firm must actually have monopoly power in some market (with monopoly power defined as the ability profitably to manipulate the prices charged to the counterparty in that market).[6] Second, some other counterparty of the firm must have sufficient power over the governance of the firm to then induce the firm to exploit its ability to charge monopoly prices by actually charging them and then turning the resulting profits over to the controlling counterparty. In the classic case, the firm that charges consumers high prices does so only because (1) the firm has a monopoly position in the market in which the firm sells its products and (2) shareholders of the firm – counterparties in the market for financing in which the firm also participates – use their control over the governance of the firm to insist that the firm charge consumers the highest possible prices and turn the resulting profits over to shareholders in the form of dividends or share buybacks.

The law, therefore, has not one but two possible ways of dealing with the problem of monopoly. The first is to prevent firms from acquiring monopoly power in

[5] See Hansmann (n 2) 54 (observing that '[t]he capital market today is so large relative to the size of any individual firm that no firm has market power as a borrower of capital.'). A firm can nevertheless always interact with shareholders as would a monopolist because shareholders cannot withdraw their funds from the firm – they have no general right to return of capital and so are locked into the firm. See *ibid* at 71–72. Selling their shares is no alternative, for they can obtain their investment from a share buyer only if the buyer can expect the firm to pay out the same amount or more on the shares in future in the form of dividends or buybacks.

[6] See J Kirkwood, 'Market Power and Antitrust Enforcement' (2018) 98 BU L Rev 1169, 1172.

markets. That is the traditional role of antitrust law. But antitrust is an imperfect fix because often monopoly power results from superior performance, rather than anticompetitive conduct, and, in such cases, antitrust cannot intervene to eliminate monopoly power without running the risk of slowing economic growth.[7] The second way of dealing with the problem of monopoly is to prevent any one counterparty of the firm from acquiring so much power over the governance of the firm as to be able to direct the firm to charge monopoly prices to counterparties in markets in which the firm has monopoly power. The great advantage of this second, governance-based solution is that, unlike antitrust laws, it can be used to stop monopoly pricing even when the firm has acquired its monopoly position through superior performance and the elimination of that position would therefore be destructive.

But how to prevent any one counterparty from taking control over firm governance? None of the familiar approaches to governance fits the bill. Shareholder-run firms give shareholders control.[8] Employee-run firms give employees control.[9] Consumer cooperatives give consumers control.[10] Supplier-run firms give suppliers control.[11] Management-dominated firms give managers control. The solution proposed here is to give each major category of counterparty apart from managers – workers, shareholders, consumers, and suppliers – an equal vote in the election of the corporate board that manages the firm. Thus, management will be checked by the other counterparties, and the other counterparties will check each other. This approach will tend to leave managers with a lot of discretion, because oversight will be dispersed among firm counterparties rather than concentrated in one. But it will also provide a democratic check on any attempt by one counterparty to exploit the firm's monopoly power to oppress the others, one that does not exist when only one counterparty dominates firm governance. The benefit of less exercise of monopoly power may outweigh the cost of less oversight over management.

The fact that the exploitation of monopoly power divides counterparties by enabling some to take from others, combined with the fact that monopoly can strike any market, making all counterparties potential victims of the exploitation of monopoly power by the firm, means that counterparties as a group have an interest in working together to block the exploitation of monopoly power in relation to any one counterparty, much the way a country's citizens have the incentive to oppose the oppression of any one group of citizens by any other because all are potentially vulnerable to abuse. Counterparties can express this common interest, however, only if they all have a voice in firm governance.

7 See *United States v Aluminum Co of America* 148 F 2d 416, 429–30 (2d Cir 1945); R, 'The Obsolescence of Advertising in the Information Age' (2018) 127 Yale LJ 2270, 2309–14; R Woodcock, 'Digital Monopoly without Regret' [2020] (1) Concurrences 53, 54–55.

8 See Hansmann (n 2) 53–66.

9 See *ibid*. at 66–120.

10 See *ibid*. at 149–68.

11 See *ibid*. at 120–49.

7.2 USING CORPORATE GOVERNANCE TO PREVENT THE EXPLOITATION OF MONOPOLY POWER

7.2.1 *The Exploitation of Monopoly Power by Firms as a Function of the Governance Power of Counterparties*

To see why corporate governance determines whether a firm will exploit monopoly power, consider how wealth is distributed between the counterparties of a firm.

All transactions create surplus understood as the difference between the value the buyer places on the goods and the necessarily lower value the seller places on them.[12] Price divides the surplus between buyer and seller.[13] Netting the firm's cash inflows and outflows gives the overall amount of surplus kept by the firm through all of its transactions in all of the markets in which the firm does business. The rest of the surplus goes to each of the firm's counterparties. Thus, the worker who would work for $7 but is paid $12 by the firm takes $5 in surplus. The consumer who would pay $20 but is charged $18 by the firm takes $2 in surplus, the supplier who would sell for $1 but is paid $2 by the firm takes $1 in surplus, and so on. This calculus applies even to the firm's suppliers of cash qua commodity, the shareholders.[14] The shareholder who would invest $10 for a 10% return of $1 but receives the equivalent of a 20% return in the form of $2 in dividends takes 10% – $1 – as surplus.

In competitive markets, the surplus taken by counterparties of the firm through the markets in which they transact with the firm is fixed because the firm has no power to vary the prices the firm charges in competitive markets.[15] The competitive price guarantees counterparties a certain level of surplus that the firm cannot eliminate.[16] If $12 is the competitive wage, the firm cannot pay $11, because then workers would go to work for the firm's competitors instead. If the competitive product price is $18, then the firm cannot raise the price to $19, because then consumers would buy from competitors instead. If the competitive supply price is $2, then the firm cannot pay $1 because then suppliers would supply to the firm's competitors instead. If the competitive rate of return is 20%, then the firm cannot pay a 10% return to shareholders, because then investors will not buy any new shares that the firm wishes to sell and will invest in competitors instead.

[12] See R Woodcock, 'The Antitrust Case for Consumer Primacy in Corporate Governance' (2020) 10 UC Irvine L Rev 1395, 1403–09.

[13] This follows immediately from the basic definitions of consumer and producer surplus in partial equilibrium. See H Hovenkamp, *Federal Antitrust Policy: The Law of Competition and Its Practice* (6th edn, West Academic Publishing 2016) 6.

[14] See D Greenwood, 'The Dividend Puzzle: Are Shares Entitled to the Residual?' (2006) 32 J Corp L 103, 117 ('[T]he stockholders [are] a factor of production that has sold capital to the firm[.]').

[15] See Varian (n 3) 289.

[16] See *ibid.* at 410–12.

The competitive price also guarantees the firm a certain level of surplus – the profit that the firm makes in competitive markets.[17] As a surplus, this profit is technically not necessary to make the firm function.[18] It represents the excess of receipts over the payments the firm must make to counterparties in order to operate. But, despite representing an excess in receipts over the amount needed by the firm to function, this profit is not due to monopoly – not a monopoly profit – because it is earned in competitive markets. Instead, this profit is due to scarcity, the fact that the firm's other counterparties are more productive than those with which the firm's competitors contract. The profit the firm earns in competitive markets is therefore properly called scarcity rent.[19]

The counterparty that dominates the governance of the firm takes this scarcity rent. In an investor-owned firm, that counterparty is the shareholder, whose right to the firm's share of the surplus – the firm's profits – is known as the shareholder's right to the 'residual' earnings of the firm.[20] Thus, the investor of $10 who would be perfectly happy with a competitive $2 return on this investment nevertheless takes an additional $4, $20, or $100 – whatever the amount of the scarcity rents generated by the firm may be. Corporate governance and tax scholars debate what should be done with those scarcity rents.[21] Putting workers in control of the firm would ensure that workers take them. Putting consumers in control of the firm would ensure that consumers take them. Allowing managers to manage without supervision from other counterparties would ensure that managers take them. A properly designed corporate tax would ensure that the government takes them.[22] And so on.

But we are not concerned in this chapter with the distribution of the surplus generated by the firm in competitive markets. Monopoly interests us. Suppose, therefore, that the firm monopolizes at least one of its markets. Monopoly power is the power to dictate price, and so it is the power to extract more surplus from a counterparty than the firm would be able to extract in a competitive market. The firm can now pay the worker $7, charge the consumer $20, pay the supplier $1, or pay the shareholder a 10% return, for example, depending on which market the firm monopolizes. But will the firm actually exercise its monopoly power and extract

[17] See *ibid.* at 412–14.

[18] See Woodcock, 'The Antitrust Case for Consumer Primacy in Corporate Governance' (n 14) 1413–15. The seller necessarily places a lower value on the goods, otherwise the buyers would not be willing to pay a price that the seller would accept.

[19] See D Teece and M Coleman, 'The Meaning of Monopoly: Antitrust Analysis in High-Technology Industries' (1998) 43 Antitrust Bull 801, 819–20; R Woodcock, 'Antimonopolism as a Symptom of American Political Dysfunction' (2021) Social Science Research Network Working Paper No. 3864585 https://papers.ssrn.com/sol3/papers.cfm?abstract_id=3864585 accessed 7 July 2021.

[20] See Hansmann (n 2) 11.

[21] See generally L Kaplow, *The Theory of Taxation and Public Economics* (Princeton University Press 2011); Hansmann (n 2).

[22] See Kaplow (n 23) 236–38.

extra surplus from the counterparty in the market that the firm monopolizes? This is where corporate governance meets antitrust. If the counterparty in the market monopolized by the firm has control over the governance of the firm, then the answer is no. The firm will not exploit its monopoly power to extract additional surplus from the counterparty. If the firm monopolizes capital markets (to pick an unlikely example), and shareholders are willing to accept a minimum of a 10% return, then the firm could insist on paying only that 10% return, rather than the 20% that the firm would pay in a competitive capital market. But if the shareholders are in control of the firm, that will not happen. Instead, shareholders will continue to pay themselves the 20% competitive return, plus any scarcity rents generated by the firm in other markets. Similarly, if a firm is dominated by labour, the firm will not exploit any monopoly power the firm may have in labour markets to pay $7 to the worker who would receive $12 in a competitive labour market. Instead, the firm will pay $12 – the competitive wage rate – despite having the power to pay less. And the firm will pay out to workers, as bonuses at the end of the year, any scarcity rents that the firm earns in other markets.

If, however, governance of the firm is dominated by a counterparty other than the one operating in the market that is monopolized by the firm, then the firm will exploit its monopoly power to charge prices that extract additional surplus from the monopolized market. The governance-dominating counterparty will then arrange to appropriate that additional surplus from the firm. The shareholder-dominated firm will, for example, pay $7 to the worker if the firm monopolizes the labour market or $20 to consumers if the firm monopolizes the product market. The shareholders will pay the additional surplus extracted thereby – $5 more from the worker or $2 more from the consumer – to themselves in the form of higher dividends or share buybacks. The additional surplus extracted by the firm due to the exercise of its monopoly power is monopoly rent.[23] When a governance-dominating counterparty induces a monopolist to exercise its monopoly power, the counterparty extracts from other counterparties not only the scarcity rents that the governance-dominating counterparty would enjoy were the firm to operate in competitive markets but also additional monopoly rents.[24]

This is possible, however, only if the firm has a governance-dominating counterparty. If instead, no counterparty dominates governance of the firm, then the firm will not exploit its monopoly power, and the firm will instead behave as if it were operating in competitive markets even when the firm is in fact monopolizing the markets in which the firm does business. Imagine a firm in which workers, suppliers, shareholders (suppliers of cash subject to no absolute repayment obligation), and consumers were each collectively to have one vote for each member of the board that manages the firm. Management – understood to mean both the board

[23] See Teece and Coleman (n 21) 822.

[24] See *ibid.*

and the managers responsible for day-to-day operations – would, as under current shareholder-dominated business forms, have no vote, but management's day-to-day control over the firm would presumably give management equal power to defend its own interests, which power would, as under current forms, be checked by those voting on the membership of the board. Under this new structure, each counterparty would insist upon competitive pricing for other counterparties in exchange for others' insistence upon competitive pricing for itself. For each counterparty would fear that, absent others' support, the firm might one day seek to charge the counterparty monopoly prices. Thus, each counterparty would vote for board members who insist upon competitive pricing in all markets in which the firm does business, notwithstanding any power the firm may have to charge monopoly prices.

One might reasonably ask why counterparties with equal governance power might not instead seek to demand prices that equalise the division of surplus between the counterparties. In every market in which a firm does business, the firm stands on one side of the transaction, either taking money in or paying money out. After deducting outflows from inflows, the firm divides any resulting profits (such as, in competitive markets, scarcity rents) among counterparties by making cash payments to them (e.g., to the shareholders in a shareholder-dominated firm). One can imagine a firm choosing prices in every market in which the firm does business to ensure that the surplus enjoyed by each counterparty, after accounting both for the value the counterparty derives from market transactions with the firm and for the share of firm profits paid to the counterparty by the firm, is equal.

For example, imagine that a worker, supplier, shareholder, and manager were each to place a value of $8 on what they supply to the firm, the firm were to pay $8 to each, a consumer were to place a value of $42 on the firm's product, and the firm were to charge $40 to the consumer. In that case, the firm could pay its profit of $8 ($40 less the $32 total cost of buying from the other counterparties) in equal parts of $2 each to the worker, supplier, shareholder, and manager, equalising the surplus enjoyed by each counterparty. The consumer, who would receive no transfer of profits from the firm, would nevertheless retain $2 of surplus in the product market thanks to having purchased a product the consumer values at $42 for a price of $40. There is no reason why the prices required to achieve this equal distribution of surplus – prices of $8 in each buyside market and a price of $40 to the consumer – should be competitive prices. If counterparties with equal governance power were to seek to equalise the surpluses they enjoy, then they would likely not compel the firm to charge competitive prices.

Counterparties having equal governance power would not seek to equalise their surpluses, however, because in order for counterparties to equalise their surpluses, they must reveal private information to each other regarding the value they place on what they supply or buy from the firm. To be able to equalise the surpluses in the example above, the firm must know that the worker, supplier, shareholder, and manager place an $8 value each on what they supply and that the consumer places a $42 value on the firm's product. To obtain a larger share of firm profit payouts, each has an incentive to lie about this value. The competitive price is, by contrast, one that the firm can find, at least in principle, in an objectively verifiable fashion, even in monopolized markets, by making bids or offers until supply is maximised in sell-side markets or until demand is maximised in buy-side markets. Because the competitive price is an externally determined benchmark, each counterparty can be certain that, in defending the competitive prices enjoyed by others, the counterparty is not falling victim to fraud.

We can, then, state the following theorem: *In order for the firm to exploit a position of domination in relation to one counterparty, that counterparty must itself occupy a position of subordination in relation to another counterparty – a counterparty that dominates governance of the firm. Absent that subordination of one counterparty to another, a firm will behave as if it were operating in competitive markets even when the firm is in fact a monopoly.*

7.2.2 *A Democratic Check on Management*

None of the business forms in use today suffices to ensure that no counterparty dominates; they all allow one counterparty or another to dominate governance. The most common type, the investor-owned firm, puts shareholders in control.[25] Consumer cooperatives put consumers in control.[26] Supplier cooperatives put suppliers in control.[27] Employee-owned firms put employees in control.[28] Non-profits tend to put managers in control thanks to tunnelling.[29] And so on. To the extent that the favoured counterparty in each of these business organisations actually succeeds at using its power to overcome management – something that is often debatable – these business forms shift the locus of domination away from managers but do not eliminate it.[30] Shareholder-run businesses will oppress all counterparties but shareholders. Consumer-run businesses will oppress all counterparties but consumers. Worker-run businesses will oppress all counterparties but workers. Supplier-run businesses will oppress all counterparties but suppliers.

One solution would be to expand the corporate board to enable each category of counterparty to choose an equal number of seats, effectively diffusing control over management among all counterparties in a bid to balance power between them.[31] But that would make the board vulnerable to deadlock, as the interests of the firm's

25 See Hansmann (n 2) 53–66.
26 See *ibid.* at 149–68.
27 See *ibid.* at 120–49.
28 See *ibid.* at 66–120.
29 See *ibid.* at 238–40.
30 See Greenwood (n 16) 152–53.
31 See R Kraakman and others, *The Anatomy of Corporate Law: A Comparative and Functional Approach* (3rd edn, Oxford University Press 2017) 95.

various counterparties are heterogeneous.[32] A better solution is to grant each category of counterparty the right to vote for all board seats: one vote each for shareholders collectively, workers collectively, other suppliers collectively, and consumers collectively. This would ensure that individual board members would not be beholden to any particular counterparty and so the board, once elected, would be able to act decisively as a unit. Indeed, the effect would be to strengthen management because there would be no possibility of total subordination to a controlling shareholder or other single counterparty. But this stronger management would still be subject to a check: the ability of the firm's counterparties as a group to vote the board out of office at the next election.[33] That would ensure that collective control does not result in paralysis, while still giving counterparties the power to restrain management if management undertakes actions that threaten all other counterparties as a group. Managers, control over the day-to-day administration of the firm would permit them to protect their own interests as counterparties. Indeed, the challenge will be to prevent managers from oppressing the other counterparties rather than to save managers from oppression.

A majority of counterparties would vote to replace the board in two circumstances. First, a majority would vote against the board when mismanagement threatens the fortunes of the firm generally. An underperforming firm both has less scarcity rent to divide among counterparties and generates less surplus for counterparties through market transactions with them. If a high-performing firm introduces an advanced product, for example, consumer demand goes up, increasing the surplus enjoyed by consumers, and the firm's profits go up, allowing the firm to write consumers a check for still more value in the form of consumers' share of the firm's profits. (In a firm governed by a board elected by all counterparties, as proposed here, counterparties would insist that the firm distribute profits to all counterparties, not just shareholders, as in the traditional shareholder-dominated firm.) The increase in demand also increases the firm's own demand for labour, investment dollars, and supplies, and that in turn enables counterparties in those markets to increase their own profits – meaning to increase the surplus they take from their market interactions with the firm – in addition to receiving larger payouts of the firm's profits. Thus, a firm creates a 'residual' through high performance that each counterparty captures in part through distributions by the firm to the counterparty and in part directly through doing business with the firm. As a result, all of the firm's counterparties have an interest in checking management when mismanagement threatens that broadly defined residual.

High performance by a firm sometimes creates winners and losers among the firm's counterparties, but that is unlikely to prevent the firm from performing at a high level.

[32] See R Clark, *Corporate Law* (Little, Brown 1986) 781. German law, which gives workers the right to elect half of board seats, handles this problem by giving the chairman of the board, who is elected by shareholders, the right to cast a tie-breaking vote. See Kraakman and others (n 33) 90–91. That means, however, that ultimately shareholders remain in control of German firms. In a board controlled by all counterparties, there would be no equivalent method of forcing a decision in the face of deadlock.

[33] See Hansmann (n 2) 58–59.

A firm's decision to adopt a transformative technology might benefit consumers and shareholders but shift business away from current suppliers and workers, who would then oppose the board.[34] Or adoption of new technology might benefit a minority of workers but harm a majority of them, causing workers as a group to oppose the board. But so long as the new technology were to increase demand, meaning that it were to expand the pie, counterparties would in aggregate gain enough to compensate the losers for their losses while still forging ahead with the project. Dealmaking between counterparties should, therefore, permit profitable projects to proceed.

Second, a majority of counterparties would vote against the board if management were to attempt to wield the firm's monopoly power to oppress any one counterparty. All counterparties are vulnerable to oppression, and so each has an interest in maintaining a norm that prohibits oppression for all. A firm has some amount of power to dictate prices in all markets in which the firm operates because every firm is differentiated to some extent from every others firm. Every firm offers a unique set of employment conditions, if only because employment locations differ. Every firm purchases supplies in a unique fashion, at different locations, with differing levels of reliability. Every firm offers a unique investment opportunity to shareholders, and sells a differentiated product to consumers.[35] The counterparties that do business with a firm therefore prefer the firm to other firms, otherwise, they counterparties would take their business elsewhere. They are, therefore, to the extent of this preference, at the mercy of the firm with respect to the terms the firm dictates to them.[36] It follows that each counterparty stands to benefit if the firm pursues a policy of competitive pricing instead of exercising its power. Management, or other counterparties working with management, might try to oppress some counterparties and reward others with the proceeds of that oppression, so dividing counterparties against each other that they cannot effectively check the oppression. This is unlikely to work, however, because counterparties cannot safely assume that a counterparty coalition that rewards them one day will not turn against them the next. As a result, all counterparties have the incentive to defend each other against attempts to exploit monopoly power, lest they, too, one day find themselves victimised by other counterparties. Political democracies run on the same general principle: no one knows who will be next, so it is in everyone's interest to censure bad behaviour, regardless of whom the target happens to be.[37] This is true even for investors, who, despite

[34] cf. Hansmann (n 2) 138–39 (giving an example of conflict of interest between suppliers in a supply cooperative).

[35] See E Chamberlin, *The Theory of Monopolistic Competition: A Re-orientation of the Theory of Value* (7th edn, Harvard University Press 1956) 71–74.

[36] See *ibid.*

[37] See A Vermeule, 'Veil of Ignorance Rules in Constitutional Law Essay' (2001) 111 Yale LJ 399, 399 ('A veil of ignorance rule … is a rule that suppresses self-interested behavior on the part of decisionmakers; it does so by subjecting the decisionmakers to uncertainty about the distribution of benefits and burdens that will result from a decision.').

doing business in highly competitive capital markets, are locked into the firm by their investment, and therefore relate to the firm as they would to a monopolist.[38]

The same principle applies to explain why counterparties that operate in markets in which the firm has less monopoly power are likely to vote to protect those that operate in markets in which the firm has more monopoly power: a counterparty never knows when markets will shift and the firm will acquire more monopoly power in the markets in which the counterparty operates. Competition, after all, is more fragile than monopoly, which is why there are antitrust laws.[39] No counterparty can rely on competition to protect it from the firm in the long run. So every counterparty has the incentive to vote against the exploitation of monopoly power regardless of the identity of the current victim. Consumers enjoying competitive prices today, for example, will want to vote to prevent the firm from using its monopoly power in labour markets to pay below-market wages because tomorrow the firm may monopolize its product markets and try to charge consumers supracompetitive prices. Consumers will then need workers to come to their aid.[40]

To enable counterparties to vote for each board seat, corporate law must extend to all counterparties the organisational support that the law currently affords only to shareholders.[41] The law must provide workers, consumers, and suppliers, all of whom are often numerous and disorganised, with the same voting rights, majority decision rules, and proxy options as shareholders currently enjoy in electing board members.[42] But now each member of a counterparty class (i.e. each worker, supplier, shareholder, or consumer) would vote to determine how the counterparty class of which he is a member will vote for each board seat, rather than vote directly for each seat. Workers will vote to determine the board members for which the worker class casts its single vote. Suppliers will vote to determine the board members for which the supplier class casts its single vote. And so on. Thus, corporate law must work to overcome the barriers to collective action that each counterparty class faces

38 See Hansmann (n 2) 55–56. While holders of shares in publicly traded companies can always sell their shares, the price the shares fetch is determined by expectations regarding future dividends or buybacks. So current shareholders are always at the mercy of firm decisionmaking regarding how much cash to pay to shareholders.

39 See R Atkinson and M Lind, *Big Is Beautiful: Debunking the Myth of Small Business* (MIT Press 2019) 19–26; J Foster and others, 'Monopoly and Competition in Twenty-First Century Capitalism' (2011) 62 *Monthly Review* 1, 3 ('Monopoly … is the logical result of competition, and should be expected. It is in the DNA of capitalism.').

40 Might all of the counterparties gang up on the firm and each insist on receiving better-than-competitive prices? The answer is no, because the firm is just the sum of its counterparties, and so in taking from the firm counterparties take from each other. See Hansmann (n 2) 18–20. It follows that attempts to obtain better-than-competitive terms from the firm will pit counterparties against each other, and counterparties will therefore vote to prevent such conduct for the same reasons that they will vote to prevent attempts by management to divide them or to oppress one but not another: they never know when other counterparties will choose to gang up on them.

41 See Kraakman and others (n 33) 59–62 (discussing 'the extent to which the law seeks to assist dispersed shareholders in overcoming their collective action problems').

42 See *ibid.*

and indeed that workers, suppliers, and consumers in particular face to a greater extent than shareholders.[43]

7.2.3 *But Is Not Shareholder Control Efficient?*

Giving each category of counterparty the right to vote for board members violates the tenet of modern corporate governance theory that efficiency requires that shareholders alone control management.[44] The principal ground for this tenet is collective action.[45] In most firms, workers have heterogeneous interests (they work different jobs and receive different levels of pay), consumers have heterogeneous interests (they buy some of a firm's products but not others, at different times, and for different purposes), and suppliers have heterogeneous interests (they supply different goods). But shareholders all want one thing: the highest possible cash return on their investment.[46] It follows, the argument goes, that if you put workers, consumers, or suppliers in charge of the firm, their members will fight among themselves and so fail to control management.

Putting all types of counterparties in control of the firm will lead to even more gridlock and indecision than if any one category of counterparty were to control the firm independently. With oversight paralyzed, management would have even more power than it would have under other corporate governance forms, including shareholder control. But the harm to firm performance associated with inadequate oversight of management must be offset by the benefit associated with the democratic check on the exercise of monopoly power that nevertheless would remain, however weak that check might be. It is not clear that the harm outweighs the benefit.

Indeed, my proposal to give a measure of control to all counterparties addresses a glaring defect in another key tenet of modern corporate governance theory. Theorists argue that the group that is entitled to the residual profits of the firm – the shareholders in a shareholder-owned firm – should have exclusive control over governance. Maximising the residual is efficient and, the theorists argue, the group that is entitled to the residual will act to maximise the residual.[47] This view of how to achieve efficiency in corporate governance is correct, but only so long as firms make their profits in competitive markets. If instead firms profit by charging monopoly prices, then maximising the residual, which residual includes monopoly rents as well as scarcity rents, ceases to be efficient, and indeed magnifies inefficiency the more effectively it is undertaken. The more that a monopolist's prices are pushed

[43] See Hansmann (n 2) 4–5.

[44] See H Hansmann and R Kraakman, 'The End of History for Corporate Law' (2000) 89 Geo LJ 439, 440–41.

[45] See H Hansmann, 'All Firms Are Cooperatives – and so Are Governments' (2014) 2 JEOD 1, 4–5.

[46] See Hansmann (n 2) 62–64.

[47] See M Jensen and W Meckling, 'Theory of the Firm: Managerial Behavior, Agency Costs and Ownership Structure' (1976) 3 J Financ Econ 305, 320–23.

beyond the competitive level in order to maximise the residual, the greater the deadweight loss that the monopoly creates.[48]

Corporate governance theorists have traditionally left it to the antitrust laws to solve this problem by ensuring that markets are competitive.[49] But antitrust is an imperfect tool. Some firms have monopoly power because they have made their own products better than those of competitors, not because they have taken steps to degrade competitors' products.[50] Antitrust rightly does not condemn monopoly based on product improvement, and so these firms can charge monopoly prices without fear of antitrust sanction, at least in the United States.[51] That does not mean, however, that a product-improving monopolist's monopoly prices cannot create deadweight loss. They do. It follows that corporate governance cannot fob the problem of monopoly off on antitrust, but must address the problem itself.[52]

48 See Woodcock, 'The Antitrust Duty to Charge Low Prices' (n 2) 1751–52; M Jensen, 'Value Maximization, Stakeholder Theory, and the Corporate Objective Function' (2010) 22 J Appl Corp Finance 32, 35 n7.

49 See Hansmann and Kraakman (n 46) 442; Jensen (n 49) 39.

50 See Teece and Coleman (n 21) 820–22.

51 See F Scherer and D Ross, *Industrial Market Structure and Economic Performance* (3rd edn, Houghton Mifflin 1990) 613–60; R Woodcock, 'How Antitrust Really Works: A Theory of Input Control and Discriminatory Supply' (2021) Social Science Research Network Working Paper No. 3794816 https://papers.ssrn.com/abstract=3794816 accessed 7 July 2021.

52 See Woodcock (n 14) 1403–08, 1433–35. Is corporate governance really capable of filling in the gaps that antitrust cannot address? Suppose that a firm that uses research to produce innovative products needs to be able to charge high prices for the products, pay low wages to workers, or pay low prices to suppliers in order to cover the costs of the research. Using antitrust to break the firm up would lead to competitive pricing that fails to cover those costs, and therefore to a reduction in research and innovation. See R Woodcock, 'Inconsistency in Antitrust' (2013) 68 U Miami L Rev 105, 126–36. But so too would the firm's unilateral resort to competitive pricing as a result of governance pressure exerted by counterparties. This suggests that governance-based restrictions on the exercise of monopoly power might be just as destructive as antitrust remedies such as the breakup of large firms.

The nice thing about a governance-based solution to the problem of monopoly, however, is that counterparties will not, in fact, impose competitive pricing on a monopolist when doing that would make the firm unable to cover costs, because making the firm unable to cover costs would harm all counterparties. A firm's costs are what the firm pays to counterparties. If the firm cannot cover costs and exits the market, counterparties end up with nothing. Thus, in cases in which competitive pricing would not cover costs, and would therefore be inefficient, counterparties can be expected not to act to check attempts by management to charge supracompetitive prices. But Counterparties will still act to check attempts by management to charge prices that more than cover costs, because such prices would represent an attempt to redistribute surplus, and therefore to oppress some counterparties for the benefit of others. Antitrust cannot police such a fine distinction between competitive pricing, fixed-cost-covering pricing, and monopoly pricing, because antitrust does not regulate prices directly and therefore can act only to achieve competitive pricing through remedies that promote competition. See H Hovenkamp, *Federal Antitrust Policy, the Law of Competition and Its Practice* (6th edn, West Academic Publishing 2020) 356–58. But a governance-based solution can police such a distinction because it acts directly on the administration of the firm. Indeed, the governance approach leads to a regime that more closely resembles public utility regulation than antitrust, for managers choosing pricing that covers fixed costs would need to identify an allocation of fixed costs across counterparties that does not cause a majority of counterparties to revolt, much as rate regulators today strive to allocate utility costs among different categories of consumers without triggering a political backlash. See W Viscusi and others, *Economics of Regulation and Antitrust* (5th edn, MIT Press 2018) 528–30.

Embracing my proposed democratic check on management would address the problem of monopoly by ensuring that firms strive to maximise only that part of the residual that is due to scarcity rents rather than the entire residual consisting of both scarcity rent and monopoly rent. That is because, as described earlier, when the governance power of all counterparties is in balance, as it would be under my proposed governance form, the firm will not seek to exploit any monopoly power that the firm may acquire.[53] The firm will charge competitive prices and earn only scarcity rents. Because of the equality of governance power among all counterparties, the firm will likely distribute the scarcity rent equally to all counterparties, giving each counterparty an incentive to push for maximisation of that rent. Thus, the firm will strive to operate at a lower cost than competitors or to produce better products than competitors, in pursuit of scarcity rent. But the firm will not strive to exploit any monopoly power the firm may acquire along the way. Under my proposed governance form, all counterparties would *own* the firm, in the sense that all would take some of the residual, and all would, collectively, *control* the firm, through their democratic check on the board. But because no one counterparty would dominate governance, the firm's counterparties would take only the healthful, efficient part of the residual – the scarcity rent – and not the unhealthful, inefficient part – the monopoly rent. The unity of ownership and control that is another name for the rule that the taker of the residual should control the firm would be preserved but the profit motive of the owners would be fundamentally altered, due to the equal distribution of power among them, to encompass only maximisation of scarcity rent and not of monopoly rent.

7.3 MANAGERIALISM AS A GUIDE

The mid-twentieth century American experience with managerialism hints at what a democratic check on management might accomplish.[54] Large shareholders dominated firms in the nineteenth and early twentieth centuries.[55] But management instead came to dominate firms during the long period of economic growth that followed World War II. Small shareholders, who could not muster the majorities required to impose shareholder interests on management, replaced controlling shareholders.[56] Adolf Berle and Gardiner Means famously fretted during this period that unaccountable managers would exploit their newly democratised shareholders.[57] They failed to appreciate that other forces worked during this period to

53 See above Section 7.2.1

54 See G Davis, *Managed by the Markets: How Finance Reshaped America* (Oxford University Press 2011) 32–33.

55 See J Coffee, Jr., 'The Rise of Dispersed Ownership: The Roles of Law and the State in the Separation of Ownership and Control' (2001) 111 Yale LJ 1, 24–25.

56 *Ibid.* at 70–71.

57 See A Berle and G Means, *The Modern Corporation and Private Property* (Transaction Publishers 1932) 46, 313; L Stout, *The Shareholder Value Myth: How Putting Shareholders First Harms Investors, Corporations, and the Public* (Berrett-Koehler Publishers 2012) 17–18; Davis (n 56) 71–72.

constrain managers. Unions gave labour bargaining power in labour markets that prevented managers from exploiting the firm's monopoly power to depress wages.[58] And the public sentiment in favour of the regulation of big business made regulation or antitrust breakup an ever-present threat if firms failed to satisfy consumers, who were also voters.[59] The result was a management that was powerful but nevertheless checked by its counterparties. Subject to this balance of power, managers shrank from the price discrimination that so troubled nineteenth-century consumers, favouring instead uniform and even average cost pricing.[60] And firms offered workers stable employment, competitive wages, and defined-benefit pension plans.[61] AT&T, for example, was a pioneer in progressive labour practices in the post-war period. The company also strove for two generations to ensure that the price of a month of local calling would not exceed the price of a medium pizza with two toppings, bundling directory services into the deal.[62]

The success of this mid-twentieth century managerialism reflects the crucial role the balance of power between counterparties plays in restraining the exercise of monopoly power.[63] Shareholders were the dominant counterparty in the nineteenth century because they tended to own controlling stakes in firms.[64] Power shifted to managers in the mid-twentieth century because the legal trigger for shareholder power – a majority stake – was no longer pulled, as shareholdings democratised.[65] This in turn devolved power to managers because corporate governance rules give

58 See M Goldfield, *The Decline of Organized Labor in the United States* (University of Chicago Press 1989) 12.

59 See M Pertschuk, *Revolt against Regulation: The Rise and Pause of the Consumer Movement* (University of California Press 1982) 5–45. The dynamic between antitrust regulation and corporate good behavior is nicely illustrated by commitments made by AT&T in 1913 and again in 1956 to avoid antitrust action by the Justice Department pursuant to which the company agreed not to expand out of the telephone industry into adjacent businesses, such as telegraph or television. See R Vietor, *Contrived Competition: Regulation and Deregulation in America* (Harvard University Press 1996) 172–73, 185. The agreements followed a pioneering public relations campaign by AT&T in which the company sold itself to the public as a mom and pop owned operation dedicated to providing "universal service" to all Americans. See Davis (n 56) 70–71; R John, *Network Nation: Inventing American Telecommunications* (Harvard University Press 2015) 385–95. The company in effect negotiated the right to dominate telephone service in exchange for a promise of good behavior that the company mostly honored.

60 See H Hovenkamp, 'Regulatory Conflict in the Gilded Age: Federalism and the Railroad Problem' (1988) 97 Yale LJ 1017, 1044–58 (discussing the controversy over 'unjust discrimination' by railroads); T McCraw, *Prophets of Regulation: Charles Francis Adams, Louis D. Brandeis, James M. Landis, Alfred E. Kahn* (Harvard University Press 1984) 239–43.

61 See Davis (n 56) 87–91.

62 See John (n 61) 408; McCraw (n 62) 256–59; Davis (n 56) 78–79.

63 For more on managerialism, see generally H Wells, 'Corporation Law Is Dead: Heroic Managerialism, Legal Change, and the Puzzle of Corporation Law at the Height of the American Century' (2012) 15 U Pa J Bus L 305.

64 See D Smith, 'The Shareholder Primacy Norm' (1998) 23 J Corp L 277, 291–305; Coffee, Jr (n 64) 24–25.

65 See Kraakman and others (n 33) 79–80; L Bebchuk, 'The Case for Increasing Shareholder Power' (2005) 118 Harv L Rev 833, 24–25.

managers free reign when shareholders lack the votes to replace them.[66] But managers could not exploit their power because other counterparties, namely workers and consumers, obtained countervailing power during this period.[67] Unlike what would happen under my proposed democratic check, however, neither workers nor consumers obtained power through corporate governance rules, which remained largely static.[68] Instead, workers obtained power out in labour markets through unionisation.[69] And consumers obtained power in the sense that antitrust enforcers, rate regulators, and Congress used threats of enforcement and regulation effectively to cow firms into making concessions to consumers.[70] But though workers and consumers obtained power by ad hoc means, they nevertheless succeeded at checking managers when necessary. As a result, monopolies such as AT&T shared the wealth despite being under the complete control, as a formal matter, of unaccountable managers.[71] At the same time, these monopolies were free to leverage their size to achieve economies of scale – something that they could not have done had antitrust enforcers broken them up.

In typical American fashion, a felicitous outcome had been achieved not through reform of the rules that directly bear on the balance of power inside the firm – the rules of corporate law – but instead through a hodgepodge of private solutions (unionisation) and government intervention (antitrust and economic regulation).[72] Democratising the election of the board, as I propose here, would broaden and institutionalise within corporate law itself the balance of power so haphazardly constructed in the heyday of managerialism.

The collapse of managerialism starting in the late 1970s shows just how important institutionalising the balance of power within the firm really is.[73] Scholars sometimes suggest that corporate raiders killed managerialism by reconstituting the old controlling ownership stakes in firms or otherwise shifting the balance of power back in favor of shareholders.[74] But corporate raiding and the cult of shareholder value maximisation it instilled in managers is more likely a symptom of the collapse

66 See Kraakman and others (n 33) 12.

67 See the text accompanying n 68–69.

68 See Smith (n 66) 323 (observing that shareholder primacy became a 'fixture' of corporate law).

69 See Goldfield (n 60) 12.

70 See the text of n 69.

71 See Kraakman and others (n 33) 12; John (n 61) 408.

72 See R Skidelsky, *John Maynard Keynes: Fighting for Freedom, 1937–1946* (Viking 1986).

73 See Davis (n 56) 81–87.

74 See *ibid.* at 85. The argument here is not that as a result of takeovers every American corporation has come to have a controlling shareholder, although the sharp decline in the number of publicly-traded corporations in the United States in recent decades suggests that the economy is moving in that direction (due more to a preference on the part of startups for private financing than to going-private transactions, however). See C Doidge and others, 'Eclipse of the Public Corporation or Eclipse of the Public Markets?' (2018) 30 *Journal of Applied Corporate Finance* 8, 11–13, 15. Instead, the argument is that the *threat* of takeover, which is meaningful only if a raider that acquires a controlling stake is able to use it to dominate management, has forced managers to act in shareholder interests, even when the firm has no controlling shareholder. This change in the locus of governance power within firms from

of the balance of power that underpinned managerialism, rather than a cause. After all, if workers and consumers had continued to enjoy countervailing power, it is not clear why that power would have been less effective in checking a corporate raider or other powerful shareholder than it was in checking powerful management.

The real cause of the collapse of managerialism was the demise of the balance of power upon which it depended. That balance required both the persistence of unions and of public sentiment in favour of the regulation of business, neither of which lasted.[75] Public support for the regulation of business collapsed in the 1970s, giving rise to deregulation and a drastic weakening of antitrust enforcement in the late 1970s and 1980s.[76] Because government was no longer willing to provide consumers with bargaining power, management – or anyone in control of management – now could extract surplus from consumers and give that surplus to itself. That in turn meant that there were now rewards associated with buying a controlling stake in the firm and dominating management that had not existed for decades. Those rewards created the figure of the corporate raider. They also enabled managers, acting on behalf of shareholders – or indeed themselves – to finance attacks on the last powerful counterparty of the old order – unions – which went into decline. Profits derived from lower wages and canceled pensions rewarded the attacks.[77]

The part that managers themselves played in the demise of managerialism highlights the role of the balance of power in this story. Managers themselves often raided their own firms.[78] Perceiving that the government was no longer willing to protect counterparties, managers sought to use their controlling position in corporate governance to take as much of the value that now could be extracted from counterparties as possible. The easiest way for managers to do that was to become controlling shareholders themselves because corporate governance orthodoxy continued to give shareholders the legal right to extract all excess value from the firm.[79]

7.4 CONCLUSION

In an age characterised by weak antitrust enforcement, it is tempting to respond with a full-throated call for across-the-board promotion of competition.[80] This temptation

managers to shareholders is reflected in the cult of shareholder value maximization among managers that arose in the wake of the 1980s takeover wave. See Stout (n 59) 2–4. The shareholder value maximization ideal was a major departure from managerialism, for which maximizing shareholder value was a secondary concern. See Davis (n 56) 74.

75 See Goldfield (n 60) 12; Pertschuk (n 61) 69–119.

76 See Davis (n 56) 84; J Baker, 'Taking the Error Out of Error Cost Analysis: What's Wrong with Antitrust's Right' (2015) 80 Antitrust L J 1, 506–09; Pertschuk (n 61) 69–119.

77 See Goldfield (n 60) 19–20.

78 See L Lowenstein, 'Management Buyouts' (1985) 85 Colum L Rev 730, 730.

79 See Kraakman and others (n 33) 13.

80 See Zephyr Teachout, *Break' Em Up: Recovering Our Freedom from Big Ag, Big Tech, and Big Money* (All Points Books 2020); T Wu, *The Curse of Bigness: Antitrust in the New Gilded Age* (Columbia Global Reports 2018).

must be resisted, because sometimes bigger really is better.[81] A wiser approach is to recognise that a firm is just the sum of its counterparties, and so the firm will not exercise monopoly power against one counterparty unless some other counterparty of the firm has sufficient control over firm governance to cause the firm to engage in such oppressive behaviour. This suggests that by altering corporate governance rules to prevent firms from coming under the control of any one counterparty and instead leaving firms in the hands of a management subject to a democratic check from firm counterparties, the law can defang monopolists without depriving the economy of the virtues of size. But to do that, antitrust – or rather the antitrust spirit, operating through the law of corporate governance – must strike at the interior of firms, rather than at the markets that surround them.[82]

[81] See Atkinson and Lind (n 41) 63–81; A Hirschman, *Exit, Voice and Loyalty: Responses to Decline in Firms, Organizations and States* (Harvard University Press 1970) 55 (arguing that 'if exit is ineffective as a recuperation mechanism, but does succeed at draining from the firm or organization its more quality-conscious, alert, and potentially activist customers or members' then 'a tight monopoly is preferable … to a looser arrangement in which competition is present').

[82] For the argument that existing antitrust rules compel a reinterpretation of prevailing corporate governance rules, albeit in favor of consumer dominance rather than a balance of power, see Woodcock (n 14) 1396–403.

8

Directors' Duty of Loyalty

Corporate Opportunity Rules as Restrictions of Competition

Marco Corradi and Julian Nowag

8.1 INTRODUCTION

When a company's director encounters new business opportunities, a question arises whether they can privately exploit such opportunities or whether such opportunities 'belong' to the cooperation. This question is the core issue addressed by corporate opportunity rules in different corporate law systems around the world. This chapter explores how corporate opportunity rules may restrict competition and proposes that further evidence on the effects of such restrictions should be collected. The chapter starts out by setting out the origins and the basic principles of corporate opportunity rules and how their fiduciary origin aims to prevent insiders from becoming competitors. The chapter provides a general account of how these rules might potentially compete focusing on unilateral effects and examines in more detail possible negative effects on dynamic efficiencies. It highlights the importance of collecting further evidence to better understand this complex phenomenon.

8.2 WHAT ARE CORPORATE OPPORTUNITY RULES

Instances of protection of a collective business from the misappropriations of material or immaterial assets by insiders have been around for millennia. Roman imperial Rescripta and medieval gilds' organisational rules already reflected the tension between the necessity to keep assets and trade secrets within the boundaries of the association on the one hand and the attempt to protect the freedom of enterprise of the individual associate on the other.[1] In the modern corporation, these rules are a manifestation of the directors'[2] duty of loyalty.[3] Hence, they are deemed as

This chapter is based on previous work by the authors and presents the core of the paper 'Enforcing Corporate Opportunities Rules: Antitrust Risks and Antitrust Failures' forthcoming 2023 European Business Law Review.

1 M Corradi, Corporate Opportunities: A Law and Economics Analysis (Hart 2021)

2 Or other fiduciaries' duties.

3 For the UK law, see P Davies and S Worthington (eds), *Gower and Davies' Principles of Modern Company Law* (9th edn, Sweet & Maxwell 2012), ch 16; in Spain, article 228 of the *Ley de Sociedades*

being one of the core sets of rules that characterise modern corporate law. Besides their primary function of protecting the proprietary's boundaries of the corporation from misappropriations by insiders, corporate opportunity rules may also create monetary counterincentives to competition by directors with the corporation that employs them.

In modern times, corporate opportunity rules were first introduced in the Anglo-American jurisdictions and subsequently imported also into the German legal system.[4] Only since early 2000, they have become widespread in most civil law jurisdictions and at times they are included in national corporate governance codes.[5] Hence, any potential anticompetitive harm, both in terms of static as well as dynamic efficiency[6] deriving from the enforcement of corporate opportunity rules, might increase in future with any further expansion of these rules. Regardless of their future expansion through case law, their mere presence may strongly affect the allocation of many kinds of rights among economic actors *ex ante*. As we will argue in the following sections, the rules may consolidate the power of firms and discourage their insiders from attempting to enter the market.

The essence of these rules is the retention of the value and the fruits of business information within the corporation. Therefore, directors (and other insiders) have to disclose information on new business opportunities before any eventual company-authorised appropriation of corporate opportunities can take place.[7] An example of a sophisticated version of this kind of rule is point 4.3.1 of the German Corporate Governance Code, as amended in 2015: 'Members of the Management Board are bound by the interests of the company. When making their decisions they must not pursue any personal interests, are subject to a comprehensive prohibition to compete during their work for the company and must not exploit for themselves business opportunities to which the company is entitled'. If the corporation has not

de Capital identifies directors' obligations deriving directly from their duty of loyalty; The German Federal Court has also expressly reminded that corporate opportunities are a direct derivation of the duty of loyalty and not of the directors' duty not to compete with the corporation. See BGH 4.12.2012, II ZR 159/10, DStR 2013, 600 = NZG 2013. 216.

4 In Germany, the *Bundesgerichtshof* introduced these rules through an extensive interpretation of the principle of loyalty of directors to the company (*die Trueupflicht*), and more specifically of their duty to avoid conflicts of interests (*das Gebot der Vermeidung von Interessenkonflikten*). See BGH WM 1977, 361, 362; BGH WM 1983, 498; BGH NJW 1986, 584, 585; BGH WM 1989, 1335, 1339. Corporate opportunity rules were discussed in a very thorough way before being introduced, thanks to an exemplary jurisprudential effort. Awareness of the problem was already revealed in EMestmäker, *Verwaltung, Konzerngewalt und Recht der Aktionare* (Müller 1958) 166ff. Further references to the first jurisprudential contribution to German corporate opportunity rules are found in M Löhnig, *Treuhand* (Mohr Siebeck 2006) 372, in particular n 2.

5 See for instance the German Corporate Governance Code, Rule 4.3.1

6 For details see Section 8.4.

7 For comments see H Wilsing (ed), *Deutscher Corporate Governance Kodex Kommentar* (Verlag CH Beck 2012) para 4.3.3. [Treupflicht] 363, paras 12ff.

authorised a given appropriation by a director, but the director still appropriates the business opportunity, the corporation can address the situation with the various remedies described in the following paragraphs.

For the analysis of this chapter, the following three specific aspects are particularly relevant and briefly discussed: (1) the industrial relevance of corporate opportunity rules; (2) the remedies that are available against a non-authorised appropriation of a corporate opportunity by a director or another insider; (3) the question of whether corporate opportunity rules are mandatory or not. Section 8.4 then builds upon these aspects and highlights their possible anticompetitive harm.

First, in terms of industrial relevance, corporate opportunity rules may cover a very wide set of cases. To provide an idea of the variety of the situations commonly discussed under the 'label' of corporate 'opportunity', consider the following. From an industrial perspective, a corporate opportunity can consist of the possibility to acquire the following assets: a trade secret, such as the Pepsi-Cola secret formula;[8] a cellular telephone service;[9] a mining licence[10] a specific piece of land;[11] technical equipment (at ordinary market price);[12] a business (cinema);[13] stock of the corporation by one of its directors from a third party, at a convenient value[14] or in the case of an initial public offering.[15] A corporate opportunity could also be the offer of a contract to be the developer of a given line of business on the behalf of a third party.[16]

Second, the remedies against misappropriation[17] can range from damages[18] to an action for unjust enrichment[19] or even, in certain jurisdictions, a disgorgement

8 *Guth* v *Loft* 5 A2d 503 (Del. 1939)

9 *Broz v Cellular Information Systems, Inc.* 673 A2d.

10 *Queensland Mines Ltd.* v *Hudson* (1978) AJLR 399 and *Peso Silver Mines (NPL)* v *Cropper* (1976) SCR 673 (Supreme Court of Canada).

11 *Bhullar* v *Bhullar* [2003] EWCA Civ 424

12 *American Metal Forming Corporation v W Pittman* 52 F3d 504; *Knox Glass Bottle Co v Underwood* 89 So 2d 799 (Miss. 1956)

13 *Regal (Hastings) v Gulliver* [1967] 2 AC 134

14 *Faraclas* v *City Vending Co* 194 A2d 298 (Md. 1963). But see an opposite view in *Weigel v Shapiro J W* 608 F2d 268. The question has been debated for a long time. On this point see Victor Brudney, 'Insider securities dealing during corporate crisis' (1962) 61 Mich L Rev 1–38.

15 *In re eBay Inc. Shareholders Litigation* 2004 WL 253521 (Del Ch 2004). *Canadian Aero Service Ltd* v *O'Malley* [1974] SCR 592 (Supreme Court of Canada).

16 *Industrial Development Consultants Ltd v Cooley* [1972] 1 WLR 443.

17 For a comparative analysis of remedies against misappropriations of corporate opportunities, See M Corradi, 'Securing corporate opportunities in Europe–comparative notes on monetary remedies and on the potential evolution of the remedial system' (2018) 18 J CLS 439–473.

18 Damages in for of 'damnum emergens' or 'lucrum cessans' or both. See for instance Italian Civil Code, Article 2391 (5).

19 M Corradi, 'Securing Corporate Opportunities in Europe – Comparative Notes on Monetary Remedies and on their Potential Evolution' (2018) J CLS (forthcoming) offers a comparative analysis of this remedy within a sample of European jurisdictions.

of profits,[20] eventually assisted by a constructive trust (in its personal or proprietary form).[21]

The essence of all corporate opportunity rules could, therefore, be described as the ability of the company to prevent an insider from appropriating part or all of the profits generated from the business opportunity. In other words, corporate opportunity rules may create monetary counterincentives to competition by insiders.

8.3 CORPORATE OPPORTUNITY RULES: A THEORY OF UNILATERAL EFFECTS

From an economic perspective, corporate opportunities can possibly be understood in light of the theory of the firm.[22] As a manifestation of directors' duty of loyalty to the corporation – along with self-dealing – they are one of the main corporate law rules that are functional to containing agency costs and therefore attract potential equity investors.[23] Moreover, in those jurisdictions where they are formulated according to the 'no-conflict' paradigm or where they include the 'line of business test', those rules can be understood as a way to protect what Oliver Williamson refers to as 'idiosyncratic investments'.[24] We, therefore, recognise that the enforcement of corporate opportunity rules has an economic justification. The rules' efficiency justification is based on law and finance considerations by majoritarian doctrine. This means that it is appropriate to protect corporate opportunities against misappropriations by insiders because such protection contains agency costs and stimulates investments in equity. In other words, corporate opportunity rules provide for a regime in which the company has the incentive to invest in insiders or the development of its business because any potential returns cannot be expropriated but are secured by those rules.

20 Disgorgement of profits is the typical Anglo-American remedy that assists corporate opportunities misappropriations. For the UK, see for instance *Bhullar v Bhullar* [2003] EWCA Civ 424. The situation in US law differs from state to state, as corporate law is not federal. Nevertheless, the general remedy available in almost every US state corporate law is disgorgement of profit. See Eric Orlinsky, 'Corporate Opportunity Doctrine and Interested Director Transactions: A Framework for Analysis in an Attempt to Restore Predictability' (1999) 24 Del J Corp L 451. The only continental European law that assist misappropriations with a similar remedy is Spain. See Ley de Sociedades de Capital, art 227 (2): '[l]a infracción del deber de lealtad determinará no solo la obligación de indemnizar el daño causado al patrimonio social, sino también la de devolver a la sociedad el enriquecimiento injusto obtenido por el administrador'.

21 At least in the UK it is now clear that in this case the constructive trust that applies is proprietary. This point is finally clear in the recent statements of Lord Neuberger in *FHR v Mankarious* [2014] UKSC 45 (paras 7 and 33).

22 M Corradi, 'Corporate Opportunities Doctrines Tested in the Light of the Theory of the Firm – A European (and US) Comparative Perspective' (2016) 27 EBLR 755, for a detailed analysis of the rules in the light of the theory of the firm.

23 Robert Sitkoff, 'The Economic Structure of Fiduciary Law' (2013) 91 BU L Rev 1039, 1043.

24 Corradi (n 23) 771ff.

Unfortunately, corporate insiders[25] may often be the most effective potential competitors for a company – especially in highly innovative environments. These individuals have acquired a solid knowledge of the market in which they have operated on behalf of their corporation, often for decades. Especially when they are directors or high-ranking officers, they are usually well aware of production processes, upstream and downstream markets, the relationship between fixed and marginal costs, and the state of the art with reference to innovation.[26] Not only are insiders well aware of market variables, but also of the specific business strategy of the firm they work for. Once they leave the corporation, the insiders' competitive advantage may enable them to act much faster as potential competitors than an outsider, pointing straight to the weaknesses of the corporation they have worked for.

Corporate opportunities, which are basically growth and development opportunities, can be the object of a negotiation between a company and its insiders.[27] But non-zero transaction costs might mean that such negotiations are inefficient.[28] If the rights to exploit a business opportunity are allocated to the already existing company, that company will tend to grow more easily. In the opposite case, that company's market power might be progressively eroded.[29] To a certain extent, corporate opportunity rules can also be compared to non-compete clauses.[30] Both provide the company with rights against agents working under its umbrella and both have developed from the idea of fiduciary duties towards the company. In this sense, both corporate opportunity rules and non-compete clauses or contracts can be seen as a way of containing hold-up costs. Both provide the company with incentives to invest in their staff/agents so that these individuals provide their principal – the company they work for – with a higher return. However, in contrast to corporate opportunity rules, many States are rather restrictive with regard to non-compete arrangements[31] or even prohibit such arrangements, for example as does California. Moreover, collusion between companies to the same end has attracted strong enforcement action

25 Whether directors, officers, or controlling shareholders.

26 And of all the other relevant variables in a business setting. See D Carlton and J Perloff, *Modern industrial organization* (Pearson 2015).

27 See the models proposed by E Talley, 'Turning Servile Opportunities to Gold: A Strategic Analysis of the Corporate Opportunity Doctrine' (1998) 108 Yale LJ 277–375 and M Whincop, 'Painting the Corporate Cathedral: The Protection of Entitlements in Corporate Law' (1999) 19 OJLS 19–50.

28 Corradi (n 23) 763ff.

29 *Ibid.* at 770ff. See Section 8.4.

30 For a functional law and economics analysis of the relationships between corporate opportunity rules and no compete clauses see M Corradi, 'Corporate Opportunity Doctrines Tested in the Light of the Theory of the Firm – a European (and US) Comparative Perspective' (2016) 27 Issue 6, EBLRev 755–819

31 For a law and economics analysis of such agreements see, Office of Economic Policy U.S. Department of the Treasury, *Non-Compete Contracts: Economic Effects and Policy Implications* (March 2016) https://home.treasury.gov/system/files/226/Non_Compete_Contracts_Econimic_Effects_and_Policy_Implications_MAR2016.pdf.

by antitrust agencies, as the example of the non-poaching and wage-fixing agreements between Silicon Valley companies shows.[32]

To understand how the corporate opportunity doctrine may be employed strategically to create barriers to entry, one has to distinguish between at least two situations. First, the corporate opportunity doctrine may well be employed appositely to prevent an insider from becoming a direct competitor, on the horizontal plan. This is the most straightforward case. If an insider tries to set up a new company on the basis of business information they obtained during their time in the company, the company will simply ask the court to declare that the new company is held on constructive trust (with subsequent transfer order and/or disgorgement of profits) or ask for damages or for unjust enrichment, depending on the remedies available in the jurisdiction. Second, corporate opportunity rules may serve potentially anticompetitive investment strategies. Companies may revert to (side) strategies that entail operating in upstream or downstream markets. For example, this may happen when a given resource is indispensable for producing a given product at a certain stage of technological development.[33] An example of such strategic behaviour could be the taking of an opportunity to acquire relevant shares of an upstream market in raw materials that are necessary for the production process downstream. Through the enforcement of corporate opportunity rules, an incumbent company may prevent the insider from setting up a company that operates upstream.

Another related case of strategic use of corporate opportunities might be the possibility to secure the fidelity of distributors. As to contracts with distributors, such practice enables the company to recruit agents for retail operations. There may be different strategies that a company may adopt to try to monopolise downstream markets, when this is crucial for the success of the corporation (for instance, in the case of high-end fashion products). First, if an insider succeeds in setting up a new corporation in the same line of business as the company they work for, the original company may invalidate any newly signed contracts with distributors through the enforcement of corporate opportunity rules.[34] Second, if a director wants to set up

[32] District Court of Columbia (2011) *United States v Adobe Systems, Inc, Apple Inc, Google Inc, Intel Corporation, Intuit, Inc, and Pixar*, 1:10-cv-01629; District Court for the Northern District of California San Jose Division (2014) *United States v eBay, Inc* Case No 12-CV-05869-EJD-PSG, District Court Columbia (June 3, 2011) *United States v Lucasfilm Ltd* 1:10-cv-02220-RBW. See also, FTC and DoJ Antitrust 'Guidance for Human Resource Professionals' (October 2016) www.justice.gov/atr/file/903511/download accessed 5 March 2017.

[33] This phenomenon is usually known as 'vertical foreclosure' (upstream foreclosure in this case). See in general P Rey and J Tyrole, *Handbook of Industrial Organization* (Elsevier 2015) 2145–2220. On the issues of vertical foreclosure from a competition law perspective see G Bonanno and J Vickers, 'Vertical separation' (1988) 36 J Industrial Econ 257–265; D Carlton and M Waldman, 'The strategic use of tying to preserve and create market power in evolving industries' (2002) 33 Rand J Econ 194–220; Guidance on the Commission's enforcement priorities in applying Article 82 of the EC Treaty to abusive exclusionary conduct by dominant undertakings [2009] OJ C45/7, paras 18ff.

[34] In this case the actual line of business of the corporation.

a company in the downstream market, the company again can proceed to vertical integration, claiming the new business through the enforcement of corporate opportunity rules.[35]

There may also be cases that are not related to horizontal competition or vertical integration but that would still be the taking of a corporate opportunity. These cases would usually arise under the 'potential line of business clause'. Examples are cases involving new commercial practices, such as the US tobacco case in 1940, where the idea was to launch lower quality cigarettes from lower quality blends of tobacco.[36] Although such commercial ideas may not be innovative in the classical sense, the commercial strategy adopted in this case shares many features of disruptive innovation, to which a significant part of Section 4(b) will be devoted.

There are at least two different categories of anticompetitive harm that may arise by way of the enforcement of a company's rights in relation to a corporate opportunity. The first category of anticompetitive harm derives from different types of foreclosure (for example, upstream or downstream foreclosure) which we have analysed in detail elsewhere.[37] The second category pertains to harm to the so-called dynamic competition.

8.4 POTENTIAL NEGATIVE EFFECTS ON DYNAMIC COMPETITION

One may be tempted to start the discussion on the competitive harm deriving from the enforcement of corporate opportunity way through the 'classic' static to a dynamic crescendo. But harm to the so-called dynamic competition[38] seems more significant in these cases and is therefore the focus of this chapter. When considering the enforcement of corporate opportunity rules and the effects on dynamic competition, the picture is rather complex, if not contradictory. This complex picture is not only the result of the different kinds of business opportunities[39] but also of the different types of dynamic effects.[40] A dynamic analysis can take place along the more traditional lines – innovation in connection with research and development (R&D) or the analysis can focus on disruptive innovation. Below we will examine both separately, adding to traditional considerations also more original ones, based on a disruptive innovation approach. In fact, companies are presented with both kinds

35 Here in form of the potential line of business.

36 See this case as reported by CS Hemphill and T Wu, 'Parallel Exclusion' (2012–2013) 122 Yale LJ 1182, 1201 and 1203. See also general references in Bishop and Walker, The Economics of EC Competition Law: Concepts, Application and Measurement (Sweet & Maxwell, 2010).

37 See Corradi and Nowag (n 2).

38 With all the caveats inherent to the use of this term, see V Kathuria 'A Conceptual Framework to Identify Dynamic Efficiency' (2015) 11(2–3) ECJ 319–339.

39 See Sections 8.2 and 8.3.

40 See Kathuria (n 39).

of innovation. Finally, we will highlight some empirical studies that examine the effects of non-compete clauses on innovation because such clauses are similar to corporate opportunity rules in their effects.

The traditional dynamic competition analysis focuses largely on the relationships between IP rights and competition.[41] One of the core tenets of IP theory suggests a high degree of temporary protection for fruits of innovation derived from R&D.[42] Starting with these traditional dynamic efficiency considerations, corporate opportunity rules that attribute to the company the innovative business opportunities seem in line with several ideas grounded in the most established analysis of this type of competition *for* rather than *in* the market. First, in markets with high fixed costs and low marginal costs, IP rights are crucial. In fact, it is well known that R&D competition for certain kinds of patents is extremely fierce and that R&D is cost-intensive.[43] Second, in such markets, investment in R&D carries a very high risk, so the expected returns to the winner must be high. Third, there is an inherent tension between competition, that is competition for innovation on the one hand and monopoly power that is granted temporarily on inventions through IP rights on the other hand.

Business opportunities might take forms that can be protected by means of IP rights, for example, as patents. However, issues related to business opportunities may occur typically before questions about IP and competition arise. Similarly, corporate opportunity rules allow a company to appropriate the fruits of innovations that are not patentable, at least on a temporary basis. Therefore, the rules may be complementary to IP rights in their role of providing incentives for innovation, in particular, where the company has spent resources to support an insider's invention. Moreover, corporate opportunity rules seem less harmful in terms of competition than IP protection. IP rights are enforceable against everyone, while corporate opportunity rules only give rights to the insider. By contrast, here it could be said that the protection offered by corporate opportunities to innovation is in line with emerging doctrine on IP. Hovenkamp has described the evolution of IP rights as a shift from monopoly to property rights which is visible both in the IP and competition analysis.[44] Enforcement of corporate opportunity rules can be seen as an expression of a property right expressed through a constructive trust and a subsequent transfer order.

One might therefore argue that enforcing corporate opportunity rules is typically not detrimental from a traditional dynamic efficiency perspective.

41 See the traditional *Schumpeter v Arrow* debate.

42 On the economics of innovation see in general C Antonelli and others (eds), *New Frontiers in the Economics of Innovation and New Technology* (Edward Elgar 2006); G Silverberg and L Soete (eds), *The economics of growth and technical change* (Edward Elgar 1994); N Rosenberg and others (eds), *Technology and the Wealth of Nations* (Stanford UP 1992)

43 *Ibid.*

44 H Hovenkamp, 'Parents, Property, and Competition Policy' (2008) 34 J Corp L 1243.

By contrast, certain cases of corporate opportunities may be more interesting from another dynamic efficiency, though so far less-explored perspective – disruptive innovation. Christensen's research on disruptive innovation has shown that innovation derives not necessarily from high expenditures in R&D.[45] Disruptive innovation usually consists of simplifications brought to an existing product, which has been over-refined by incumbent companies because of sustained innovation. Hence, certain consumers become progressively uninterested in the product because of over-sophistication. Moreover, the innovative simplifications introduced by the disruptive innovator usually are techniques that are not patentable. Quite often disruptive competition comes at a low cost, so there is no need to protect a company's financial R&D expenditure.

What does that mean for corporate opportunities cases? In such cases, the innovator is an insider. Therefore, the legal framework should provide incentives to innovate. Such incentives can certainly be generated by more liberal corporate opportunity rules, which allow the insider to take at least some corporate opportunities.[46] In this context, it should also be noted that strict corporate opportunity rules will lower insiders' incentives to undertake inventions in their free time. In other words, if an insider knows they cannot appropriate the fruit of their invention, there will be no incentive to spend time creating such innovations.

Furthermore, disruptive products tend to offer a set of attributes that is different from the ones offered in the mainstream market. While being innovative, disruptive products typically address a niche of the existing market and serve the low-end rather than the high-end market. Christensen provides many examples[47] where low-end innovation conquering a market completely in the medium-long term because incumbent firms were busy refining their old product. From the perspective of corporate opportunity rules, the question is therefore: what would an incumbent company do, knowing that disruptive innovation by means of low-end innovation, in which it is not presently interested, may become a potential foe? Such a company has, in effect, two options: it could develop the opportunity or it could appropriate it and kill it, thereby eliminating potential competition.

The first solution looks like the most efficient one, even from the point of view of a corporation. However, there are several potential drawbacks. First, it would be rather difficult to address all the possible innovations that could be developed by insiders. For example, if ten innovative opportunities arise in a given time, the incumbent company carefully analyses them all and decides that only one is potentially disruptive. Therefore, it uses all its resources for the development of that one

45 See for instance J Bower and C Christensen, 'Disruptive Technologies: Catching the Wave' (1995) 73(1) *Harv Bus Rev* 43–53; C Christensen, *The Innovator's Dilemma* (Harper Business 2000); C Christensen and M Raynor, *The Innovator's Solution* (Harvard Business Review Press 2003); C Christensen, S Anthony and Erik Roth, *Seeing What's Next* (Harvard Business School Press 2004).

46 If not by a corporate opportunities waiver.

47 Many examples are provided in Christensen, *Innovator's Dilemma* (n 46).

innovation. What will the company do with those innovative opportunities it has discarded? While benevolence towards insiders would suggest that these business opportunities may be left to the insiders to take, there is also another, more likely, option. Aware of disruptive innovation and of the limits to predicting accurately whether a given opportunity is disruptive or not, it is rational to appropriate and kill those opportunities that the company is not able or willing to pursue. Practically, the company would enforce the corporate opportunity rule on any kind of innovative opportunity even if it decides not to develop the opportunity and simply let it die. From the point of view of dynamic competition, such behaviour would be extremely harmful.

However, problems might arise even regarding those opportunities that the company appropriates to develop. In fact, the company may decide to use corporate opportunity rules to slow down innovation. In other words, the company may be slower than an insider in implementing innovation, because it is still able to earn from a previous technology without aiming to maximise the speed of innovation. Ezrachi and Stucke have shown this in relation to quality.[48] Another example is the already mentioned case of tobacco companies in the 1940s. If an insider had taken the opportunity and launched lower-quality cigarettes from lower-quality blends of tobacco, it may well have provided a springboard to later engage in competition with the 'normal' tobacco companies.

Finally, as we have explained above,[49] from the point of view of their economic function, corporate opportunity rules can be compared to non-compete clauses. The effects on innovation of such clauses also provide insights into the possible effects of corporate opportunity rules. There is some evidence that non-compete clauses have a negative effect.[50] Moreover, Gilson convincingly argued that the absence of non-compete clauses may be an incentive for Silicon Valley inventors. According to Gilson, the unenforceability of employee's non-compete covenants under Californian law[51] fosters intercompany knowledge spillovers, which are renowned as one of the main reasons for Silicon Valley's economic success over Route 128.[52] The impact of legal structure on innovation is confirmed by the likelihood of enforcement of the same kind of covenant under Massachusetts law and the lesser success of Route 128.[53]

[48] M Stucke, and A Ezrachi, 'When Competition Fails to Optimise Quality: A Look at Search Engines' (2016) 18 Yale J L & Tech 70 http://ssrn.com/abstract=2598128

[49] See text to (n 31–33).

[50] See for example the negative effects of non-compete and trade secrets, see C Graves and J DiBoise, 'Do Strict Trade Secret and Non-Competition Laws Obstruct Innovation' 1 (2006) *Entrepreneurial Bus LJ* 323–344; O Amir and O Lobel, 'Driving Performance: A Growth Theory of Noncompete Law' (2013) 16 Stan Techn L Rev 833–874.

[51] R Gilson, 'The Legal Infrastructure of High Technology Industrial Districts: Silicon Valley, Route 128, and Covenants Not to Compete' (1999) 74 NYUL Rev 575, 607ff.

[52] *Ibid.* at 620ff.

[53] *Ibid.* at 603ff.

From a rational perspective, it seems rather surprising that companies would choose to be subject to Californian law that allows former employees to compete freely. One reason why they may choose to do so may be the sociological features of Silicon Valley, as Saxenien highlights. First, in Silicon Valley, loyalty to networks seems to prevail over loyalty to the company.[54] As a consequence, the boundaries between employers and employees are depicted as 'blurring'.[55] Second, despite the existence of a sort of network loyalty, competitive pressure is particularly strong, due to the demand for increasing innovation.[56] If Silicon Valley's success in terms of dynamic efficiency is related to the unenforceability of non-compete clauses, then one may have reason to question a strict and inflexible enforcement of corporate opportunity rules.[57]

The unenforceability of non-compete rules seems to highlight the close relationship between competition by insiders and dynamic innovation. Openness to a more flexible approach could be expected in the context of competition by insiders regulated by corporate opportunity rules: this is reflected in the introduction in Delaware corporate law of the possibility to approve an *ex ante* waiver for corporate opportunity rules. By contrast, such flexibility has not been reached yet by European corporate opportunity rules.[58]

8.5 OPEN QUESTIONS AND THE NEED FOR FURTHER EVIDENCE

Corporate opportunity rules are among a range of tools that can be employed to prevent insiders from competing with the corporation. As already mentioned, other examples may include for instance non-compete agreements and clauses. In this chapter, we have taken the first step in exploring new frameworks for the analysis of this multifaceted problem. And given the novelty of such a paradigm, it is not surprising that the framing of the competitive harm issue highlighted in this chapter proves difficult in the present competition law framework.

Having outlined the potential of corporate opportunities for significant effects on competition, static and dynamic considerations can be explored. Beyond the static concerns about exclusion on a horizontal level and about foreclosure on a vertical level, dynamic concerns seem far more pressing given the centrality of innovation in contemporary economic systems. Unfortunately, neither the current corporate nor competition rules can presently address these concerns sufficiently. Corporate opportunity rules are usually concerned with a containment of agency costs – although innovation dynamics have been considered in the last reform of

54 A Saxenian, *Regional Advantage* (Harvard UP 1996) 36.
55 *Ibid.* at 50.
56 *Ibid.* at 46.
57 Corradi (n 2) ch 5.
58 *Ibid.* ch 7.

Delaware corporate legislation.[59] In Europe, the absence of such flexibility calls for a strict enforcement of corporate opportunity rules, to defend investors' incentives to invest in equity. Thus, at least until the focus is on short-term investment returns, it is less surprising that corporate law does not address these concerns.

Indeed, even competition law is not able to provide sufficient tools to address the relevant competition concerns as we have explored elsewhere.[60] This has in particular to do with the *ex post* nature of the majority of competition laws. The classical tools of competition law, the cartel, and abuse/monopolisation rules are applied *ex post* and are ill-equipped to address dynamic and innovation concerns which are naturally forward-looking. The *ex ante* approach of the merger rules with its focus on future developments would seem better equipped to deal with the dynamic competition issues. Moreover, the comparison to a merger situation seems also closer to the situation at hand. In corporate opportunities cases, it is the future developments that are at issue. Seen from a competition perspective, the question is whether the enforcement of business opportunities would block a (future) competitor.

Elsewhere, we have suggested that a flexibilisation of corporate opportunity rules can help to address the competition problems stemming from such rules.[61] Crucial is further evidence resulting from cases, as it helps to inform policy discussion and helps in the design of any new corporate opportunity rules regime that takes account of potential negative effects on dynamic efficiency. Thus, future evidence-based research should explore whether the current corporate opportunity rules are in the majority of cases beneficial or harmful from a competition perspective with a special focus on dynamic efficiency. Ideally, such an examination would even go a step further and explore and categorise situations where corporate opportunity rules are more likely to be beneficial and those where this is not the case. For any such examination, the comparison to non-compete clauses might be fruitful comparison.

Case-based evidence should inspire the flexibilisation of standard rules and the relevant burden of proof. As establishing *ex ante* which kind of opportunity is beneficial to whom would often be a difficult operation, bargaining between the company and directors should play a crucial role – and corporate opportunity rules should inform such bargaining.[62] Keeping in mind the specific needs related to dynamic efficiency, one might explore whether the rules should allow the director faced with a claim to a corporate opportunity by the incumbent company to argue in its defence a potential harm to dynamic efficiency. In other words, while the standard rule could be that the opportunity remains with the company the director should then be entitled to abduct evidence that it would be more beneficial for dynamic efficiency if s/he were to receive the opportunity instead of the company. This adds

59 See text to (n 24–26).

60 See Corradi and Nowag (n 1).

61 *Ibid.*

62 Corradi (n 2) ch 4.

a further potential variable to the already complex set of arguments that normally surround 'classic' corporate opportunity rule cases.

8.6 CONCLUSION

Since the Standard Oil saga, competition law has been characterised by periods of harsh enforcement and periods of milder 'wait and see' and in this sense it is described as having a highly political connotation when compared to for example corporate law.[63] Moreover, antitrust agencies are renowned for their periodical focus on specific sectors often requiring the full-time dedication of most of their staff. Therefore, it seems not surprising that a topic such as the one we have dealt with in this chapter has never attracted any attention of any enforcer at all. In this sense, the chapter is not only a call for the collection of more evidence on this topic. It is a starting point of a reflection about certain interactions between corporate and competition law rules, rather than a call for urgent action in this area. Yet, what might be in need of urgent and thorough rethinking are the core aspects of dynamic competition. Today, corporate founders and directors have become the carriers of sophisticated technological knowledge and insight. Rules that affect their freedom to develop their innovative ideas and potential definitely raise questions about potential harms to dynamic competition. And again, this area proves to be challenging and has so far escaped the traditional antitrust metrics inspired by structural analysis which is still based on the structure-conduct-performance paradigm with a focus on significant market shares. Overall, corporate law rules escape the present antitrust prohibitions, and the enforcement of these rules may prevent rare plants' seeds to sprout into Esperidis golden apple-bearing trees. In other words, the loss in innovation maybe not only be to the detriment of the inventors but also to consumers and society as a whole.

63 W Kovacic, 'Politics and Partisanship in US Federal Antitrust Enforcement' (2013) 79 Antitrust LJ 687.

PART IV

Beyond the Boundaries of the Corporation

9

Horizontal Directors Revisited

Yaron Nili

9.1 INTRODUCTION

In this article, prepared for a special JCLE symposium, I revisit my initial findings regarding the prevalence of 'horizontal directors' in the United States.[1] 'Horizontal directors' serve on the board of multiple companies operating within the same industry. I have previously spotlighted the prevalence of horizontal directors in the US, despite a prima facie prohibition on director service among competitors.

Despite that spotlight and increasing attention to common ownership and to director interlocks, this Article explores six additional data years to further demonstrate the prevalence of horizontal directors as recently as the end of 2019.

In fact, in this project, the original dataset has been enhanced with bookend data from 2007 to 2009 and 2017 to 2019 for the director-level analysis. These expanded data confirm the rise of horizontal directors previously discussed and highlight their continued prevalence even against a backdrop of increased attention to the effects of common ownership and directors' interlocks.

Horizontal directors are significant because they stand at a unique intersection of antitrust law and corporate governance. They offer many legitimate governance and operational benefits to companies and shareholders but at the same time pose significant concerns both to the governance of the corporation and to antitrust policy. Despite that significance, horizontal directors have yet to receive the proper attention from regulators, stock exchanges, and investors.

This lack of attention to the horizontal aspect of director interlocks is particularly surprising for two reasons. First, existing US antitrust regulation specifically prohibits directors from serving on the boards of two competitors,[2] so sharing a director across companies in the same industry may violate these laws. Second, antitrust law has re-emerged in recent years[3] commanding increased attention to market concentration

1 Yaron Nili, *Horizontal Directors*, 114 N.W. L. Rev. 1179 (2020).

2 *See infra* section 9.4.1.

3 *See generally, e.g.* Herbert Hovenkamp, *Whatever* Did *Happen to the Antitrust Movement?*, 94 Notre Dame L. Rev. 583 (2018); John B. Kirkwood & Robert H. Lande, *The Fundamental Goal*

and consumer welfare (specifically in merger decisions[4] and 'horizontal shareholding'[5] by institutional investors). This emerging literature has sparked a vivid academic and public debate regarding the effects of shareholder concentration on antitrust policy.[6] Specifically, scholars have raised concerns regarding the incentives of companies to compete where major institutional shareholders hold large equity positions in all competitors. While market concentration by large investors has been widely acknowledged, a vivid debate has ensued on whether such concentration materialises in ways that promote anticompetitive behaviour.[7] As a by-product of this debate, recent focus has been directed to the question of which channels common owners use to effect anticompetitive behaviour.

For instance, one channel prominently discussed in recent years is executive compensation. Some suggest that common owners may either actively discourage

of Antitrust: Protecting Consumers, Not Increasing Efficiency, 84 Notre Dame L. Rev. 191 (2008); Barak Y. Orbach, *The Antitrust Consumer Welfare Paradox*, 7 J. Comp. L. & Econ. 133 (2010); Sean P. Sullivan, *What Structural Presumption?: Reuniting Evidence and Economics on the Role of Market Concentration in Horizontal Merger Analysis*, 42 J. Corp. L. 403 (2016); Samuel N. Weinstein, *When Systemic Risk Meets Antitrust: Dodd-Frank's Impact on Competitive Markets in the Wake of an Economic Crisis*, 21 Stan. J. L. Bus. & Fin. 286 (2016).

4 *See generally* Herbert Hovenkamp & Carl Shapiro, *Horizontal Mergers, Market Structure, and Burdens of Proof*, 127 Yale L.J. 1996, 2017–18 (2018) ('In practice, merger policy has sought to promote competition by applying the consumer welfare standard, under which a merger is judged to be anticompetitive if it disrupts the competitive process and harms trading parties on the other side of the market'); D. Daniel Sokol, *Antitrust, Institutions, and Merger Control*, 17 Geo. Mason L. Rev. 1055 (2010) (analysing antitrust institutions); D. Daniel Sokol & James A. Fishkin, *Antitrust Merger Efficiencies in the Shadow of the Law*, 64 Vand. L. Rev. En Banc 45 (2011) (providing an overview of antitrust merger practice).

5 Einer Elhauge, *Horizontal Shareholding*, 129 Harv. L. Rev. 1267, 1267 (2016) (defining horizontal shareholding as 'when a common set of investors own significant shares in corporations that are horizontal competitors in a product market').

6 *See id.*; Fiona Scott Morton & Herbert Hovenkamp, *Horizontal Shareholding and Antitrust Policy*, 127 Yale L. J. 2026 (2018); Edward B. Rock & Daniel L. Rubinfeld, *Defusing the Antitrust Threat to Institutional Investor Involvement in Corporate Governance* (NYU Sch. of Law, Law & Econ. Research Paper Series, Working Paper No. 17-05, 2017), https://papers.ssrn.com/a=2925855 [https://perma.cc/ULZ2-EEHJ]; José Azar et al., *Anticompetitive Effects of Common Ownership*, 73 J. Fin. 1513 (2018); Miguel Antón et al., *Common Ownership, Competition, and Top Management Incentives* (Fin. Working Paper No. 511/2017, 2018), https://papers.ssrn.com/a=2802332 [https://perma.cc/28VT-Q8KN]; Einer Elhauge, *New Evidence, Proofs, and Legal Theories on Horizontal Shareholding* (Jan. 4, 2018), https://papers.ssrn.com/a=3096812 [https://perma.cc/UR4Q-K9TQ]; Andrea Pawliczek & A. Nicole Skinner, *Common Ownership and Voluntary Disclosure* (June 8, 2018) (unpublished manuscript), https://papers.ssrn.com/a=3002075 [https://perma.cc/X455-T96Y]; John R. Woodbury, *Can Institutional Investors Soften Downstream Market Competition?* (June 2017), and https://papers.ssrn.com/a=2993433 [https://perma.cc/VY2Q-FK5B]; *see also* Martin C. Schmalz, *Common-Ownership Concentration and Corporate Conduct*, 10 Ann. Rev. Fin. Econ. 413 (2018).

7 Manesh S. Patel, *Common Ownerhsip, Institutional Investors & Antitrust*, 82 Antitrust L. J. 279 (2018) (explaining that the extent to which common ownership results in anticompetitive harm depends on a number of market factors); Edward B. Rock & Daniel L. Rubinfeld, *Antitrust for Institutional Investors*, NYU L. and Econ. Rsch. Paper No. 17–23, https://ssrn.com/abstract=2998296 or http://dx.doi.org/10.2139/ssrn.2998296; Scott Hemphill & Marcel Kahan, *The Strategies of Anticompetitive Common Ownership*, 129 Yale L. J. 1392, 1420 (2020).

performance-sensitive compensation or not actively push for a particular compensation plan and instead promote the status quo which lets executives 'get away with high performance-insensitive pay'.[8] While less plausible, another channel is through a targeted strategy of specific actions that is communicated to management that promotes portfolio value even at the expense of firm value.[9] In this channel, a common owner obtains leverage over management with its voting power and its ability to sell shares and decrease the market price of firm stock in order to promote its strategy.[10] Interestingly, and surprisingly, the role of directors as potential conduits of common ownership has been left underexplored. Specifically, horizontal directors might create this exact channel for common owners' influence, therefore facilitating anticompetitive effects on the market.[11] Alternately, horizontal directors may alone serve as the channel through which anticompetitive practices are achieved, without the need to pin such results on common owners.[12]

Equally important, horizontal directors are not a rarity: in fact, as shown below, empirical data reveal hundreds of directors concurrently serving on boards of companies operating in the same or similar industries. More so, the prevalence of horizontal directors is on the rise. Yet, despite the rise in horizontal directorships over time, proactive corporate disclosure of horizontal directors remains sparse.[13] Notably, the presence of horizontal directors across industry lines is not equal. Some industries are more prone to having horizontal directors than others. For example, while the construction industry has on average 10.6% industry-level horizontal directors serving on two or more companies' boards, the manufacturing industry has 33.7%.[14] This variance across industries invites for further research trying to connect industry levels of anticompetitiveness and horizontal directorships.

8 José Azar, Martin C. Schmalz & Isabel Tecu, *Common Ownership, Competition, and Top management Incentives* (Ross School of Business, Working Paper No. 1328, 2021) https://poseidon01.ssrn.com/delivery.php?ID=193021116117101011104086085118075018050053039063074059107023113074026011125098008122062055115111018120051030090026086029000017011005029023065116120091073093022001028030057095102102102071111113006109112123112120108025093068023014079076091009001004115&EXT=pdf&INDEX=TRUE.

9 Hemphill & Kahan, *supra* note 7, at 1420.

10 *Id.* at 1420–21.

11 Hubert Buch-Hansen, *Interlocking Directorates and Collusion: An Empirical Analysis*, 29 IN'L SOC. 249, 250–53 (2014) (describing research suggesting that interlocking directorates could facilitate collusion); James T. Halverson, *Should Interlocking Director Relationships Be Subject to Regulation and, If So, What Kind?*, 45 ANTITRUST L.J. 341, 347–49 (1976) ('While it seems unlikely, with counsel in attendance and recordation of minutes, that the boardroom serves today as a center of collusion, the potential for competitive abuses inherent in a horizontal interlocking relationship has not abated'); Maralynne Flehner, *Section 8 of the Clayton Act Applicable to Corporations* (SCM v. FTC), 53 ST. JOHN'S L. REV. 234, 239 (1979).

12 In new forthcoming work, my co-authors and I find a connection between the rise in horizontal directors and common owners, a connection that makes horizontal directors more likely to serve as a channel connected to common ownership rather than independently. Draft is on file with the Author.

13 *See infra* Sections 9.3.2 & 9.4.1.

14 See Nili *supra* note 1 at 1216–1217.

This Article proceeds as follows. Part II starts by providing an overview of the unique case of horizontal directors. Part III then provides a refreshed empirical analysis of the S&P 1500 director dataset and also revisits the company-level analysis of disclosure practices. Part IV then provides an overview of the current US legal framework governing and regulating horizontal directors. Part V discusses and analyses the implications of those results in more detail in light of the potential benefits and concerns horizontal directors may bring.

9.2 FROM INTERLOCKS TO HORIZONTALNESS

Directors' service on multiple boards has drawn both investor and academic attention,[15] mostly focusing on one of two areas: (1) the number of board seats a director holds and whether directors who hold several board positions have an impact on company performance or other governance metrics[16] or (2) the 'interlocks', or the connections and bridges, created between two (or more) companies by having a director that serves on both (or multiple) boards.[17]

Busy directors, and the interlocks they create, are a natural and inevitable by-product of a corporate culture that taps directors to serve on multiple boards at once.[18] The benefits of serving on multiple boards are tangible. Busy directors have more experience, provide more connections and develop more industry expertise at a

[15] The finance literature often uses the term 'busy directors', while the legal literature has used 'interlocks' more often. *See e.g. supra* note15. ____. Often, investors and proxy advisors also use the term 'overboarding', which is similar in concept to the term 'busy director'. *See e.g.* Kosmas Papadopoulos, *Director Overboarding: Global Trends, Definitions, and Impact*, ISS ANALYTICS (Aug. 28, 2019), www.issgovernance.com/library/director-overboarding-global-trends-definitions-and-impact/ [https://perma.cc/G2H6-7R6Q].

[16] Some studies consider a director as busy if she serves on more than one board. *See e.g.* Antonio Falato et al., *Distracted Directors: Does Board Busyness Hurt Shareholder Value?*, 113 J. FIN. ECON. 404, 405 (2014); Jeremy C. Kress, *Board to Death: How Busy Directors Could Cause the Next Financial Crisis*, 59 B.C. L. REV. 877, 878 (2018); Stephen P. Ferris et al., *Too Busy to Mind the Business? Monitoring by Directors with Multiple Board Appointments*, 58 J. FIN. 1087, 1091 (2003); Eliezer M. Fich & Anil Shivdasani, *Are Busy Boards Effective Monitors?*, 61 J. FIN. 689, 689 (2006) (using the larger, 'three or more' metric). This article will consider directors busy if they serve on more than one board, as serving on even two boards operating in the same industry brings the potential dangers and benefits of horizontal directorship.

[17] Director 'interlocks' refers to the connection between two companies that is facilitated by sharing a director. *See e.g.* Michal Barzuza & Quinn Curtis, *Board Interlocks and Outside Directors' Protection*, 46 J. LEGAL STUD. 129 (2017) (examining the relationship between interlocks and indemnification protection); Michal Barzuza & Quinn Curtis, *Board Interlocks and Corporate Governance*, 39 DEL. J. CORP. L. 669, 669 (2015); Eliezer M. Fich & Lawrence J. White, *CEO Compensation and Turnover: The Effects of Mutually Interlocked Boards*, 38 WAKE FOREST L. REV. 935 (2003) (empirical analysis finding that mutual interlocks increase CEO compensation and decrease CEO turnover).

[18] *See* Anil Shivdasani & David Yermack, *CEO Involvement in the Selection of New Board Members: An Empirical Analysis*, 54 J. FIN. 1829, 1846 (1999); Todd Wallack & Sacha Pfeiffer, *Debate Swirls on How Many Board Directorships Are Enough*, BOS. GLOBE (Dec. 10, 2015), www3.bostonglobe.com/metro/2015/12/09/some-corporate-directors-overboard-joining-many-boards-and-raising-performance-questions/pQBVAGZmCBJ4fzaKTGdziP/story.html?arc404=true [https://perma.cc/63SD-9GZ8].

rate that exponentially increases with the number of boards they serve.[19] Conversely, less-busy directors provide fewer tangential benefits derived from busyness to firms.[20]

While there is no shortage in attention to busy directors,[21] missing from current discourse is a more nuanced account of the boards on which busy directors serve. While by definition directors serving on more than one board fall into the definition of a 'busy director', some of these busy directors *also* serve on more than one board in the same industry – these are what I termed as horizontal directors.[22]

Horizontal directors are particularly important because their prevalence, as discussed below, raises both governance and antitrust concerns. Horizontal directors raise antitrust concerns since their concurrent board seats provide a channel between companies in the same industry. These channels can lead to either collaboration and/or collusion.[23] Additionally, horizontal directors also raise corporate governance concerns, such as reduced independence and increased conformity in governance practices that could lead to systemic governance risk.[24] Moreover, the rise in horizontal directors comes against a backdrop of heightened concentration in the US markets. More than 75% of US industries experienced a rise in concentration levels[25]

[19] Jeremy McClane & Yaron Nili, *Social Corporate Governance*, 89 GEO. WASH. L. REV. (forthcoming, 2021).

[20] *See e.g.* Laura Field et al., *Are Busy Boards Detrimental?*, 109 J. FIN. ECON. 63, 63–64 (2013) (finding that venture-backed IPO firms benefit from busy director expertise, as busy directors serve more as advisors than monitors); Ira C. Harris & Katsuhiko Shimizu, *Too Busy to Serve? An Examination of the Influence of Overboarded Directors*, 41 J. MGMT. STUD. 775, 775 (2004) (finding that busy directors enhance acquisition performance through expertise); Wolfgang Drobetz et al., *Industry Expert Directors*, 92 J. BANK. & FIN.195, 195 (2018) (analysing 'the valuation effect of board industry experience and channels through which industry experience of outside directors relates to firm value', and finding that 'firms with more experienced outside directors are valued at a premium compared to firms with less experienced outside directors').

[21] *See e.g.* George D. Cashman et al., Going Overboard? *On Busy Directors and Firm Value*, 36 J. BANK. & FIN. 3248, 3252 (2012); Harris & Shimizu, *supra* note 20, at 775 (finding that 'overboarded directors' – the paper's term for busy directors – enhance corporate governance, but focusing solely on the amount of boards as a measure). Field et al., *supra* note 20, at 65 (arguing that smaller, less established firms might benefit from busy directors' connections and experience); *see also* David J. Denis et al., *The Selection of Directors to Corporate Boards* 1 (2018), https://ssrn.com/abstract=3215474 [https://perma.cc/HB7N-KKLR] (finding that 'post-spinoff unit and remaining parent firms are more likely to select pre-spinoff parent directors who have []relevant industry expertise'). *See* Ferris et al., *supra* note 16, at 1097 ('[F]irms with larger boards present greater opportunities for board members to make connections leading to additional invitations to serve on other boards'); Nili, *supra* note 1.

[22] *See* Nili, *supra* note 1.

[23] *See e.g.* Scott A. Sher & Andrea Agathoklis Murino, *Unilateral Effects in Technology Markets:* Oracle, H&R Block, *and What It All Means*, 26 ANTITRUST 46, 46–47 (2012), www.wsgr.com/publications/PDFSearch/sher-summer-12.pdf [https://perma.cc/75J9-5F5V]; *see also Competitive Effects*, FED. TRADE COMM'N, www.ftc.gov/tips-advice/competition-guidance/guide-antitrust-laws/mergers/competitive-effects [https://perma.cc/C5UU-ETD9].

[24] *See* Section 9.5.

[25] Concentration, in this context, is used as a measure of competition in the industry. A low concentration number indicates a high level of competition, while a high concentration level indicates a lower level of competition in the industry. *See* Sean P. Sullivan, *What Structural Presumption?: Reuniting*

in recent years.[26] As the distribution of a given market among participating companies becomes less spread out, the anticompetitive effects of collusion and price-fixing intensify. Therefore, the potential impact of horizontal directors is also amplified.

A final factor contributing to the profound effect horizontal directors can have in the corporate landscape is a product of the fact that demarcation lines among industries are becoming increasingly more difficult to ascertain.[27] Because horizontal directors are identified based on industry, the murkier industry lines become, the harder it will be to identify and monitor horizontal directors for anticompetitive behaviour.

9.3 REVISITING HORIZONTAL DIRECTORS: EMPIRICAL FINDINGS

This Part provides augmented data on the prevalence of horizontal directors in the US as well as information disclosed to investors on horizontal directors. The data presented herein extend prior analysis,[28] expanding the analysis to include data from 2007 to 2009 and 2017 to 2019, therefore providing an even more broad view of the rise of director horizontalness and the persistence of it even as recently as January 2020.

9.3.1 *Horizontal Directors in S&P 1500 Companies*

9.3.1.1 Methodology

This Part examines the prevalence of horizontal directors on boards in the same industry for companies within the S&P 1500 from 2007 and through 2019. The data for this sample were originally compiled from Equilar's BoardEdge dataset.[29] Both director-level data and company-level data were obtained for each company within the S&P 1500 for each year previously mentioned. These separate datasets were merged to create one panel dataset at the director-company-year level where each individual case describes a director's service on a specific S&P 1500 board as well as any additional boards that specific director served on and that were outside of the

Evidence and Economics on the Role of Market Concentration in Horizontal Merger Analysis, 42 J. CORP. L. 403, 408–410 (2016).

26 Gustavo Grullon et al., *Are U.S. Industries Becoming More Concentrated?* 2, 6–11 (Rev. Fin. Swiss Fin. Inst. Research Paper No. 19–41, 2018), https://ssrn.com/abstract=2612047 [https://perma.cc/P9TA-9M3U] (finding that more than 75% of US industries have experienced an increase in concentration levels over the last two decades).

27 *See e.g.* Charlene L. Nicholls-Nixon & Dale Jasinski, *The Blurring of Industry Boundaries: An Explanatory Model Applied to Telecommunications*, 4 INDUS. & CORP. CHANGE. 755, 755–56, 758 (1995); Eamonn Kelly, *Blurring Boundaries, Uncharted Frontiers*, *in* DELOITTE, BUSINESS ECOSYSTEMS COME OF AGE 17, 19 (2015) (ebook), www2.deloitte.com/us/en/insights/focus/business-trends/2015/business-ecosystems-boundaries-business-trends.html#endnote-sup-9 [https://perma.cc/MM4B-DV9E].

28 *See* Nili, *supra* note 1.

29 *See* EQUILAR, www.equilar.com/boardedge-issuers.html [https://perma.cc/2VJU-778B].

S&P 1500. For the purposes of analysis all directors were included, whether they were designated as independent or not. This consolidated dataset was subsequently supplemented with company-level data from FactSet and the North American Industry Classification System (NAICS) Association to add NAICS codes[30] and industry classifications for groups of SIC and NAICS codes.

Directors were coded as 'horizontal' using four classifications: whether a director served on more than one board in the same (1) SIC code, (2) SIC industry, (3) NAICS code, or (4) NAICS industry. Because an 'industry' contains multiple SIC codes or NAICS codes, the industry-horizontal classifications are a broader measure than the classifications based on specific SIC or NAICS codes. However, using both SIC and NAIC classifications allows for a more robust analysis. Directors were given a binary variable (0 or 1) for each classification indicating their horizontal status. These variables were used to calculate the number of horizontal boards on which the director served in a given year. Directors were also coded as 'busy' – serving on more than one board at a time – regardless of whether those boards are horizontal. Each busy director was individually coded with an indicator variable as well as a count of the number of boards on which they served each year.

9.3.1.2 Director-Level Analysis

As depicted in Table 9.1, the expanded data show the number and percentage of directors in the S&P 1500 who served on more than one board. From 2007 to 2019, more than 30% of all directors sat on more than one board, and a substantial number of directors (around 12%) held three or four board positions. The data covering the 2010–2016 years ('The Original Data') pointed out that the percent of busy directors did not vary more than 2% from 2010 to 2016. However, the supplemented data from 2007 to 2009 and 2017 to 2019 show a more prominent incline in busy directors over time. For example, the number of directors that served on two boards increased by 17% from 2007 to 2019, and the number of directors that served on three boards increased by 39% for this same time period.

Additionally, the percent of directors that serve on two or more boards has increased despite the fact that the total number of directors in the sample has decreased by 3% on average each year (total decline of 28% from 2007 to 2019).

30 'The North American Industry Classification System is unique among industry classifications in that it is constructed within a single conceptual framework. Economic units that have similar production processes are classified in the same industry, and the lines drawn between industries demarcate, to the extent practicable, differences in production processes.... In the design of NAICS, attention was given to developing production-oriented classifications for (a) new and emerging industries, (b) service industries in general, and (c) industries engaged in the production of advanced technologies'. Office of Mgmt. & Budget, Exec. Office of the President, North American Industry Classification System (2017), www.census.gov/eos/www/naics/2017NAICS/2017_NAICS_Manual.pdf [https://perma.cc/5FNS-XM86].

TABLE 9.1 *Number of boards a director sits on*

	1	2	3	4	5	6	7+	N
2019	61.93%	24.99%	9.21%	3.11%	0.63%	0.09%	0.04%	100.00%
	6,159	2,485	916	309	63	9	4	9,945
2018	60.81%	24.91%	10.14%	3.22%	0.75%	0.12%	0.05%	100.00%
	6,175	2,530	1,030	327	76	12	5	10.155
2017	60.42%	25.08%	10.43%	3.16%	0.78%	0.09%	0.03%	100.00%
	5,943	2,467	1,026	311	77	9	3	9,836
2016	65.14%	22.44%	9.08%	2.66%	0.52%	0.10%	0.04%	100.00%
	8,191	2,822	1,142	335	66	13	5	12,574
2015	63.75%	23.49%	9.05%	2.92%	0.59%	0.13%	0.07%	100.00%
	7,937	2,925	1,127	363	74	16	9	12,451
2014	63.55%	23.37%	9.22%	2.83%	0.79%	0.18%	0.07%	100.00%
	7,960	2,927	1,155	354	99	22	9	12,526
2013	63.31%	23.28%	9.78%	2.70%	0.70%	0.17%	0.07%	100.00%
	7,822	2,877	1,208	333	86	21	9	12,356
2012	63.92%	23.24%	9.40%	2.44%	0.78%	0.14%	0.07%	100.00%
	7,755	2,820	1,141	296	95	17	8	12,132
2011	64.23%	23.25%	9.11%	2.44%	0.75%	0.19%	0.03%	100.00%
	7,650	2,769	1,085	291	89	23	3	11,910
2010	63.63%	23.41%	9.20%	2.68%	0.74%	0.30%	0.03%	100.00%
	7,564	27,83	1,094	318	88	36	4	11,887
2009	72.88%	18.76%	6.03%	1.71%	0.50%	0.12%	0.01%	100.00%
	10,090	2,597	835	237	69	16	1	13,845
2008	71.60%	19.88%	6.35%	1.56%	0.49%	0.11%	0.02%	100.00%
	10,164	2,822	902	221	69	15	3	14,196
2007	69.60%	21.35%	6.64%	1.80%	0.47%	0.11%	0.02%	100.00%
	9,675	2,968	923	250	66	15	3	13,899

As I have previously underscored, horizontal directors are not outliers among directors of public companies – the opposite is true. Table 9.2 shows that the trends previously highlighted with respect to the Original Data are amplified by the additional years included. Although the data show that the percent of busy directors that share an industry within their boards served does not vary more than 8% in this 13-year period, a closer look at the data shows more nuanced patterns. For example, the number of directors that served on boards of at least two companies within the same industry slowly increased from 2007 to 2009. However, from 2009 to 2010 there was a 20% decrease in the number of directors that served on two or more boards within the same industry, showing some year-to-year volatility in the appointment of horizontal directors.

Although industry classification is broader than a single SIC or NAICS classification, combining multiple codes, the number of horizontal directors is substantial under both metrics. There were 1,888 directors that served on the board of more

TABLE 9.2 *Number and percentage of busy directors sharing an industry within boards served*

# of boards	2007	2008	2009	2010	2011	2012	2013	2014	2015	2016	2017	2018	2019
2	895 (34%)	994 (35%)	1473 (46%)	952 (34%)	1002 (36%)	1056 (37%)	1077 (37%)	1094 (37%)	1075 (37%)	1051 (37%)	936 (38%)	960 (38%)	954 (38%)
3	519 (62%)	571 (63%)	618 (65%)	676 (62%)	687 (63%)	724 (63%)	800 (66%)	769 (67%)	751 (67%)	767 (67%)	675 (65%)	674 (65%)	596 (65%)
4	197 (79%)	184 (78%)	266 (83%)	258 (81%)	237 (81%)	237 (81%)	267 (80%)	289 (82%)	300 (83%)	282 (84%)	262 (84%)	281 (85%)	269 (86%)
5	63 (90%)	62 (90%)	97 (92%)	80 (91%)	81 (91%)	89 (94%)	79 (92%)	93 (94%)	67 (91%)	62 (94%)	75 (95%)	73 (95%)	56 (90%)
6	16 (100%)	15 (100%)	25 (93%)	33 (92%)	22 (96%)	16 (94%)	21 (100%)	22 (100%)	16 (100%)	13 (100%)	9 (100%)	12 (100%)	10 (100%)
7+	1 (100%)	4 (100%)	10 (100%)	4 (100%)	3 (100%)	8 (100%)	9 (100%)	9 (100%)	9 (100%)	5 (100%)	2 (67%)	4 (80%)	3 (75%)

TABLE 9.3 *Number and percentage of busy directors sharing SIC/NAICS within boards served*

# of boards	SIC/NAICS	2010	2011	2012	2013	2014	2015	2016	2017	2018	2019
2	SIC	140 (5%)	149 (5%)	180 (6%)	183 (6%)	195 (7%)	208 (8%)	209 (8%)	170 (7%)	169 (7%)	184 (7%)
	NAICS	104 (4%)	120 (4%)	144 (5%)	155 (5%)	165 (6%)	159 (5%)	147 (5%)	143 (6%)	151 (6%)	156 (6%)
3	SIC	101 (9%)	103 (9%)	123 (11%)	139 (12%)	129 (11%)	148 (13%)	150 (13%)	146 (14%)	154 (15%)	129 (14%)
	NAICS	80 (7%)	81 (7%)	99 (9%)	118 (10%)	115 (10%)	129 (11%)	132 (12%)	121 (12%)	123 (12%)	107 (12%)
4	SIC	45 (14%)	43 (15%)	53 (18%)	70 (21%)	68 (19%)	85 (25%)	102 (29%)	73 (23%)	77 (23%)	67 (21%)
	NAICS	36 (11%)	40 (14%)	41 (14%)	57 (17%)	65 (18%)	62 (17%)	56 (17%)	65 (21%)	65 (20%)	63 (20%)
5	SIC	21 (24%)	19 (21%)	28 (29%)	28 (33%)	31 (31%)	24 (32%)	26 (39%)	38 (48%)	29 (38%)	22 (35%)
	NAICS	14 (16%)	14 (16%)	28 (29%)	23 (27%)	23 (23%)	19 (26%)	24 (36%)	35 (44%)	23 (30%)	14 (23%)
6	SIC	13 (36%)	8 (35%)	9 (53%)	8 (38%)	13 (59%)	9 (56%)	10 (77%)	7 (78%)	7 (58%)	9 (90%)
	NAICS	13 (36%)	10 (43%)	7 (41%)	5 (24%)	11 (50%)	7 (44%)	8 (62%)	5 (56%)	6 (50%)	9 (90%)
7+	SIC	1 (25%)	0 (0%)	5 (62%)	7 (78%)	6 (67%)	4 (44%)	2 (40%)	2 67%)	3 (60%)	1 (25%)
	NAICS	1 (25%)	0 (0%)	5 (62%)	6 (67%)	5 (56%)	3 (33%)	2 (40%)	2 (67%)	3 (60%)	1 (25%)
Total	SIC	321 (7.4%)	322 (7.5%)	398 (9.2%)	435 (9.5%)	442 (9.7%)	478 (10.5%)	499 (11.3%)	436 (11.1%)	449 (11.2%)	412 (10.8%)
	NAICS	248 (5.7%)	265 (6.2%)	324 (7.5%)	364 (8%)	384 (8.4%)	379 (8.3%)	369 (8.4%)	371 (9.5%)	371 (9.2%)	350 (9.2%)

TABLE 9.4 *Time trend of horizontal directors*

Year	2010	2011	2012	2013	2014	2015	2016	2017	2018	2019
% of Industry-Horizontal Directors out of All Directors	16.9	17.1	17.6	18.2	18.2	17.8	17.3	19.7	19.5	18.8
% of Industry-Horizontal Directors out of Busy Directors	46.3	47.7	48.7	49.7	49.8	49.1	49.7	50.2	50.2	49.6
% of SIC-Horizontal Directors out of All Directors	2.7	2.7	3.3	3.5	3.5	3.8	3.9	4.4	4.3	4.2
% of SIC-Horizontal Directors out of Busy Directors	7.4	7.6	9.1	9.6	9.7	10.6	10.9	11.2	11	10.8
% of NAICS-Horizontal Directors out of All Directors	2.1	2.2	2.7	2.9	3.1	3	2.9	3.7	3.6	3.6
% of NAICS-Horizontal Directors out of Busy Directors	5.7	6.2	7.4	8	8.4	8.4	8.4	9.5	9.3	9.2

than one company within the same industry in 2019. On a more granular level, there were 412 directors (10.8% of directors serving on more than one board) who served on at least two companies in the same industry per four-digit SIC code. Similarly, there were 250 directors (9.2% of the directors serving on more than one board) that served on at least two companies' boards within the same NAICS code.

The number of directors that serve on more than one company with the same NAICS or SIC code has decreased by only 3% from 2016 to 2019 (Table 9.3). Therefore, there has not been a significant change in the striking presence of horizontal directors since the Original Data.

Table 9.4 further shows that the percentage of horizontal directors as a percent of busy and total directors has been trending upwards over time with a merely a slight

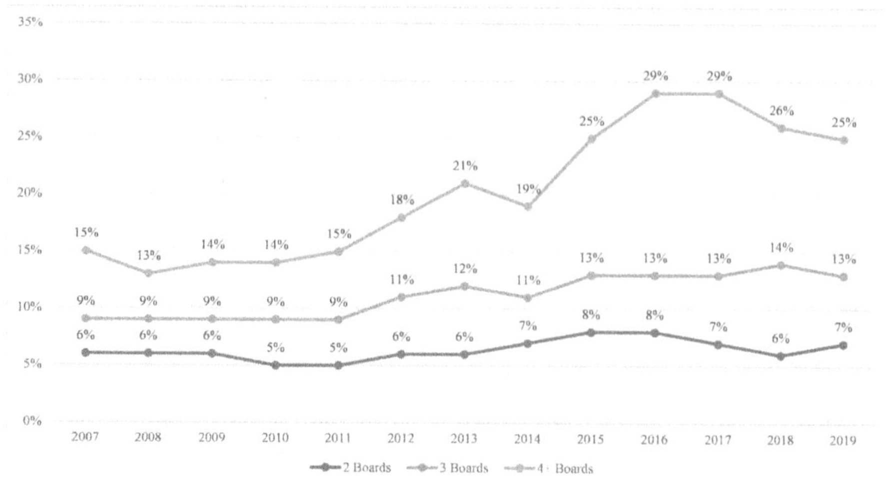

FIGURE 9.1 Percentage of busy directors sitting on at least two boards with the same SIC code

decline seen in the last two years. For example, in 2010, 7.4% of all horizontal directors sat on at least two boards of within the same SIC classification. This number increased by 7% on average each year from 2010 to 2016 but decreased by 2% in both 2018 and 2019. A similar trend was observed under the NAICS classification with an average increase in that metric of 8% each year with a decline of 3% in the last two years.

The pattern of steady growth followed by a slight decline is magnified in Figure 9.1. As depicted below, there has been a significant amount of growth from 2007 to 2016, particularly among directors serving on three or more boards. However, the expanded data show that the number of busy directors who sit on boards for companies within the same SIC code has slightly decreased in the last couple of years especially for directors serving on four or more boards, though it is still at significantly higher levels compared to 2010.

9.3.2 *Disclosure Practices*

The SEC imposes disclosure requirements on publicly traded companies in regard to their independent directors. Under Item 407 of Regulation S-K, companies are required to disclose which directors have been determined to be independent by the board of directors.[31] Companies must also disclose any non-independent members

[31] 17 C.F.R. § 229.407(a) (2019). Companies usually satisfy the Item 407 requirements by including the disclosures within their annual proxy statement or annual 10-K. NYSE and NASDAQ rules also effectively defer to Item 407 for disclosure. *See* N.Y.S.E. Listed Company Manual (CCH) § 303A.02(a); NASDAQ Stock Mkt. Rules (CCH) 5605(b)(1).

of the compensation, nominating, or audit committees.[32] And lastly, if any company has adopted its own director independence standards, in addition to the existing stock exchange rules, the company must disclose whether its own definition of 'independence' is available online.[33]

Alongside the director independence disclosure requirements, companies are required to provide general information on their directors. Notably, Item 401(e)(2) requires companies to '[i]ndicate any other directorships held, including any other directorships held during the past five years, held by each director'.[34] Thus, Items 401 and 407 collectively require companies to disclose which directors are considered independent and to detail each director's position on the board and any directorships held over the past five years.

The disclosure of board positions enables investors to better monitor and influence companies regarding board composition, including horizontal directors. However, companies vary in their disclosure practices and many lack several elements that would give shareholders access to information about horizontal directors.

To analyse the disclosure practices for companies within different market capitalisations, data were hand collected for fifty large-cap companies that make up the Fortune 50 and fifty small-cap companies that make up the Russell 2000. Data regarding the service of directors for other companies were collected from each company's most recent form DEF 14A – an annual proxy filing required by the SEC.

Of the 100 companies surveyed, 99 had directors that served on another board. 97 of those companies disclosed this information, but only 24 of those companies provided a description of the other company or identified the company's industry, as shown in Table 9.5. As previously noted, given the scarcity of information disclosed, it is very difficult to ascertain the presence of a horizontal director.

Additionally, companies are only required to disclose a director's prior roles for the last five years. Considering many companies (53%) only disclose the minimum required and some (6%) didn't disclose any past information at all, this causes a great concern as the social and professional ties that a director develops while serving on other boards generally last for much longer than five years. Even when this information was disclosed, it is often buried within a paragraph and not presented in an easy-to-digest format that highlights this information. This leaves shareholders in the dark about the true prevalence of horizontal directors in their portfolio companies.

32 17 C.F.R. § 229.407(a) (2019).

33 § 229.407(a)(2). If the internal standards are available online, the site must include a hyperlink for shareholders to access. *Id.*

34 17 C.F.R. § 229.401(e)(2) (2019).

TABLE 9.5 *Director disclosures*

Level of proxy statement disclosure	Percent of companies
Name of other boards served	97
Industry of other boards served	24
Current boards served	95
Past boards served	90
More than minimum disclosure of past five years	53

9.4 THE PECULIAR PRESENCE OF HORIZONTAL DIRECTORS

9.4.1 *The Regulatory Framework*

Horizontal directorships are not completely unchecked, they are subject to several regulatory and market restrictions. While corporate and securities laws do not explicitly prohibit horizontal directorships,[35] a mosaic of regulatory and market-based restrictions does provide outer limits on their prevalence. Similarly, and more explicitly, antitrust laws attempt to target collusion between competitor companies with common directors.[36] Yet, these constraints may have not yielded the expected results. Indeed, despite the various constraints on horizontal directors, they remain prevalent.

9.4.1.1 Antitrust: Section 8 of the Clayton Act

The major aim of antitrust regulation is to promote healthy, fair, and robust competition among companies.[37] Horizontal directors may provide an avenue for companies to collude at the expense of consumers, in direct violation of antitrust regulatory goals.[38] Section 8 of the Clayton Act directly addresses this concern by prohibiting

[35] *See infra* Section 9.4.1.1.

[36] *See* Press Release, U.S. Dep't of Justice, Tullett Prebon and ICAP Restructure Transaction After Justice Department Expresses Concerns About Interlocking Directorates (July 14, 2016) [hereinafter Press Release, U.S. Dep't of Justice, Tullett Prebon], www.justice.gov/opa/pr/tullett-prebon-and-icap-restructure-transaction-after-justice-department-expresses-concerns [https://perma.cc/TZE9-XMRE] ("'Robust competition depends on competitors being actually independent of each other – that's what Section 8 [of the Clayton Act] requires", said Principal Deputy Assistant Attorney General Renata Hesse of the department's Antitrust Division. "As originally proposed, this deal would have violated that core principle – creating a cozy relationship among competitors"'); United States v. Sears, Roebuck & Co., 111 F. Supp. 614, 616 (S.D.N.Y. 1953).

[37] Andrea Agathoklis Murino & Kirby H. Lewis, *Board Interlocks on Antitrust Enforcement Hot Seat: A Must-Read Guide for Board Members and Officers*, GOODWIN ALERT (Aug. 17, 2016), www.goodwinlaw.com/publications/2016/08/08_17_16-board-interlocks-on-antitrust-enforcement [https://perma.cc/6QEG-A2EX]; *see also* KEITH N. HYLTON, ANTITRUST LAW: ECONOMIC THEORY AND COMMON LAW EVOLUTION 40 (2003); Daniel A. Crane, *Antitrust's Unconventional Politics*, 104 VA. L. REV. ONLINE 118, 123 (2018).

[38] Buch-Hansen, *supra* note 11, at 249–50 ('It is widely believed that interlocking directorates – situations in which directors sit on more than one company board – have the potential to facilitate collusion').

an individual or entity from serving on the board or as an officer of two *competing* corporations.[39] The crux of Section 8 revolves around the requirement that the two companies be competitors. Horizontal directors risk violating Section 8 if the two (or more) companies in question are considered 'competitors', as the Clayton Act requires.[40] Companies that produce the same products, companies that sell 'reasonably interchangeable products within the same geographic area',[41] and 'companies that vie for the business of the same prospective purchasers, even if the products they offer, unless modified, are sufficiently dissimilar to preclude a single purchaser from having a choice of a suitable product from each' all fall into the category of 'competitors' for purposes of Section 8.[42]

The government can also target horizontal directors under Section 5 of the Federal Trade Commission Act (FTC Act) as an unfair practice or method of competition,[43] which provides the FTC with broader power to pursue per se violations and activities that violate the spirit of the Clayton Act.[44] It follows that horizontal directors do not have to overtly collude to violate antitrust law. The FTC recently demonstrated that anticompetitive effects outside of direct coordination could still violate antitrust principles, relying on evidence of unilateral effects.[45] Interestingly, horizontal directors are also prevalent in the EU.[46] However, unlike the US, horizontal directors in direct competitors are not prohibited in Europe, with the exception of Italy.[47] Italy prohibited interlocking in 2011 to promote competition in the banking, insurance, and financial sectors.[48]

9.4.1.2 *Fiduciary Duty Law*

Directors are agents of the corporation, and therefore, they owe fiduciary duties to the corporation.[49] Because horizontal directors serving on the board of two companies owe concurrent fiduciary duties to each company, they are at a heightened risk of violating their fiduciary duties.[50]

39 *See* 15 USC § 19 (2018).
40 *See* Murino & Lewis, *supra* note 37.
41 1 Earl W. Kintner et al., 5 Federal Antitrust Law § 42.11 (2019) (*citing* Am. Bakeries Co. v. Gourmet Bakers, Inc., 515 F. Supp. 977, 980 (D. Md. 1981).
42 TRW, Inc. v. F.T.C., 647 F.2d 942, 946 (9th Cir. 1981).
43 15 USC § 45 (2018); *see e.g. In re* Perpetual Fed. Sav. & Loan Ass'n, 90 F.T.C. 608 (1977).
44 *See* Federal Trade Commission Act, 15 USC § 45 (2018) (as generally applied to interlocks).
45 *See* Sher & Murino, *supra* note 23.
46 Florence. Thépot, and Florian Hugon, and Mathieu Luinaud, *Interlocking Directorates and Anti-Competitive Risks: An Enforcement Gap in Europe?*, Concurrences No 1-2016, (February 15, 2016).
47 *Id.*
48 Florence Thépot, *Interlocking Directorates in Europe – An Enforcement Gap?, in this volume.* TJ; Federico Cesare Guido Ghezzi & Chiara Picciau, *The Curious Case of Italian Interlocking Directorates, in this volume.*
49 *See e.g.* Guth v. Loft, Inc., 5 A.2d 503, 510 (Del. 1939).
50 *See* John K. Wells, *Multiple Directorships: The Fiduciary Duties and Conflicts of Interest that Arise When One Individual Serves More than One Corporation*, 33 J. Marshall L. Rev. 561 (2000).

Delaware law has well-developed case law interpreting allegations of conflicting loyalties and corporate opportunity violations.[51] Loyalty conflicts typically arise in the parent–subsidiary setting. Delaware courts have declined to hold that dual-seated directors on parent–target subsidiary boards are per se conflicted,[52] but have found a violation of good faith and fair dealing and the 'absence of any attempt to structure [the] transaction on an arm's length basis', and on that basis held that the directors were conflicted.[53]

Additionally, under the corporate opportunity doctrine, directors may not take for themselves 'a new business opportunity that belongs to the corporation, unless they first present it to the corporation and receive authorization to pursue it personally'.[54] Horizontal directors are more susceptible to potential corporate opportunity concerns due to their increased access to intra-company information.[55] The potential for these directors to, even unintentionally, violate their fiduciary duties is reason for them to limit their service on other boards, or at the very least restrict their exposure through corporate opportunity waivers,[56] recusals, and nondisclosure agreements.[57]

9.4.1.3 Interlocking Director Committee Limitations

Horizontal directors are theoretically also restricted by The New York Stock Exchange (NYSE) and the NASDAQ Stock Market, both of which require that a majority of a company's board of directors be independent.[58] Because director

[51] For a recent case explaining and applying this line of case law, see Pers. Touch Holding Corp. v. Glaubach, No. 11199-CB, 2019 Del. Ch. LEXIS 66, at *34–49 (Feb. 25, 2019).

[52] Weinberger v. UOP, Inc., 457 A.2d 701 (Del. 1983).

[53] *Id.* at 710–11.

[54] *Id.* at 1087.

[55] *See e.g.* Nicole Huberfeld, *Tackling the 'Evils' of Interlocking Directorates in Healthcare Nonprofits*, 85 Neb. L. Rev. 681 (2007) (discussing the increased potential for fiduciary duty breaches in the context of director interlocks in healthcare nonprofits); Wells, *supra* note 50 (analysing the fiduciary duty conflicts arising out of holding multiple directorships).

[56] *See generally* Gabriel Rauterberg & Eric Talley, *Contracting out of the Fiduciary Duty of Loyalty: An Empirical Analysis of Corporate Opportunity Wiavers*, 117 Colum. L. Rev. 1075 (2017) (discussing the use of corporate opportunity waivers); Alarm.com Holdings, Inc. v. ABS Cap. Partners Inc., No. CV 2017-0583-JTL, 2018 WL 3006118 (Del. Ch. June 15, 2018), aff'd, 204 A.3d 113 (Del. 2019) (dismissing a claim for misappropriation of trade secrets by a horizontal director because multiple agreements between the two companies memorialized that the horizontal director could engage in competing businesses).

[57] James E. Berchtold, *Dual Directorship: The Perils of Serving Two Masters*, Martindale (July 30, 2003), www.martindale.com/business-law/article_Lewis-Roca-LLP_22410.htm [https://perma.cc/SLK3-LNH7]; Charles M. Nathan, *Maintaining Board Confidentiality*, Harv. L. Sch. F. Corp. Governance (Jan. 23, 2010), https://corpgov.law.harvard.edu/2010/01/23/maintaining-board-confidentiality/ [https://perma.cc/Y4X4-23U3] (explaining the dearth of case law on confidentiality requirements of directors and the difficulties in ensuring director confidentiality).

[58] *See SEC Approves NYSE and NASDAQ Proposals Relating to Director Independence*, FindLaw, http://corporate.findlaw.com/finance/sec-approves-nyse-and-nasdaq-proposals-relating-to-director.html [https://perma.cc/W7V9-X9GY]; Securities Exchange Act Release No. 34-48745 (Nov. 4, 2003) (approving NYSE § 303A(1) & NASD Rule 4350(c)(1)).

TABLE 9.6 *Audit committee participation by busy directors*

Audit participation	2010	2011	2012	2013	2014	2015	2016	2017	2018	2019
4+ Boards	8.33%	9.09%	6.06%	2.90%	2.33%	1.87%	1.80%	0.54%	0.54%	0.51%

independence can depend on the director's or her family members' service in other companies, a horizontal director who serves on the board of multiple companies risks corroding her independence.[59]

A specific restriction imposed by the NYSE that could impact the service of horizontal directors requires that simultaneous service on more than three public company audit committees be disclosed and approved by the board.[60] NASDAQ does not have the same rule, but in recent years there has been a marked drop-off in participation on more than three audit committees by directors.[61] As Table 9.6 demonstrates, the percentage of directors serving on the audit committees on four or more boards has declined dramatically, going from 8.33% in 2010 to 0.51% in 2019.

9.4.1.4 ISS/Glass Lewis

Institutional Shareholder Services, Inc. (ISS) and Glass Lewis wield influence in potentially comparable ways to that of governmental regulators by shaping corporate governance practices and corporate board policies.[62] Both ISS and Glass Lewis have adopted policies providing additional boundaries on the service of directors on multiple boards that companies will be expected to follow in order to win the support of ISS and Glass Lewis.

Because support of these proxy advisory firms is critical, their adopted policies likely increase the pressure on firms to reduce the number of busy directors, including horizontal directors. Even though their policies only serve as an outer limit on extreme cases of horizontal directorships and are unlikely to curb a large percentage of the cases, these standards still have an impact. As Part II demonstrated, the

59 NASDAQ Stock Mkt. Rules (CCH) 5605(a)(2)(E).

60 This disclosure can be made 'either on or through the listed company's website or in its annual proxy statement or, if the listed company does not file an annual proxy statement, in its annual report on Form 10-K filed with the SEC. If this disclosure is made on or through the listed company's website, the listed company must disclose that fact in its annual proxy statement or annual report, as applicable, and provide the website address'. N.Y.S.E. Listed Company Manual (CCH) § 303A.07(a).

61 Data were obtained from the BoardEdge database and is valid through 12 June, 2017. The BoardEdge data file contains various statistics on all public companies in the United States, including board committee service. *See supra* Section 9.3.1.

62 *See* Timothy M. Doyle, *New Report: Proxy Advisory Firms Operate with Unchecked Power*, AMERICAN COUNCIL FOR CAPITAL FORMATION (May 1, 2018), http://accf.org/2018/05/01/outsized-influence-minimal-oversight-new-accf-report-finds-that-proxy-advisory-firms-operate-with-unchecked-power/ [https://perma.cc/EMV3-DVAZ].

ratio of horizontal directors dramatically increases as they serve on more boards. Therefore, limiting – even modestly – the number of boards on which a director can hold a position has a stronger impact on those directors that have horizontal directorships.

9.4.1.5 Disclosure Rules

Finally, as discussed above, the SEC imposes disclosure requirements on publicly traded companies requiring them to provide general information on their directors, including information regarding their service on other boards. To the extent companies comply with such requirements, it may deter them from appointing horizontal directors if they anticipate regulatory pressure or investor push-back.

9.4.2 *Horizontal Directors: Contrasting the Law with the Data*

Antitrust laws prohibit horizontal directorships in competing corporations. Yet, as discussed herein, a significant number of directors serve on boards in the same industry, even if narrowly defined by NAICS and SIC classifications. While industry measures are only a crude proxy for the potential of two companies to compete, it is more likely that two companies operating in the same space will in fact compete. This is especially true given the wide definition of competition that has been applied to Section 8.[63] How can one explain this disparity of law and reality?

As I discussed in a prior writing, there are several key factors that help explain the prevalence of horizontal directors against this regulatory backdrop. First, it could be that companies sharing a director, even in the same industry, are not competitors, and therefore are not in violation of Section 8. However, this is unlikely given the fact that Section 8 applies to 'companies that vie for the same purchasers' even if dissimilar products.[64] Second, although Section 8 is a strict liability offense,[65] several practical and structural barriers hinder its enforcement. Historically, the FTC and DOJ have not brought Section 8 enforcements in court,[66] but instead have relied on self-policing and behind-the-scenes actions to pressure violators.[67] Additionally,

[63] Debbie Feinstein, *Have a Plan to Comply with the Bar on Horizontal Interlocks*, FED. TRADE COMM'N (Jan. 23, 2017), www.ftc.gov/news-events/blogs/competition-matters/2017/01/haveplan-comply-bar-horizontal-interlocks [https://perma.cc/8JLS-3ZL5] (stating that competition under Section 8 can encompass more than the market definition analysis, especially in the context of emerging industries).

[64] TRW, Inc. v. FTC, 647 F.2d 942, 946 (9th Cir. 1981).

[65] Brian Desmarais et al., *Board Interlocks on Antitrust Enforcement Hot Seat: A Must-Read Guide for Board Members and Officers*, JD SUPRA (Mar. 22, 2019), www.jdsupra.com/legalnews/board-interlocks-on-antitrust-80619/ [https://perma.cc/K6WX-DF4M].

[66] Feinstein, *supra* note 63.

[67] *See e.g.* James T. Halverson, *Interlocking Directorates – Present Anti-Trust Enforcement Interest Placed in Proper Analytical Perspective*, 21 VILL. L. REV. 393, 399 (1976) (describing that because Section 8 was 'so fraught with loopholes and so easily evaded that it was hardly worth the allocation of resources

private plaintiffs may be disincentivised from bringing a claim due to the lack of remuneration for individual shareholders, especially in cases where horizontal directors advance shareholder value. Furthermore, as discussed above, information regarding horizontal directors is not clearly disclosed or readily available to shareholders to identify these situations.[68]

Section 8 also gives the FTC a lot of discretionary power and lacks clarity and a bright-line rule in applying the 'competition' requirement. This is further complicated by the fact that it is not always obvious to discern the market in which a company operates. The lack of a clear and public enforcement process adds a layer of difficulty in projecting FTC/DOJ enforcement and in deterring companies from violating Section 8 ex-ante.

9.5 HORIZONTAL DIRECTORS: ZERO-SUM PROPOSITION?

Some level of collaboration between companies within the same industry can be beneficial to consumers; therefore, antitrust laws only target efforts that lead to anticompetitive outcomes or collusion.[69] Horizontal directors may provide value to the company and investors, such as contributing to the diffusion of beneficial corporate governance practices, networking, and expertise. By sitting on boards of multiple companies in the same industry, horizontal directors gain intimate knowledge can be a valuable asset to a director's ability to advise and monitor the management team.[70] However, the presence of horizontal directors also presents concerns, such as an increased risk of antitrust collaboration, an increased risk of systemic governance risk,[71] and decreased director independence.[72] Furthermore, horizontal directors may facilitate anticompetitive practices that could further insulate management from market pressures which may lead to a loss of shareholder value in the long term.

required to enforce it', more often horizontal interlocks were dissolved as a result of FTC pressure than actual litigation); Victor H. Kramer, *Interlocking Directorships and the Clayton Act After 35 Years*, 59 YALE L.J. 1266, 1270–71 (1950) (describing a 1947 survey by the DOJ of '10,000 persons in 1600 leading corporations....[A]pproximately 1500 ... held directorships in more than one concern ... most of those persons holding directorships in violation of Section 8 resigned without contest').

68 *See supra* Section 9.2.

69 *See* FED. TRADE COMM'N & U.S. DEP'T OF JUSTICE, ANTITRUST GUIDELINES FOR COLLABORATIONS AMONG COMPETITORS 2–3 (Apr. 2000), www.ftc.gov/sites/default/files/documents/public_events/joint-venture-hearings-antitrust-guidelines-collaboration-among-competitors/ftcdojguidelines-2.pdf [https://perma.cc/YEN5-MWLV] [hereinafter FTC–DOJ COLLABORATION GUIDELINES].

70 *Id.*

71 The presence of horizontal directors may lead to the adoption of similar best practices across companies in which they serve and for better overall governance practices and adoption. Yet, uniformity in governance procedures, through the adoption of similar governance arrangements, may form a 'weak spot' in corporations' compliance or other best practices that could lead to a cascade of similar issues across corporations. *See* Veronica Root, *The Compliance Process*, 94 IND. L.J. 203, 216 (2019).

72 *See infra* Section 9.3.2.

As previously explored, this Article re-emphasises the need to shine a spotlight on horizontal directors and to address the accompanying concerns. Even though there has been a slight decline in the number of directors serving on companies within the same industry in the last few years, the overall prevalence of horizontal directors remains a concern.

Yet, horizontal directors are not necessarily a zero-sum proposition. Companies could still tap the valuable aspects of horizontal directors while at the same time minimising the concerns that they may present.

First, legislation that targets higher risk companies will be more effective at mitigating antitrust risks and will be easier to enforce uniformly, which will mitigate some of the current Section 8 underenforcement concerns. As I previously discussed,[73] some industries and SIC codes are more likely to have horizontal directors, and some of these horizontal-director-saturated industries also exhibit strong levels of industry concentration, perhaps making them a key starting point for evaluation.

Focusing the prohibition on concentrated industries might strike a desired balance. The right balance would allow companies to enjoy the benefits these directors provide while prohibiting their presence in cases where the costs to competition are more likely to outweigh these benefits. For instance, Section 8 could be revised to exempt from the prohibition industries with an HHI that is below a certain threshold. Aggressively enforcing Section 8 for that subset of public companies would reduce significant antitrust risk. Italy took a similar approach, in focusing on the banking sector. The main provision dealing with interlocking directors prohibits members of boards and any top manager of a company operating in the banking, insurance, and financial sectors from holding one of those offices in a competing company.[74] However, the Italian legislation was criticised for its inflexibility and lack of clarity.[75] For example, the Act did not include a de minimis exemption for very small firms that did not prompt the same concerns as larger companies.[76] If policymakers choose to amend the Clayton Act, they should take care to incorporate flexibility to strike the desired balance.

Second, regulators could consider an ex-ante design to Section 8 of the Clayton Act that would allow directors to apply for a waiver before accepting a horizontal directorship. By obtaining an ex-ante 'no action' waiver,[77] companies would be more certain about nominating potential directors. Furthermore, companies would

[73] *See* Nili, *supra* note 1.

[74] *See* Ghezzi & Picciau, *supra* note 48.

[75] *Id.* at 12.

[76] *Id.*

[77] This would be similar to the no-action process employed by the SEC in exclusion of shareholder proposals. *See* Note, *Proxy Rule 14a-8: Omission of Shareholder Proposals*, 84 HARV. L. REV. 700, 717 (1971); Scott Lesmes, *Frequently Asked Questions About Shareholder Proposals and Proxy Access* 1–3 (2017), https://media2.mofo.com/documents/frequently-asked-questions-about-shareholder-proposals-and-proxy-access.pdf [https://perma.cc/R99U-GBWR].

be able to justify the nomination of directors that would technically violate the Act. Giving the FTC a veto right ex-ante would also reduce the need for costly ex-post enforcement and may lead to more consistent enforcement.

In fact, a similar arrangement is already employed in the context of interlocking bank directorships. The Federal Reserve's (the Fed) Regulation L is similar to the Clayton Act in that it prohibits an officer or director of a bank from serving as an officer or director for more than one of any bank's holding companies with over $10 billion in assets.[78] However, Regulation L allows the Fed to grant waivers when it determines that an interlock would not substantially lessen competition.[79] While the banking industry is more regulated than other industries, one can easily find ways to implement this rule in a cost effective way across other industries. For instance, the FTC may require a public notice to be filed, with a presumption of approval unless otherwise indicated within 20 days. The notice in turn will also allow shareholders, stock exchanges, and proxy advisors to apply private ordering restrictions if they so desire.

Third, and as previously mentioned, horizontal directors toe the line between antitrust and corporate governance, and a comprehensive reform should highlight the benefits of these directors as well as address the corporate governance risks. As Part II highlighted, many companies currently keep disclosures to the bare minimum required.[80] Thus, it is often difficult to even identify the industry of the other boards on which horizontal directors serve. Regardless of whether shareholders see horizontal directors as positively or negatively impacting the company, improved transparency via more comprehensive disclosures would enable shareholders to more effectively participate in corporate governance by making more informed director nominations and board recommendations.

An alternative approach to consider for reform would be updating stock exchanges' self-regulation to better incorporate horizontal directorship concerns. One concern of horizontal directorships is the ability of directors to serve as independent directors when they have extensive experience in one industry. From a shareholder perspective, including directors with deep industry experience may add significant value to the

78 12 C.F.R. § 212.3 (2019).

79 *See e.g.* Letter from Margaret McCloskey Shanks, Deputy Secretary of the Board, to Jason J. Cabral, Esq., Sullivan & Cromwell LLP (Sept. 7, 2017), www.federalreserve.gov/supervisionreg/legalinterpretations/bhc_changeincontrol20170907.pdf [https://perma.cc/5PDT-TYHD]; Letter from Ann E. Misback, Secretary of the Board, to Jason J. Cabral, Esq., Sullivan & Cromwell LLP (June 9, 2017), www.federalreserve.gov/supervisionreg/legalinterpretations/bhc_changeincontrol20170609b.pdf [https://perma.cc/4WCX-AC3Y]; Letter from Margaret McCloskey Shanks, Deputy Secretary of the Board, to Patricia M. Schaubeck, Esq., Sun Bancorp, Inc. (Apr. 14, 2017), www.federalreserve.gov/supervisionreg/legalinterpretations/bhc_changeincontrol20170414.pdf [https://perma.cc/EAJ5-LR82].

80 *See supra* Section 9.2; *see also* Yaron Nili, *Out of Sight, Out of Mind: The Case for Improving Director Independence Disclosure*, 43 J. Corp. L. 35, 53 (2017) (discussing the current flaws in the disclosure regime).

company. Accordingly, stock exchanges may consider revising their independence definitions to exclude directors from being considered independent if they serve on the boards of two companies in the same SIC code, whether or not they are considered competitors. This restriction could strike a better balance between enabling companies from benefitting from horizontal directorship and preventing boards and directors from becoming too dependent on their specific industry connection.

Finally, state law and fiduciary law can also evolve to increase restrictions to mitigate the concerns that arise from the prominence of horizontal directors. Additionally, tightening judicial review of non-compete agreements, corporate opportunity waivers, and board fiduciary duties may position common law jurisprudence to more effectively address potential governance issues that stem from the presence of horizontal directors. For example, courts may examine corporate opportunity waivers more skeptically where a horizontal director is involved and where the opportunity is given to a horizontal company. The common law route can provide the flexibility and adaptability that regulatory intervention often lacks; however, it will depend on litigants voicing concerns.

9.6 CONCLUSION

In many ways, horizontal directors epitomise the push and pull of our corporate governance system. Directors are expected to monitor management, to provide expertise and networking, and to make the corporation's most important decisions.[81] Yet, we lean on outsiders to serve as directors, and we allow, and even encourage, their service on other boards, potentially undermining their ability to appropriately serve their director role. Indeed, many directors serve on more than one board when given the opportunity. Director is a desired position due to the relatively limited time commitment to each board, significant salary and perks, and limited exposure to legal risk.[82] Additionally, serving on several boards across industries, within the same industry, and even within the same SIC code can benefit not only the director but also the companies she serves – at least under certain conditions.[83]

Yet, there is an open question as to how horizontal directors should fit within our current antitrust regulatory framework and corporate governance regime. Moreover, how to appropriately balance the competing interests remains unresolved. Similarly, it remains unclear how we should view horizontal directorships given increased industry concentration and vivid discourse regarding horizontal mergers and horizontal shareholdings.

81 *See supra* text accompanying notes 34–37.

82 *See* Bernard S. Black et al., *Outside Director Liability: A Policy Analysis*, 162 J. Inst. & Theoretical Econ. 5, 5 (2006); Christopher M. Bruner, *Good Faith, State of Mind, and the Outer Boundaries of Director Liability in Corporate Law*, 41 Wake Forest L. Rev. 1131, 1175 (2006).

83 *See supra* Section 9.5

This Article demonstrates that horizontal directors remain a prevalent feature (and bug) of the US corporate landscape. Future research into horizontal directorships is still needed, given the increased reliance on the board as an institution,[84] and the emergence of contemporary antitrust discourse regarding horizontal ties between companies through common shareholders. Understanding that not all companies are created equal, investors may be better situated than regulators to account for the rise in horizontal directorships and offer market-based solutions to the inherent tension that these directors present.

[84] *See supra* Section 9.2.

10

Interlocking Directorates in Europe

An Enforcement Gap?

Florence Thépot

10.1 INTRODUCTION

Interlocking directorates refer to situations in which one or more companies have one or more members of their boards in common. In the US, under Section 8 of the Clayton Act, competing companies are prohibited from having common board members.[1] In application of this prohibition, Eric Schmidt, CEO of Google, stepped down from the board of Apple in 2009. In the EU, however, such links between companies' boards are not uncommon. In the EU, as well as in the different Member States,[2] there is no such express prohibition of interlocking directorates between competitors. Some economies have even been characterised by very dense networks of companies owing to multiple links among their boards[3].

This chapter highlights the potential anticompetitive risks raised by interlocking directorates between competitors. The anticompetitive effects stem both from the increased ability to collude enabled by interlocks, as well as the reduced incentive to compete fiercely on markets characterised with numerous social and corporate links. In addition, this chapter touches upon the questions of conflict of interest and problems of directors' independence that are inherent when a board member sits on the boards of two competing companies.

The main claim of this chapter is that there may be an enforcement gap around anticompetitive effects of interlocking directorates in Europe. Although Article 101 TFEU and EU Merger Control regulation theoretically apply to the coordinated

University of Strasbourg. Among other sources, this chapter builds on developments in F Thépot, *The Interaction between Competition Law and Corporate Governance* (Cambridge University Press 2019).

1 15 USC § 19.

2 Apart from Italy in the financial sector since 201. See F Ghezzi and C Picciau, chapter 11 of this book.

3 See e.g. F Ferraro and others, 'Structural Breaks and Governance Networks in Western Europe' in B Kogut (ed), *The Small Worlds of Corporate Governance* (MIT Press 2012); Brullebaut, B., Allemand, I., Prinz, E. and Thépot, F. Persistence in corporate networks through boards of directors? A longitudinal study of interlocks in France, Germany, and the United Kingdom (2022) 16 Rev Manag Sci 1743–82.

and unilateral effects of interlocks, these provisions are of very limited use in practice. Company law in some Member States, such as France, limits the number of board appointments a director may hold, but such solutions are specific to certain types of companies and are largely insufficient to address the anticompetitive effects of interlocking directorates. Principles of corporate governance, such as fiduciary duties, are not binding and seem inappropriate to prevent anticompetitive effects and issues of conflict of interests.

Issues raised by interlocking directorates do not attract the attention they deserve and are notably absent from discussions on possible issues raised by financial links at the EU level.[4] In the US, the discussion about anticompetitive effects of common ownership should also grant more attention to interlocking directorates, particularly in the light of recent findings on the prevalence of interlocking directorates in the US.[5] This is because financial ownership links and interlocking directorates raise similar concerns, critically at the edge of competition law and corporate governance.[6] Therefore, this chapter draws attention on the need to tackle potentially significant issues that are currently largely undebated in Europe.

This chapter demonstrates that the anticompetitive effects of interlocking directorates (Section 10.1) may fall short of EU competition law (Section 10.2). Section 10.3 explains how interlocking directorates may be regulated in other jurisdictions, including in the US, and discusses whether tools of corporate governance may remedy the identified anticompetitive concerns (Section 10.4).

4 Unless attached to minority interests, the issue of interlocks was absent from discussion around Merger control reform in 2014 (that was later abandoned). Renewed interest for issues of structural links at EU level (but no discussion of interlocks) M Vestager, 'Competition in Changing Times' (FIW Symposium, Innsbruck, 16 February 2018) https://ec.europa.eu/commission/commissioners/2014–2019/vestager/announcements/competition-changing-times-0_en; Commission, Management Plan 2017 of DG Competition, Ref Ares(2016)7130280 16; Recent European Parliamenet study: S Frazzani and others, 'Barriers to Competition through Common Ownership by Institutional Investors' (European Parliament 2020) Study for the Committee on Economic and Monetary Affairs, Policy Department for Economic, Scientific and Quality of Life Policies.

5 Y Nili, 'Horizontal Directors' 114 NWUL Rev 1179 (2020) Y. Nili, Horizontal Directors Revisited, in this Volume. A recent speech shows that joint effect of common ownership and interlocks are clearly acknowledged. A Finch, 'Concentrating on Competition: An Antitrust Perspective on Platforms and Industry Consolidation' (Tech, Media, and Telecom Competition Conference, Washington DC, 14 December 2018) www.justice.gov/opa/speech/principal-deputy-assistant-attorney-general-andrew-finch-delivers-keynote-address-capitol.

6 See chapters in Part IV of this book. Overview of the debate on common ownership, see e.g. Federal Republic of Germany, 'Common Ownership by Institutional Investors and Its Impact on Competition' (OECD Competition Policy Roundtable, December 2017) Contribution by Germany, OECD DAF/COMP/WD(2017)87, 10; CPI Antitrust Chronicle 'Common Ownership revisited' (2019) 2; CPI Antitrust Chronicle 'Index Funds – a New Antitrust Frontier?'(2017) 3. For more particular legal and economic analysis, see e.g. J Azar, M Schmalz and I Tecu, 'Anti-Competitive Effects of Common Ownership' (2018) 73(4) J Fin; E Elhauge, 'Essay: Horizontal Shareholding' (2016) 129 Harv L Rev 1267; J Baker 'Overlapping Financial Investor Ownership, Market Power, and Antitrust Enforcement: My Qualified Agreement with Professor Elhauge' (2016) 129 Harv L Rev *Forum* 212.

10.2 ANTICOMPETITIVE EFFECTS OF INTERLOCKING DIRECTORATES

Various studies highlighted that corporate networks across industries, based on interlocking directorates, have been particularly dense in continental Europe, although networks have tended to become less dense and more diffuse over the past decades.[7] These studies also demonstrate that corporate networks based on interlocks have been comparatively less dense in the US and in the UK.[8] Germany has long been characterised by dense networks of companies where banks play a central role, leading to the qualification of 'cooperative capitalism' as a feature of the German economy.[9] In France, large companies were typically connected through their boards with a high number of CEOs sitting as independent board members of competitors.[10] A recent study analysed the structure and evolution of corporate networks of the top 100 French, British, and German companies over a 14-year period (2006–2019). It found that although networks are composed of weaker links (individuals hold less appointments on average), they are wider in scope (more companies are now part of the networks).[11] While it does not specifically provide intra-sectoral information, this study demonstrates the existence of traditionally dense corporate networks in Europe comprising companies from the same industry. As explored by various corporate governance scholars, the existence of interlocking directorates may enhance the firm performance owing to the cognitive input of an experienced board member, and resource potential the link may create.[12]

When held among competing companies, interlocking directorates may give rise to unilateral and coordinated effects.[13] The first impact on competition stems from

[7] P Windolf, *Corporate Networks in Europe and the United States* (Oxford University Press 2002); S Chabi and J Maati (2005), 'Les réseaux du CAC40' (2005) 153 *Revue du Financier* 45–65; Brullebaut and others (n 4). Among the possible reasons for the reduced density may be the limits set by corporate law or governance codes on the number of board seats individuals may hold. For example, in France or Germany, gender diversity requirements may explain that companies appoint directors from a greater pool of individuals.

[8] See e.g. P Windolf and J Beyer, 'Co-operative Capitalism: Corporate Networks in Germany and Britain' (1996) 47 Bri Journal of Sociol 205–231; K Van Veen and J Kratzer, 'National and International Interlocking Directorates within Europe: Corporate Networks within and among Fifteen European Countries' (2011) 40(1) Economy and Society 1–25; Brullebaut and others (n 4).

[9] F Ferraro and others, 'Structural Breaks and Governance Networks in Western Europe' in B Kogut (ed), *The Small Worlds of Corporate Governance* (MIT Press 2012); Windolf and Beyer (n 9) 205–23.

[10] HJ Yeo, C Pochet and A Alcouffe, 'CEO Reciprocal Interlocks in French Corporations' (2003) 7 J Manag Gov 87–108.

[11] Brullebaut and others (n 4), see appendix – visual representation of corporate networks in 2019.

[12] According to the resource-based and resource dependence theories; see e.g. C Drago and others, 'Corporate Governance Reforms, Interlocking Directorship and Company Performance in Italy' (2015) 41 *Int'l Rev L & Econ* 38–49; M Macus, 'Board Capability: An Interactions Perspective on Boards of Directors and Firm Performance' (2008) 38(3) Int Stud Manag Organ 98–116.

[13] EM Fich and LJ White, 'Why do CEOs Reciprocally Sit on Each Other's Boards?' (2005) 11 J Corp Finan 175; MS Mizruchi, 'What Do Interlocks Do? An Analysis, Critique, and Assessment

the information and communication flows facilitated by interlocking directorates. Board members have access to strategic, accounting, and commercial information as well as information regarding the appointment and compensation of executives.[14] Information and communication between competitors have been shown to facilitate collusion, even when not specifically related to prices and quantities. Information flows may help in reaching a collusive agreement and also provide monitoring tools for competitors to prevent deviation from the collusive agreement.[15] As an example, a network of interlocking directorates has helped stabilise a number of cartels, including the international uranium and diamond cartels.[16] Accordingly, the purpose of the US prohibition of interlocking directorates is expressly to 'avoid the opportunity for the coordination of business decisions by competitors and to prevent the exchange of commercially sensitive information by competitors'.[17] Anticompetitive agreements can also be facilitated by indirect interlocks where competitors sit on the board of a third party. Information exchanges can be more discrete with indirect rather than direct interlocks.[18]

Interlocks may also affect unilateral incentives to compete. Social ties created by the attendance of common board meetings may discourage aggressive commercial strategies towards rivals. If interlocks are widespread within industries, this may reduce the overall intensity of competition.[19] When attached to financial interests, interlocking directorates may provide the ability to influence a competitor's conduct. The remuneration schemes in place may also affect the incentive to compete, especially if closely tied to the firm's performance.[20]

of Research on Interlocking Directorates' (1996) 22 Annu Rev Sociol 273; e.g. H Buch-Hansen, 'Interlocking Directorates and Collusion: An Empirical Analysis' (2014) 29 Int Sociol 253; V Petersen, 'Interlocking Directorates in the European Union: An Argument for Their Restriction' (2016) 27 EBL Rev 821–864; F Thépot, F Hugon, and M Luinaud, 'Cumul de mandats d'administrateur et risques anticoncurrentiels: Un vide juridique en Europe?' (2016) 1 Concurrences 1–11; Nili (n 6).

14 UK Office of Fair Trading (OFT), 'Minority Interests in Competitors: A Research Report prepared by DotEcon Ltd' (2010) OFT Economic Discussion Paper Series, OFT1218, 11; JP Schmidt, 'Germany: Merger Control Analysis of Minority Shareholdings – A Model for the EU?' (2013) 2 Concurrences 16.

15 KU Kühn, 'Fighting Collusion by Regulating Communication between Firms' (2001) 16 *Economic Policy* 167; X Vives, *Oligopoly Pricing: Old Ideas and New Tools* (MIT Press 1999) in P Buccirossi and G Spagnolo, 'Corporate Governance and Collusive Behavior', WD Collins (ed), *Issues in Competition Law and Policy 1* (American Bar Association 2008) 10.

16 V Petersen, 'Interlocking Directorates in the European Union: An Argument for Their Restriction' (2016) 27 (6) EBL Rev 821, 842.

17 *Square D Co v Schneider SA* 760 F Supp 362 (SDNY 1991). Nonetheless, directors may still belong to a close network of business elites, linked via common educations or social values through which they can somehow coordinate business decisions. For a discussion of interlocks and business elites, see e.g. WK Carroll and JP Sapinski, 'Corporate Elites and Intercorporate Networks', in John Scott and Peter Carrington (eds), *The Sage Handbook of Network Analysis* (SAGE Publishing 2011) 180.

18 Buch-Hansen (n 14).

19 L Flochel, 'The Competitive Effects of Acquiring Minority Shareholdings' (2012) (1) Concurrences 16–17; D Spector, 'Some Economics of Minority Shareholdings' (2011) (3) Concurrences 14.

20 UK OFT (n 15) 60–63.

Nevertheless, economic efficiencies are more likely to exist in the area of interlocking directorates than in the situation of minority shareholdings (e.g. where used to align incentives in joint ventures).[21] Information exchange, enabled by such links, may reduce strategic uncertainty which may under certain circumstances be pro-competitive if it improves business decision-making. The presence of the board member of a competitor offers the benefit of his expertise and experience which may improve decision-making. Moreover, the exchange of information can create synergies in the control and management of companies facing similar technical and economic issues. A business can also benefit from the reputation of an independent board member and use it in situations where the asymmetry of information may be an obstacle in negotiations to obtain financing from banks or investors. Similarly, the expertise and reputation of the board member of a competitor can facilitate contractual negotiations with suppliers and customers – especially in small businesses.[22]

The anticompetitive effects of interlocking directorates are exacerbated if the corporate governance of the competing companies is weak. Directors sitting on several boards may influence the decision process in one company, as a way of favouring another company of which they are a board member. Directors may also be tempted to disclose confidential information of a company at another company's board meeting. These issues may be mitigated by the quality of the fiduciary duty. A strong fiduciary duty, which indicates good corporate governance, may prevent the director from engaging in these types of practices. A director's fiduciary duty to one company, however, may naturally conflict with their fiduciary duty in another company.[23] Overall, bad quality of corporate governance is more likely to induce directors with shared directorship to compete less aggressively.[24]

10.2.1 *Empirical Studies on Competitive Effects*

The few existing empirical studies draw contrasting conclusions regarding the actual effectiveness of interlocks as a collusive device. Based on data of a sample composed of 225 firms convicted for participating in cartels between 1986 and 2010,

[21] *Ibid.*

[22] The welfare effect of a reduction in uncertainty depends on the type of decision variable (price or quantity), the type of uncertainty (common demand v idiosyncratic costs), and the characteristics of the goods (substitutes or complements, homogeneous or heterogeneous products). KU Kühn and X Vives, *Information Exchanges among firms and their impact on Competition* (Office for Official Publications of the European Communities 1995). For a comprehensive analysis of the impact of board interlocks on the firms' performance, see e.g. E Prinz, *Les effets des liens personnels interconseils sur la performance de l'entreprise : une analyse comparée entre France et Allemagne* (Peter Lang 2011).

[23] OECD, Common Ownership by Institutional Investors and its Impact on Competition, DAF/COMP/WD (2017)10.

[24] UK OFT (n 15) para 6.5. For a discussion of how loyalty to competing companies can articulate in the context of venture capital, see e.g. T Woolf 'The Venture Capitalist's Corporate Opportunity Problem.' Colum Bus L Rev (2001): 473; and M Corradi, *Corporate Opportunities: A Law and Economic Analysis* (Hart 2021) ch.6

Gonzales and Schmidt found that there is a greater likelihood of collusion when companies have a higher fraction of 'busy' board members, referring to members sitting on the board of other companies, owing to the impact of board connections on collusion.[25] Based on data of EU cartel cases between 1969 and 2012 and corporate links between the companies, a study by Hubert Buch-Hansen concluded that only 12 of the 3318 corporate ties among the 890 companies involved in the cartel cases seem to have been conducive to collusion. Three of them were direct and nine indirect interlocks. Interestingly, however, earlier cases of cartels seem to have been more correlated to interlocking directorates than today.[26] A possible interpretation is that since the 1990s, there is a stricter enforcement against cartel practices. Consequently, companies would refrain from using interlocking directorates to sustain collusion, possibly to avoid attracting the authority attention. Although inherent to the study of typically hidden illegal practices, the correlation was limited to cases of detected explicit collusion. This prevents any conclusion to be made on corporate links and undetected collusion between competitors. Based on estimation of the probability of detection (of cartels that were eventually detected), we can imagine that the population of undetected collusion largely outweighs that of detected cases.[27] A few older studies by Pennings and Burt based on US firms establish a positive correlation between an industry concentration and interlocks.[28] The latter study, however, found a negative relationship between interlocks and concentration, as of intermediate level of concentration. This may be explained by the fact that firms in highly concentrated industries have little need for interlocks to achieve collusive outcomes.[29]

Finally, the following data further supports the idea that interlocks may have facilitated collusive agreements in the past.[30] Building on Connor's statistics on international cartels between 1990 and 2009, I computed the rate of cartel recidivism according to the companies' country of incorporation.[31] Among the 52 leading recidivist companies involved in international cartels, 17 companies originated in France and Germany, and those companies engaged in a total of 213 cartels. This means that French and German companies were liable for 35.3% of the international cartels in

25 TA Gonzales and M Schmid 'Corporate Governance and Antitrust Behavior' (2012) Swiss Institute of Banking and Finance, University of St Gallen Working Paper. www.efmaefm.org/oefmameetings/efma%20annual%20meetings/2012-Barcelona/papers/ArtigaGonzalezSchmid.pdf (accessed March 2021).

26 Buch-Hansen (n 14) 253.

27 E Combe, C Monnier and R Legal, 'Cartels: The Probability of Getting Caught in the European Union' (2008) Bruges European Economic Research Papers, 2.

28 JM Pennings, *Interlocking Directorates: Origins and Consequences of Connections among Organizations' Board of Directors* (Jossey-Bass Inc 1980); RS Burt RS, *Corporate Profits and Cooptation* (Academic 1983) (as cited in Mizruchi (n 14) 273–274). For an overview of existing older studies in the US, see Nili (n 6) fn 16 p 1186.

29 Mizruchi (n 14) 273.

30 Although no causation ought to be established here – merely suggesting one among other possible factors.

31 JM Connor, *Annex: Table 1. Fifty-Two Leading Recidivists*, 1990–2009 in 'Recidivism Revealed: Private International Cartels 1990–2009' (2012) 6 Competition Policy International 101.

that period. In contrast, a total of nine UK and US companies, traditionally characterised by less dense corporate networks, were among the top cartel recidivists, engaging in a total of 88 cartels, which amounts to 14.6% of the international cartels accounted for.[32] Furthermore, France and Germany's combined economies (reflecting possibly, the number of companies in it) amount only to 1/3 or the combined US and UK economies. Thus, weighing this, the proportion of French and German companies involved in cartels may appear to be comparatively even stronger[33].

Characteristics of the French and German industries, prone to cartel formation, surely plays a key role in explaining the substantial difference in cartel participation.[34] Corporate features, including dense corporate networks – particularly during the period covered by the statistics, may also explain the higher rate of cartel prosecution in France and Germany. Indeed, in Germany, it was suggested that corporate networks played a role as an 'institutional infrastructure for coordination, information exchange, and control in Germany'.[35] In France, on top of interlocking directorates, during the 1990s and 2000s, cross-shareholdings among major companies increased, intensifying the network of corporate ownership.[36] Therefore, corporate ties that establish a 'small world' of corporations may have also been correlated with the multiple cartel convictions in France and Germany between 1990 and 2010.

10.3 THE REACH OF EU COMPETITION LAW OVER INTERLOCKING DIRECTORATES

In the EU, a structural link is scrutinised under the Merger Regulation if it is part of an acquisition that confers a 'lasting change in the control of the undertaking'.[37] Interlocking directorates which are not part of an acquisition conferring control

[32] Interestingly, recent data on US firms contrast with this idea, showing that interlocking directorates are more common, including among companies active in the same industry. Nili (n 6)

[33] Based on 2020 GDP data, OECD, *OECD Data: Gross domestic product* (GDP) https://data.oecd.org/gdp/gross-domestic-product-gdp.htm (accessed 1 March 2021)

[34] Both economies are characterised by industries that are particularly prone to cartel formation because of the type of goods produced and the high barriers to entry into the market. It has been shown that cartel formation is more likely in industries producing homogeneous goods, which are characterised by rather stable demand, or a demand affected by common shock. Moreover, cartel formation is deemed more likely in markets where entry and exit are difficult. If barriers to entry are low, new entrants are attracted by the high profits realised in such market. Gains from collusion are then reduced, while the costs of punishment in case of a deviation are relatively lower. UK OFT, 'Predicting Cartels: A Report Prepared for the Office of Fair Trading by PA Grout and S Sonderegger' (2005). See also RC Marshall and LM Marx, *The Economics of Collusion* (MIT Press 2012).

[35] B Kogut and G Walker, 'The Small World of Germany and the Durability of National Networks' (2001) 66 Am Soc Rev 317.

[36] Some related these new ties to the wave of liberalisation in the 1990s. VA Schmidt, 'Privatization in France: The Transformation of French Capitalism' (1999) 17 Environment and Planning C: Government and Policy 445. In subsequent periods, the intensity of these links seems to have reduced, with the emergence of foreign investors in French major companies.

[37] EU Merger Control Regulation, Recital 20.

can be captured by Article 101TFEU only to the extent there is an agreement or concerted practice between undertakings, or by Article 102 TFEU if there is dominance.

10.3.1 *EU Merger Control*

According to the EU Merger regulation, 'control shall be constituted by rights, contracts or any other means which, either separately or in combination and having regard to the considerations of fact or law involved, confer the possibility of exercising decisive influence on an undertaking, in particular by: (a) ownership or the right to use all or part of the assets of an undertaking; (b) rights or contracts which confer decisive influence on the composition, voting or decisions of the organs of an undertaking'.[38] Therefore, the existence of 'decisive influence' is central to the existence of control triggering the application of merger review. Interlocking directorates that confer influence are therefore theoretically part of merger control scrutiny. In addition, the Commission notice on remedies specifically addresses the removal of structural links, including financial or board links to remedy possible competition concerns raised by a merger.[39] The termination of interlocking directorships are thus examples of remedies imposed in the context of a merger raising competitive issues.[40] While the Commission and courts grasp the potential anticompetitive effects of structural links that do not confer control, such effects are unchallenged on a stand-alone basis.[41] The existence of an enforcement gap results from the reliance of EU merger review on the concept of control – which excludes from its scope structural links that do not confer control. relation.

10.3.2 *Article 101TFEU*

The main obstacle to the application of Article 101 TFEU to capture the effects of interlocking directorates is distinguishing a unilateral from a joint conduct, through the finding of an agreement or a concerted practice.[42] If the nomination of a board

[38] *Ibid.* at art 2.

[39] Commission Notice on remedies acceptable under Council Regulation (EC) No 139/2004 and under Commission Regulation (EC) No 802/2004 [2008] OJC 267/1, para 58.

[40] See e.g. in *AXA/GRE* (Case COMP/M.1453), para 34: one of the undertakings to address the competitive issues raised by the merger was that members of the board of directors nominated by GRE would resign upon their replacement by an individual, approved by the Commission, and not employed by AXA. Para 34. Other cases where board links were required to be unwound include *Thyssen/Krupp* (Case COMP/M.1080) *Nordbanken/Postgirot* (Case COMP/M.2567), *Generali/INA* (Case COMP/M.1712).

[41] GD Pini, 'Passive – Aggressive Investments: Minority Shareholdings and Competition Law' (2012) 23 EBL Review 575, 653.

[42] 'The concept of concerted practice does in fact imply the existence of reciprocal contacts [...]. That condition is met where one competitor discloses its future intentions or conduct on the market to another when the latter requests it or, at the very least, accepts it' Joined Cases T-25/95 and others *Cimenteries CBR* [2000] ECR II-491 para 1849.

member emanates from an appointment by the general assembly of shareholders, this will not constitute an agreement between undertakings. Yet, if the right to nominate a board member is part of a shareholding agreement, the board nomination may constitute an agreement between undertakings and therefore fall within the Article 101(1) TFEU prohibition.[43]

A relevant question is whether flows of information stemming from interlocking directorates could fall within the scope of Article 101 TFEU. The mere exchange of information between competitors can be an object restriction of competition, if the information relates to individualised and future price information.[44] In practice, to what extent could strategic information received at a board meeting, be in breach of Article 101 TFEU? In *Suiker Unie*, the Court established that Article 101 TFEU 'preclude[d] any direct or indirect contact between [competitors], the object or effect whereof is either to influence the conduct on the market [...] or to disclose to such competitor the course of conduct which they themselves have decided to adopt or contemplate adopting on the market'.[45] In addition, *Hüls* provides that the presumption that competitors take into account the information in determining their conduct is even greater 'where the undertakings concert together on a regular basis over a long period'.[46] Therefore, the nature of the contact is irrelevant as long as such contact produces an anticompetitive effect. A concerted practice may exist even in the event of a passive reception of information, provided that there is reciprocity of acceptance.[47] Interlocking directorates may amount to a direct and close contact between undertakings. Depending on the nature of the information disclosed at the occasion of board meetings, and the manner in which it is circulated within the companies, such conduct can in principle meet the requirements of a concerted practice.

Having a common board member does not bring the two companies within the same economic entity. Therefore, information exchange between those two companies cannot be considered as an intra-corporate relation precluding the application of Article 101 TFEU.[48] It is, however, difficult to consider that the mere exchange of information during a board meeting, which is internal to the company, can be sufficient to establish a concerted practice. To my knowledge, there is no case where a

43 F Caronna, 'Article 81 as a Tool for Controlling Minority Cross Shareholdings between Competitors' (2004) 29 EL Rev 494; Elhauge (n 7) however, takes the view that the requirement of agreement or concerted practice is no obstacle to the application of Article 101 TFEU.

44 Communication from the Commission – Guidelines on the applicability of Article 101 of the Treaty on the Functioning of the European Union to horizontal co-operation agreements Text with EEA relevance OJ C 11/1 ('Horizontal Guidelines') General Principles on the competitive assessment of information exchange.

45 Case 40/73 *Suiker Unie v Commission* [1975] ECR 1663 para 174.

46 Case C-199/92 *P Hüls* [1999] ECR I-4287 para 162.

47 See (n 43).

48 T Staahl Gabrielsen, E Hjelmeng, and L Sorgard, 'Rethinking Minority Share Ownership and Interlocking Directorships – The Scope for Competition Law Intervention' (2011) 36 EL Rev 839, 84.

concerted practice was identified in such context, reflecting the practical difficulty for competition authorities to produce tangible evidence of a concerted practice based on the mere existence of structural links.[49] In sum, Article 101 TFEU theoretically applies to an information exchange related to structural links, but the establishment of an agreement or concerted practice between undertakings may prove difficult.[50]

10.3.3 *Article 102 TFEU*

In addition, anticompetitive effects could be reviewed in the context of collective dominance, the abuse of which may also be in breach of Article 102 TFEU.[51] Collective dominance can exist when economic links between undertakings make them together hold a dominant position vis-à-vis other competitors on the same market.[52] In *Irish Sugar*, a situation of collective dominance was established based on a combination of economic and corporate ties between two companies, including interlocking directorates.[53] Therefore, anticompetitive effects of structural links falling short of Article 101 TFEU could be theoretically be reviewed under Article 102 TFEU even if undertakings are individually not dominant, provided there is an 'abuse' of this collective dominance. The main difficulty would be, however, to establish an abuse of that position of collective dominance. To date, there are only very few cases of collective dominance. One of the reasons is that anticompetitive issues raised in such cases may not fit the analytical framework and legal standards developed in cases of single undertaking abuses, more focused on exclusionary conduct. Cases of collective dominance based on structural links would, instead, be exploitative types of abuses, typically involving higher prices, which are far more difficult to establish.[54]

To sum up, limits to applying Article 101 TFEU relate to the difficulty of finding an agreement between undertakings as the corporate relation may not be reciprocal.

49 F Thépot, F Hugon, and M Luinaud (2016), 'Cumul de mandats d'administrateur et risques anticoncurrentiels: Un vide juridique en Europe?' (2016) 1 Concurrences 1–11.

50 Elhauge clearly states that the requirement of concerted practice or agreement is no obstacle in the case of structural links. Although he's right in theory, in practice the obstacles presented complicate the reach of Article 101 TFEU to structural links. E Elhauge, 'Tackling Horizontal Shareholding: An Update and Extension to the Sherman Act and EU Competition Law' (OECD Competition Policy Roundtable, November 2017) Background Paper for 128th meeting of the OECD Competition Committee, OECD DAF/COMP/WD(2017) 95.

51 'Any abuse by one or more undertakings of a dominant position within the internal market or in a substantial part of it shall be prohibited' (emphasis added). Article 102 TFEU.

52 O Okeoghene, 'Collective Dominance Clarified?' (2004) 63(1) CLJ 44.

53 *Irish Sugar* (Case COMP 97/624) Commission Decision 7/624/EC [1997] OJ L 258/1, para 112.

54 A Jones, B Sufrin, N Dunne, *EU Competition Law: Text, Cases, and Materials* (7th edn, Oxford University Press 2019) 696. Elhauge, however, argues that a case of excessive pricing could have better substantial grounds where high prices result from structural links rather than from monopoly power or tacit collusion. See Elhauge (n 51) 2. However, usual difficulties related to administrability, and willingness of authorities to bring exploitative abuse cases remain. In addition, the limited decisional practice on collective dominance provides little guidance on how to handle the anticompetitive effects of structural links.

Coordinated effects stemming from information flows may be caught, but to date, there is no case of violation based on the type of information usually communicated within the private remit of a board. Article 102 TFEU potentially enabling an extension of the concept of influence to capture non-coordinated effects only applies in the context of dominance. Collective dominance may provide a better avenue to control the negative impacts of structural links in concentrated markets; this would, however, require willingness from the Commission to re-open excessive prices line of cases.

10.4 INTERLOCKING DIRECTORATES IN OTHER JURISDICTIONS

10.4.1 *In the US: a* per se *Prohibition*

In the US, interlocking directorates are subject to a specific provision. Section 8 of the Clayton Act prohibits any 'person' from simultaneously serving as a director or officer of two competing corporations.[55] The degree of competition required for the application of Section 8 is such that its elimination 'by agreement between [the companies] would constitute a violation of any antitrust laws'.[56] Section 8 prohibition only applies to companies of a certain size.[57] In addition the section does not apply when the overlap between the competing companies is *de minimis*.[58]

The US has a particular approach to interlocking directorates. A specific provision on the issue of interlocking directorates only exists in very few jurisdictions.[59] In addition, those jurisdictions enable the interlock to be justified based on a lack of competitive injury, which contrasts with the per se prohibition in Section 8.[60] A brief historical background sheds some light on the US antitrust peculiarity. The introduction of Section 8 in 1914 is closely related to concerns about monopolies in a period of broad public mistrust in business.[61] Following a proposal by the

[55] 15 USC §19 (a)(1) (A).

[56] 15 USC §19 (a)(1) (B).

[57] The Act applies if each of the corporations has capital, surplus, and undivided profits of more than $10,000,000, adjusted for inflation.

[58] 'A) the competitive sales of either corporation are less than $1,000,000, adjusted for inflation;
(B) the competitive sales of either corporation are less than 2 per centum of that corporation's total sales; or
(C) the competitive sales of each corporation are less than 4 per centum of that corporation's total sales'.

[59] Chile expressly prohibits interlocking directorates through Art 3, Letter d) of the Decree Law 211 www.fne.gob.cl/en/antitrust/interlocking-directorates/ Japan, Act on Prohibition of Private Monopolization and Maintenance of Faire Trade, Act No 54 of 1947, ch IV, Art 13; Indonesia: Indonesia Competition Law No 5 of 1999, Art 26; Italy for the financial sector: Art 36 of Decree Law No 201 of December 6, 2011, converted into Law No 214/2011: 'Protection of competition and personal cross-shareholdings in credit and financial markets'.

[60] American Bar Association (ABA) Section of Antitrust Law, *Interlocking Directorates: Handbook on Section 8 of the Clayton Act* (ABA Publishing 2011) 94–96. Except for Chile which has a similar 'per se' prohibition; and Italy, which prohibits interlocks in the financial sector. See chapter by F Ghezzi and C Picciau, Chapter 11 of this book.

[61] *Ibid.* at 1.

Democratic Party in 1908, all three political parties called for legislation on interlocking directorates in 1912. In that context, several reports were issued to publicise the scope of interlocking directorates in sectors, such as the railroad and steel markets, as well as in financial institutions.[62]

Section 8 is the outcome of a political and legislative process, largely influenced by the work of Louis Brandeis, advisor to President Wilson. His position with regard to the harm created by interlocking directorates was as follows:

The practice of interlocking directorates is the root of many evils. It offends laws human and divine. Applied to rival corporations, it tends to the suppression of competition and to violation of the Sherman law. Applied to corporations which deal with each other, it tends to disloyalty and to violation of the fundamental law that no man can serve two masters. In either event it tends to inefficiency, for it removes incentives and destroys soundness of judgment. It is undemocratic, for it rejects the platform: 'A fair field – and no favors' – substituting the pull of privilege for the push of manhood.[63]

In an address to Congress, President Wilson defended the necessity for stricter antitrust laws with the necessity to 'open the field to scores of men who have been obliged to serve when their abilities entitled them to direct'. Interlocking directorates were then perceived as an obstacle to the opportunities that the American economy was supposed to provide.[64] Therefore, much broader concerns than unilateral and coordinated effects, also including the issue of conflicts of interests between shareholders and directors, drove the introduction of Section 8. The Act finally adopted in 1914 reflected a narrower approach taken by Congress to limit the scope of the prohibition to certain types of interlocks.[65] The last amendment of the Act, in 1990, was aimed at providing greater exceptions to the per se prohibitions (raising the jurisdictional threshold and exempting interlocks having de minimis overlap) while extending the prohibition to officers in addition to directors.[66] Section 8 of the Clayton Act is enforced by counsels to corporations, and there has been very little litigation.[67] Private litigation cases show that Section 8 is closely related to issues of corporate governance. Claims have typically been lodged by corporations in order to prevent an acquisition or proxy fight, or to remove an interlocked director; they have also been brought by shareholders of an alleged interlocked company to reject a merger or in support of a derivative action.[68] Recent investigations by the FTC

62 See, for example, the Stanley Committee and Pujo Committee reports, *ibid.* at 3.

63 LD Brandeis, *Other People's Money and How Bankers Use it* (Seven Treasures Publications 1914) 51.

64 AH Travers, 'Interlocks in Corporate Management and the Antitrust Laws' (1968) 46 Tex L Rev 819, 830.

65 ABA Section of Antitrust Law (n 61) 4.

66 *Ibid.* at 8–9.

67 *Ibid.* at 2. Cases include *US v WT Grant* Co 345 US 629 (1953); *SCM Corp v FTC* 565 F2d 807 (1977); *TRW, Inc v FTC* 647 F2d 942 (9th Circ 1981); *Borg-Warner Corp v FTC* 746 F2d 108 (2nd Circ 1984).

68 *Ibid.* at 22–23, e.g. *Charming Shoppes v Crescendo Partners* II 557 T Supp 2d 621 (ED Pa 200): attempt to prevent an acquisition or proxy fight; *Protectoseal Co. v Barancik* 484 F2d 585 (7th Circ 1973): or to remove an interlocked director.

led, for example, to the resignation from the board of Google of Arthur Levinson, a member of Apple's board. Google's CEO Eric Schmidt, who was director of both companies, stepped down from Apple's board.[69] In 2016, the DOJ obtained the restructuring of a transaction that would have given a company the right to appoint a member on its competitor's board.[70]

In addition, anticompetitive effects of interlocking directorates that may not be reached by Section 8 can be reviewed under Section 1 of the Sherman Act as well as under Section 5 of the Federal Trade Commission Act.[71] A specific historical and economic context in which the US provision emerged explains the far-reaching prohibition of interlocking directorates between competitors, irrespective of whether they actually harm competition.

Recent evidence shows, however, that interlocking directorates persist (and even tend to increase) despite this far-reaching prohibition. A study by Nili of 1500 S&P US companies over the years 2010–2016 demonstrates that intra-industry links are very common.[72] It shows that, in 2016, around 25% of companies shared at least one common board member with a company operating in the same narrowly defined sector (corresponding to one code of the SIC/NAICS classification systems). These links constitute potential Section 8 violations.[73]

10.4.2 *Interlocking Directorates in EU Member States*

In EU Member States, the problem of interlocking directorates is rather a matter of corporate law. In France, the French Commercial Code governs different aspects of the composition and functioning of the board of directors of limited companies.[74] The law limits the number of seat appointments held as top executive or board member to five. In addition, the 'Macron law'[75] has reduced that number to

69 Federal Trade Commission, 'Statement of FTC Chairman Jon Leibowitz Regarding the Announcement that Arthur D. Levinson Has Resigned from Google's Board' (12 October 2009).

70 US Department of Justice, 'Tullett Prebon and ICAP Restructure Transaction after Justice Department Expresses Concerns about Interlocking Directorates' (14 July 2016) www.justice.gov/opa/pr/tullett-prebon-and-icap-restructure-transaction-after-justice-department-expresses-concerns.

71 D Feinstein, 'Have a Plan to Comply with the Bar on Horizontal Interlocks' (*Federal Trade Commission*, 23 January 2017) www.ftc.gov/news-events/blogs/competition-matters/2017/01/have-plan-comply-bar-horizontal-interlocks; FTC Commissioner J Thomas Rosch, 'Remarks before the University of Hong Kong: "Terra Incognita: Vertical and Conglomerate Merger and Interlocking Directorate Law Enforcement in the United States"' (Hong Kong, 11 September 2009); s 5 of FTC Act prohibits 'unfair methods of competition' 15 USC §45.

72 In 2016, 81% of companies have interlocks within industries broadly defined (possibly involving competitors but not strictly).

73 Nili (n 6) 1215.

74 Art L 225–17 of the French Commercial Code.

75 Law N° 2015–990 of 6 August 2015.

three appointments for publicly listed companies of more than 5,000 employees in France, or at least 10, 000 worldwide.[76]

Italy is the only country having adopted a specific regulation entitled 'Protection of competition and cross corporate ties in the banking and finance industry' to deal with the anticompetitive effects of interlocks among competitors.[77] In 2011, following a report of the competition authority on problems of corporate governance and competition in the financial industry, Italy adopted a series of specific economic measures.[78] These measures aim at increasing competition and ethical governance in industries where low economic performance seemed to stem from the multitude of personal ties linking corporate governance bodies.[79] This regulation prohibits any person appointed as a manager, supervisor, or auditor of a company operating in the financial and insurance industry, from holding a similar appointment with a competitor. Persons holding more than one such appointment must comply within 90 days and decide which one to keep. Failure to comply leads to the termination of all appointments, either by the company or by the national regulator.[80]

With the exception of Italy in the banking and financial industry, limitations of interlocking directorates do not specifically target competitors. These tools, existing at the national level in a few EU Member States, offer a variety of different solutions and have, in practice, a limited impact on cross-border operations.

10.5 PRINCIPLES OF CORPORATE GOVERNANCE

Structural links are at the heart of corporate governance systems. This section discusses whether principles of corporate governance can set constraints over the anticompetitive effects of interlocking directorates. Competition law may adjust its boundaries to address common issues that corporate laws and corporate governance fail to address. This overall shows that the discussion at the EU level require a multidisciplinary approach to the issue of interlocking directorates.

While protection of minority shareholders and the freedom to appoint board members are essential to corporate governance, these corporate arrangements can also hinder rivalry between companies. In addition, policies regarding corporate governance encourage an active role by institutional investors in the corporate

[76] This gives binding force to the provision set by the non-binding AFEP/MEDEF code of conduct that provides that 'the board member of a public company may not hold more than two other appointments in public companies outside of his own group, including foreign companies', Article 19.

[77] V Falce, 'Interlocking Directorates: An Italian Antitrust Dilemma' (2013) 9 JCL & E 457–472. See chapter by F Ghezzi and C Picciau, chapter 11 of this book.

[78] Article 36 Protection of Competition and Personal Cross Shareholdings in the Credit and Financial Markets of the Law Decree N° 201/2011, converted by Law N° 214/2011.

[79] Falce (n 79) 460.

[80] F Ghezzi, 'Interlocking Directorates in the Financial Sector: The Italian Job (art 36 law 214/2011) – An Antitrust Perspective' (Università Bocconi 2012).

governance, which seems to conflict with the competitive concerns raised by common ownership.[81]

Yet, corporate governance and competition law seem to converge on other issues. A core principle of corporate governance is the fiduciary duty of management to shareholders.[82] Fiduciary duty may mitigate the anticompetitive effects of structural links. In the context of interlocking directorates, a strong fiduciary duty may prevent a common board member from disclosing information from one company to the other. However, a director's fiduciary duty to one company may naturally conflict with their fiduciary duty to another company.[83]

Independence of decision-making is another important principle of corporate governance.[84] Accordingly, decisions should be made in the company's best interest, without consideration of other companies.[85] The French Asset Management Association warns against the risk of interlocking directorates as undermining transparency and independence of decision-making, unless associated with a strategic economic alliance.[86] In practice, however, an increase in price taken in the interest of a competitor may be difficult to identify. Collecting evidence and taking action, such as voting to remove a director in breach of a fiduciary obligation, could be difficult and risky for the shareholders. Further exploration of corporate governance mechanisms is therefore critical to understanding the practical ability of a board to raise prices unfavourably for the company, for the financial benefits of a competitor.[87]

As an example, the French Court of Cassation reaffirms the legal requirement of fiduciary duty for top executives, which then applies to those sitting on the board of a competing company. In addition, the court clarified that this duty forbids the chief executive from commercial negotiation in his capacity as manager of another

81 OECD (n 7) 36. See also Chapter 12 by Schmalz and Chapter 13 by Rock and Rubinfeld in this book.

82 As an example, the French Court of Cassation reaffirms the legal requirement of fiduciary duty for top management: Cass com, 27 February 1996, *JCP* G 1996, II, 22665, note J Ghestin.

83 OECD Policy Roundtable (n 7) 34. In addition, fiduciary duty which was for long considered as one 'mandatory' rule of corporate law, is being increasingly 'waived' across jurisdictions. In such instances, fiduciary duty no longer acts as a safeguard against identified negative impacts of interlocks. For an account of this process, see e.g. G Rauterberg and E Talley 'Contracting Out of the Fiduciary Duty of Loyalty: An Empirical Analysis of Corporate Opportunity Waivers' (2017) 117 Colum L Rev 1075–151; M Corradi, *Corporate Opportunities: A Law and Economic Analysis* (Hart 2021)

84 See e.g. AFEP-MEDEF Code of Corporate Governance of Listed Corporations (2016) s 8 and s 19.

85 See the scenario of fiduciary duty limiting the anticompetitive effects of partial acquisitions in SC Salop and DP O'Brien, 'Competitive Effects of Partial Ownership: Financial Interest and Corporate Control' (2000) 67 Antitrust LJ 568, 580.

86 AFG, 'Recommandations sur le gouvernement d'entreprise' (2020) 19 www.afg.asso.fr/wp-content/uploads/2020/01/recommandations-sur-le-gouvernement-d-entreprise-2020-fr.pdf.

87 'Real-world' corporate governance factors that affect the financial incentives on competition – incomplete information, management's incentives, and ability to capture benefits. JB Dubrow, 'Challenging the Economic Incentives Analysis of Competitive Effects in Acquisitions of Passive Minority Equity Interests' (2001) 69 Antitrust LJ 131.

company within the same industry.[88] However, such requirement, rather limited to apprehend the whole spectrum of anticompetitive effects, only applies to executives (and not to all directors) of French companies. In addition, the code of corporate governance recommends that as an ethical rule, a board member should be bound to report to the board any actual or potential conflict of interest, and refrain from voting on the related resolution.[89] Although no express mention is there made of conflicts of interests arising from individuals sitting within multiple board meetings, generic rules on conflicts of interest are likely to encompass such instances.

Interlocking directorates may pose additional problems both for corporate governance and competition law, if top managers favour the selection (or exclusion) of board members based on how passive (or active), they are on other boards, in an effort to retain control over the board.[90] In addition, mutual interlocks can reflect and contribute to CEO entrenchment, resulting in higher compensation and lower turnover.[91]

10.5.1 *Conclusion: Competition Law 'stepping in'?*

Legal constraints provided by corporate laws do not bridge the regulatory gap that exists at the EU level. General principles of corporate governance, such as independence of decision-making, have a limited ability to address competitive concerns, even when they closely relate to common issues. In Italy, for example, a competition approach may have stepped in to address issues that corporate governance modernisation has so far insufficiently addressed.[92] Some have argued that interlocking directorates should remain beyond the realm of competition law.[93] Corporate laws of Member States may provide effective *ex ante* solutions to the problem, especially if the practice of interlocks primarily has national features. The need of an EU-wide solution also depends on whether there is a growing tendency for cross-border interlocking directorates.[94] If an EU-wide regulation prohibiting interlocks among

88 *Affaire Clos du Baty*, Chambre commerciale de la Cour de cassation, 15 novembre 2011, n° 10–15049. The scope of this duty seems to be expending as illustrated by recent decisions. See F Thépot et al (n 5050) fn 47.

89 AFEP-MEDEF, Code of Corporate Governance of Listed Corporations (2016) s 19.

90 EJ Zajac and JD Westphal, 'Director Reputation, Power, and CEO-Board the Dynamics of Board Interlocks' (1996) 41 Admin Sci Q 507.

91 EM Fich and LJ White, 'CEO Compensation and Turnover: The Effects of Mutually Interlocked Boards' (2003) 38 Wake Forest L Rev 935.

92 L Enriques and P Volpin, 'Corporate Governance Reforms in Continental Europe' (2007) 21 J Econ Perspect 117.

93 BM Gerber, 'Enabling Interlock Benefits While Preventing Anticompetitive Harm: Toward an Optimal Definition of Competitors Under Section 8 of the Clayton Act' (2007) 24 Yale J on Reg 107, 112.

94 Studies reach contrasting conclusions in respect of cross-border interlocks. Carroll et al, for example, show that from 1996 to 2006, while national ties started to slightly decrease, European networks were increasing. WK Carroll, M Fennema, and EM Heemskerk, 'Constituting corporate Europe: A study of elite social organization' (2010) 42 Antipode 811–843; Brullebaut and others (n 4) find no evidence of increasing transnational board links between France, Germany, and the UK over the period 2006 to 2019.

competitors may seem too ambitious, significant limitations of interlocking directorates could be introduced nationally to remedy issues that are of concern for both corporate governance and competition law. In any case, a comprehensive impact assessment of the extent of such issues in Europe should form part of any proposal for reform and would supplement the identification of theoretical concerns provided here.[95] Finally, the issues of common ownership, currently highly debated especially, and that of interlocking directorates, should be approached jointly.[96] They raise similar competitive concerns and solutions to remedy those are critically at the junction of competition law and corporate governance. Mapping corporate networks created by both types of structural links would illuminate this debate.

Appendix[97] *Corporate networks in France, Germany, and the UK – largest 100 companies in 2019*

95 Example of such studies: Brullebaut and others (n 4).

96 Especially in light of recent evidence by Nili (n 6) and study by Azar, J. Common Shareholders and Interlocking Directors: The Relation Between Two Corporate Networks (2022) 18 Journal of Competition Law & Economics 75–98.

97 In Brullebaut, B., Allemand, I., Prinz, E. and Thépot, F. Persistence in corporate networks through boards of directors? A longitudinal study of interlocks in France, Germany, and the United Kingdom (2022)16 Rev Manag Sci 1743–82.

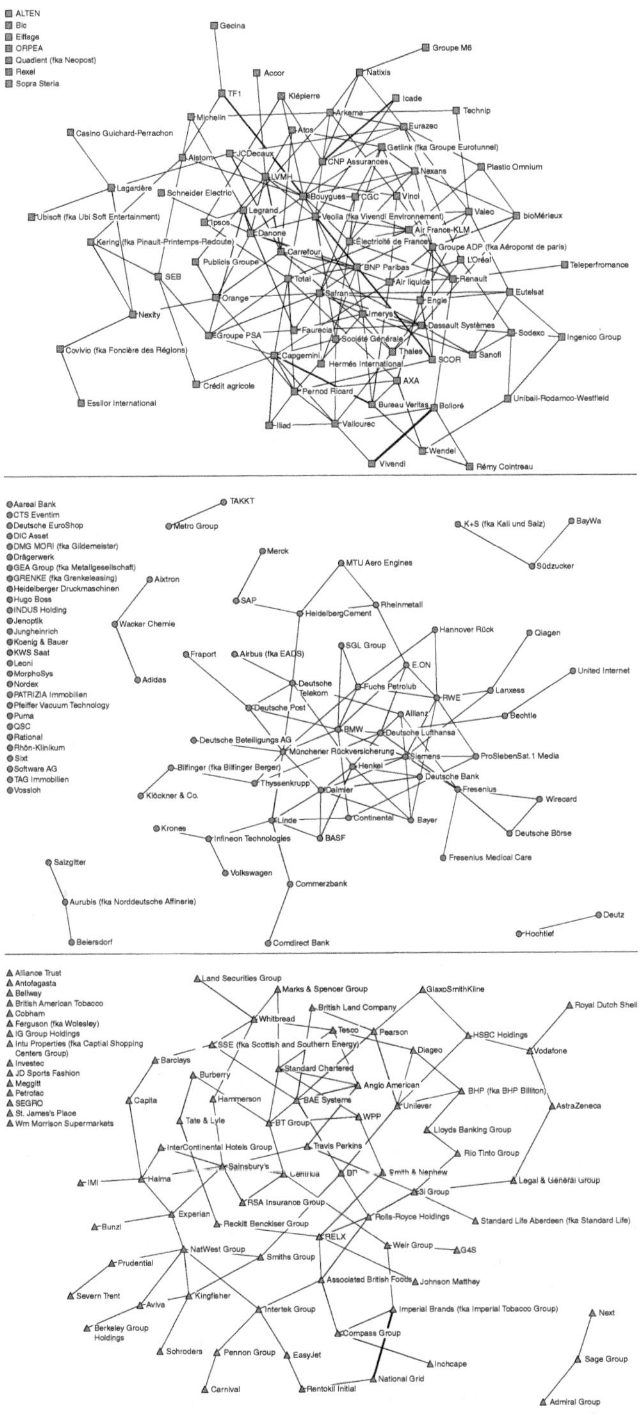
ALTEN
Bic
Eiffage
ORPEA
Quadient (fka Neopost)
Rexel
Sopra Steria
Gecina
Groupe M6
Accor
Natixis
TF1
Klépierre
Icade
Technip
Michelin
Arkema
Eurazeo
Atos
Casino Guichard-Perrachon
Getlink (fka Groupe Eurotunnel)
Alstom
JCDecaux
CNP Assurances
Plastic Omnium
Nexans
LVMH
Lagardère
Schneider Electric
Bouygues
CGC
Vinci
Legrand
Ubisoft (fka Ubi Soft Entertainment)
Veolia (fka Vivendi Environnement)
Valeo
bioMérieux
Ipsos
Air France-KLM
Danone
Kering (fka Pinault-Printemps-Redoute)
Électricité de France
Groupe ADP (fka Aéroporst de paris)
Carrefour
L'Oréal
Publicis Groupe
BNP Paribas
Teleperfromance
SEB
Total
Air liquide
Renault
Eutelsat
Safran
Orange
Engie
Nexity
Imerys
Dassault Systèmes
Faurecia
Sodexo
Ingenico Group
Groupe PSA
Société Générale
Thales
Covivio (fka Foncière des Régions)
Capgemini
Sanofi
SCOR
Hermès International
AXA
Crédit agricole
Pernod Ricard
Unibail-Rodamco-Westfield
Essilor International
Bureau Veritas
Bolloré
Iliad
Vallourec
Wendel
Vivendi
Rémy Cointreau
Aareal Bank
CTS Eventim
Deutsche EuroShop
DIC Asset
DMG MORI (fka Gildemeister)
Drägerwerk
GEA Group (fka Metallgesellschaft)
GRENKE (fka Grenkeleasing)
Heidelberger Druckmaschinen
Hugo Boss
INDUS Holding
Jenoptik
Jungheinrich
Koenig & Bauer
KWS Saat
Leoni
MorphoSys
Nordex
PATRIZIA Immobilien
Pfeiffer Vacuum Technology
Puma
QSC
Rational
Rhön-Klinikum
Sixt
Software AG
TAG Immobilien
Vossloh
TAKKT
Metro Group
K+S (fka Kali und Salz)
BayWa
Merck
MTU Aero Engines
Südzucker
Aixtron
SAP
Rheinmetall
HeidelbergCement
Wacker Chemie
Hannover Rück
Qiagen
SGL Group
Fraport
Airbus (fka EADS)
E.ON
United Internet
Adidas
Deutsche Telekom
Fuchs Petrolub
Lanxess
RWE
Deutsche Post
Allianz
Bechtle
BMW
Deutsche Lufthansa
Deutsche Beteiligungs AG
Münchener Rückversicherung
Siemens
ProSiebenSat.1 Media
Henkel
Bilfinger (fka Bilfinger Berger)
Deutsche Bank
Thyssenkrupp
Fresenius
Daimler
Klöckner & Co.
Wirecard
Linde
Continental
Bayer
Krones
Infineon Technologies
BASF
Deutsche Börse
Fresenius Medical Care
Salzgitter
Volkswagen
Commerzbank
Aurubis (fka Norddeutsche Affinerie)
Deutz
Hochtief
Beiersdorf
Comdirect Bank
Alliance Trust
Antofagasta
Bellway
British American Tobacco
Cobham
Ferguson (fka Wolesley)
IG Group Holdings
Intu Properties (fka Captial Shopping Centers Group)
Investec
JD Sports Fashion
Meggitt
Petrofac
SEGRO
St. James's Place
Wm Morrison Supermarkets
Land Securities Group
Marks & Spencer Group
GlaxoSmithKline
British Land Company
Royal Dutch Shell
Whitbread
Tesco
Pearson
HSBC Holdings
SSE (fka Scottish and Southern Energy)
Diageo
Vodafone
Barclays
Standard Chartered
Burberry
Anglo American
BHP (fka BHP Billiton)
Capita
Hammerson
BAE Systems
Unilever
AstraZeneca
Tate & Lyle
WPP
BT Group
Lloyds Banking Group
InterContinental Hotels Group
Travis Perkins
Rio Tinto Group
Sainsbury's
IMI
Halma
Centrica
BP
Smith & Nephew
Legal & General Group
3i Group
RSA Insurance Group
Experian
Rolls-Royce Holdings
Standard Life Aberdeen (fka Standard Life)
Bunzl
Reckitt Benckiser Group
RELX
Weir Group
G4S
NatWest Group
Smiths Group
Prudential
Associated British Foods
Johnson Matthey
Severn Trent
Kingfisher
Aviva
Intertek Group
Imperial Brands (fka Imperial Tobacco Group)
Next
Berkeley Group Holdings
Compass Group
Schroders
Pennon Group
EasyJet
Sage Group
Inchcape
National Grid
Carnival
Rentokil Initial
Admiral Group

11

The Curious Case of Italian Interlocking Directorates

Federico Ghezzi and Chiara Picciau

11.1 INTRODUCTION

In this chapter, we provide an overview of the Italian legislation on interlocking directorates and its enforcement in the last decade. Italy has introduced an anti-interlocking provision to promote competition in the banking, insurance, and financial sectors. Even if it is not easy to make comparisons with other EU Member States, many studies claimed that the number and relative dimension of the Italian financial companies linked by interlocking directorates were greater than in other Member States.[1] This is why, in 2011, in the aftermath of a very harsh financial crisis, Italy enacted a statutory provision forbidding the simultaneous appointment of the same person to the board of directors (or to other corporate bodies)[2] of two or more competing financial companies.

Although this chapter is the result of common research and discussion between the authors, Sections 11.3, 11.4, 11.5, and 11.7 shall be attributed to Federico Ghezzi, while Sections 11.1, 11.2, 11.6, 11.8, 11.9, and 11.10 shall be attributed to Chiara Picciau. The analysis in this chapter has been further expanded in two other works, to which the reader may refer: F Ghezzi and C Picciau, 'Il divieto di *interlocking* nel settore finanziario: spunti da un'analisi empirica sui principali 25 gruppi bancari italiani' (2020) 65 Rivista delle società 1659–93; F Ghezzi and C Picciau, 'Evaluating the Effectiveness of the Italian Interlocking Ban: An Empirical Analysis of the Personal Ties among the Largest Banking and Insurance Groups in Italy' (2022) 18 J Compet Law Econ 29–74. The authors finished working on this chapter in August 2021 and very limited amendments could be made after that date.

1 See e.g. the Italian Competition Authority's (AGCM) sector inquiry on the corporate governance of banking and insurance companies: AGCM, *La corporate governance di banche e compagnie di assicurazioni (IC 36)* (2008) 96–97 www.agcm.it/dotcmsCustom/getDominoAttach?urlStr=192.168.14.10:8080/C12564CE0049D161/0/26FE72DE86F8B4D9C1257546004B404D/$File/IC36%20.pdf accessed on 20 August 2021.

2 Italian corporations may adopt one of three different governance models: (1) the traditional model, in which the shareholder meeting appoints a board of directors with management powers and a board of statutory auditors with control duties; (2) the two-tier system, consistent with the German tradition, in which the shareholder meeting appoints a supervisory board that in turn appoints a management board; and (3) the one-tier system, consistent with the Anglo-American experience, in which the shareholder meeting appoints a board of directors, which entrusts some of its members, constituting a management control committee, with monitoring functions. See F Ghezzi and C Malberti, 'The Two-Tier Model and the One-Tier Model of Corporate Governance in the Italian Reform of Corporate Law' (2008) 5 Eur Co Financ Law Rev 1–47.

After explaining why, without regulation, these personal ties may facilitate or reinforce the achievement of a collusive or quiet life equilibrium among competitors, we provide a brief description of the main features and scope of the 2011 Italian interlocking ban. We then attempt to evaluate its effectiveness and limits. Using the banking sector as a case study, we gathered data on the number of interlocking directorates that persisted among the 25 largest banks and banking groups in Italy at the end of 2018. The result of our study is that interlocking directorates among major Italian banks seem to have disappeared. This is at odds with the prevailing empirical literature which has claimed that interlocking directorates are still a widespread reality of Italian capitalism, with possible persisting anticompetitive effects in many markets. To counter this claim, we also considered some empirical studies showing that, in the period following the entry into force of the interlocking ban, bank lending rates fell, which suggests more vigorous competition.

We conclude the chapter by questioning whether the 2011 interlocking ban has had any effect on the ownership structure of the relevant market players – for instance, contributing to the disposal of minority and cross-shareholdings held by companies operating in the sectors concerned – as well as on the composition of their governing bodies.

11.2 INTERLOCKING DIRECTORATES, OWNERSHIP TIES, AND THEIR EFFECT ON COMPETITION

While there are different justifications to establish interlocking directorates,[3] these personal links may produce anticompetitive effects when the linked firms operate on the same markets. The conclusion is straightforward when the personal tie is one of the elements of a wider collusive scheme in which a director sitting on the board of two horizontal competitors helps make sure that each firm sticks to the terms of an agreed-upon behaviour.

However, even when there is no anticompetitive agreement in place, interlocking directorates can still limit competition by facilitating the establishment of a quiet life equilibrium.[4] This often happens when interlocking directorships are coupled with ownership ties. To be sure, not all ownership ties are relevant in an antitrust perspective. For instance, common majority shareholdings are usually not relevant, since companies belonging to the same group generally constitute a single economic entity and

3 Interlocking directorates may also serve legitimate purposes, including monitoring (for example, in a bank-firm relationship). See e.g. MS Mizruchi, 'What Do Interlocks Do? An Analysis, Critique, and Assessment of Research on Interlocking Directorates' (1996) 22 Annu Rev Sociol 271–98. For an overview of the literature on the positive and negative effects of interlocking directorates, see NH Lamb and P Roundy, 'The "Ties that Bind" Board Interlocks Research: A Systematic Review' (2016) 39 Manag Res Rev 1516–42.

4 For an overview of the theories of harm see Chapter 10 by F Thépot, 'Interlocking Directorates in Europe: An Enforcement Gap?'.

are thus not considered independent competitors.[5] Other ownership ties may, however, pose antitrust concerns. This is the case for minority shareholdings (e.g., firm A holds a minority stake in competitor firm B),[6] cross-shareholdings (e.g., competitors A and B hold shares in one another), and horizontal shareholdings (e.g., horizontal competitors A and B have, in all or in part, the same minority shareholders).[7] In all these cases, the horizontal competitors might have an incentive to forego or limit competition, as the higher profits that each firm would earn from competition could be, in all or in part, offset or even outweighed by a loss in the value of the stake held in the competitor (directly by the company or by its common minority shareholders).

The incentives are mostly the same when the ownership ties between the competing firms are only indirect and include companies operating in other markets or sectors, as it would happen if the cross-shareholding involved one or more interposed companies. This is probably why, in the Italian experience, interlocking directorates and ownership ties have often gone hand in hand. It is also why, considering that Bank of Italy regulations restrict ownership ties between financial firms,[8] they have typically involved not only these companies but listed companies more generally.[9] Empirical studies based on data collected before the 2011 statutory ban on interlocking directorates showed, for instance, that the ownership patterns of large Italian listed companies, including major financial firms, closely resembled the interlocking directorates among them.[10] At least until 2011, many listed companies that shared one or

5 In the Italian case law see, for example, TAR Lazio, 14 November 2018, n 11002. In fact, the Italian interlocking ban does not apply to personal ties within the same group of companies. See Section 11.5 of this chapter.

6 On the anticompetitive effects of minority shareholdings, see OECD, 'Antitrust Issues Involving Minority Shareholding and Interlocking Directorates' (Competition Committee Roundtable DAF/Comp[2008]30 23 June 2009) www.oecd.org/competition/mergers/41774055.pdf accessed on 20 August 2021. See also Chapter 15 by A Tzanaki, 'Common Ownership and Minority Shareholding at the Intersection of Competition and Corporate Law: Looking Through the Past to Return to the Future?'.

7 A well-known study on the subject, examining the anticompetitive effects of common ownership in the US domestic airline industry, is that of J Azar, MC Schmalz, and I Tecu, 'Anticompetitive Effects of Common Ownership' (2018) 73 J Finance 1513–65. For further discussion, mostly in a US perspective, and references, see Chapter 12 by MC Schmalz, 'Conceptual Breakthroughs on Common Ownership and Competition: A Framework for Evaluating Policy' and Chapter 13 by EB Rock and DL Rubinfeld, 'Does Common Ownership Explain Higher Oligopolistic Profits?'. On the topic, also with respect to the European Union, see Chapter 14 by M Corradi, 'Common Ownership by Investment Management Corporations and EU Policies: Please, Play Puzzles and not Mikado!' and Chapter 15 by A Tzanaki, 'Common Ownership and Minority Shareholding at the Intersection of Competition and Corporate Law: Looking Through the Past to Return to the Future?'.

8 For instance, the acquisition of relevant shareholdings in other banks or in insurance and financial firms must be authorised by the Bank of Italy when certain conditions are met. See Section V, Chapter 1, Part III of the Bank of Italy's prudential supervisory regulations: Bank of Italy, *Disposizioni di vigilanza per le banche. Circolare n. 285 del 17 dicembre 2013* (17 December 2013), as subsequently amended.

9 See e.g. F Bertoni and PA Randone, 'The Small-World of Italian Finance: Ownership Interconnections and Board Interlocks amongst Italian Listed Companies' (2006) https://papers.ssrn.com/sol3/papers.cfm?abstract_id=917587 accessed 20 August 2021.

10 C Drago, S Manestra, and P Santella, 'Interlocking Directorships and Cross-Shareholdings among Italian Blue Chips' (2011) 12 Eur Bus Organ Law Rev 619, 629–36, 638, 641. See also Bertoni and

more directors also directly or indirectly shared some stockholders and/or held shares in one another. Interlocking directorates have hence likely enhanced or strengthened the anticompetitive pressure created by the ownership links of Italian capitalism.

However, interlocking directorates may have anticompetitive effects also in other circumstances[11] and even if the competing firms are not linked by ownership ties. For instance, before and during board meetings, strategic information is shared among the directors and officers of the firm. The interlocked directors receive this information together with the other members of the board and may use it to the benefit of the competing firm in which they also serve.

Even when the interlocked directors do not actively use the information to the advantage of the competitor, the information may influence their opinions and votes at board meetings.[12] This is because a director sitting on the boards of two competing companies owes fiduciary duties to both of them and must try to maximise the profits of both. That may *per se* lead to a quiet life equilibrium, since the director will vote for the solution that maximises the joint profits of the two companies or that increases the profit of one without damaging the other.[13] Indeed, if 'X is a director of both Corporation A and Corporation B', 'X could hardly vote for a policy by A that would injure B without violating his duty of loyalty to B; at the same time he could hardly abstain from voting without depriving A of his best judgment'.[14] If the director is an executive officer in at least one of the interlocked companies, the impact on the company's management and day-to-day decisions is straightforward.[15] In other cases he/she may still signal to both boards the choice that would maximise joint profits.[16]

Randone (n 9) (observing, at 16 and 20, that the ownership and interlocking networks in Italy seemed to be strongly related).

11 In this chapter, we do not consider vertical interlocking directorates, which, under some circumstances, may favour market foreclosure effects. See V Petersen, 'Interlocking Directorates in the European Union: An Argument for Their Restriction' (2016) 27 Eur Bus Law Rev 821, 855–58.

12 GD Pini, 'Passive – Aggressive Investments: Minority Shareholdings and Competition Law' (2012) 23 Eur Bus Law Rev 575, 589–90; Petersen (n 11) 846–48.

13 See e.g. F Ghezzi, 'Legami personali tra intermediari finanziari e diritto della concorrenza. Sull'opportunità di introdurre uno specifico divieto «anti-interlocking» nell'ordinamento italiano' (2010) 55 Rivista delle società 997, 1006–07. See also F Ghezzi, 'La nuova disciplina dei legami personali in Italia' (2012) 14 Mercato Concorrenza Regole 199, 210–11; Petersen (n 11) 846–47. Among the decisions of the Italian Competition Authority, see AGCM, *Banche Popolari Unite/Banca Lombarda e Piemontese*, 12 April 2007, Bollettino 13/2007, § 139–40. Some empirical studies have found that interlocking directorates rarely facilitate collusion in practice. See H Buch-Hansen, 'Interlocking Directorates and Collusion: An Empirical Analysis' (2014) 29 Intl Sociol 1–19. However, according to other studies, in the past interlocking directorates had a role in building trust between participants in a collusive scheme. See CR Leslie, 'Trust, Distrust, and Antitrust' (2004) 82 Tex Law Rev 515, 583–84. In any case, we simply suggest that personal ties among competitors may lead to a quiet life equilibrium without that necessarily amounting to collusion.

14 AH Travers Jr, 'Interlocks in Corporate Management and the Antitrust Laws' (1968) 46 Tex Law Rev 819, 840; also cited by Petersen (n 11) 847.

15 cf Ghezzi, 'La nuova disciplina' (n 13) 212.

16 Ghezzi, 'Legami personali' (n 13) 1007. For an example, see Petersen (n 11) 846.

Holding a directorship position in two competing firms should thus be prohibited not only when it helps competitors reach a common understanding about future behaviour or detect each other's deviations from that common understanding[17] but also when it enables them to establish a quiet life equilibrium. The question remains, however, as to what is the best way to address this potential information-sharing mechanism.

Absolute prohibitions may be too strict.[18] Indeed, based on the circumstances of the relevant markets, lawmakers typically choose between *ex-post* antitrust enforcement and *ex-ante* limits or bans. In the first case, personal ties are eradicated if a reduction in competition has been observed, but there is a chance that they escape regulation and enforcement. The pervasiveness of the phenomenon and a history of collusive behaviour in the relevant market might thus suggest the need for an *ex-ante* ban on interlocking directorates, eventually accompanied by exceptions for situations that, due to the size of the firms involved or to other circumstances, do not pose actual dangers to competition.

11.3 THE UNCOMMON SPREAD OF INTERLOCKING DIRECTORATES IN THE ITALIAN BANKING, INSURANCE, AND FINANCIAL SECTORS

Interlocking directorates have always been a common feature of Italian capitalism. In 1928, statistician Luzzatto Fegiz wrote that

> [f]lipping through a yearbook of joint-stock companies one is struck by the frequency with which the same names repeat themselves on the boards of several companies; and indeed a closer look only confirms the first impression, because not only is it that many people take up two or three seats, but it is not rare that one person occupies fifteen, twenty or even more seats.[19]

Interlocking directorates and ownership ties have been used in Italy, typically by families, as a mechanism to secure control of the biggest privately owned corporations across different sectors (conglomerate interlocks), as well as a defensive tool

[17] See JT Halverson, 'Should Interlocking Director Relationships Be Subject to Regulation and, If So, What Kind?' (1976) 45 Antitrust LJ 341, 345–46. See also P Buccirossi and G Spagnolo, 'Corporate Governance and Collusive Behavior', in WD Collins and J Angland (eds), *Issues in Competition Law and Policy* (ABA Section of Antitrust Law 2008) vol 2, 1228; ME Jacobs, 'Combating Anticompetitive Interlocks: Section 8 of the Clayton Act as a Template for Small and Emerging Economies' (2014) 37 Fordham Intl LJ 643, 652–53.

[18] cf V Falce, 'Interlocking Directorates: An Italian Antitrust Dilemma' (2013) 9 J Compet Law Econ 457, 459 (arguing that interlocking directorates should not be prohibited *per se* and underscoring the importance of evaluating the relevant circumstances of the market).

[19] P Luzzatto Fegiz, 'Il consiglio di amministrazione e l'interdipendenza delle imprese' (1928) 68 Giornale degli Economisti e Rivista di Statistica 197, 197 (our translation from Italian).

against hostile takeovers.[20] They reinforced the ability of coalitions and weak owners to maintain control and extract private benefits.[21]

However, interlocking directorates were a common feature even within industrial and financial sectors, thus affecting the relationship between horizontal competitors. Empirical studies suggest that, after World War II, interlocking directorates were a persistent and endemic phenomenon especially within the Italian banking, insurance, and financial sectors.[22] The Mediobanca-Generali conglomerate group was at the centre of a galaxy of interlocking directorates, passive investments, and active minority shareholdings among directly or indirectly competing firms and groups. Some authors referred to this characteristic as the circular ownership of Italian listed companies:[23] a 'petrified forest' where structural links represented an objective limit to the competitive dynamic that these markets could have otherwise exhibited.[24]

Some tables and figures illustrate the impressive thickness and density of the web of personal links between Italian banks, insurance companies, and financial firms before 2011.

According to the Italian Competition Authority, at the beginning of 2008 many banks (roughly 40% of the sample) had no members of their governing bodies interlocked with other banks. However, some had ten or even more interlocked persons. In terms of firm dimension, banks having seven or eight interlocked directors represented more than 47% of the total asset value in the sample. Similar results were found in the insurance and financial sectors.[25]

[20] Note that even if firms do not compete horizontally or vertically, personal and ownership ties may have anticompetitive effects. They reinforce minority control against hostile takeovers, preventing the positive effects that an efficient market for corporate control may have on firm performance. On the use of these ties as a means to secure control, see e.g. M Bianchi, M Bianco, and L Enriques, 'Pyramidal Groups and the Separation between Ownership and Control in Italy', in F Barca and M Becht (eds), *The Control of Corporate Europe* (Oxford University Press 2002) 156; A Rinaldi and M Vasta, 'The Structure of Italian Capitalism, 1952–1972: New Evidence Using the Interlocking Directorates Technique' (2005) 12 Financ History Rev 173–98; RM Barker, *Corporate Governance, Competition, and Political Parties: Explaining Corporate Governance Change in Europe* (Oxford University Press 2010) esp 258–66; L Bellenzier and R Grassi, 'Interlocking Directorates in Italy: Persistent Links in Network Dynamics' (2014) 9 J Econ Interact Coord 183–202.

[21] For further references and a review of the literature on the Italian case, see L Fattobene, M Caiffa, and E Di Carlo, 'Interlocking Directorship across Italian Listed Companies: Evidence from a Natural Experiment' (2018) 22 J Manag Gov 393, 397–400.

[22] See e.g. M Bianco and E Pagnoni, 'I legami creati tra le società quotate dagli *interlocking directorates*: il caso delle banche' (1997) Moneta e credito 215–44; P Santella, C Drago, and A Polo, 'The Italian Chamber of Lords Sits on Listed Company Boards: An Empirical Analysis of Italian Listed Company Boards from 1998 to 2006' (2010) https://papers.ssrn.com/sol3/papers.cfm?abstract_id=1027947 accessed on 20 August 2021.

[23] M Bianchi, S Fabrizio, and G Siciliano, 'La proprietà "circolare" nei gruppi quotati italiani', in *Rapporto IRS sul mercato azionario 1998* (Il Sole 24 Ore Libri 1998) 203–22.

[24] See Pini (n 12) 578.

[25] AGCM (n 1) 78–79, 84–95. The data refer to the period 31 December 2007–20 May 2008. With respect to banks, the sample included 53 banking enterprises considered at the group level, thus excluding interlockings within the same group.

TABLE 11.1 *Percentage of listed and non-listed banks, insurance companies, and asset management companies with interlocking directorates in competing companies (sample: 145 companies; period: 31 December 2007–20 May 2008)*

	Listed companies	Non-listed companies
% of companies with interlocking directorates	89.2	62.3
% of companies with interlocking directorates (in terms of total assets)	97.3	71.3

Note: Interlocking directorates within the same group were excluded.
Source: adapted from AGCM, La corporate governance di banche e compagnie di assicurazioni (IC 36) (2008), table 27, 88

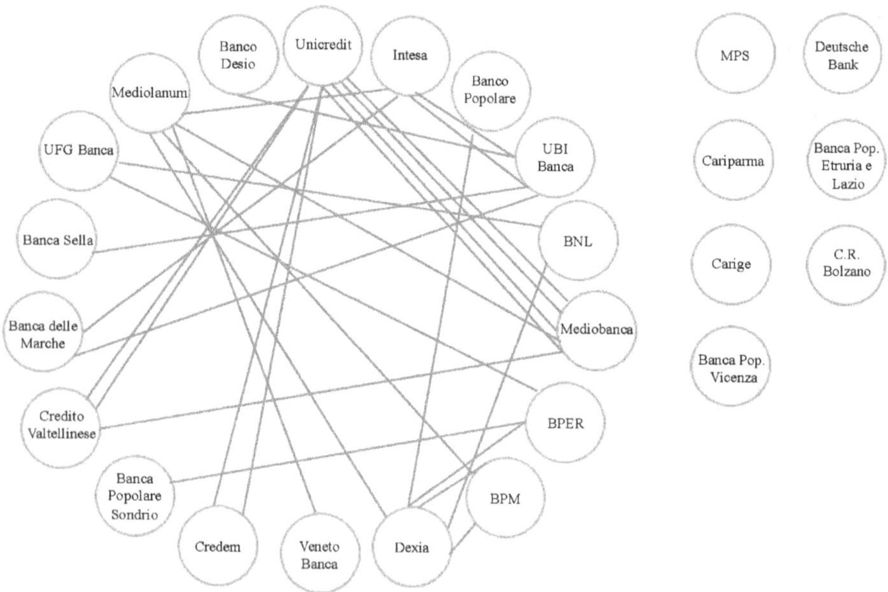

FIGURE 11.1 Interlocking directorates between the 25 largest banking groups in Italy on 31 December 2010
Source: Federico Ghezzi and Chiara Picciau, 'Il divieto di *interlocking* nel settore finanziario: spunti da un'analisi empirica sui principali 25 gruppi bancari italiani' (2020) 65 *Rivista delle società* 1659, 1680

Table 11.1 gives an idea of the widespread use of interlocking directorates in the Italian financial sector more generally.

Figure 11.1 instead shows the degree of concentration in the Italian banking sector on 31 December 2010. The lines represent interlocking directorates between the

25 largest banking groups in Italy (controlling at the time a total of 130 banks). In a perfectly competitive market, one should expect a picture only made up of isolated points.[26] Figure 11.1 instead displays only a few isolated firms.

11.4 REASONS FOR THE INTRODUCTION OF AN *EX-ANTE* BAN ON INTERLOCKING DIRECTORATES BETWEEN FINANCIAL FIRMS

Despite the prevalence of interlocking directorates, the Italian antitrust legislation, which is largely modelled on the EU legislation, had the same limits and gaps of the latter, including the absence of specific tools and remedies to counteract the potential anticompetitive effects of interlocking directorates.[27] While the Italian Competition Authority could and did intervene on several occasions to sever interlocking directorates,[28] its enforcement tools were not designed to deal specifically with these inter-company links, nor were they always effective and timely for that purpose.[29] Yet, the financial sector exhibited at that time all the characteristics that, according to economic theory, would justify the introduction of an *ex-ante* interlocking prohibition: (*i*) significant market power of the main interlocked companies; (*ii*) a history of underdeveloped competition in the affected markets (due to state ownership, past regulation on premiums, interest rates, and credit allocation, as well as evidence of collusive behaviour and information exchanges);[30] and (*iii*) stability and pervasiveness of the interlocking directorates' network, which may have functioned as a reciprocal trust creator in a context of tacit collusion. For this reason, the Italian

26 D Carbonai and G Di Bartolomeo, 'Interlocking directorates as a trust substitute: The case of the Italian non-life insurance industry' (2006) University of Teramo Department of Communication Working Paper No 1–2006, 13–14 https://papers.ssrn.com/sol3/papers.cfm?abstract_id=953648 accessed on 20 August 2021 (also showing a strongly interconnected picture within the insurance sector in 2004).

27 A ban on interlocking directorates is still absent in the European legislation. See, also for further references, Chapter 10 by F Thépot, 'Interlocking Directorates in Europe: An Enforcement Gap?'.

28 See e.g. the following merger authorisations: AGCM, *Banca Intesa/San Paolo IMI*, 20 December 2006, Bollettino 49/2006; AGCM, *Banche Popolari Unite/Banca Lombarda e Piemontese*, 12 April 2007, Bollettino 13/2007; AGCM, *Unicredito Italiano/Capitalia*, 18 September 2007, Bollettino 33/2007; AGCM, *Banca Monte dei Paschi di Siena/Banca Antonveneta*, 7 May 2008, Bollettino 18/2008; AGCM, *Istituto Centrale delle Banche Popolari Italiane/SI Holding*, 26 March 2009, Bollettino 12/2009.

29 Italian company law deals with interlocking directorates among competitors from a duty of care and a duty of loyalty standpoint, but it does not completely prevent them. See e.g. R Santagata, '*Interlocking directorates* ed «interessi degli amministratori» di società per azioni' (2009) 54 Rivista delle società 310–46; M Miola, 'Interlocking directorates e doveri degli amministratori', in R Santagata (ed), *I legami personali negli organi amministrativi delle società tra autonomia privata e regole di mercato* (Giappichelli 2011) 1–73; M Cera, '*Interlocking directorates* nelle società bancarie, finanziarie e assicurative: evoluzioni e problemi' (2010) 63(I) Banca borsa titoli di credito 276–94. On the inadequacy of the Italian antitrust legislation and enforcement, see Ghezzi, 'Legami personali' (n 13) 1014–18; Falce (n 18) 460–61.

30 cf P Coccorese, 'Information Exchange as a Means of Collusion: The Case of the Italian Car Insurance Market' (2010) 10 J Ind Compet Trade 55–70.

Competition Authority, in its sector inquiries,[31] public speeches, advocacy activity,[32] and annual reports,[33] strongly favoured creating an *ad hoc* provision prohibiting interlocking directorates between banking, insurance, and financial companies.

An additional reason for introducing an interlocking ban came at the end of 2008, when the global financial crisis hit Italy with particular severity. While every sector of the Italian economy was affected by a harsh recession, the financial sector experienced the most severe effects. The weakness of the financial sector and its inability to react promptly to the crisis were ascribed, among other factors, to a lack of competition and to the presence of a net of personal and ownership links between banks and other financial firms.[34]

These circumstances led a new 'government of experts' – appointed at the end of 2011 to fight the crisis and headed by former EU Competition Commissioner Mario Monti – to introduce a statutory provision dealing with interlocking directorates in the financial sector.[35]

11.5 THE MAIN FEATURES OF THE 2011 PROVISION DEALING WITH INTERLOCKING DIRECTORATES IN THE BANKING, INSURANCE, AND FINANCIAL SECTORS

Article 36 of the so-called 'Save-Italy' Decree[36] provides that the members of boards of directors, supervisory boards or boards of statutory auditors, as well as the 'top managers' of a company or group of companies operating in the banking, insurance, and financial sectors[37] shall not accept or hold any such offices in a competing

31 AGCM (n 1) 99–100, 147–48.

32 See the hearing of the President of the Italian Competition Authority before the Finance and Treasury Committee of the Italian Senate, addressing the relationship between banks and firms: Senato della Repubblica, XVI legislatura, 6° commissione permanente (Finanze e Tesoro), 'Indagine conoscitiva sui rapporti tra banche e imprese con particolare riferimento agli strumenti di finanziamento' – Audizione del Presidente dell'Autorità garante della concorrenza e del mercato (10 February 2009) www.senato.it/service/PDF/PDFServer/DF/210365.pdf accessed on 20 August 2021.

33 See e.g. the presentation of the Italian Competition Authority's annual report for 2009 by the Authority's President: AGCM, *Relazione annuale. Presentazione del Presidente Antonio Catricalà* (15 June 2010), 6 www.agcm.it/dotcmsDOC/relazioni-annuali/relazioneannuale2009/Presentazione10.pdf accessed on 20 August 2021, where the President complained that 'our repeated calls for a legislation on principles of banking governance remained unheard' (our translation from Italian).

34 cf A Baccini and L Marroni, 'Regulation of Interlocking Directorates in the Financial Sector: A Comparative Case Study' (2016) 41 Eur J Law Econ 431, 436 (recalling that the aim of the interlocking ban was 'to improve competition in the financial system').

35 The scope of the provision is limited to the banking, insurance, and financial sectors, even though the decisional practice of the Italian Competition Authority showed that personal links characterised many other industrial sectors and markets.

36 Article 36 was originally introduced by Law Decree No 201 of 6 December 2011 (the so-called 'Save Italy Decree'), later converted with amendments into Law No 214 of 22 December 2011.

37 Banking, insurance, and financial markets are regulated and supervised. For a discussion regarding which activities fall within the scope of the interlocking ban, see Falce (n 18) 464–65.

company or group of companies.[38] These offices are deemed to be incompatible with one another.

Persons holding two or more incompatible offices must choose which one to terminate within 90 days of the appointment. If the term has expired without a decision being made by the interested person, the interlocker is dismissed from all offices by a decision of the corporate bodies in which he/she serves or, if they do not take action, by the regulatory agency supervising the company (the Bank of Italy for banks; Consob for financial firms; and IVASS for insurance companies).

With the entry into force of the prohibition in 2012, hundreds of people had to step down from one or more incompatible offices,[39] with some of the largest Italian banks and insurance companies, including Intesa Sanpaolo, UniCredit, Mediobanca, and Generali, deeply affected by the measure.[40]

Yet, the interlocking ban raised many interpretive issues and was harshly criticised for its inflexibility and lack of clarity.[41] For this reason, the regulatory agencies decided to issue a joint set of interpretive guidelines.[42] An initial complication

[38] The guidelines on the application of Article 36 issued by the competent Italian supervisory authorities (see n 42 of this chapter) reference actual – not merely potential – competition in one or more relevant product and geographic markets. Given that the boundaries between different geographic markets can change over time and that financial entities can enter new markets or expand their activity in new product markets, the competitive relationship between banking, insurance, and financial firms may evolve over time. Interlocking directorates that were previously allowed under Article 36 may therefore become forbidden at a later date. This implies that directors and firms should monitor compliance with Article 36 on an ongoing basis.

[39] See Assonime, *Rassegna stampa* (11 October 2012) www.assonime.it/_layouts/15/Assonime.CustomAction/GetPdfToUrl.aspx?PathPdf=http://www.assonime.it/assonime/area-stampa/comunicati/Documents/241685/Rassegna_Stampa_11_ottobre_2012.pdf accessed on 20 August 2021; also cited by S Brugnoli, 'Il divieto di interlocking nel Decreto Salva Italia. Analisi normativa e criteri per l'applicazione' (2015) Rivista di diritto societario 425, 439–40.

[40] Unfortunately, data on the application of Article 36 are not available. The regulatory authorities do not publish any data on the subject. The only information generally available comes from press releases of financial firms stating that, in compliance with Article 36, a member of the board of directors or of the internal control body had to resign because of a concurring appointment in a competing firm.

[41] This was partly due to the fact that the interlocking ban was included in an emergency law decree aimed at addressing Italy's difficult financial situation, which contained hundreds of different provisions.

[42] The competent regulatory authorities issued a set of guidelines on the application of Article 36. See Banca d'Italia, Consob, and ISVAP, *Criteri per l'applicazione dell'art. 36 del d.l. 'Salva Italia' (c.d. 'divieto di interlocking')* (20 April 2012). The same authorities subsequently issued a 'FAQ' document also dealing with enforcement and procedure: Banca d'Italia, Consob, and ISVAP, *Criteri per l'applicazione dell'art. 36 del d.l. 'Salva Italia' (c.d. 'divieto di interlocking'). Frequently Asked Questions* (13 June 2012). They also signed a protocol with the Italian Competition Authority to coordinate their enforcement actions under Article 36: Banca d'Italia, Consob, ISVAP, and AGCM, *Protocollo d'intesa per il coordinamento tra Banca d'Italia, CONSOB, ISVAP e AGCM ai fini dell'applicazione dell'art. 36 del d.l. Salva Italia (c.d. 'divieto di interlocking')* (14 June 2012). The guidelines on the application of Article 36 were updated in 2018: Banca d'Italia, Consob, and IVASS, *Aggiornamento dei criteri per l'applicazione dell'art. 36 del d.l. 'Salva Italia' (c.d. 'divieto di interlocking')* (21 December 2018). All these documents are available at www.bancaditalia.it/compiti/vigilanza/accordi/accordi-consob/index.html accessed on 20 August 2021.

stemmed from the fact that Article 36 does not establish any *de minimis* exemption for situations in which the same person holds office in two very small firms that have no market power and thus are no threat to competition. The guidelines hence introduced a threshold based on the turnover of the companies involved.[43] The interlocking directorates' prohibition applies when at least two of the companies (or groups of companies) involved achieve a net (group) turnover exceeding 30 million euros.[44]

According to Article 36, the competitive relationship must be evaluated at the group level. It is reasonable to apply the ban when the interlocked companies are directly competing in the same markets or when one of them controls one or more companies that are in direct competition with the interlocked company.[45] In the latter case, even though there is no direct competition between the interlocked companies, the controlling company may influence the decisions of the subsidiaries that are direct competitors of the interlocked company. However, as the guidelines specify, once a competitive relationship between two financial groups has been ascertained, any interlocking between them is prohibited under Article 36. This applies regardless of the competitive relationship between the interlocked companies or the possibility to (indirectly) affect competition. Imagine two groups that are deemed to compete on the life insurance market because each has a subsidiary operating in that market. Since the two groups are considered to compete in a relevant market, any interlocking directorate between any company belonging to each of the two groups – even that between a bank subsidiary of the first group and a leasing company of the second group, neither of which controls a company in the life insurance market – is prohibited.

The wide reach of the prohibition is partly mitigated by the fact that the guidelines introduced a second *de minimis* threshold. If the personal tie concerns two non-competing companies belonging to different groups and the turnover of each company is less than 3% of the total turnover of the group, the interlocking ban does not apply.[46] However, it remains true that the scope of Article 36, as applied in the context of competing financial groups, may include interlocking directorates that do not and cannot restrict competition, not even on a theoretical level. This result is at odds with the purpose of the provision and may unduly limit the freedom of a

[43] The introduction of this threshold is welcome, but there is no basis for it in Article 36. The guidelines therefore seem to have *amended* the statute by introducing *de minimis* exemptions that were not included in Article 36. This may raise problems, since Italian courts are certainly not bound by the guidelines.

[44] For banks and other financial intermediaries, turnover means one-tenth of their total assets, excluding memorandum accounts. For insurance companies, it is the value of the gross premiums collected.

[45] For example, no interlocking should exist between a leasing company of group A and the parent company of another leasing company belonging to group B.

[46] Consider groups A and B, both operating in the banking market. A has a leasing subsidiary which represents 2% of the total turnover of group A, and B has an insurance subsidiary representing 1% of the total turnover of group B. In this case, according to the *de minimis* threshold mentioned in the text, the interlocking ban should not apply.

financial company to select the members of the board of directors (or of other corporate bodies) that it deems fittest for the office.

Article 36 applies not only to executive and non-executive members of the board of directors and to top managers but also to members of the board of statutory auditors and, in two-tier governance systems, to members of the supervisory board, whose main task is to monitor compliance with sectoral laws and regulations that are often complex. In order to efficiently perform this activity, many Italian banks and insurance companies used to 'share' the same skilled professionals. The broadening of the interlocking ban to these other bodies was thus strongly opposed by both the companies and the professionals involved. While these objections seem understandable,[47] they are not founded in an antitrust perspective. Members of the board of statutory auditors (as well as members of supervisory boards in two-tier systems) participate in the meetings of the board of directors and have an ongoing relationship with the directors and officers of the company. They may hence influence board decision-making and management and are in a position to obtain, share, or release strategic information about the company.

On a final note, the 'sanction' set forth in Article 36 is rather peculiar. The burden of non-compliance is on individuals, not on companies. In fact, if the director does not opt in due time for one of the incompatible offices, he/she must step down from *all* of them. The purpose is, clearly, to provide the interlocker with a strong incentive to promptly put an end to the forbidden multiple appointments. The role given to supervisory agencies is thus a residual one. They must intervene only if (*i*) the director didn't opt in a timely manner for one of the incompatible offices and (*ii*) the interlocked companies didn't declare the director's removal.[48]

11.6 NO MORE INTERLOCKING DIRECTORATES? THE DISPUTED EFFECTS OF THE ITALIAN ANTI-INTERLOCKING PROVISION

One of the main open questions regarding Article 36 concerns its effectiveness at eliminating interlocking directorates in the financial sector. To be sure, the sanction for non-compliance might not deter interlockings, as it may not always be administered in practice. If the people appointed to multiple incompatible offices do not point out the existence of a prohibited interlocking, it is for the firms involved (and for their boards) to uncover the situation and ask the person to choose between

47 From the company's perspective, Article 36 may require the substitution of a reliable and skilled professional with someone less talented or competent (in this respect, see also Section 11.9 of this chapter). From the standpoint of the professional involved, the obligation to step down from all offices but one also implies a loss of salary and reputation.

48 Even if no specific powers are provided for by Article 36, the supervisory authorities and the Italian Competition Authority could play a more active role, for example by making available detailed product and geographic market definitions and/or inviting interlocked firms to terminate a specific interlocking directorate prior to adopting formal measures. On this point, see Ghezzi, 'La nuova disciplina' (n 13) 222–23.

the incompatible offices. This may not be easy. Therefore, a prohibited interlocking may go undetected and unsanctioned because of the silence of the interested party and the inaction of the firm.

It is true that the competent supervisory authorities should also be aware of the prohibited interlocking, given the availability of databases on the composition of the corporate bodies of the supervised firms, and could thus remove the interlocker from all incompatible offices. However, these proceedings are not public. We therefore do not know whether the authorities have actually intervened or instead tolerated violations of the interlocking prohibition that did not raise antitrust concerns in specific cases.

In the absence of official data, a first indication on the possible effect of the interlocking ban is provided by studies that have examined the density of the interlocking directorates' network in general. Some studies seem to confirm that the interlocking ban has led to a reduction in personal ties among listed companies,[49] even though companies at the centre of the network, which often include financial firms, appear to have maintained some relevant connections.[50] This is probably due to the fact that the interlocking ban applies only within the banking, insurance, and financial sectors. Personal ties between financial and non-financial firms are therefore still allowed. It is also possible that direct personal (and ownership) links between financial firms have been substituted by indirect links, that is, by interlocking directorates involving a non-financial firm in between the previously interlocked financial firms.[51]

A more specific study on the effectiveness of the interlocking ban, which considered 95 financial firms and adopted a broad definition of 'competition', compared the interlocking directorates detected in the financial sector in 2008 with those observed in 2015.[52] According to the study, the number of interlockings in the financial industry appears to have decreased after the introduction of the ban, but not by much, at least with respect to personal ties across different sectors (for example, between a bank and an insurance company or between the latter and a financial firm). Even within sectors interlocking directorates seemed to still be widespread. For instance, the study claims that, in 2008, 60% of banks had personal links with

[49] See Fattobene, Caiffa, and Di Carlo (n 21) 395 (claiming that the 'reduction of the personal ties among directors is certainly due to the regulatory reform of the Interlocking Ban'). With specific reference to banks, see G Barone, F Schivardi, and E Sette, 'Interlocking Directorates and Competition in Banking' (2020) CEPR Discussion Paper DP14654, 3 https://repec.cepr.org/repec/cpr/ceprdp/DP14654.pdf accessed on 20 August 2021.

[50] C Drago, R Ricciuti, and P Santella, 'An Attempt to Disperse the Italian Interlocking Directorship Network: Analysing the Effects of the 2011 Reform' (2016) FEEM Working Paper No 82.2015 https://papers.ssrn.com/sol3/papers.cfm?abstract_id=2715441 accessed on 20 August 2021; C Drago and R Ricciuti, 'Communities Detection as a Tool to Assess a Reform of the Italian Interlocking Directorship Network' (2017) 466 Physica A 91–104.

[51] This possibility is envisaged by Baccini and Marroni (n 34) 449.

[52] R Creatini and O Main, '*Interlocking directorates*: un problema risolto?' (2015) 17 Mercato Concorrenza Regole 539–60.

other banks, compared with a slightly lower 50% in 2015, while interlocking directorates among insurance firms only declined from 71% to 45% in the same period.[53] In other words, the study suggests that the Italian interlocking ban cannot reach all existing interlockings and/or that its enforcement has been vastly ineffective.[54]

However, the implications of the study seem to be limited, considering that it adopted a very broad definition of competitor in the financial sector, even broader than the already extensive notion employed in Article 36.[55] Moreover, it does not account for the *de minimis* exemptions introduced by the supervisory authorities, nor does it explicitly assess whether the interlocked firms were horizontal competitors within each sector.[56]

11.7 INTERLOCKING DIRECTORATES IN THE ITALIAN BANKING SECTOR: A CASE STUDY

We have therefore gathered our own data on the number of interlocking directorates after the introduction of the interlocking ban, focusing for the time being only on personal ties between banks.[57] Specifically, we determined whether, at the end of 2018, there were any interlocking directorates between the 25 largest banking groups in Italy.[58] This is a representative sample (consisting of more than 90% of the market

53 *ibid.* at 549 (esp table 1).

54 While the measures taken by the Italian Competition Authority when assessing concentrations have allegedly been more effective. See Creatini and Main (n 52) 553–57. In the United States, a similar claim has been made with respect to the application of Section 8 of the Clayton Act to horizontal directors, i.e. directors who serve on boards of companies operating within the same industry. At least some of these companies would in fact qualify as competitors under Section 8. See Y Nili, 'Horizontal Directors' (2020) Northwest Univ Law Rev 1179–1262.

55 For instance, in the study conducted by Creatini and Main (n 52), a bank and an insurance company are considered competitors regardless of whether they actually compete in any relevant market or control a competitor.

56 These last factors could explain why personal ties have persisted especially among non-banking financial firms, provided that many of them are of limited size in terms of assets or operate in different product and geographic markets. See Creatini and Main (n 52) 557, with reference to asset management companies and other financial firms.

57 The findings and data reported in this section are part of (and draw from) a broader empirical study, to which the reader may refer, in which we examined the interlocking directorates among the 25 largest banking groups in Italy on the following dates: 31 December 2010 (before the introduction of the interlocking ban); 31 December 2012 (after the interlocking ban entered into force); and 31 December 2018. See F Ghezzi and C Picciau, 'Il divieto di *interlocking* nel settore finanziario: spunti da un'analisi empirica sui principali 25 gruppi bancari italiani' (2020) 65 Rivista delle società 1659–93. In another study, we extended the empirical analysis to the insurance sector: see F Ghezzi and C Picciau, 'Evaluating the Effectiveness of the Italian Interlocking Ban: An Empirical Analysis of the Personal Ties among the Largest Banking and Insurance Groups in Italy' (2022) 18 J Compet Law Econ 29-74.

58 The 25 largest banking groups operating in Italy on 31 December 2018 were the following: UniCredit, Intesa Sanpaolo, Cassa Depositi e Prestiti, Banco BPM, Banca Monte dei Paschi di Siena, UBI Banca, BNL, Mediobanca, BPER Banca, Crédit Agricole Italia, Banca Mediolanum, Credito Emiliano, Banca Popolare di Sondrio, Credito Valtellinese, Deutsche Bank, Banca Carige, Dexia Crediop, Banca Sella

both in terms of assets and bank branches).[59] Given the size of the banks and banking groups involved, we can assume that they are competitors in at least some geographic or product markets and that they do not fall within the exemption thresholds.

For each bank, we identified the members of the board of directors, the members of the internal control body, and the general manager. In the case of banks controlled by other firms, we extended the analysis to the parent company (with the exclusion of foreign parent companies, to which the ban does not apply). This process ensured that we captured in our data the potential cases of a director, general manager, or member of the internal control body of a bank or of a bank controlling company holding an analogous office in a rival bank, which are equally prohibited by Article 36.

The results of our analysis, carried out using 31 December 2018 as a reference point, are clear. Among the banks and banking groups considered, there is not even a single relevant interlocking directorate.[60] More precisely, using a concept of competition closer to traditional antitrust principles (comprising companies that are active in the same geographic or product banking markets and their controlling firms), we can conclude that the anti-interlocking provision was meticulously followed, at least as of 31 December 2018 and by the Italian banking sector's largest players.[61]

This conclusion helps assess whether the interlocking ban affected the degree of competition in banking markets. A second, more general issue is, in fact, whether the reduction in the number of interlocking directorates has in any way enhanced competition in the relevant markets.

If interlocking directorates can have anticompetitive effects, then the introduction of an interlocking ban should have a positive impact on price (e.g., the interest rates in the banking sector or insurance premiums in the insurance market). Unfortunately, it is very difficult to find any data on the causal relationship between the interlocking ban and prices (or quantities). However, a recent study focusing on the effects of the interlocking ban in the Italian banking sector tried to fill the gap by using a difference-in-differences framework. The study takes advantage of the fact that the legislative reform took place almost unexpectedly, which allows a comparison between the situation before and after the introduction of the ban as a

Holding, Banca Popolare di Bari, Banco di Desio e della Brianza, Cassa di Risparmio di Asti, Banca di Credito Cooperativo di Roma, Unipol Banca, Banca Popolare dell'Alto Adige, and Banca Generali. Several of these groups comprised more than one bank. Our study considered a total of 58 banks.

59 Note that the banks and groups not included in the 25 largest banking groups were of very limited size. In 2018, the total assets of the first Italian banking group (UniCredit) amounted to 828 billion euros, compared with 9.09 billion euros of assets of the Cassa di Risparmio di Bolzano, the first group excluded from our study. It is thus fair to assume that the latter's market share was very small on a national basis.

60 Interlocking directorates persist, however, within the same group.

61 In a separate study, we show a similar result using 31 December 2012 as a reference point. See Ghezzi and Picciau, 'Il divieto di *interlocking*' (n 57) 1679, 1682–83. See also Ghezzi and Picciau, 'Evaluating the Effectiveness' (n 57) 58. One can thus conclude that the ban has generally been effective at eliminating the most troublesome interlocking directorates in an antitrust perspective.

quasi-natural experiment.[62] The results seem to support the procompetitive effects of the interlocking prohibition. In fact, the major finding of the study is that the severance of interlocking directorates resulted in a drop in the interest rates applied to 'treated' relationships: that is, credit relationships between a firm and a bank interlocked with another bank that also granted credit to the same firm. The drop was between 10 and 30 basis points vis-à-vis all other credit relationships, defined as 'controls'.[63] The study also showed that interest rates became more dispersed after the introduction of the ban, and provided some evidence of a slight increase in the quantity of credit used for treated relationships.[64]

11.8 THE BAN ON INTERLOCKING DIRECTORATES AND ITS CONSEQUENCES ON OWNERSHIP TIES

A related issue is whether the reduction in interlocking directorates has caused a corresponding decrease in the strength or number of ownership links that previously connected Italian listed firms, including banking, insurance, and financial companies. The available empirical evidence does not specifically address this question, and economists have actually suggested that further research be undertaken to investigate if and how ownership ties between these firms have changed since the enactment of the ban.[65]

Indeed, it could be expected that Italian ownership patterns have been influenced by the anti-interlocking provision. Recall that some ownership links might have been established, in whole or in part, for collusive or anticompetitive purposes. If the interlocking ban makes it more difficult to obtain this result, by severing an important communication channel among previously interlocked companies, the existing ownership connections between those companies could also lose importance.

According to the Italian financial market authority (Consob), concentrated ownership still largely prevailed among Italian listed companies in 2019 (50 of the 228 companies listed on the Italian stock exchange at the end of 2019 were financial companies).[66] However, the number of companies not belonging to any group has

62 For further details on the empirical design of the study and on the data and robustness checks performed to confirm the results, see Barone, Schivardi, and Sette (n 49).

63 See *ibid.* According to the study, 'a relationship between firm *i* and bank *j* [is] *treated* if firm *i* is also borrowing from another bank which shares a board member with bank *j* in December 2011' (*ibid. at* 1). Obviously, the relationship between the firm and the second bank is also considered 'treated'. Relationships are defined as 'controls' in all other cases.

64 *ibid.* at 2, 12, 14.

65 See Fattobene, Caiffa, and Di Carlo (n 21) 422; G Di Bartolomeo and P Canofari, 'Interlocking Directorates and Concentration in the Italian Insurance Market' (2015) 15 J Ind Compet Trade 351, 361 (stressing the need for further research on the relationship between minority shareholdings and interlocking directorates).

66 Consob, 2020 *Report on corporate governance of Italian listed companies* (2021) 10, 13 (esp table 1.1) www.consob.it/documents/46180/46181/rcg2020.pdf/023c1d9b-ac8b-49a8-b650-3a4ca2aca53a accessed on 20 August 2021.

TABLE 11.2 *Stakes held by banks and insurance companies in Italian listed companies (years 2010 to 2019)*

	Banks and insurance companies (Italian and foreign)		Italian banks and insurance companies	
	Number of stakes held in Italian listed companies	Mean stake	Number of stakes held in Italian listed companies	Mean stake
2010	56	5.3	44	5.3
2011	55	5.3	46	5.2
2012	51	5.3	42	5.2
2013	41	5.4	36	5.3
2014	40	5.2	33	5.3
2015	24	5.1	19	5.4
2016	12	6.4	8	7.2
2017	11	6.8	7	6.8
2018	8	6.7	5	6.7
2019	14	5.7	6	6.8

Source: adapted from Consob, 2020 Report on Corporate Governance of Italian Listed Companies (2021), tables 1.10–1.11

continued to increase in the recent past.[67] Moreover, the '[d]ata confirm the decline in the number of major holdings owned by banks and insurance companies, especially by Italian ones'.[68] As Table 11.2 shows, the mean stake held by Italian banks and insurance firms in Italian listed companies has remained more or less stable in the period between 2010 and 2019, with only a slight increase after 2015. However, the number of holdings that these financial firms have in Italian listed companies has sharply decreased from a total of 44 in 2010 to six in 2019.

These data do not allow us to draw any sure conclusion with respect to the effect of the interlocking ban on the ownership patterns in the Italian financial sector. The

[67] cf Consob (n 66) 10–11, 19 (esp table 1.13). This and other similar trends have, however, been documented even earlier. For a review of previous work on the changing ownership patterns of Italian listed firms since the reforms enacted in Italy starting in the 1990s, see A Zattoni and F Cuomo, 'Institutional Change and Ownership Patterns in Italy', in M Goranova and L Verstegen Ryan (eds), *Shareholder Empowerment: A New Era in Corporate Governance* (Palgrave Macmillan 2015) 280–89.

[68] Consob, 2019 *Report on corporate governance of Italian listed companies* (2020) 13 www.consob.it/documents/46180/46181/rcg2019.pdf/941e4e4e-60db-4f89-afb3-32bddb8488e0 accessed on 20 August 2021. To be sure, with respect to 2019, the Italian securities market supervisory authority (Consob) observed that 'data on the major holdings by Italian institutional investors, especially banks and insurance companies, show a reversal in the declining trend experienced in the last decade'. cf Consob (n 66) 11. However, as mentioned in the text, the number of shareholdings held by Italian banks and insurance firms in Italian listed companies in 2019 was still significantly lower than the number observed in 2010 (*ibid.* at 18, esp table 1.11), confirming a general decline over time. It is in any case too soon to determine whether this is a temporary reversal or not.

data merely show that banks and insurance firms have curtailed their investments in listed companies, but do not enable us to establish the cause of this reduction. More specifically, on the basis of the available data it is not possible to ascertain whether the shareholdings that have been sold by banks and insurance firms were previously held in interlocked companies. Nor is it possible to determine whether the severance of the ownership connections corresponds in any way to a reduction in personal ties. Nevertheless, and despite a significant degree of stability in the ownership of Italian listed firms,[69] the data show that transformations have been underway precisely with respect to some of the financial firms (Italian banks and insurance companies) to which the interlocking prohibition applies.

Identifying what propelled these changes remains in any case difficult. The task is made even more daunting by the fact that at least some of the aforementioned trends seem to have a more distant origin. For instance, even before the introduction of the 2011 interlocking ban some commentators had pointed out a decline in ownership links,[70] and the same is true with respect to the decrease in the number of firms belonging to pyramidal or other groups and to the reduction of the average stake held by controlling shareholders in listed companies.[71] As a matter of fact, these and other transformations might also be explained by a number of other reforms that have been enacted in Italy in recent decades: from the privatisations of the early 1990s to the introduction of new legislation on issuers and public offerings, among others.[72] Therefore, while one might have a hunch that the interlocking ban did have some effect on ownership ties, there is yet no sure way to tell.

11.9 INTERLOCKING DIRECTORATES AND THE COMPETENCE OF FINANCIAL FIRMS' BOARDS

Unambiguous conclusions cannot even be reached with respect to the impact of the interlocking ban on the composition and competence of corporate boards in Italy. Some commentators have pointed out that interlocking directorates may serve the positive function of enabling companies to attract scarce expertise[73] that might

69 See Zattoni and Cuomo (n 67) 282, 288–90.

70 See e.g. M Bianco and others, 'The evolution of ownership and control structure in Italy in the last 15 years' (2008), esp table 9, www.bancaditalia.it/pubblicazioni/altri-atti-convegni/2008-corporate-governance-ita/evolution_ownership_control_structures.pdf accessed on 20 August 2021; Bertoni and Randone (n 9) (showing that while ownership links among Italian listed companies became sparser in the period between 1999 and 2004, personal ties increased).

71 See e.g. Bianco and others (n 70).

72 See Zattoni and Cuomo (n 67) 275–89.

73 See e.g. BM Gerber, 'Enabling Interlock Benefits While Preventing Anticompetitive Harm: Toward an Optimal Definition of Competitors Under Section 8 of the Clayton Act' (2007) 24 Yale J on Regulation 107, 112–15; PC Dooley, 'The Interlocking Directorate' (1969) 59 Am Econ Rev 314, 316; Travers Jr (n 14) 834–38.

be valuable especially when firms undergo complex operations (such as a listing or a takeover);[74] in highly regulated businesses (such as the banking, insurance, and financial sectors);[75] or for small firms.[76] One may thus fear that an interlocking ban would prevent companies from selecting and sharing the most competent and talented professionals, in a context where expertise, competence, and talent are rare.

While this argument is surely appealing and has some foundation, it is impossible to determine whether the Italian anti-interlocking provision has actually diminished the overall competence of the governing bodies of companies operating in the financial sector. The interlocking ban is just one of the many provisions that, over the last decades, have affected the composition and diversity of corporate boards.

For instance, the Italian Consolidated Law on Finance,[77] which was introduced in 1998 and amended several times afterwards, limits the number of directorships and control offices that members of the internal control bodies of issuers, including many financial firms, may hold at the same time.[78] It also provides that issuers must have at least one independent director or two independent directors when the board is composed of more than seven members[79] (the fraction raises to one-third of the board for firms adopting the one-tier corporate governance model).[80]

74 More generally, on the correlation between firm complexity and board interlocks, S Johnson, K Schnatterly, JF Bolton, and C Tuggle, 'Antecedents of New Director Social Capital' (2011) 48 J Manag Stud 1782–1803.

75 See e.g. Ghezzi, 'La nuova disciplina' (n 13) 208 (esp at fn 28); Pini (n 12) 591.

76 With respect to the potential benefits of interlocking directorates for small firms, see e.g. Nili (n 54) 1193; Brugnoli (n 39) 430.

77 Legislative Decree No 58 of 24 February 1998 (Italian Consolidated Law on Finance).

78 Art 148-*bis* of the Italian Consolidated Law on Finance empowers Consob to limit the number of directorships and control positions that may be concurrently held by members of the internal control bodies of companies whose financial instruments are either listed or widely distributed among the public (cf Art 116 of the same statute). Pursuant to Art 144-*terdecies* of Consob Regulation No 11971 of 14 May 1999 as subsequently amended, the members of the internal control body of companies whose financial instruments are listed or widely distributed among the public may not hold the same position in more than five of such companies. Art 144-*terdecies* also places limits on the number of directorships that they can hold (cf Annex 5-*bis*, Model I, to the same Regulation). These provisions do not address the simple cumulation of directorships in multiple companies. However, according to Art 3, Recommendation No 15, of the Italian Corporate Governance Code (2020), the boards of directors of large listed companies should establish the maximum number of directorships or control positions in other issuers or large firms that are considered compatible with the exercise of the duties of director of the company. The goal is to ensure that the members of the issuer's governing bodies have sufficient time to devote to their role.

79 Art 147-*ter*, para 4, of the Italian Consolidated Law on Finance.

80 Pursuant to the combination of Art 147-*ter*, para 4, of the Italian Consolidated Law on Finance and Art 2409-*septiesdecies*, para 2, of the Italian Civil Code, if a company has adopted the one-tier system of corporate governance, at least one-third of the members of the board of directors must, in any case, satisfy independence requirements. If the issuer has instead adopted the two-tier system of governance, Art 147-*quater* of the Italian Consolidated Law on Finance establishes that when the management board has more than four members, at least one of them must satisfy independence requirements.

For certain large listed companies, an even higher number of independent directors is recommended, under a comply-or-explain approach, by the Italian Corporate Governance Code.[81]

Italian issuers must also make sure that at least two-fifths of the members of the board of directors and of the board of statutory auditors (or the supervisory board in two-tier governance systems) consist of the less-represented gender (typically, women).[82] Other specific personal requirements apply to board members of financial firms.[83]

Clearly, these provisions, which have only been briefly sketched here, may already limit the freedom of financial firms to select which people to appoint to their governing bodies.[84] As a result, it may be hard, if not impossible, to discern whether any observed change or decline in the competence of the boards of financial firms is due to the interlocking ban or to these other requirements.

However, upon closer inspection, several reasons indicate that the interlocking prohibition does not (significantly) prevent financial firms from acquiring and sharing valuable talent and competence.

First, if competence and skill are hard to find, the solution should be investing in training and education, inside and outside the firm, not enabling the same person to serve on a large number of boards at the same time. Indeed, nudging firms to go beyond the usual panel of candidates for a job may foster investment in managerial and technical skills by aspiring candidates. Such investments are particularly important because even the most talented and competent professionals may not do their job well when overworked by holding offices in many different firms.[85]

Second, one may very well doubt that competence and expertise are so hard to find. Education rates have improved across the developed world,[86] and financial firms increasingly draw from a wider set of candidates, including women and

[81] Pursuant to Art 2, Recommendation No 5, of the Italian Corporate Governance Code (2020), boards of directors of listed companies should comprise at least two independent directors (who do not also chair the board). In large listed companies with concentrated ownership, independent directors should represent at least one-third of the board. In other large listed companies, at least half of it.

[82] See Art 147-*ter*, para 1-*ter* and Art 148, paras 1-*bis* and 4-*bis* of the Italian Consolidated Law on Finance. Pursuant to Art 147-*quater*, para 1-*bis*, the same gender quotas apply to the management board in two-tier governance systems if the board has at least three members. Board diversity is also encouraged by the Italian Corporate Governance Code. See Art 2, Principle VII and Recommendation No 8 of the Italian Corporate Governance Code (2020).

[83] See, for example, Art 26 of Legislative Decree No 395 of 1 September 1993, as subsequently amended (Italian Consolidated Law on Banking) and the Decree of the Ministry of Economy and Finance No 169 of 23 November 2020.

[84] See Brugnoli (n 39) 443–46.

[85] On all these aspects, F Ghezzi, 'Interlocking directorates in the financial sector: the Italian way' (Antitrust Alliance Meeting conference presentation, Turin, 11 May 2012).

[86] See, for instance, the data on the expansion of tertiary education in OECD countries: OECD, *Education at a Glance 2019: OECD Indicators* (OECD Publishing 2019), https://read.oecd-ilibrary.org/education/education-at-a-glance-2019_f8d7880d-en#page3 accessed on 20 August 2021. cf Petersen (n 11) 850.

foreign professionals.[87] With respect to the Italian case, one must also consider that interlocking directorates are prohibited only between competing banking, insurance, and financial companies or groups. The prohibition thus does not prevent financial firms from sharing skilled and talented board members with non-financial companies or groups.[88]

To be sure, one might argue that financial firms do not simply need competent and talented individuals, but people with very specialised knowledge and expertise, and with the additional personal requirements set forth in prudential regulation. Finding the right people may therefore be particularly difficult. Yet, consider that, according to the guidelines on the application of Article 36, the notion of 'top managers' – to whom the interlocking ban applies, in addition to board members and members of the internal control body of financial firms – only comprises the general manager and the manager responsible for the corporate financial reporting of the firm.[89] This leaves out a variety of highly specialised, high-ranking officers and managers who could serve as directors or members of the internal control body of other financial companies. If these people do not hold multiple offices is because financial firms generally do not allow it (consider that top managers typically are employees). In short, the Italian interlocking ban, by itself, does not seem to significantly limit the ability of financial firms to acquire skills that are already fruitfully employed elsewhere.

Third, and most importantly, there is yet no empirical support for the proposition that limiting interlockings has a negative impact on the competence of the board or on firm value. Similar concerns have been raised in the past with respect to gender quotas and have been disproven by empirical studies that show that increasing board diversity, also with respect to gender, generally improves performance.[90] Indeed, even artificially intelligent algorithms, programmed to select the best performing directors for a given firm, suggest that diversity is the right way to go.[91]

[87] Going forward, opening national markets for board positions to international candidates could bring interlocking directorates to the attention of European lawmakers. Notably, some commentators have already shown the existence of an emerging network of interlocking directorates at the European level. See EM Heemskerk, 'The Rise of the European Corporate Elite: Evidence from the Network of Interlocking Directorates in 2005 and 2010' (2013) 42 Econ Soc 74–101; Bellenzier and Grassi (n 20) 187 (also citing Heemskerk's work).

[88] Ghezzi (n 85).

[89] Banca d'Italia, Consob, and ISVAP, *Criteri per l'applicazione dell'art. 36 del d.l. 'Salva Italia' (c.d. 'divieto di interlocking'*) (n 42) para 3, no 1.1.

[90] See e.g. DA Carter, BJ Simkins, and WG Simpson, 'Corporate Governance, Board Diversity, and Firm Value' (2003) 38 Financ Rev 33–53; NL Erhardt, JD Werbel, and CB Shrader, 'Board of Director Diversity and Firm Financial Performance' (2003) 11 Corporate Gov: An Intl Rev 102–11; S Terjesen, E Barbosa Couto, and P Morais Francisco, 'Does the Presence of Independent and Female Directors Impact Firm Performance? A Multi-country Study of Board Diversity' (2016) 20 J Manag Gov 447–83; G Bernile, V Bhagwat, and S Yonker, 'Board Diversity, Firm Risk, and Corporate Policies' (2018) 127 J Financ Econ 588–612.

[91] See I Erel, LH Stern, C Tan, and MS Weisbach, 'Selecting Directors Using Machine Learning' (2021) 34 Rev Financ Stud 3226, 3229, 3251–53.

In any case, the impact of these reforms is still uncertain and needs to be evaluated over time, in light of the perhaps unexpected effects of many of these new measures. For instance, while the introduction of gender quotas in listed firms has increased the number of women sitting on corporate boards, it has perhaps also led to the spread of female interlockings across issuers.[92] Issuers have started to appoint women on company boards, but they continue to draw from a limited set of candidates who sit on the boards of many listed firms at the same time. It remains to be seen whether this is just an adjustment phase or a new future trend.

11.10 CONCLUSIONS

Interlocking directorates among competitors may facilitate collusion and endanger competition. In Italy, they typically accompanied direct and indirect ownership ties and were a systemic and widespread phenomenon particularly in the banking, insurance, and financial sectors. This is why, in 2011, the Italian lawmaker introduced an *ex-ante* prohibition on interlocking directorates in the financial sector. Despite the breadth of the prohibition, which arguably even covers situations in which a threat to competition is not likely or lacking, some empirical studies questioned the effectiveness of the ban, claiming that relevant personal links persisted, together with possible anticompetitive effects.

Using the banking sector as a case study, we have argued instead that there is some indication that the Italian interlocking ban has met its goal. The data we collected on interlocking directorates among the 25 largest banking groups in Italy on 31 December 2018 show that, on that date, there were no relevant personal ties among the largest banks and banking groups. This result is in line with other studies that claim that, after the introduction of the prohibition, bank lending rates in Italy fell, which should indicate that the interlocking ban had a procompetitive effect.

However, further research is needed not only to ascertain the effects of the ban but also to determine whether it had any impact on the ownership of Italian firms and on the competence of their governing bodies. While it is highly unlikely that board competence was significantly affected by the ban, ownership ties might have changed as a result. Indeed, it is curious that the Italian lawmaker decided to ban interlocking directorates without also intervening on ownership ties, such as minority shareholdings. However, at least in some cases the interlocking ban might have killed two birds with one stone.

92 cf Consob (n 66) 33, 54 (esp table 2.29). Consob's data show that the number of female interlockers holding office on the corporate boards of Italian listed companies rose from 80 in 2013 to 283 in 2019 and then decreased to 280 at the end of 2020.

12

Conceptual Breakthroughs on Common Ownership and Competition

A Framework for Evaluating Policy

Martin C. Schmalz

12.1 INTRODUCTION

Common ownership is the phenomenon of ownership of natural competitors in an industry by an overlapping set of institutional investors. Ignited by an empirical study of US airline competition under common ownership[1], a recent literature exploring the possibility of anticompetitive effects caused by common ownership has not only raised long dormant conceptual questions in corporate finance, organizational and labour economics, and industrial organization[2] but also raised questions in antitrust law,[3] corporate law,[4] and securities law[5]. Moreover, the original common ownership paper has triggered a policy discussion[6]

Schmalz is Professor of Finance and Economics at the University of Oxford Saïd Business School, OMI, CEPR, ECGI, CESIfo, University of Cologne, and C-SEB, Martin.Schmalz@sbs.ox.ac.uk. I am grateful to Marco Corradi, Einer Elhauge, Julian Nowag, Gabriel Rauterberg, and Fiona Scott Morton for helpful comments. I thank Deutsche Forschungsgemeinschaft (DFG, German Research Foundation) under Germany's Excellence Strategy – EXC 2126/1–390838866 for funding.

1 J Azar, M Schmalz and I Tecu, 'Anticompetitive Effects of Common Ownership' (2018) 73 J Fin 1513.

2 *See* M Schmalz, 'Common-Ownership Concentration and Corporate Conduct' (2018) 10 Annu Rev Financial Econ 413.

3 *See* E Elhauge, 'Horizontal Shareholding' (2016) 109 Harv L Rev 1267 [hereinafter *Elhauge*] and the literature that followed, including E Elhauge, 'How Horizontal Shareholding Harms Our Economy – And Why Antitrust Law Can Fix It' (2020) 10 Harv Bus L Rev 207; E Elhauge, 'The Causal Mechanisms of Horizontal Shareholding' (2021) 82 Ohio St LJ 1.

4 Shareholders with heterogeneous portfolios generally only agree on firm value maximization as the firm's objective when firms are price takers; *see* O Hart, 'On Shareholder Unanimity in Large Stock Market Economies' (1979) 47 *Econometrica* 1057. Therefore, when shareholder have heterogeneous portfolios and preferences – or agree on alternative objective functions – the entire corporate governance ecology that interacts with the firm's objective changes. This change affects optimal executive compensation, voting, and fiduciary duty.

5 Commissioner Robert J Jackson Jr, 'Common Ownership: The Investor Protection Challenge of the 21st Century' (Federal Trade Commission Hearing on Competition and Consumer Protection, New York, 6 December 2018) www.sec.gov/news/testimony/jackson-testimony-ftc-120618 Jackson.

6 *See*, e.g. EPosner and others, 'A Proposal to Limit the Anticompetitive Power of Institutional Investors' (2017) 81 Antitrust LJ 669; E Rock and D Rubinfeld, 'Antitrust for Institutional Investors' (2017) NYU Law and Economics Research Paper No 17–23 https://ssrn.com/abstract=2998296; D Lund, 'The Case Against Passive Shareholder Voting' (2018) 43 J *Corp* L 493.

that arguably challenges the business practices of the asset management industry as we know it[7].

In a review of the economics and finance literature[8] on common ownership in 2018, I laid out the conceptual challenges this line of inquiry brings to the surface, and suggested directions for future research. In a second review,[9] I reported on the exploding empirical literature that responded to some of these directions, but mainly documented robustness of the basic premise: the effects of common ownership on corporate behaviour and market outcomes have now been documented in a host of different industries and settings and using a variety of different methodologies. Further, many early criticisms of the literature were proven incorrect and have been withdrawn.[10]

In this paper, I analyse conceptual challenges that the original 'airlines' paper left for future research to address, and which many believed would need to be addressed before a consideration of policy changes would be appropriate. These questions include: how would estimates or (anti-)competitive effects of common ownership of horizontal competitors be affected if agency problems, informational frictions, and organizational complexities were considered? Are estimates of horizontal common ownership links on product market outcomes affected by considering the effect of common ownership links between vertically related firms as well? Are there methods to ensure that effects are truly causal? And perhaps most importantly: how does the lifting of data limitations change researchers' ability to measure effects of common ownership on firm behaviour and market outcomes? Given the data limitations, is there a consensus now on how much common ownership there is? The first part of this paper brings the reader up to speed by addressing these questions.

In the second part of the paper, I develop a framework and use it to evaluate policy proposals others have made to address the antitrust and governance challenges posed by the rise of 'common ownership' and the related rise of 'passive investing'. The objective of that discussion is primarily to provide a clear framework to help organize and analyse the various proposals, and to view their conceptual commonalities and differences from an economic perspective. The framework is meant to clarify which directions have which likely costs and benefits, and which uncertainties come with which approach. The objective is not to engage with detailed – though important – issues of implementation, or to provide a final answer to what should or shouldn't be done, but to help shape a more informed and perspicuous debate. As such, the present paper is not meant to substitute for or contain the state of debate

7 T Hunnicutt, 'BlackRock says outside commentaries on index funds could pose risk' (*Reuters*, 28 February 2018) www.reuters.com/article/us-blackrock-funds-index-idUSKCN1GC345.

8 Schmalz (n 2).

9 M Schmalz, 'Recent Studies on Common Ownership, Firm Behavior, and Market Outcomes' (2021) 66(1) Antitrust Bull 12–38.

10 *See* J Azar, M Schmalz, and I Tecu, 'Research on the Competitive Consequences of Common Ownership: A Methodological Critique' (2021) 66(1) Antitrust Bull 113–122.

between the authors of various proposals. Instead, I focus on overlooked dimensions relevant to the policy debate that arise from the recent economics and finance literature's application to law and policy.

12.2 NEW CONCEPTUAL BREAKTHROUGHS

In this part, I explore how our conceptual understanding of important features of common ownership has advanced by recent research responding to questions that arose with the publication of Azar, Schmalz, and Tecu's paper[11].

12.2.1 *How Do Agency Frictions, Informational, and Organizational Complexities Affect How Common Ownership Affects Product Market Outcomes?*

At the 2018 FTC Hearings on Common Ownership, FTC Commissioner Noah J. Phillips remarked that '… areas of research that I, as an antitrust enforcer, would like to see developed before shifting policy on common ownership [are]: Whether a clear mechanism of harm can be identified …'[12] At the same event, SEC Commissioner Robert Jackson Jr. added: 'The organizational complexity of today's largest public companies makes it far from clear how – even if top managers receive an anticompetitive signal from their pay packages – those incentives affect those making pricing decisions throughout the organization. […] For these reasons, I worry that the evidence we have today may not carry the heavy burden that … I would require imposing costly limitations'.[13] I focus on two recent contributions to the literature that have pushed the boundaries of knowledge in these dimensions.

My recent co-authored work[14] offers both an economic model and empirical analysis identifying a mechanism of harm. Our 'Antón and others' model makes two modifications to a standard model of optimal executive compensation amid a moral hazard problem. The first modification is that we do not restrict the firm to be a price taker. Instead, firms strategically interact, as in a standard model of industrial organization. The second modification is that we allow shareholders to hold more than one firm, as standard diversification motives would dictate. This latter assumption contrasts with arrived models in industrial organization, which implicitly assume that shareholders do not diversify across competitors (or that firms entirely

11 Azar, Schmalz, and Tecu (n 1).

12 N Phillips, 'Protection in the 21st Century Corporate Governance, Institutional Investors, and Common Ownership' (FTC Hearing #8: Competition and Consumer, NYU School of Law, 6 December 2018) www.ftc.gov/system/files/documents/public_statements/1454690/phillips_-_ftc_hearing_8_opening_remarks_12-6-18.pdf.

13 Jackson (n 5).

14 M Antón and others, 'Common Ownership, Competition, and Top Management Incentives' (2021) Ross School of Business Paper 1328, European Corporate Governance Institute – Finance Working Paper 511/2017 https://ssrn.com/abstract=2802332].

ignore thus-arising shareholder incentives). The baseline prediction of the Antón and others model is that more common ownership leads to less performance sensitive managerial incentives. The reason is that more performance-sensitive incentives induce stronger managerial incentives to exert 'effort', which reduces the firm's cost. Taking product prices as given – as in standard agency models – such a cost reduction would increase margins and profits. However, when firms strategically interact, a firm with lower costs will also optimally produce more output and set lower prices in industry equilibrium. Doing so imposes a negative externality on competitors. The shareholder of a single firm may still favour that, but common owners of competitors internalize such externalities, and therefore are less keen on spending resources to improve governance in any one target firm. As a result, commonly owned firms feature less performance-sensitive managerial incentives, and weaker corporate governance in general, and their costs are higher.

As a result of these higher costs – as opposed to because of higher margins – product prices are higher. Therefore, the view that common owners are relatively 'lazy' or low-cost principals that underinvest in stewardship and are 'excessively deferential' to managers (as Bebchuk and Hirst argue)[15] is not incompatible with anticompetitive effects of common ownership. To the contrary, in the Antón and others model, common ownership is the reason, endogenously, the owners choose to underinvest in stewardship, which in turn harms productivity and increases product prices. Phrased differently, the general insight is that *cost-reducing good governance imposes a negative externality on competitors*. This is one reason – among others identified elsewhere in the literature -- why common owners underinvest in 'good governance', compared to otherwise similar investors who do not also own large stakes in competing firms. As a result, common ownership induces a 'productive inefficiency' – an inward shift in supply curves – as opposed to only a redistribution of rents from consumers to producers and a small deadweight loss. This insight is important for the evaluation of policy proposals that would limit the ability of common owners to influence their product market firms but without reallocating such control rights to other investors. In the context of the Antón and others model, everything else equal, such a policy could make the problem worse.[16] I will get back to these points in Part 2 of this essay.

The theoretically proposed mechanism is empirically identified by Antón and others using the index inclusion of competitors.[17] To illustrate the strategy, assume Delta and United Airlines are already in the S&P 500 index. Southwest gets added to the index. Southwest's ownership structure changes because of the index inclusion – after all the S&P 500 index trackers now have to buy Southwest – but Delta

[15] L Bebchuk and S Hirst, 'Index Funds and the Future of Corporate Governance: Theory, Evidence, and Policy' (2019) NBER Working Paper No w26543 https://ssrn.com/abstract=3282794.

[16] Antón and others (n 14).

[17] *Ibid.* at Table 9

and United's ownership structure is unaffected. Yet, Delta and United are 'treated' with a dose of common ownership: their pre-existing owners now have greater holdings of Southwest shares as well. This treatment with 'common ownership' is followed by reductions in the wealth-performance sensitivity of Delta and United's top executives' compensation packages, as predicted by theory.

This mechanism of harm can explain cross-market correlations between common ownership and higher product prices: in markets in which a commonly owned high-cost provider competes with a not-commonly owned low-cost provider, naturally, product prices are lower. In markets in which only commonly owned peers compete, prices are higher. Hence, common ownership correlates positively with product prices, even within firms and across markets. Because a low-cost provider will also produce a relatively greater quantity, the theory also correctly predicts that common ownership is negatively related to market concentration. In fact, it is the only theory to date that can organize the set of empirical results the literature has produced to date.[18]

The model thus proves that there are no particular informational requirements necessary for common ownership to affect market-level competition via standard governance channels. The mechanism does not even require firm managers to know who their largest shareholders are for the managers to act in the shareholders' interest: the manager simply takes her incentive contract as given and acts accordingly. The informal conjecture – promoted by prominent commentators[19] – that for common ownership to have market-level effects, an elaborate corporate governance mechanism would be required simply does not hold up to the scrutiny of mathematical logic. The theory of harm the model proposes, and the empirics identifies, is thus not complicated, but rather follows long-established standard theories and practices of 'normal' corporate governance activities.

The Antón and others model also features the organizational complexity that Commissioner Jackson wanted to get clarity about. In the model, it is not the top manager (whose proposed compensation is approved by shareholders) who makes market-level decisions. Instead, it is a market-level pricing specialist, who knows nothing about either common ownership, the top manager's incentives, or the desire of the firm's shareholders. Instead, the specialist maximizes profits market by market, taking the firm's cost as given – as in standard models of industrial organization. This feature is in fact necessary for the theory to correctly predict the wide range of facts the empirical literature has documented. To name one example, if shareholders contracted with the top manager on costs and prices, common ownership would lead to lower costs and higher margins – which is not what is observed empirically.

Whereas the empirical analysis in Antón and others identifies a corporate governance mechanism using reduced-form empirical techniques, a second, more

[18] *Ibid.* at Table 1

[19] L Summers, 'Dinner Speech' (Global Corporate Governance Colloquium, Cambridge, MA, June 2018) https://gcgc.global/presentations/gcgc-dinner-speech-2018-lawrence-h-summers.

recent paper by Azar and Ribeiro[20] offers a structural estimation of a model featuring agency conflicts that also links to product market outcomes, again using the airlines industry as a laboratory. What they find is that the 'conduct parameter' that identifies the extent to which managers take shareholders' portfolio interest into account is significantly positive – but also significantly below the level one would expect without agency conflicts. Hence, the rejection of full internalization by structural models that ignore agency conflicts does not reject the presence of large anticompetitive effects; such a rejection would instead indicate a mis-specified model. What is exciting conceptually is that this is the first time that a structural model not only considers common ownership but also agency problems.

The take-away from these two papers is that the recognition of agency problems in otherwise standard models of competition under common ownership by no means undoes or puts in doubt that there are anticompetitive effects from common ownership of horizontal competitors. Instead, agency problems are a feature that either gives rise to productive inefficiencies and thus higher prices in the first place, or at least is a feature that increases the precision of estimates of how strong the competitive effects of common ownership are. Both aspects become important as we think about policy proposals in Part 2 of this paper.

The structural estimation by Azar and Ribeiro also features and shows the empirical importance of vertical common ownership links. However, the importance of this feature is perhaps best illustrated by describing a reduced-form investigation into this matter.

12.2.2 *How Do Vertical Common Ownership Links Affect Estimates of the Effect of Horizontal Common Ownership Links on Product Market Outcomes?*

Since the start of the asset management industry's involvement in the debate on competitive effects of common ownership and its regulation, a central argument of their advocates has been that ignoring vertical common ownership would cause the papers to 'lack economic logic and factual support from the real world. For instance, why would passive managers want airline prices to be higher given the air travel is a cost to nearly any other business that is owned by the index funds?'[21] Does that argument hold up to scrutiny?

Formal economic theories on partial vertical integration with multiple upstream and downstream firms tend to be analytically intractable, and thus offer little guidance to inform the question. However, it is possible to study the question

[20] J Azar and R Ribeiro, 'Estimating Oligopoly with Shareholder Voting Models' (2021) IESE Business School Working Paper https://ssrn.com/abstract=3988265.

[21] B Novick, 'How Index Funds Democratize Investing' Wall St J (9 January 2017) www.wsj.com/articles/how-index-funds-democratize-investing-1483914571.

empirically, and a recent paper has done just that – and produced a clear answer. Azar and Vives[22] show that controlling for the extent to which airlines have vertical common ownership links has a negative effect on prices – but that controlling for these effects increases the positive estimate of price effects of horizontal common ownership links. Omitting a variable capturing vertical common ownership links from the horizontal-ownership regressions leads to a bias of the estimates. The finding suggests also that policies that have the effect of reducing horizontal common ownership while strengthening vertical common ownership links may be best suited to deal with the anticompetitive effects of common ownership. Some of the proposals covered in Part 2 have that feature.

Azar and Vives's contribution not only captures vertical common ownership links, but also offers a methodological alternative over the Azar, Schmalz and Tecu regressions: instead of using a modified Herfindahl-Hirschman-Index of market concentration – which includes potentially endogenous market shares – as the main explanatory variable, Azar and Vives follow Antón and others and others in the more recent literature and use the primitive of the common ownership theory, the profit weights that firm managers are presumed to put on commonly owned firms' rivals. Azar and Vives is thus also the first academic study that shows with a reduced-form methodology that market shares do not drive the results in Azar, Schmalz and Tecu's original analysis[23] of US airline competition under common ownership, as some have speculated.[24]

22 J Azar and X Vives, 'Revisiting the Anticompetitive Effects of Common Ownership' (2021) IESE Business School Working Paper https://ssrn.com/abstract=3805047. The authors verbally connect these findings to a theoretical investigation by the same authors based on the 2018 Walras-Bowley lecture, J Azar and X Vives, 'General Equilibrium Oligopoly and Ownership Structure' (2021) 89 Econometrica 999–1048. The mechanism driving the results of this theory is however quite different from the internalization of interests of vertically related firms. The prediction that economy-wide common ownership can reduce prices in this theory requires that shareholders also consume all inside goods and thus internalize effects on consumption. Further, reducing the price of good *i* increases the *relative* price of goods in other industries and thus profits in other industries, as measured in this numeraire-free price system. As such, the mechanism proposed in that paper is driven by cross-sector horizontal externalities, and unrelated to a reduction double marginalization through common ownership – although the latter may drive the empirical results in the empirical paper described above.

23 Azar, Schmalz and Tecu (n 1).

24 J Gramlich and S Grundl, 'Estimating the Competitive Effects of Common Ownership' (19 February 2019) FEDS Working Paper No 2017–29 https://ssrn.com/abstract=2940137 claim to have made that same methodological choice before – but their actual regressions do not in fact estimate the effect of profits weights on prices. The ICI-sponsored paper by P Kennedy and others, 'The Competitive Effects of Common Ownership: Economic Foundations and Empirical Evidence' (24 July 2017) SSRN Electronic Journal, https://ssrn.com/abstract=3008331 has previously offered one specification with profit weights; A Park and K Seo, 'Common Ownership and Product Market Competition: Evidence from the U.S. Airline Industry' (2019) 48 Korean J Finance *Stud* 617 estimate with a structural model that rules out the market-share channel that there are likely anticompetitive effects from common ownership in the U.S. airline industry; the above-discussed study by Azar and Ribeiro (n 20) offers another structural approach that also rules out a role of market shares and at the same time recognizes agency frictions.

In sum, the recognition of vertical common ownership links does not challenge the finding that horizontal common ownership links increase prices – at least in the US airlines industry as the poster child for such studies. Instead, recognition of a role of vertical common ownership links in also affecting firm behaviour strengthens the finding that common ownership of horizontal competitors increases product prices.

12.2.3 *Methodological Novelties*

A good part of the past five years of the literature on competitive effects of common ownership has been spent debating the relative virtues and merits of reduced-form versus structural approaches – which rely on different assumptions and are suited for different purposes. (A standard view would hold that these approaches are complementary: reduced-form approaches tend to be suited to identify causal links, whereas structural estimations are suitable to make welfare estimations and to analyse counterfactuals.) A thus-far overlooked third set of methods concerns laboratory experiments. Should there be any doubt that the variation in ownership that the empirical studies to data have interpreted to have *caused* an increase in prices is truly exogenous, these doubts can be examined in a laboratory setting. Hariskos, Königstein, and Papadopoulos[25] show that exogenously imposed increases in partial cross-ownership increases product prices in the laboratory, and as such, break new ground. Given their study does not feature agency problems, there is no clear distinction between cross-ownership (firms holding direct stakes in competitors) and common ownership (industry outsiders holding stakes in competing firms), but this paper nevertheless opens the door for future work using this methodology as a complement to reduced-form and structural approaches.

12.2.4 *Endogeneity of Portfolio Choice in the Presence of Strategic Interactions between Product Market Competitors*

The key challenge for empirical economists working on the question whether firm ownership affects firm behaviour is to assess whether observed correlations in the data likely have a causal interpretation – or if they are just that: correlations. The emphasis of industrial organization economists, as it comes to scrutinizing the correlation between common ownership and higher prices, has been to focus on the potential endogeneity of market shares in polluting such estimates. I have explained above how this concern has been addressed by recent research, both with structural methods that explicitly model that endogeneity, and with reduced-form methods that avoid the problem simply by using measures of common ownership that don't contain market shares in the first place.

[25] W Hariskos and others, 'Anti-Competitive Effects of Partial Cross-Ownership: Experimental Evidence' (2021) 193 J Econ Behav Organ 399 https://doi.org/10.1016/j.jebo.2021.11.027.

However, there is another source of endogeneity that is much less well understood – but plays a crucial role in understanding the likely effect and thus desirability of the various policy proposals: *it is the endogenous choice of portfolios by investors*. If investor portfolios affect both firm behaviour and market outcomes, including firm profits, asset prices and the asset market equilibrium are affected by investor portfolio choice. Of course, in turn, portfolio choice is also affected by asset prices. A model capturing these mutual dependencies did not exist in the economics literature to date. In other words, we don't know how investors choose portfolios when firms strategically interact and the ownership structure affects firm behaviour.

The empirical literature deals with this lack of theoretical understanding by finding quasi-exogenous 'shocks' to the ownership of a particular set of firms that is unlikely to be related to the product market dynamics in question. However, policy proposals can't avail themselves of such techniques to predict what the likely effect of the proposals on asset prices and asset market equilibria is going to be. Such predictions will have to be made based on theoretical considerations, as emphasized in Part 2 of this paper. As a foundation, I therefore assess where we stand in our formal understanding of this complex system.

In recent years, more than half a dozen papers have attempted to address this question.[26] In particular, each paper shows that strategic considerations determine whether a particular portfolio allocation is an equilibrium or not. However, there are severe limitations. The literature does not prove but appears to suggest that anything beyond duopoly settings (or otherwise extremely specific parameter) are analytically intractable. In other words, the progress in this dimension is far from offering practically relevant predictions on how new policies may change the asset market equilibrium. This negative result is useful – because it tells us that we may have to accept that we are unlikely to learn much more in this dimension in the near future, and there is no point in waiting for 'more research' before policy decisions are made. Instead, the uncertainty must be taken as a given when trading off the cost of waiting, and potentially continued harm from lessened competition and governance against the uncertain costs (or benefits!) that some of the proposed policies may bring. I will get back to this tradeoff in Part 2.

[26] *See* D Moreno and El Petrakis, 'The impact on market outcomes of the portfolio selection of large equity investors' (2022) 212 Economics Letters https://e-archivo.uc3m.es/bitstream/handle/10016/33659/we2114.pdf?sequence=1&isAllowed=y; A Piccolo and J Schneemeier, 'Ownership and Competition' (1 November 2020) SSRN Electronic Journal https://ssrn.com/abstract=3733795; C Hemphill and M Kahan, 'Endogenous Choice of Stakes Under Common Ownership' (2021) European Corporate Governance Institute – Finance Working Paper No 805/2021 https://ssrn.com/abstract=3914327; R Stenbacka and G Van Moer, 'Cross Ownership and Divestment Incentives' (2021) 201 Econ Lett, https://doi.org/10.1016/j.econlet.2021.109748≥; A Bayona and others, 'Common Ownership, Corporate Control and Price Competition' (11 February 2021) SSRN Economic Journal, https://ssrn.com/abstract=3784072; K Papadopoulos, 'Advantageous Symmetric Cross-Ownership' (1 April 2021) SSRN Electronic Journal https://ssrn.com/abstract=3813415.

12.2.5 *The Gradual Lifting of Data Limitations*

Limitations on high-quality and comprehensive ownership data have been a bottleneck for the literature ever since its inception. Lifting those limitations is important for at least two reasons.

For one, studies that claim evidence of absence of competitive effects of common ownership (reviewed by Azar, Schmalz, and Tecu[27]) make these statements based on analyses that lack data on some of the most important and powerful investors. Such studies are run using 13F filings filed by passive institutional investors alone – but omit other blockholders, whether they are activist investors (who must file SEC 13Ds rather than 13Fs) or individual blockholders or large insiders (who file 13Gs). Such research thus attempts to explain the competitive behaviour of Facebook, Google, and Amazon, without considering the economic interests and control rights of Mark Zuckerberg, Larry Page and Sergey Brin, and Jeff Bezos. Thus, much of the variation in the measures of common ownership is missed, resulting in biased estimates.[28] The original Azar, Schmalz, and Tecu paper[29] hand collected ownership from the various SEC filings and alternative sources for that industry – however, for studies beyond a specific industry that approach is impractical. The paper on top manager incentives under common ownership by Antón and others makes qualitative progress in that dimension, by combining ownership information from 13F filings with information on 13D and 13G blockholders, while controlling in their regressions for direct effects of institutional ownership on managerial incentives. The results of this improvement in data quality are that the effects of common ownership on incentives are more than two times larger than when only 13F institutions are taken into consideration.[30] This result proves the point that accurate ownership data is a key ingredient in better empirical research on the question.

The second reason it is important to lift these data limitations is that it is difficult for scholars, policymakers, and lawmakers to know who owns Corporate America, and hence what precisely is the problem that needs fixing, and how big it is.[31] To answer that question, and to implement of any one of the policy proposals discussed in what follows, we need high-quality ownership data. Regulators have

[27] Azar, Schmalz, and Tecu (n 10).

[28] The import of this concern is difficult to ascertain because none of these critiques have made code and data available for that purpose, also on request. Azar, Schmalz, and Tecu's code and data are available since publication of the paper on the Journal of Finance website, https://onlinelibrary.wiley.com/doi/abs/10.1111/jofi.12698.

[29] Azar, Schmalz, and Tecu (n 1).

[30] Antón and others (n 14); compare Table 5 in 2021 version to 2022 version.

[31] Indeed, some policymakers were until recently under the mistaken belief that the majority of large shareholders in US airlines were not also common owners of competitors, *see* Phillips (n 12). Rock and Rubinfeld (n 6) have claimed as much in their 2017 article – yet without a factual basis an indeed in contradiction to the facts supplied by Azar, Schmalz, and Tecu (n 1).

the power to supply it, but have not to date; only one academic paper exists that makes such a resource available, as I now discuss.

12.3 DISCUSSION OF POLICY PROPOSALS

Legal scholars have made a number of proposals, taking at face value that there are competitive effects of common ownership and/or governance problems caused by large institutional investors, and that those problems are as widespread as the phenomenon of common ownership itself – i.e. across all firms and industries held by institutional investors. An interesting and worthwhile discussion of these proposals' strengths and weaknesses followed in recent years. What I find to be missing in the discussion is a clear and simple economic framework to organize that discussion. I aim to provide such a framework. I will then illustrate how some of the more prominent proposals fit in the framework, and which arguments and questions naturally arise that are thus far missing from the debate.

12.3.1 *A Framework to Discuss Policy Proposals*

The conceptual problem that causes anticompetitive effects of common ownership is when within-industry diversification is achieved at the same level at which corporate control is exercised. This insight is easily forgotten but has a long lineage in US policy. The 1934 Senate Securities ('Pecora') Report proposes that Congress must '*prevent the diversion of these trusts from their normal channels of diversified investment to the abnormal avenues of control of industry*'; the Investment Company Act bill opines that '*the national public interest … is adversely affected … when investment companies [have] great size [and] excessive influence on the national economy*'[32]. Accordingly, the Investment Company Act of 1940 limits the fraction of any issuer's shares a fund can hold to 10% of the outstanding stock.[33] It was obvious even to the 'father' of index investing that this rule was meant to apply not to funds but to the level at which corporate control is exercised – in practice the fund family – and that the existing rule does not technically cover that spirit: 'But when and if our index fund gets to 10%, all we have to do is start a second one and that would be in technical compliance. There should be limits'.[34] By my own calculations based on scraped SEC filings, Vanguard already in 2020 held more than 10% on average in the S&P 500's companies.

32 M Roe, 'Political and Legal Restraints on Ownership and Control of Public Companies' (1990) 27 J Financ Econ 7; US Senate Committee on Banking and Currency, *Stock Exchange Practices* (Rep No 1455 pursuant to S Res 84, 1934) www.senate.gov/about/resources/pdf/pecora-final-report.pdf.

33 Investment Company Act of 1940 15 USC § 80–1 et seq.

34 J Bogle, 'Bogle Sounds a Warning on Index Funds' Wall St J (New York, 29 November 2018) www.wsj.com/articles/bogle-sounds-a-warning-on-index-funds-1543504551.

A clear understanding of what the problem is also makes clear the basic directions that all effective solutions to the competition problem must take: solutions to the competition problem need to separate the levels at which diversification is achieved and at which corporate control is exercised. This can logically happen in two principal ways: either asset managers diversify across competitors but then have to leave influencing portfolio firms to other investors, or asset managers have to limit themselves to diversifying *across* industries, and leave diversification within industries (by diversifying across asset managers) to the ultimate asset owners.

A first insight that arises from recognizing a distinction between the levels of asset manager and asset owner as in the above framework is that full diversification can be achieved at the household level even if no asset manager or fund holds more than one firm in any one industry. Therefore, there is not necessarily a tradeoff between household diversification and product market competition, as the early theoretical contributions to this literature[35] and some policy proposals[36] may have suggested. I will get back to this point in my evaluation of proposals below.

The second insight to keep in mind is that it is not possible to *independently* address the antitrust and governance problems generated by the rise of concentrated institutional ownership. For example, any intervention in governance that affects the firm's cost structure also has competitive consequences, as the Antón and others model shows. In that model, any strengthening or weakening of the governance rights of institutional investors will induce a strengthening or weakening of the implementation of competitive or anticompetitive incentives implied by their portfolio. As such, desirable proposals should not narrowly address governance mechanisms that some suspect causes common ownership to increase profit margins (there is no evidence that common ownership increases profit margins). Instead, proposals should also address the lack of incentives for good governance practices that can lead to a lessening of productive efficiency and *thus* increased product prices, reduced output, and other harms.

A tertiary goal of any proposal is, or should be, to minimize disruptions to asset markets and the asset management industry, subject to attaining the first two goals.

With light of this framework, how should we evaluate the policy proposals made by various legal scholars, considering the research that has accumulated in the past five years? I first summarize the most prominent contributions' main arguments and then proceed to analysing their likely effects.

35 J Rotemberg, 'Financial Transactions Costs and Industrial Performance' (1984) Massachusetts Institute of Technology – Alfred P Sloan School of Management WP 1554–84, https://dspace.mit.edu/bitstream/handle/1721.1/47993/financialtransacoorote.pdf.

36 Posner and others (n 6).

12.3.2 *Summary of Extant Policy Proposals*

The first policy proposal in response to Azar, Schmalz, and Tecu's paper[37] being circulated was contained in Elhauge's 'Horizontal Shareholding'[38]. The opinion advanced therein is that existing law provides sufficient power to adjudicate competition problems created by common ownership of horizontal competitors, and that this power should be used to that effect. Whereas Elhauge discussed other applicable laws as well, including the Hart-Scott-Rodino Act, the main argument is that Clayton Act Section 7 already prohibits '*any acquisition of assets that [has] the effect … of substantially lessening competition*'.[39] The crux is that the Act does not prohibit a particular type of conduct of horizontal shareholders of competitors (or 'common owners'), but rather that it prohibits the asset acquisition itself, to the extent the resulting holding has anticompetitive effects. Also, no intent is required. The so-called passive investment exemption does not apply, as long as investors vote their shares.[40] As a result, a consequential enforcement of the law would result in a reduction of common ownership links between horizontal competitors, to the extent that they are likely to have anticompetitive effects. This idealized result from enforcement of existing law has some similarities to the intended effects of several other proposals that followed.

One of them is Posner and others[41], who agree with Elhauge's legal assessment, but point to practical and administrative problems with Elhauge's proposal to enforce anticompetitive common ownership links as Section 7 violations. In particular, Posner and others note, correctly, that the extent to which one institution's holdings has anticompetitive effects depends on the holdings of other institutions. Therefore, 'institutions obeying the law at one moment could become liable simply because other institutions changed their holdings and thereby made an industry less competitive. Institutional investors would need to determine other institutions' ownership shares plus an appropriate definition of hundreds or even thousands of industries to comply with the Clayton Act. Thus, a large institutional investor acting unilaterally in the current environment cannot ensure it is not violating the Clayton Act. That is a difficult position for institutional investors, who require clarity about where they can legally invest'.[42] Further, there could – and perhaps

[37] Azar, Schmalz and Tecu (n 1).

[38] Elhauge (n 3).

[39] I omit a discussion of a potential enforcement of Hart-Scott-Rodino Act notifications, which some have remarked the law may also require for the so-called 'passive' investors, given the similarity of their engagement practices with so-called 'active' investors, *see* M Flaherty and R Kerber, 'US lawsuit against activist ValueAct puts mutual funds on alert' *Reuters* (London, 12 April 2016) www.reuters.com/article/us-valueact-lawsuit-funds-idUSKCN0X92E6.

[40] Elhauge (n 3) 1305–08.

[41] Posner and others (n 6).

[42] *Ibid.* at 9.

would – be lawsuits for each transaction in each oligopolistic industry, which seems unwieldy.[43] To avoid such mayhem, Posner and others propose a safe haven for institutional investors, which would exempt institutional investors from antitrust scrutiny as long as they do not hold more than 1% of the shares of more than a single effective firm in an oligopoly *or* are index funds that are unable to make discretionary trades and are entirely passive not only with respect to their portfolio choice but also their governance activities, including voting.[44] Hence, investors have to choose if they want to hold large stakes in competitors or influence portfolio firms. Posner and others anticipate that large institutional investors will find this safe haven sufficiently attractive to divest from all but one firm in each oligopolistic industry, and concentrate their holdings in one target firm per industry, which would have the benefit, in Posner and others' estimation, of improving investors' incentives to engage in good governance in their chosen target firms. This idea has appeal as it both promises to address both the competition and the governance challenge laid out above. It would also reduce the cost of operating an index fund, due to saving on governance costs.

Rock and Rubinfeld[45] disagree both with Elhauge's and Posner and others' reading of Clayton Act Section 7 and with the logic behind Posner and others' proposal of a safe haven at 1% ownership limits; they propose a safe haven for institutional investors that hold less than 15% of the issuer's stock, don't have board representation (whereas it is left unexplained what that means for an institution that votes 15% of the shares and thus very likely is pivotal in director elections), and only engage in 'normal' governance activities, including the setting of executive compensation (which itself is likely to be a problematic mechanism as per Antón and others).[46] Rock and Rubinfeld's reasoning is based on the assumption that passivity in corporate governance matters would protect investors from suits under Clayton Act Section 7 (which contradicts Elhauge's and Posner and others' legal assessment). Based on that legal opinion, Rock and Rubinfeld don't believe investors would choose to reduce within-industry diversification in response to PSW's safe harbour. Nor do Rock and Rubinfeld believe investors would simply not react to the PSW proposal – which would be indicated if investors truly believed, like Rock and Rubinfeld, that there is no substantive antitrust violation to be concerned about. Instead, Rock and Rubinfeld believe investors would choose to become entirely passive to protect

43 Further concerns include the transactions costs, endless litigation, the risk of idiosyncratic judgments, changing patterns who competes with whom, and a risk to thus severely impair or destroy a socially desirable fund industry.

44 Posner and others (n 6) 33. Frequent mischaracterizations of Posner and others present it not as a safe harbour, but as a prohibition to hold competitors, and present the proposed exemption as applying to any funds that merely don't communicate with firm executives or directors as opposed to remaining entirely passive in matters of corporate governance.

45 Rock and Rubinfeld (n 6).

46 *Ibid.* at 43.

themselves from Clayton Act 7 violations and avoid changing their business model of holding horizontal competitors. They believe this would lead to a worsening of corporate governance standards; they do not discuss why no other investor would respond to the power vacuum. Notwithstanding Rock and Rubinfeld's criticism of the logic of PSW's proposal, they propose a qualitatively similar rule, namely a safe harbour but with a 15% instead of 1% limit, implying that four asset managers (or individuals) could jointly control 60% of the voting shares of *all* firms, in any, every, and all industries or 7 asset managers could control 100% of all shares -- and yet be exempt from antitrust scrutiny. They do not explain why this policy would have the effect of protecting consumers and competition, in addition to protecting investors from antitrust suits under present law.

Lund's[47] proposal is similar to Posner and others' in that she proposes to restrict the voting rights of index investors, but differs in that she does not propose a size threshold below which indexers would be allowed to engage in governance. Also, she does address index funds specifically, rather than common owners more generally, which also can – and often does – include non-indexer investors. Posner and others by contrast aim to remove anticompetitive incentives arising from all types of common owners, but *exempt* index funds that don't engage in governance activities. The idea behind Posner and others' proposal to target common ownership by all types of investors and not just index funds is that common owners can be individuals, conglomerates such as Berkshire Hathaway, and in some cases even activist hedge funds. Posner and others' idea behind exempting index funds is that the threat to sell shares can itself be used to influence firms; index funds that cannot make discretionary trades do not have that lever at their disposal. Lund's argument to target index funds per se, by contrast goes as follows. Lund points out a variety of reasons why asset managers that predominantly offer 'passive' investment products have reduced incentives to engage in governance with the aim of maximizing individual firms' value. Those reasons include lacking financial incentives, free-rider problems, and cost pressure. For these reasons, passive funds may encumber votes and thus prevent other investors with stronger incentives to govern and improve firm performance, but not use their power to that effect themselves. Further, 'even if a fund does choose to intervene, it will rationally adhere to a low-cost, one-size-fits-all approach to governance that is unlikely to be in the company's best interest'. She thus proposes that lawmakers consider restricting passive funds from voting at shareholder meetings altogether, thus leaving governance to other investors – namely, those that have incentives to be better informed and discipline management.

I have myself never made or endorsed a policy proposal, except for advocating for the collection and provision of high-quality ownership data that would allow for

[47] Lund (n 6).

more and higher-quality research into the problem.[48] To date, no such efforts have been made to my knowledge by the federal agencies to provide such a public good. Amel-Zadeh and others have since scraped and parsed the SEC's EDGAR system for ownership records and make the resulting data base freely available for academic research; it is the first and thus far only directly sourced, complete dataset on the ownership of US firms that is usable in academic research.[49]

12.3.3 *An Analysis of Extant Policy Proposals*

Elhauge's proposal to enforce existing law may first appear to be the least disruptive, by virtue of not changing the law but merely enforcing it. Further, as his proposal attacks the anticompetitive incentives implied by the holdings rather than specific governance channels, one would expect there to be no detrimental 'chilling' effect on investors' governance activities from intensified enforcement, which satisfies the second goal to some extent. However, upon inspection, the proposal may be not much less disruptive to asset markets and the asset management industry than the alternative proposals to change rules or laws: after all, a large fraction of extant institutional owners' portfolios would be affected by litigation. Abstracting away from this practical concern, the main substantive question mark with the proposal may be whether relevant judges would agree with Elhauge's reading of the Act and the burden of proof Elhauge deems necessary to proof a lessening of competition. To the extent a common ownership case under Section 7 would be difficult to win in practice, the main risk of Elhauge's proposed policy would be underenforcement, and thus an insufficient strengthening of competition – the first objective in my proposed framework. Hence, Elhauge's proposal would be least disruptive mainly to the extent it fails to satisfy the primary objective, which is restoring vigorous competition.

Regarding the second goal, one would expect improvements in governance insofar as ownership structure would change from heightened enforcement, and investors with greater incentives and ability to manage agency problems would become relatively more powerful owners. The result would be increases in productive

48 M Schmalz, 'Common Ownership' (8th Hearing on Competition and Consumer Protection in the 21st Century, New York City, 6 December 2018) www.ftc.gov/news-events/audio-video/audio/martin-schmalz-presentation-common-ownership.

49 A Amel-Zadeh, F Kasperk, and M Schmalz, 'Measuring Common Ownership: the Role of Blockholders and Insiders', *Working Paper*, 2022. Amel-Zadeh and others show that much of the variation in common ownership between S&P500 firms is driven by blockholders, whose ownership is disclosed in 13-G or 13-D filings as well as insiders who report their ownership on Forms 3, 4, and 5 with the SEC. Therefore, research using datasets based on 13-F forms alone, such as those provided by Thomson Reuters via WRDS or those by Backus, Conlon, and Sinkinson, is of limited validity, because omitting block holders and insiders leads to potentially grave bias in the econometric analysis of studies that rely on the ownership by passive investors alone. More research is needed to expand the database to firms outside the S&P500.

efficiency. As such, Elhauge's proposal seems a modest push in the right direction, in both dimensions. It has that feature in common with Posner and others' proposal.

Posner and others' concern about liability being caused by other investors' changing portfolio weights can be illustrated as follows: suppose two tech firms, Mazebook and Poodle, were 'competitors' in some meaningful sense, and suppose one individual controlled each firm via dual class share structure. Further, suppose diversified institutional investors hold voting shares in both firms but have no influence due to the presence of the controlling founders. As there is no influence by common owners, there are no anticompetitive effects from common ownership. Now, suppose one of the individuals or both sell their shares to many small investors, who don't exercise the voting rights. Suddenly, the institutional common owners are the largest investors, and their anticompetitive incentives begin to materialize, for no fault of the investors, but simply because of the absence of the formerly present controlling founders. This is the motivation to consider safe havens for investors.

In terms of evaluation, Posner and others' proposal is more attractive in some dimensions than they describe it to be, because of the first insight from my proposed framework: whereas Posner and others argue the loss of diversification benefits due to restricting portfolios to only one firm per oligopolistic industry was minimal, I have argued that the loss of theoretically possible diversification to households is zero. There is no loss of diversification to the ultimate investors.[50] The households would be made poorer in their identity as shareholders (whose portfolio firms' profits would drop because of firms operating in more competitive markets), but richer in their identity as consumers. Given the facts about the US wealth and consumption distribution, for the vast majority of the population – and certainly for the population as a whole – the latter effect dominates.[51]

Whereas the asset market disruptions of such a change and other practicalities are not discussed in detail, the appeal of this solution is that not only would it remove anticompetitive incentives from holding competitors, but it would also strengthen corporate governance, both by increasing the stake investors hold in firms and thus reducing free riding by other investors, and by removing disincentives to engage due to the externality on other firms that drives the Antón and others model. Hence, the proposal addresses both goals I have declared to be desirable above. Concerning

[50] As with all of the proposals discussed here, there are enormous practicalities that would need to be addressed before such policies would be enacted. In PSMW's case, it may be impossible for an asset manager the size of Vanguard to concentrate all their, say, bank holdings in a single bank, without having to take the bank private. I will abstract away from such considerations, to retain the focus on an analysis which principal directions are likely to be most desirable.

[51] See J Gans and others, 'Inequality and Market Concentration, When Shareholding Is More Skewed than Consumption' (2019) 35 Oxford Rev Econ Pol 550. The concern that institutional investors would internalize the heterogeneous preferences of ultimate shareholders for more or less competition seems remote, given informational frictions that appear to give rise already to investors with diverging interests homogeneously paying a fixed percentage of the market value of assets under management to asset managers.

the third goal, it certainly would be disruptive, but it is not clear whether more or less disruptive than a barrage of suits to the industry under existing law! Moreover, some of the feared disruptions – such as a dramatic reduction of the profitability of portfolio firms, would be a feature not a bug in this proposal, to the extent these profits are 'excessive' as they are illegally derived from anticompetitive incentives from common ownership, and a reflection of the social harm of reduced competition.

As a further reflection, a key element of the proposal is not to allow investors to qualify as 'passive' if they merely not communicate with top management: there are many other channels by which investors can influence governance and competitive outcomes. Indeed, not engaging with companies while encumbering voting rights is a mechanism that can itself cause a lessening of productive efficiency and thus cause higher product prices. Investors should have to choose between any corporate governance interventions at all – including voting – or not holding large stakes in competitors. Stated this way, the Posner and others' proposal is not dissimilar to Lund's proposal, whose idea mainly differs in that she proposes to outright limit index funds' voting rights, rather than giving investors the freedom to self-assess their likely antitrust liability and choose whether they want to engage in governance or become purely passive in both meanings of the word.[52]

Rock and Rubinfeld's proposal, by contrast, appears to have the effect of protecting institutional investors from antitrust liability, even if they do in fact cause a lessening of competition, up to a limit at which it is virtually assured that there would be a lessening of competition by common ownership: I am not aware of economic theories that would predict that if 100% of a firm's shareholder base identically overlaps with the shareholder base of all competitors, that one could expect no lessening of competition. Yet, this would be explicitly covered and exempt from scrutiny under Rock and Rubinfeld's proposal. The proposal therefore is likely to be ineffective at addressing any anticompetitive effects of common ownership, but in fact removes concerns about enforcement some institutional investors may have that engage in strategies that are likely to have anticompetitive effects.

Rock and Rubinfeld's proposal further appears to do worse than either Elhauge's or Posner and others' in the second dimension. The reason may be that Rock and Rubinfeld rely on an erroneous understanding of the economic theory at the core of the common ownership problem. Rock and Rubinfeld appear to believe that active involvement in corporate governance is necessary for common ownership to bring about a lessening of competition. Their proposal holds that not-too-large investors

[52] Further proposed refinements of PSMW's proposal could address concerns about being both over-inclusive and under-inclusive, spelled out by E Elhauge, 'The Growing Problem of Horizontal Shareholding' (June 2017) 3 Antitrust Chronicle. The same paper also responds to PSMW's motivating concern about the practicability of enforcement under the Clayton Act, noting that PSMW's proposal is itself subject to the same concern, to the extent it should be viewed as a concern; *see* also E Elhauge, 'How Horizontal Shareholding Harms Our Economy – And Why Antitrust Law Can Fix It' (2020) 10 Harv Bus Law Rev 2.

should be exempt from antitrust scrutiny as long as they pursue only 'normal governance activities', including setting executive compensation, which they expect would not change competitive outcomes, and hence not fall under what Clayton Act Section 7 is meant to capture. Yet, Antón and others are the last paper in a long line of economic literature that has shown that compensation can cause anticompetitive outcomes.

Recall that Rock and Rubinfeld's proposal would protect corporate control rights of institutions that have questionable incentives to use them for the benefit of society. The incentives are doubtful be it because asset managers face agency problems of their own (as in Bebchuk and Hirst), because governance improvements in one firm harm other firms (as in Antón and others), because they don't sufficiently care about individual firms (as in Lund), or because of excessive competition to reduce fees in the market for asset management product, and thus limit the resources devoted to governance.

As such, the Rock and Rubinfeld proposal achieves either of the two aims I outlined in the framework to evaluate the policy proposals. I conclude that whereas this proposal appears suitable to deal with the SEC's concern to help investors deal with the 'investor protection challenge of the 21st century',[53] the proposal seems to have the effect of weakening existing consumer protections afforded by the Clayton Act.

Lund's proposal to limit the voting rights of institutions at first seems like a recipe for a corporate governance catastrophe.[54] By main own calculations, in typical US publicly traded firms, the largest shareholder who does not also own similarly large stakes in competitors (and who should therefore be captured by a version of her proposal for the purposes of addressing the antitrust concern, whether a passive fund or not) tends to rank above the top 50 and tends to hold less than 1% of the cash flow rights. Giving this investor a disproportionate share of the control rights would dramatically misalign cash flow and control rights, and thus lead to the definition of a corporate governance problem.

However, this thinking overlooks the asset market's equilibrium response. Whereas an analytic solution and precise prediction for this response remains elusive to the researchers working on the question, it is clear that some qualified investors interested would be attracted to purchase the shares of a firm in which control or significant influence can be bought by acquiring less than 1% of the outstanding stock. Indeed, the implementation of the proposal might trigger a revival of activist shareholders who in recent years have increasingly concentrated on campaigns that are agreeable to the big common owners.[55]

53 Jackson (n 5).

54 Lund (n 6).

55 For a case study on how common owners can determine the outcome of an activist campaign and thus change competitive outcomes, *see* M Schmalz, 'How passive funds prevent competition' (*View From Oxford*, 15 May 2015) https://viewfromoxford.com/how-passive-funds-prevent-competition.

In an ironic twist, the outcome of this endogenous reallocation of cash flow and control rights may lead to a similar outcome as the one Posner and others' proposal aims for. In the re-allocated equilibrium, there exist fully diversified investors, but they don't engage in governance; the only investors that engage in governance are those that have concentrated stakes in the target firm. The same benefits in terms of jointly improving competition and governance would result.

Both proposals also have in common that index funds could implement the proposals without any disruption to their business model, other than stopping their costly governance activities, leading to a further cost reduction for ultimate household investors, as well as a reduction in the concentration of corporate control.

The above discussion aims to organize the proposals along the principal directions that matter. The proposals differ in many other details, but which can be iterated and improved upon. For example, Lund's proposal to prevent index funds from voting does not capture other common owners and thus would be under-inclusive compared to Posner and others', but this feature could be adjusted to avoid such under-inclusion. A discussion of such details is beyond the scope of this paper, so as to focus attention to whether the principal direction of travel appears suitable to achieve the main goals of the policies.

In sum, the proposals that would actually address the issue – Elhauge's, Posner and others', and Lund's – differ substantially in their methods, but are essentially similar in that they all aim for the same, desirable outcome: a separation of diversification and influence over portfolio firms. My contribution is not to judge which of those means are most appropriate, politically feasible, or realistic, but to enable readers to see the commonalities and the cost and benefits from an economic perspective.

There is no doubt that each one of these proposals would lead to a substantial reorganization of asset management and asset markets, which would be disruptive, which many appear to view as per se undesirable. On the other hand, the counterfactual to implementing a version of these proposals is to allow for no less fundamental changes to occur, if incrementally day by day. Namely, it would amount to letting an unprecedented concentration of control over industry to grow ad infinitum and remain virtually unchecked, which would be at odds not only with economic theories of competitive markets but American political ideals as well.

It hence appears increasingly likely that, earlier or later, depending on the political climate, something will be done. 'Recognising this potential issue further down the line, BlackRock has taken an active step in allaying concerns by offering asset owners in 40% of its $4.8trn equity index funds[56] the opportunity to vote directly with companies, instead of the firm partaking itself'.[57] In other words, BlackRock

56 T Eckett, 'BlackRock to offer voting powers to index investors' (ETF stream, 8 October 2021) https://etfstream.com/news/blackrock-to-offer-voting-powers-to-index-investors/.

57 T Eckett, 'Common ownership is "defining battleground" for ETF industry over next decade' (*ETF Stream*, 21 December 2021) https://etfstream.com/features/common-ownership-is-defining-battleground-for-etf-industry-over-next-decade.

implemented a version of the Posner and others/Lund proposal so as to forestall regulation. This appears to be substantively desirable at first glance. However, 'While this goes some way in addressing the issue in wider indexing, the problem will continue in the ETF space where there is less transparency on who owns the ETFs due to the fact they trade on the secondary market'.[58] In other words, it remains unclear whether this move also obscures the picture of who controls Corporate America, thus disabling further research on the matter, and reemphasizing my call for more complete and correct ownership data to be made available. On second thought, it is also substantively undesirable, first because the move fails to separate the levels at which corporate control is exercised and the level at which diversification is achieved. And if the practice achieved such separation by ultimate shareholders not voting their shares, we would go back to the old Bearle and Means problem of rationally apathic shareholders who fail to control management. Therefore, a solution in which blockholders exist but in which these blockholders don't hold competitors and have strong incentives to monitor management is more desirable along all key dimensions.

12.4 CONCLUSION

As this review showed, essentially all dimensions regulators have viewed as roadblocks to regulation have been addressed by recent research: we are assured the measured correlations between common ownership and higher product prices are most likely to have a causal interpretation and that they are, in particular, not driven by endogenous market shares. We know realistic mechanisms exist, and that agency conflicts are most likely a key driver of the empirical facts the literature has uncovered. Similarly, organizational complexities are a feature of models that can make nuanced predictions that are verified in the data. When vertical links are considered, the measured effects of common ownership on prices get stronger. The same is true when more complete and more accurate ownership data are used.

Which of the proposals should be implemented? The bottom line of this paper is that this is not a question that can be answered with purely economic analysis. As this review illustrated, economic research has made progress – but not nearly enough to be able to fully predict the effect of policy proposals that aim to fundamentally change the asset market equilibrium, and hence macroeconomic performance as well. Rather than a question that can and should be decided by economic technocrats, a broader question is whether we want an economic system featuring a 'Problem of Twelve'[59] in which a very small number of players effectively controls large swathes of American industry. In the past, politicians, such as Pecora, saw no

[58] *Ibid.*

[59] J Coates, 'The Future of Corporate Governance Part I: The Problem of Twelve' (2018) Harvard Public Law Working Paper No 19-07, https://corpgov.law.harvard.edu/wp-content/uploads/2019/11/John-Coates.pdf.

need for structural estimates of competitive effects across all industries before taking action. Instead, it was clear to them that increasingly centralized control over business was not conducive to a thriving capitalist economy. Whether the resulting laws were overly restrictive (including the 10% limits for single funds) appears to be more a question of political convictions and personal incentives than rigorous economic analysis. A further concern with calls for more research is that when we insist on having 'quasi-experimental' evidence to evaluate whether a given policy is good, we are limiting the scope of analysis and allowable policies to those we have tried before. This restriction is obviously self-defeating for a phenomenon that has not occurred previously. In other words, I believe that we are at risk of relying on economic analyses that miss the forest for the trees. The danger is that economists can have the effect of hindering regulation by pointing to uncertainties, while omitting the fact that anticompetitive harm continues, at ever increasing scale, while the debate continues. In sum, I positively view it at this stage as determined rather by political processes than further economic analysis – and to the extent these political processes reflect the interests of ordinary citizens I normatively agree with that notion to some extent. The unarguable part of the debate appears to me that transparency on who controls corporate America should be fostered. The only grounds to obscure the facts to me appear to be a desire to deal with the 'investor-protection challenge' of the twenty-first century rather than with a concern about competition and governance.

13

Does Common Ownership Explain Higher Oligopolistic Profits?

Edward B. Rock and Daniel L. Rubinfeld

13.1 INTRODUCTION

There is compelling evidence that both concentration and profitability in oligopolistic industries have increased over the past two decades. Over roughly the same time period, the concentration of shareholding in the hands of the largest institutional investors has dramatically increased, with a corresponding increase in the degree to which investors (such as Vanguard, State Street, and BlackRock) own large equity stakes in competing portfolio companies. A number of authors have argued that the growth in this 'common ownership' has *caused* the increase in oligopoly profits and have proposed a variety of policy responses.

In this paper, we review the available evidence. We argue that as of now (a) the evidence that common ownership is the driving force behind the increasing oligopoly profits is unconvincing, (b) there are plausible competing explanations for the correlation between profitability and common ownership. As a result, (c) regulatory intervention directed against common ownership is not currently warranted, given the significant costs of such intervention.

This paper proceeds as follows. In Section 13.2 we provide an overview of the evidence that concentration and profitability have increased. In Section 13.3, we consider the evidence that increased common ownership is the cause of the increase in profitability. Section 13.4 considers alternative explanations for the correlation between increasing concentration, increasing profitability, and increasing common ownership, along with the available evidence in support of these alternative hypotheses. Section 13.5 considers the policy implications of the current state of play.

Edward B. Rock is the Martin Lipton Professor of Law at NYU; Daniel L. Rubinfeld is Professor of Law, NYU and Robert L. Bridges Professor of Law and Professor of Economics, Emeritus, UC Berkeley.

13.2 THE EVIDENCE: CONCENTRATION AND PROFITABILITY

Over the past two decades, major industries in the US and worldwide have become more concentrated and, over the same time period, more profitable. The US Council of Economic Advisors 2016 'Issue Brief' documents that between 1997 and 2012 changes in the revenue share of the largest firms in a variety of industries have ranged between −2% and 11.4%, with the majority of those firms showing substantial increases.[1] More recently, a study by Bajgar et al. used firm-level concentration measures and found that the share of industry sales due to the 10 largest companies in 10 European economies increased on average by 2% in manufacturing and 3% in non-financial services from 2001 to 2012.[2] The authors conclude that there has been a clear increase in industry concentration in both Europe and North America (from 2000 to 2014) by between 4% and 8%, with the absolute increase being somewhat greater in North America.[3]

Industry-specific studies support and augment this broad picture. To mention just a few, a 2010 Congressional Research Service study by Shields found that between 1971 and 2002 dairy industry concentration increased in eight of the nine agricultural industries studied.[4] Gaynor, Ho, and Town found that between the early 1990s and 2006, the average HHI for hospital markets increased by about 50% to approximately 3,200, substantially above the DOJ/FTC Guidelines' 2,500 cutoff measure of high concentration.[5] With respect to mobile wireless, concentration has steadily increased over time, highlighted by the recent successful acquisition of Sprint by T-Mobile, that left the US with only three facilities-based wireless carriers having a national footprint.[6]

Interestingly, there are significant exceptions to this overall pattern in some high-profile markets. Froeb and Werden found that US airline route-level HHIs slightly decreased over their broad period of study, ranging from 1984 through 2012.[7] Likewise,

1 US Council of Econ Advisers, 'Issue Brief: Benefits of Competition and Indicators of Market Power' (April 2016).

2 Matej Bajgar and others, 'Industry Concentration in Europe and North America' (2019) OECD Productivity Working Papers, Paper No 18, 2019.

3 The increased consolidation in the US has been echoed in the Canadian economic environment. A 2019 study by Bawania and Larkin shows that one-third of Canadian industries have seen an increase in the HHI of over 50%. See Ray Bawania and Yelena Larkin, 'Are Industries Becoming More Concentrated? The Canadian Perspective' (20 March 20 2019) (unpublished manuscript).

4 DA Shields, 'Consolidation and Concentration in the US Dairy Industry' (2010) Cong Research Service R41224. See also RJ Sexton and Tian Xia, 'Increasing Concentration in the Agricultural Supply Chain: Implications for Market Power and Sector Performance' (2018) 10 Ann Rev Resource Econ 229 (discussing concentration and coordination in the agri-food supply chain).

5 Martin Gaynor, Kate Ho, and Robert Town, '*The Industrial Organization of Health-Care Markets*' (2015) 53 J Econ Lit 235.

6 For historical perspective, see FCC, 'Eighteenth Mobile Wireless Competition Report' (2015) 30 FCC Rcd 14515 (18).

7 LM Froeb and GJ Werden, 'Don't Panic: A Guide to Claims of Increasing Concentration' (2018) Antitrust Magazine. Froeb and Werden reference three papers with differing periods of study. For the

a study by the UK Social Market Foundation found little indication of increasing concentration in most UK consumer markets over the period of 2000 to 2017.[8]

The link between concentration and profitability has been more contested. Antitrust law, scholarship, and policy have all been based on a link between the two.[9] Indeed, that link has been one of the foundations for the DOJ-FTC Horizontal Merger Guidelines. The Guidelines, in turn, were highly influenced by the 'Structure-Conduct-Performance paradigm' in Industrial Organization.[10] Convincing empirical analysis has historically been sparse for a variety of reasons that modern industrial organisation scholarship describes. For one thing, concentration is not an exogenous force; as a result, we cannot be certain of the direction of the concentration-profitability relationship. For another, published concentration measures are often not coincident with the relevant economic markets that underlie industrial organisation economics.

Studies looking for evidence from earlier periods have found weak or no correlation between these variables.[11] Indeed, the uncertain connection between industry concentration and anticompetitive outcomes is one of the reasons why, in the Guidelines, HHI levels are the starting point for further investigation and do not, on their own, trigger challenges.[12] Post-2000, however, the evidence of this link is more robust. A Swiss finance Institute Research Paper by Grullon et al, supports the correlation between concentration and profit margins.[13] The authors find that more

1984–90 period, Borenstein found that route-level HHIs on domestic US routes decreased slightly. See Severin Borenstein, 'The Evolution of U.S. Airline Competition' (1992) 6 J Econ Perspectives 45. For the 1995–2009 period, according to Hüschelrath and Müller the HHIs for the largest 100 short-, medium- and long-haul routes revealed a general downward trend in concentration. See Kai Hüschelrath and Kathrin Müller, 'Low Cost Carriers and the Evolution of the Domestic U.S. Airline Industry' (2012) 13 Competition & Regulation in Network Industries 133. Finally, for the 2007–12 period, the US Government Accountability Office (GAO) concluded that there was a slight reduction in concentration in the highest-travelled markets. See GAO, 'Airline Competition: The Average Number of Competitors in Markets Serving the Majority of Passengers has Changed Little, but Stakeholders Voice Concerns about Competition' (June 2014) 26 www.gao.gov/assets/gao-14-515.pdf.

8 Scott Corfe and Nicole Gicheva, 'Concentration not competition: the state of UK consumer markets' (*The Social Market Foundation*, October 2017) www.smf.co.uk/wp-content/uploads/2017/10/Concentration-not-competition.pdf. See also TA Lambert and ME Sykuta, 'The Case for Doing Nothing About Institutional Investors' Common Ownership of Small Stakes in Competing Firms' 13 Virginia Law and Business Review 213 (2019).

9 P. Areeda and H. Hovenkamp, Antitrust Law: An Analysis of Antitrust Principles and Their Application (CCH), Paragraph 404(d)(concentration-performance evidence). F.M. Scherer & David Ross, Industrial Market Structure and Economic Performance 4–6, 411–447 (Houghton Mifflin 1990); Herbert Hovenkamp, Federal Antitrust Policy: The Law of Competition and Its Practice 1.7, at 42–44 (1994) (describing the relationship between the structure-conduct-performance paradigm and merger law of the 1950s–1960s).

10 The SCP paradigm can be traced back to the work of Bain. See, e.g. JS Bain, 'Relation of Profit Rate to Industry Concentration: American Manufacturing: 1936 to 1940' (1951) 65 QJ Econ 293.

11 For a thoughtful early overview, see Richard Schmalensee and Robert Willig, *Handbook of Industrial Organization*, vol 2 (Elsevier 1989) 951–1009.

12 DOJ and FTC, 'Horizontal Merger Guidelines', s 1.5, ss 2–5.

13 Gustavo Grullon, Yelena Larkin, and Roni Michaely, 'Are US Industries Becoming More Concentrated?' Review of Finance, Volume 23, Issue 4, July 2019, pp. 697–743.

than three-fourths of US industry have experienced an increase in concentration levels over the past two decades and that those industries with the highest increases in concentration have seen higher profit margins.[14] The authors credit these changes in part to reduced antitrust enforcement and increased technological barriers to entry.[15]

Along the same lines, an informative paper by Gutierrez and Philippon shows clearly that there has been an increase in the HHI in most US industries and correspondingly an increase in profit margins as measured by the Lerner index.[16] The evidence that, since 2000, increased concentration is correlated with increased profitability suggests that an adequate theory must explain two things: why is there a correlation between concentration and profitability? And why has there been a strong(er) correlation post-2000 than pre-2000? Jonathan Baker tells a compelling story. According to Baker, large businesses have profited by using sophisticated pricing algorithms and customer data to secure substantial, persistent advantages over smaller players.[17]

13.3 HAS COMMON OWNERSHIP LED TO HIGHER PROFIT MARGINS? THE CLAIMS AND A CRITIQUE OF THE EVIDENCE

Much of the current debate results from the extraordinary attention attracted by Jose Azar, Martin C. Schmalz and Isabel Tecu's (AST) widely read working paper (now published in the Journal of Finance) that claims the increased common ownership by diversified investors has *caused* a significant increase in the price of airline tickets.[18] A related paper claims that the same effect is found in commercial banking.[19] In response to the dramatic claims of these papers, there has been a huge outpouring of theoretical and empirical research and analysis. In this section, we briefly review that research.

13.3.1 *The AST Claim*

Azar, Schmalz, and Tecu make two main arguments. First, they argue that managers of firms in concentrated industries characterised by high levels of common ownership will have an incentive to adopt a 'soft competition' strategy out of deference

[14] See ibid 6–11.

[15] ibid.

[16] Germán Gutierrez & Thomas Philippon, 'Declining Competition and Investment in the US' (2017) National Bureau of Economic Research Working Paper No 23583. The Lerner index is a measure of a firm's profit margin (typically the gross profit margin as a percentage of the price of the product). See e.g. RS Pindyck and DL Rubinfeld, '*Market Power: Monopoly and Monopsony*' in Microeconomics (9th edn, Pearson 2018).

[17] Jonathan B Baker, *The Antitrust Paradigm: Restoring the American Economy* (Harvard University Press 2019).

[18] José Azar, MC Schmalz and Isabel Tecu, 'Anti-competitive Effects of Common Ownership' (2018) 73 J Fin 1459.

[19] José Azar, Sahil Raina & MC Schmalz, 'Ultimate ownership and bank competition' (May 4, 2019) (unpublished manuscript) https://ssrn.com/abstract=2710252.

to their shareholders' ownership of competing firms. Second, they argue that, in fact, this is what has happened in the airline industry – with the effect of increasing ticket prices. As noted, a related paper finds that common ownership had the same effect in the commercial banking industry.

13.3.2 *Concerns with the AST Claim*

There are a variety of theoretical and empirical concerns that have been raised in response to these claims. As we have argued in detail elsewhere, it is unclear whether shareholders as a group would in fact have an *incentive* to encourage firms to adopt a 'soft competition' strategy.[20] While there is clearly a degree of common ownership among airlines, there is also substantial heterogeneity, with a mix that has varied substantially over time. Thus, while the common holdings of the largest index funds have remained fairly constant, as would be expected for funds that track an index, the holdings of actively managed investors are large and have varied substantially over relatively short time periods. AST's argument that managers of airlines will sacrifice their own airline's profits out of deference to investors' holdings in competitors assumes a degree of commonality in the holdings of investors that, in practice, does not exist. Moreover, when investors' portfolios are heterogeneous, each investor will have a different view of the right sort of competition within the industry and the extent to which managers should take into account the effect on competitors of a competitive strategy.

These concerns point to a more fundamental question: how exactly would an individual firm find a way to maximise the weighted average of the profits enjoyed by the shareholders of all of the firms in the industry, accounting for some shareholders' ownership of horizontal competitors? Does this broader more complex objective function explain the strategic behaviour of the airlines more accurately than the usual firm-based profit maximisation assumptions? We have seen no compelling evidence that firms, in fact, take their shareholders' investment portfolios into account in setting competitive strategy.

This leads directly into a second set of concerns with the AST argument: what is the basis for thinking that common owners have the *ability* to influence managers to soften competition even if doing so would increase the investors' portfolio value? The corporate governance channels by which investors would influence managers in the way that AST hypothesise remain obscure. While shareholders elect directors, who disclose vast amounts of information in proxy statements, we are not aware of any directors who have 'run' on a 'soften competition' platform. While shareholders have a periodic non-binding vote on management compensation, this is likewise too blunt an instrument to be plausible.

[20] EB Rock and DL Rubinfeld, 'Antitrust for Institutional Investors' (2018) 82 Antitrust LJ 279.

What has led the AST paper to attract such attention, however, is not the theoretical possibility but, rather, the empirical claim that common ownership has *actually* resulted in significantly higher prices in airlines and other industries. Their empirical analysis of the airline industry starts with an analysis of the correlation between the change in the degree of common ownership and airline fares (using a measure of overlapping ownership that O'Brien and Salop used in their quite different cross-ownership context – the MHHIΔ). AST then treat an exogenous event that increased ownership concentration – BlackRock's 2009 purchase of Barclay's iShares business – as a natural experiment to determine whether a change in ownership concentration leads to an increase in ticket prices.

Every step of this analysis has been subjected to substantial scrutiny. First, Hemphill and Kahan show that the use of MHHIΔ as the measure of ownership concentration is problematic because it is not the right measure for testing plausible channels of influence and the channels of influence that it tests are not plausible.[21] Others agree that the MHHIΔ is not a useful measure for a variety of other reasons and have tried to develop alternative approaches.[22]

Second, and more fundamentally, Backus et al show that looking for correlations between prices and common ownership concentration runs into all of the same issues that have long been raised about correlations between prices and market concentration, as measured by the HHI.[23] Specifically, the results are often spurious or impossible to interpret; ultimately, the relationship identified is an equilibrium outcome that may well not identify any meaningful economic relationship. Moreover, there are issues concerning the appropriate choice of profit weights and endogeneity with respect to the determination of prices, outputs, market shares, and concentration.

Third, the empirical results in the airline industry are not robust. Dennis et al and Kennedy et al have both shown that the AST results are extremely sensitive to initial assumptions.[24]

21 CS Hemphill and Marcel Kahan, 'The Strategies of Anticompetitive Common Ownership' (2020) 129 Yale LJ 1392.

22 Matthew Backus, Christopher Conlon, and Michael Sinkinson, 'Theory and Measurement of Common Ownership' (2020) 110 AEA Papers and Proceedings 1; Matthew Backus, Christopher Conlon, and Michael Sinkinson, 'Common Ownership and Competition in the Ready-to-eat Cereal Industry' (Draft, September 2018); Erik Gilje, TA Gormley and Doron Levit, 'Who's Paying Attention? Measuring Common Ownership and Its Impact on Managerial Incentives' Journal of Financial Economics, 2020, vol. 137, issue 1, 152–178.

23 Matthew Backus, Christopher Conlon & Michael Sinkinson, 'The Common Ownership Hypothesis: Theory and Evidence' (2019) Brookings Economic Studies Paper, Feb 5 2019.

24 *See* PJ Dennis, Kristopher Gerardi, and Carola Schenone, 'Common Ownership Does Not Have Anti-Competitive Effects in the Airline Industry' (2019) McIntire School of Commerce Working Paper https://papers.ssrn.com/sol3/papers.cfm?abstract_id=3063465#. For a broader criticism of AST, see Pauline Kennedy, Daniel P. O'Brien, Minjae Song and Keith Waehrer, 'The Competitive Effects of Common Ownership: Economic Foundations and Empirical Evidence' (July 2017) (unpublished manuscript) https://papers.ssrn.com/sol3/papers.cfm?abstract_id=3008331.

Fourth, if the AST theory is correct, one would expect to find similar effects in markets other than airlines and banking. To our knowledge, such attempts have failed. Backus et al, in a working paper, find that the results cannot be replicated in the ready-to-eat cereal market, despite similar levels of market and ownership concentration.[25] With respect to banking, Gramlich and Grundl find little evidence of economically large effects of common ownership on profits.[26]

Koch, Panayides, and Thomas have carried out some interesting empirical tests across a wide range of product markets. They conclude that higher industry common shareholding levels have no robust, positive effects on industry profitability measured as either the average cross-industry ratios of revenues over costs or the price-cost margin.[27] Knowing the difficulty of drawing causal conclusions absent an ideal randomised experiment (the system receives a random shock in the form of an unexpected change in the extent and/or form of common ownership) the authors looked for structural breaks in time series that might be indicative of the possibility of a related quasi-experiment. They found no systemic changes in markups or price-cost margins following dramatic changes in common ownership. The same conclusion flowed from industry-level regressions of profitability on non-price competition proxies for common ownership, with controls that take into account other aspects of institutional ownership and differences in industry structure.[28]

Although the research triggered by the AST paper reinforces our doubts about the unilateral effects theory that is at the heart of the AST analysis, we remain agnostic with respect to the more general claim that common ownership has led to higher profit margins and prices. As we explain in our most recent common ownership paper, there are a number of potential links, but we have yet to see empirical evidence establishing a compelling causal story linking the growth of common ownership with systemic coordinated anticompetitive effects.[29]

[25] Backus, Conlon, and Sinkinson, 'Common Ownership and Competition in the Ready-to-eat Cereal Industry' (n 23).

[26] Jacob Gramlich and Serafin Grundl, 'The Effect of Common Ownership on Profits: Evidence from the US Banking Industry' (2018) FEDS Working Paper No 2018-069.

[27] Koch, Andrew & Panayides, Marios & Thomas, Shawn, 2021. "Common Ownership and Competition in Product Markets," Journal of Financial Economics, Elsevier, vol. 139(1), pp. 109–137.

[28] For a study that draws similar conclusions, see Katharina Lewellen and Michelle Lowry, 'Does Common Ownership Really Increase Firm Coordination?' J Fin Economics (2021) vol. 141(1), pp. 322–344 (finding no evidence that common ownership increases the likelihood of firm coordination, as measured by joint ventures, strategic alliances, or mergers).

[29] EB Rock and DL Rubinfeld, 'Common Ownership and Coordinated Effects' (2020) 83 Antitrust LJ 201, 222–24. A recent paper by Mengde Liu ('Players Behind the Scenes: Common Ownership in the Hospital Industry,' Draft, October 31, 2019) claims to find causal price effects from common ownership in the hospital industry. The author conducts a range of statistical tests, but in the end several major conceptual flaws remain: (1) The lead–lead and other methods to treat endogeneity are not compelling; (2) There is no explanation as to the causal mechanism by which the common owners impact hospital management behaviour (while the author cites our coordination paper, the paper uses a unilateral effects methodology); and (3) There is no attempt to account for any hospital or hospital systems mergers.

13.4 ALTERNATIVE EXPLANATIONS FOR THE CORRELATION BETWEEN CONCENTRATED MARKETS, HIGHER PROFITS, AND CONCENTRATED COMMON OWNERSHIP

If the increase in common ownership is not the cause of the increase in concentration or profitability, what might that cause be? In this section, we consider some alternative explanations.

13.4.1 *Reverse Causation? Suppose that Savvy Investors Invest in Oligopolies?*

Observers have noted that Warren Buffett, a legendary investor, tends to invest in oligopolies.[30] Indeed, he has explicitly noted that the most wonderful business to invest in is one with pricing power.[31] If other savvy and successful investors follow a similar strategy, then the increase in common ownership in concentrated industries may be the *result* of concentration and profitability and not the *cause* of either.

As an explanation, this has some plausibility. Because oligopolies and monopolies tend to have high and sustained profits, it is not crazy to think that savvy investors would disproportionately gravitate to such investments and, having identified an oligopoly, invest in many if not all the firms in the market.

At the same time, this explanation has its limits. First, it does not explain the timing: why did concentration, common ownership, and profitability all increase since around 2000? Second, the persistence over time is puzzling because it is unclear why unsophisticated investors would not eventually learn to follow the lead of the sophisticated investors. Third, it may be a complementary rather than competing explanation if Buffett and the other common owners somehow put pressure on members of an oligopoly not to engage in sharp competition, or if, in anticipation of such pressure, managers tailor their strategies to the savvy investors' portfolios.

13.4.2 *Might There Be a Common Cause?*

The most interesting and puzzling finding in the literature is that the link between concentration and profitability is clearer post-2000 than pre-2000. Concerns about the limits of oligopoly competition go back decades, as do concerns with common

30 Jonathan Tepper and Denise Hearn, 'Where Warren Buffett and Silicon Valley Billionaires Agree' (*Barron's*, 11 December 2018) www.barrons.com/articles/myth-of-capitalism-book-excerpt-51544500404; Paulo Santos, 'A *Warren Buffett Insight: Buy Monopoly-Like Situations*' (*Seeking Alpha*, 28 December 2015) https://seekingalpha.com/article/3778976-warren-buffett-insight-buy-monopoly-like-situations; Vincent Fernando, 'Warren Buffett Building a Cosy Insurance Oligopoly' (*Business Insider*, 26 February 2010) www.businessinsider.com/buffett-2010-2; 'Finding Stock the Warren Buffet Way, Part 3: A Screen for Identifying Consumer Monopolies' http://web.csulb.edu/~pammerma/fin382/screener/buffett3.htm.

31 Nicholas Vardy, 'Is Warren Buffett the Ultimate Anti-Capitalist?' (*Liberty through Wealth* 20 November 2018) https://libertythroughwealth.com/2018/11/20/warren-buffett-anti-capitalist-anti-competition.

and cross-ownership.[32] The fact that the link has become stronger since 2000 raises the possibility that some other recent change is primarily responsible.

What are the main changes that plausibly could have such a significant effect? Two candidates come to mind: technology (especially in markets with strong network effects); and the old bogeyman, regulation. Might some combination of these explain the observed changes? Might the increase in concentration, the increase in profitability and the increase in common ownership all be a consequence of the impact of technology and/or regulation? In this section, we examine the plausibility of this suggestion.

In an insightful paper by Autor, et al., the authors suggest that 'superstar firms' – firms whose productivity and rate of innovation allows them to outgrow their competitors – account for the increased market shares of the leading firms in some industries.[33] Put simply, the higher productivity of the superstars allows them to cut costs and reduce price (while in many cases increasing their price/cost markups and their profitability).[34] The ability to undercut competitors allows the firm to grow market share as well.

What 'special sauce' could make a firm into a superstar and allow it to remain one? Autor and his co-authors suggest that the increase in market shares might be attributed to greater competition caused by globalisation, especially in markets in which demand is relatively elastic. This, however, seems unlikely because, as Bessen points out, there does not appear to be any correlation between the extent of globalisation and the extent of industry concentration.[35]

Bessen makes a plausible argument that the 'special sauce' is the sustained increase in productivity that derives from *proprietary* advances in information technology. Whether due to network effects, technological advances, or more generally effective competitive mechanisms, we can expect the more technologically productive firms to have a substantial competitive advantage over firms that are less productive. This offers a good explanation for the increased profitability of a number of oligopolistic industries.

Delving more deeply into the sources of IT productivity, Bessen credits the differential productivity of firms to management's ability to utilise its software development abilities to take advantage of economies of scale as well as network effects. He notes that the development of IT systems has varied substantially across firms.[36]

32 *US v EI du Pont de Nemours & Co*, 353 US 586 (1956).

33 David Autor, David Dorn, Lawrence Katz, Christina Patterson and John Van Reenen, 'The Fall of the Labor Share and the Rise of Superstar Firms' (2020) 135 QJ Econ 645.

34 ibid 6. Autor et al. point out the conditions under which higher markups are likely to be achieved.

35 James Bessen, 'Information technology and Industry Concentration' (2019) Boston University School of Law, Law and Economics Research Paper No 17–41 https://scholarship.law.bu.edu/faculty_scholarship/267.

36 Dan Andrews, Chiara Criscuolo, and PN Gal, 'The Best versus the Rest: The Global Productivity Slowdown, Divergence across Firms and the Role of Public Policy' (2016) OECD Productivity Working Papers No 5 (016); Giuseppe Berlingieri, Patrick Blanchenay, and Chiara Criscuolo, 'The great divergence' (2017) OECD Science, Technology, and Industry Policy Papers No 39.

The key is whether firms (a) have the ability to develop cutting edge systems and (b) have the management or software development skills to put new technologies into the marketplace.

This is a compelling perspective that offers a set of explanations for why there has been substantial variation in the growth and profitability of oligopolistic firms. In particular, it potentially explains why there has been a parallel increase in concentration in airlines and banking: in both, proprietary IT has arguably provided enduring competitive advantages.

With respect to banking, nearly a decade ago Hughes and Mester found evidence that IT development costs along with network effects help explain the presence of substantial-scale economies.[37] They pointed out that proprietary IT can help explain the reallocation to more productive firms, increased industry concentration, and growing profit margins. Delving more deeply into the cost functions of banks, the authors emphasise that larger banks have a greater ability to manage the scale economies that flow from the diversification of risk.[38]

Now consider airlines. The airline industry utilises highly sophisticated software technologies in managing (i) the allocation of equipment among a multitude of available routes; (ii) the allocation of available seats among the available categories (first class, economy plus, regular economy as well as 'opaque' seats sold to businesses that are heavy users); and (iii) the offering of ticket prices up to 11 months in the future for all air classes. These software technologies, along with the substantial network effects that flow from the hub and spoke business model, have allowed three of the four major US carriers to achieve reasonable levels of profitability in a competitive environment. The fourth, Southwest Airlines has been the most profitable.[39] Southwest has at best a partial network operation. It has benefitted generally by flying point to point in competition with profitable network routes, while utilising airports with relatively low utilisation fees.

It is worth considering whether the increase in common ownership is driven by the same technological changes. Asset management likewise combines extreme competition with economies of scale driven by technology. The largest managers of index strategies – BlackRock, State Street, and Vanguard – have developed systems that allow for the deployment of massive amounts of capital at an extraordinarily low cost (at Vanguard, 4 basis points), while still making money. BlackRock combines additional technological advantages with its Aladdin platform, an operating system for

37 JP Hughes and LJ Mester, 'Who Said Large Banks Don't Experience Scale Economies? Evidence from a Risk-Return-Driven Cost Function' (2013) 22 J Fin Intermediation 559.

38 For recent empirical evidence that these scale economies are significant, see DC Wheelock & PW Wilson, 'The Evolution of Scale Economies in US Banking' (February 2017) (unpublished manuscript). See also SA Asongu and NM Odhiambo, 'Size, Efficiency, Market Power, and Economies of Scale in the African Banking Sector' (2019) 5 Fin Innovation 4.

39 See, e.g. Mark Israel, Bryan Keating, Daniel L. Rubinfeld and Bobby Willig, 'Airline Network Effects and Consumer Welfare' (2013) 12 Rev Network Econ 1.

investment professionals that manages large volumes of investment data, maintains quality control, and allows for a wide range of analyses for its clients. On the other hand, it is less clear whether the technological sophistication of BlackRock, Vanguard, and State Street provides any enduring competitive advantage, given that the sort of technology necessary for running an index fund at scale is likely to be widely available. The popularity of index strategies combined with standard economies of scale provide an alternative explanation for the increased concentration in asset management, even as asset management overall remains a fragmented industry.[40]

If some version of the claim that proprietary improvements in information technology is the heart of the special sauce is correct, it could explain why AST observe a correlation between concentration, common ownership and profitability in airlines and banking while Chris Conlon and co-authors find no such relationship in breakfast cereals. Here, the suggestion would be that proprietary software and network effects play an important role in airlines and banking but a relatively minor role in a classic consumer product market like ready to eat cereals.

13.5 CURRENT POLICY IMPLICATIONS

The rise of the large institutional investors over the last 30 years has been the biggest 'story' in corporate governance.[41] With AST's pathbreaking work on the competitive effects of common ownership, we are at the beginning of what promises to be a fascinating investigation of the competitive effects of common ownership. In this section, we consider some of the policy implications of this new debate.

Some who are convinced by the AST analysis have proposed systemic solutions to what they believe is a systemic problem. Einer Elhauge argues that the current common ownership by the largest institutional investors constitutes a continuing violation of Section 7 of the Clayton Act and possibly Section 1 of the Sherman Act and advocates for government enforcement actions and private class actions.[42] As we

[40] While BlackRock, Vanguard, and State Street are the dominant players for indexed strategies, the overall asset management industry is quite unconcentrated. See e.g. Francesco Franzoni, 'Table 1' in '*The effects of concentration in the asset management industry on stock prices*' (VOX-CEPR, 3 June 2019) https://voxeu.org/article/concentration-asset-management-industry-and-stock-prices; Itzhak Ben-David, Francesco Franzoni, Rabih Moussawi and John Sedunov, 'The Granular Nature of Large Institutional Investors' (2020) National Bureau of Economic Research Working Paper 22247 www.nber.org/papers/w22247; Kenechukwu Anadu, Mathias Kruttli, Patrick McCabe and Emilio Osambela, 'The Shift from Active to Passive Investing: Potential Risks to Financial Stability?' (2018) Federal Reserve Bank of Boston Working Paper RPA 18-04 www.bostonfed.org/-/media/Documents/Workingpapers/PDF/2018/rpa1804.pdf.

[41] EB Rock, 'The Logic and (Uncertain) Significance of Institution Shareholder Activism' (1991) 79 Geo LJ 445; Bernard Black, 'Agents Watching Agents: The Promise of Institutional Investor Voice' (1992) 39 UCLA L Rev 811; LA Bebchuk, Alma Cohen, and Scott Hirst, 'The Agency Problem of Institutional Investors' (2017) 31 J Econ Perspectives 89; EB Rock and Marcel Kahan, 'Index Funds and Corporate Governance: Let Shareholders be Shareholders' 100 B.U. Law Review 1771 (2020).

[42] Einer Elhauge, 'Horizontal Shareholding' (2016) 129 Harv L Rev 1267, 1301–16.

have discussed at length elsewhere, we disagree with Elhauge's legal analysis.[43] For what it is worth, we are not aware of any enforcement actions or private class actions embracing Elhauge's legal theory.

Posner, Scott Morton, and Weyl are, likewise, convinced by the AST analysis and have proposed an alternative to complete divestiture. In their view, the danger posed by common owners is so severe that they should be put to a choice: divest all but one firm in each oligopoly; or limit holdings to less than 1% and pre-commit to governance passivity by sterilising votes.[44] Given the huge benefits of index investing for ordinary investors, and what we view as the generally positive role that the largest institutional investors play in corporate governance, we think that the Posner et al policy change is not warranted by the evidence gathered to date, and would cause significant harm.

For both Elhauge and Posner et al.'s proposals, the difficulty of replicating the AST results in other industries, discussed above, undermines the case for a global/systemic reform. Rather, any intervention addressing the anticompetitive effects of common ownership should require a specific showing of such effects, based on particularised industry findings. Although common ownership is a market wide phenomenon, there is no evidence that the supposed anticompetitive effects of common ownership obtain in every concentrated market.

Although unconvinced that common ownership undermines competition systemically, common ownership does raise significant antitrust issues that enforcement authorities should investigate. First, in oligopolies, shareholders – whether they are common owners or undiversified owners – can indisputably play an anticompetitive role. They can, for example, organise competitors into a 'hub and spokes' conspiracy and, if they do so, will violate Section 1 of the Sherman Act and be subject to criminal sanctions and treble damages.[45] Likewise, there are a variety of other plausible coordinated scenarios in which shareholders can cause competitive harm, such as if shareholders act as a trustworthy conduit for communication among competitors, or advocate an industry-wide anticompetitive compensation structure and even possibly as the spreader of anticompetitive practices.[46] In each of these cases, depending on the factual context, shareholder conduct may violate existing antitrust law and be subject to sanctions.

Finally, there may be implications for merger policy. The European Commission, in the Dow/DuPont matter, suggested that, in light of the AST analysis, the treatment of traditional measures of market concentration, such as the HHI, should be supplemented by the MHHIΔ to take into account the competitive effects of

43 Rock and Rubinfeld, *supra* note 20, at 251–262.

44 This can be implemented either by common owners committing not to vote their shares or, to avoid depriving companies of a quorum at the annual meeting, committing to vote their shares in proportion to how the non-common owners vote (what is known as 'mirror voting').

45 Rock and Rubinfeld, '*Common Ownership and Coordinated Effects*' (n 30).

46 ibid.

common ownership. This is unwarranted for a number of reasons beyond the preliminary nature of the AST results. First, in mergers of commonly owned firms, while incorporating MHHIΔ may affect the threshold at which enforcement officials look closely at mergers on the grounds that HHI understates the pre-merger competitive condition, it will likewise *reduce* the significance of any increases in HHI resulting from the merger (on the same grounds). Second, while focusing on MHHIΔ points in the right direction in the review of mergers between a large incumbent and a non-commonly owned maverick firm, merger policy already subjects such mergers to enhanced scrutiny. In such cases, focusing on MHHIΔ adds little.

But suppose that the relation between increased industry concentration, increased oligopoly profits, and increased common ownership since 2000 is all the result of a common cause. What if it turns out that the rise of superstar firms, driven by changes in information technology, network effects, regulation, and/or globalisation, is responsible for the simultaneous increase in concentration and common ownership? What are the implications?

This will be an important debate going forward. Some will argue that the rise of superstar firms should justify stricter merger control.[47] Others, however, will argue that the rise of the superstar firms – firms that become and remain superstars because they reduce costs and increase output at the same time as they increase profits – calls into question the fundamental assumptions of current merger regulation. If the superstar firm hypothesis is confirmed, these will be among the most important debates of the next era of antitrust enforcement.

[47] See Carl Shapiro, 'Protecting Competition in the American Economy: Merger Control, Tech Titans, Labor Markets' (2019) 33 J Econ Perspectives 69, 75 (noting that if Azar, Schmalz, and Tecu's claims find additional support in future research, they would provide an additional basis for stricter merger controls).

14

Common Ownership by Investment Management Corporations and EU Policies

Please, Play Puzzles and not Mikado!

Marco Corradi

14.1 INTRODUCTION

The recent literature on the anticompetitive effects of parallel holdings[1] can be seen as one of the many expressions of both a scientific and societal concern for the increasing economic influence acquired by big investment management corporations throughout the world.[2] The findings of the authors of the seminal papers in this area[3] – although highly contested –[4] may highlight the existence of a (present or potential) antitrust issue, which still needs to be understood in all its complexity.

If we widen our perspective from the mere price effects correlated to the presence of parallel holdings to a larger range of variables, we may soon understand that the parallel holdings antitrust issue is nested within a complex set of systems and subsystems, which cannot be ignored while studying the possible policy reactions to the antitrust issues arising from common ownership. For instance, the raise of common ownership has occurred during a period of increasing concentration in product markets[5] and of significant changes in corporate governance worldwide.[6] The latter also aimed at pursuing ESG objectives that were previously considered as mere externalities in corporate governance.[7]

Assistant Professor, ESSEC Business School Paris and Singapore.

1 See (n 11).

2 Such concerns go well beyond investment funds' parallel holdings. See, for example, the increasing concerns for the development of urbanization and re-urbanization investments by big investment corporations in large cities. Isabelle Rey-Lefebvre, 'Les Fonds d'Investissementscomme BlackRock Commencent à s'Intéresser aux Immeubles d'Habitation du Grand Paris' *Le Monde* (Paris, 3 September 2021) www.lemonde.fr/societe/article/2021/09/03/les-fonds-etrangers-se-disputent-les-immeubles-d-habitation-du-grand-paris_6093193_3224.html.

3 See (n 11).

4 *Ibid.*

5 See Section 14.6.

6 In particular, the rise of stewardship codes. See J Hill, 'Good Activist/bad Activist: The Rise of International Stewardship Codes' (2017) 41 Seattle UL Rev 497; D Katelouzou and M Siems, 'The Global Diffusion of Stewardship Codes' in Katelouzou and D Puchniak (eds), *Global Shareholder Stewardship: Complexities, Challenges and Possibilities* (Cambridge University Press, forthcoming).

7 See Section 14.5.

Even if common ownership was unequivocally proven to be correlated with price increases, a well-designed policy reaction would not necessarily need to target parallel holdings or parallel holdings alone. On one hand, dismantling parallel holdings may jeopardise the efficiencies of such an investment system as well as their role in promoting ESG objectives.[8] On the other hand, it would need to be proven that a shift in corporate ownership structure can effectively improve competition ceteris paribus (i.e. despite highly concentrated product markets and despite a rather unpromising promotion of stewardship).[9] On top of that, given the massive presence of the biggest investment corporations worldwide, dismantling of parallel holdings and the entry of new foreign investors may trigger a series of geopolitical consequences among the three main areas of economic influence in the world (i.e. the US, Europe, and China) whose long-term effects may be hard to predict.[10]

14.2 PARALLEL HOLDINGS: A NEW ANTITRUST FRONTIER ALSO FOR EUROPE?

The academic debate on the anticompetitive effects of common ownership[11] started as a pure US antitrust one.[12] Nevertheless, the growing weight of Indexed Funds' equity holdings in the ownership structure of US[13] and non-US corporations[14] seems to have a substantial impact on the overall structure and functioning

8 See Section 14.6.

9 See Section 14.6.

10 See Section 14.7.

11 Such new corporate ownership configuration is also known as 'parallel holdings', 'horizontal shareholding', or, more recently, it has also been depicted as 'permanent universal ownership' – to highlight the (at least apparent) long-term commitment of common owners. See J Fichtner and E Heemskerk, 'The New Permanent Universal Owners: Index Funds, (Im)Patient Capital, and the Claim of Long-Termism' (2018) https://ssrn.com/abstract=3321597.

12 The industrial organization debate stemmed especially from a seminal paper by Azar, Schmalz and Tecu, now published as J Azar, M Schmalz, and I Tecu, 'Anticompetitive Effects of Common Ownership' (2018) 73 J Fin 1513. A paper that followed fuelled the debate: J Azar, S Raina and M Schmalz, 'Ultimate Ownership and Bank Competition' (2019) https://ssrn.com/abstract=2710252. Azar, Schmalz and their co-authors' research was employed as grounds for a wider legal and policy debate. See E Elhauge, 'Horizontal Shareholding' (2015) 129 Harv L Rev 1267; E Posner, F Scott Morgan, and G Weyl, 'A Proposal to Limit the Anticompetitive Power of Institutional Investors' (2016) 81 Antitrust LJ 69. A far more articulated debate followed the seminal works by the abovementioned authors. For an exhaustive review of the debate, see M Schmalz Chapter 12 in this book.

13 A significant number of US corporations represented in the S&P 500 index, which were previously known for their dispersed ownership structure, now have the same common owners: investment funds, such as Black Rock, Vanguard, Fidelity, State Street hold substantial blocks of shares of such corporations. J Fichtner, E Heemskerk and J Garcia-Bernardo, 'Hidden Power of the Big Three? Passive Index Funds, Re-concentration of Corporate Ownership, and New Financial Risk' (2017) 19(2) Business and Politics 298, 299.

14 N Rosati and others, *Common Shareholding in Europe* (Publications Office of the European Union 2020) https://publications.jrc.ec.europa.eu/repository/handle/JRC121476. On the situation in Germany, see J Seldeslachts, M Newham, and A Banal-Estanol, 'Changes in Common Ownership of German Companies' (2017) 7 DIW Economic Bulletin 303.

of the economic, financial, and industrial systems worldwide. Hence, such a debate appears to be inherently global in nature – not only from the point of view of pure financial economics or industrial organisation theory but also for its wider policy and socio-political implications. Recent papers have argued that common ownership may produce significant wealth transfers and therefore affect the welfare of shareholders and consumers alike.[15] It may also create a sort of monopsony on the labour markets, while pushing managers to pursue cost reduction strategies, which in turn often entail dismissals and/or salary cuts.[16] The other flip of the coin is that large investment corporations – apart from their renowned capability to contain investment management costs and to promote investment efficiency and investment democracy through indexing –[17] have also become increasingly able to advance effectively ESG objectives.[18] Hence, common ownership by institutional investors seems to interact with a very wide range of stakeholders – maybe society as a whole – which makes any potential issue surrounding parallel holdings a matter of complex balance of conflicting interests.

The importance of the welfare effects (and competitive harm) attributed to common ownership seems to contrast with the limited decisional power historically enjoyed by common owners in relation to the strategic choices of most of their target corporations.[19] In most cases, none of the common owners seems to be able to exercise any control right on their target corporations, at least not on a standalone and stable basis.[20] This is a classic situation where owners could, at least in principle, acquire a degree of influence on corporations through coalitions. But, even if that was to become the case, the outcome of coalitions is often hard to predict and their stability can be challenged also by very subtle changes in the equity holdings.[21] This sort of influence, or 'potential influence' without proper control, is notably a conundrum for antirust and especially for EU competition law.[22]

15 O Shy and R Stenbacka, 'Common Ownership, Institutional Investors, and Welfare' (2020) 29 J Econ Manage Strat 706.

16 Z Goshen and D Levit, 'Common Ownership and the Decline of the American Worker' (2021) European Corporate Governance Institute Law Working Paper No 584/2021 https://ssrn.com/abstract=3832069.

17 See Section 14.3.

18 See Section 14.6.

19 In most cases, common owners are depicted as passive investors. G Strampelli, 'Are Passive Index Funds Active Owners: Corporate Governance Consequences of Passive Investing' (2018) 55 San Diego L Rev 803. Nonetheless, traditionally passive indexed funds have recently signaled their ESG engagement. See M Barzuza, Q Curtis, and D Webber, 'Shareholder value (s): Index fund ESG activism and the new millennial corporate governance' (2019) 93 S Cal L Rev 1243.

20 Control seems to be still contestable in the presence of several blockholdings of around 3% to 5% and absent any agreement among blockholders for the exercise of joint control. Such percentages are reported to be extremely frequent in praxis by Fichtner and Heemskerk (n 11) 10.

21 M Corradi, 'Bridging the Gap in the Shifting Sands of Non-Controlling Financial Holdings?' (2016) 39 World Competition 239, 248ff.

22 See further text corresponding to n 77 to 90.

The unprecedented situation triggered by common ownership does not puzzle only antitrust and competition law experts. It is also a corporate law and governance primary issue.[23] In contrast with what had been foreseen by Hansmann and Kraakmann in their famous essay on the 'end of the history of corporate law', the world financial and industrial systems, including the European ones, have not converged to a full extent and univocally towards what the authors call 'the standard model'.[24] Today, the US corporation looks increasingly dissimilar from that 'standard model' and has not become the end point of any other corporate law model in the world.[25] Hence, a degree of legal diversification is actually the standard.

In the presence of parallel holdings, corporate directors may not be as strong as they used to be (or at least as they used to be depicted) when there was more significant capital dispersion.[26] This may be the case especially when common owners adopt active strategies in relation to some of their holdings.[27] But even if they stay passive the dimension of their blockholding – the now famous '800-Pounds gorilla'[28] – may pose a potential threat to corporate directors' inefficient behaviours.[29]

Despite the primary importance of Indexed Funds in the US, the rest of the world still hosts a completely different corporate reality in terms of ownership structure. For instance, continental European corporations still are characterised

[23] It is not by chance that the most authoritative comparative corporate law book in its concluding chapter, now hints to parallel holdings as 'arguably itself becoming an important source of international convergence in corporate law'. R Kraakman and others, *The Anatomy of Corporate Law: A Comparative and Functional Approach* (Oxford University Press 2017) 270.

[24] H Hansmann and R Kraakman, 'The End of History for Corporate Law' (2000) 89 *Geo LJ* 439. For instance, at 441ff, the authors claimed that managers will respond exclusively to shareholders. Nonetheless, by examining German corporate law, it is clear that managers are also accountable in front of employees. See the *Mitbestimmungsgesetz* 1976, known in English as the Codetermination Act 1976, which enables employees to appoint members of the supervisory board which in turn will appoint the members of the management board. Unlike what the authors had predicted in 444, the German codetermination model has not disappeared. The authors also predicted the end of the stakeholder model at 447, whereas actually, in the light of the ESG corporate governance discussion, such model is re-emerging.

[25] M Roe, *Strong Managers, Weak Owners* (Princeton UP 1996).

[26] A Berle and G Means, *The Modern Corporation and Private Property* (MacMillan 1932) described the transition of the US corporate reality towards such a model in the 1930s. More modern description of the main features of the pre-common ownership US corporate system are found in F Easterbrook and D Fischel, *The Economic Structure of Corporate Law* (2nd edn, Harvard UP 1996); R Romano, *The Genius of American Corporate Law* (American Enterprise Institute Press 1993).

[27] A Hamdani and S Hannes, 'The Future of Shareholder Activism' (2019) 99 BUL Rev 971, 986.; M Mallow and J Sethi, 'Engagement: The Missing Middle Approach in the Bebchuck-Strine Debate' (2005) 12 NYUJL & Bus 385; D Lund, 'The Case against Passive Shareholder Voting' (2017) 43 J Corp L 493.

[28] Term initially by L Strine, 'The Inescapably Empirical Foundation of the Common Law of Corporations' (2002) 27 Del J Corp L 499, 509 and now adopted by Goshen & Levit (n 16) 55.

[29] Goshen & Levit (n 16) 55ff.

by the prevalence of one or a few controlling shareholders – very often an entrepreneurial family.[30] But think also of the People's Republic of China's (PRC), whose economic system may be described as 'socialism with many capitalists'.[31] In PRC, since the end of the 1970s many private corporations have emerged as significant alternatives to the traditional State-owned industries[32] – including today several cross-border active high-tech giants, such as Lenovo[33] – while the Chinese Communist Party has acquired a substantial influence on the country's private business reality.[34] An influence which seems to have increased after the mixed-ownership reform of State-Owned Enterprises (SOEs).[35] The PRC example shows that the combinations between institutional and political variables can reach levels of creativeness that perhaps we could not have expected in the 1980s, when the world was largely polarised between the capitalist and the socialist/communist models.

Even in a globalised world, the diversity of the local business and organisational models is mindboggling. Therefore, even if Indexed Funds invest worldwide, their investments in such diversified corporate environments cannot be understood in the light of a monolithic theoretical framework. The real challenge ahead is not only understanding the potential competitive consequences deriving from parallel holdings but also adapting any potential policy response in the most adequate way possible to different business and organisational realities. This may require avoiding early and easy fixes and considering the wider social and political variables triggered by the intertwining between finance, industry, and corporate governance.[36]

30 G Aminadav and E Papaioannou, 'Corporate Control Around the World' (2000) 75 J Fin 1191, 1210. Note that a family-dominated industrial system is not necessarily less efficient or less desirable than one with dispersed ownership, as highlighted by R Gilson, 'Globalizing Corporate Governance: Convergence of Form or Function' (2001) 49 The Am J Comp L 329.

31 For the political origins of such a peculiar social and economic experiment, see A Sihotang, 'Strategy of China's Political Economy on the Era of Deng Xiaoping in China to Build Economic Growth' (2020) 10 *Intl J Social Science Economics Art* 79.

32 X Chen, *Chinese Private Manufacturing Firms: The Challenges of Global Competition* (Routledge 2018).

33 L Zhijun, *The Lenovo Affair: The Growth of China's Computer Giant and Its Takeover of IBM-PC* (John Wiley & Sons 2006).

34 X Yan and J Huang, 'Navigating Unknown Waters: The Chinese Communist Party's New Presence in the Private Sector' (2017) 17 *The China Review* 37. See also the case of Huawei, which exemplifies the complexity of the relationship of the Chinese Communist Party with important private players; C Hawes, 'Why Is Huawei's Ownership so Strange? A Case Study of the Chinese Corporate and Sociopolitical Ecosystem' (2021) 21 JCLS 1.

35 J Wang and T Cheng-Han, 'Mixed Ownership Reform and Corporate Governance in China's State-Owned Enterprises' (2020) 53 Vand J Transnatl L 1055.

36 As suggested by the authors of the *Anatomy of Corporate Law* (n 23) 270, '[g]lobal institutional investors have generated pressure for the international adoption of the governance practices prevailing in developed (typically UK and US) markets. This may, however, result in a convergence that is more formal than functional, if "investor-oriented" strategies are applied beyond the extent justified by the type of agency problems they address'.

14.3 NON-CONTROLLING EQUITY HOLDINGS AND MINORITY SHAREHOLDINGS: PIECES OF A SCATTERED PUZZLE

Indexed Funds, a type of Exchanged Traded Fund – had hardly ever attracted negative public comments until 2016.[37] Indexed Funds are based on an ingenious intuition by John 'Jack' Bogle who published copious essays and books in defence and for the promotion of his investment strategies.[38] The merits of indexing as an investment technique is proven by its success: Indexed Funds have become prevalent over alternative international financial investments in 2003.[39] Bogle's investment strategy consists of mimicking financial indexes: Indexed Funds have been renowned for being rarely outperformed by alternative investment strategies.[40] Their expanded diversification system offers ideal risk containment; the prevalence of passive investment strategies for such holdings[41] entails very low management costs, with consequent lower fees for investors.[42]

Despite parallel equity holdings being mostly qualified and treated as passive investments,[43] they are significantly different from other forms of non-controlling minority holdings and/or passive investment, such as minority non-controlling holdings by competitors or cross-shareholdings in the same product market or across the supply chain – on which EU competition law literature abounds.[44] They also differ

[37] Pre-2015 US press extolled the economic and financial benefits of indexing. See for instance Edward Wyatt, 'Riding Wall St. on Autopilot: Indexed Funds Draw Investors' *The New York Times* (New York, 29 January 1997) 1.

[38] An interesting anthology of his publications is J Bogle, *John Bogle on Investing: The First 50 Years.* (John Wiley & Sons 2015). See also J Bogle, *Common Sense on Mutual Funds: New Imperatives for the Intelligent Investor* (John Wiley & Sons 1999). John Bogle later seemed to regret the 'unrestrained' success of his own creation – due to the excessive concentration and the lack of new entrants in the financial industry; J Bogle, 'Bogle Sounds a Warning on Index Funds' *Wall Street Journal* (New York, 29 November 2018).

[39] J Sommer, 'Exchange-Traded Funds Are Now in Favor' *The New York Times* (New York, 8 June 2003) 6.

[40] J Bogle, 'An Index Fund Fundamentalist' (2002) 28 J Portfolio Manage 31. Nonetheless, already in the beginning of the twenty-first century, there were voices of disagreement with respect to the efficiency of such an investment technique. G Gastineau, 'Equity Index Funds Have Lost Their Way' (2002) 28 The J Portfolio Manage 55. Moreover, alternative investment strategies, such as hedge funds, are known for being able to outperform equity markets. T Bali, S Brown, and K Demirtas, 'Do Hedge Funds Outperform Stocks and Bonds?' (2013) 59 Manage Sci 1887.

[41] Even if at times they may engage in active behaviours for larger holdings. See (n 27).

[42] Although IF's fees today are extremely differentiated – which in turns depends on a degree of product differentiation. A Hortaçsu and C Syverson, 'Product Differentiation, Search Costs, and Competition in the Mutual Fund Industry: A Case Study of S&P 500 Index Funds' (2004) 119 The QJ Econ 403.

[43] Strampelli (n 19)

[44] A seminal work is that of A Ezrachi and D Gilo, 'EC Competition Law and the Regulation of Passive Investments among Competitors' (2006) 26 Oxford J Leg Studies 327. See also S Russo, 'Abuse of Protected Position? Minority Shareholdings and Restriction of Markets' Competitiveness in the European Union' (2006) 29(4) W Comp 607; F Caronna, 'Article 81 as a Tool for Controlling Minority Cross- Shareholdings between Competitors' (2004) 29 Eur L Rev 485; E Moavero Milanesi and A Winterstein, 'Minority Shareholdings, Interlocking Directorships and the EC Competition

from the so-called circular ownership, a situation in which each firm on a given relevant market owns equity in at least one of its competitors.[45]

Even though they may at times have anticompetitive effects, holdings in a competing firm (i.e. nothing to do with holdings deriving from investment based on indexing, which are normally in non-competing firms) can be supported by a financial and/or an industrial rationale.[46] On one hand, a company may be willing to invest in one's competitor simply because that competitor is well positioned for meeting the market demand and such information is easily retrievable by other actors within the same industry.[47] On the other hand, a company may want to have a stake in one of its competitors in order to increase collaboration, for instance for the purpose of innovation – i.e. pursuing dynamic efficiency.[48] There may also be cases where two competitors set up a jointly owned corporation expressly as an R&D joint venture and their interests are (limitedly) aligned as equity owners. Finally, the acquisition of non-controlling equity holdings may anticipate an intention to merge, such as in the case of certain types of earnouts M&A operations.[49] *None* of such strategy is present in parallel holdings – where the inherent rationale is purely financial and is based on maximum diversification through indexing.

Secondly, the influence of the investment performance of one single minority holding in a competitor's balance sheet may be rather significant, as it will be diversified only against the industrial activity of the acquirer.[50] By contrast, for an indexed fund, the relevance of the investment performance of one single non-controlling equity holding will fade against the myriad of additional holdings represented in the reference index that the investment fund aims at mimicking. Therefore, the kind of action in which a competitor is ready to engage is likely to be different from the actions undertaken by an indexed fund. As a matter of fact, when Indexed Funds have been active, they have normally focused on wide common objectives and not on one single holding.[51] For the reason outlined above, one cannot consistently employ the theoretical findings on minority holdings in a competitor for tackling the problems which might arise in the case of parallel holdings.

Rules – Recent Commission Practice' (2002) 1 *Competition Policy Newsltr* 15; R Struijlaart, 'Minority Share Acquisition below the Control Threshold of the EC Merger Control Regulation: An Economic and Legal Analysis' (2002) 25(2) W Comp 173.

45 Corradi (n 21) 244.

46 Ezrachi & Gilo (n 44) 328.

47 *Ibid.*

48 As in the case of joint ventures, see R Reynolds and B Snapp, 'The Competitive Effects of Partial Equity Interests and Joint Ventures' (1986) 4 Int J Ind Org 141.

49 R Ragozzino and J Reuer, 'Contingent Earnouts in Acquisitions of Privately Held Targets' (2009) 35 J Manage 857, 862.

50 Ezrachi & Gilo (n 44).

51 See Section 14.6.

14.4 THE PECULIARITIES OF INDEXED FUNDS' PARALLEL HOLDINGS IN THE EU CORPORATE CONTEXT WITH PREVALENCE OF TRADITIONAL CONTROLLING SHAREHOLDERS

In the US, the phenomenon known as common ownership arose from the ashes of a corporate world that was previously characterised by dispersed corporate ownership structure.[52] But dispersed ownership structure is not a common feature of European corporations,[53] with the exceptions of the UK and Ireland.[54] In certain industries dispersed corporate ownership structure is present also in continental Europe – although far from being the dominant model.[55] Therefore, if we purport to understand the impact of Indexed Funds' investments on competition in European product markets, the case for a potential competitive harm deriving from common ownership needs to be analysed considering two alternative hypotheses: dispersed and concentrated corporate ownership structure – concentrated ownership being the most commonly found in practice. The literature on competitive harm in case of dispersed corporate ownership structure is already abundant; yet an overall agreement over the existence of such harm has not been reached yet.[56] Had an agreement on such harm to be reached, as we will see, US literature would not necessarily be of great use in the EU institutional context. Neither from a legal,[57] nor from a policy perspective.[58]

When it comes to concentrated corporate ownership structure, the chances that the same mechanisms described in the US literature on common ownership apply within the EU corporate context are extremely remote. In a system characterised by concentrated corporate ownership structure directors will chiefly respond to the controlling shareholder(s).[59] As recently shown, this will occur despite the emphasis put by stewardship codes on the role of institutional investors in corporate governance in those systems characterised by concentrated ownership structure.[60]

Yet, one may still hypothesise a residual anticompetitive role of common owners in a context of concentrated ownership. For instance, one might want to investigate

52 Berle & Means (n 26); F Barca and M Becht (eds), *The Control of Corporate Europe* (Oxford University Press 2001).

53 Aminadav & Papaioannou (n 30) 1216.

54 *Ibid.* at 1209. For an analysis of the process of corporate ownership dispersion in the UK, see B Cheffins, 'Does Law Matter? The Separation of Ownership and Control in the United Kingdom' (2001) 30 JLS 459; B Cheffins, *Corporate Ownership and Control: British Business Transformed* (Oxford University Press 2008).

55 Aminadav & Papaioannou (n 30). This holds particularly in certain sectors in Germany; see WG Ringe, 'Changing Law and Ownership Patterns in Germany: Corporate Governance and the Erosion of Deutschland AG' (2015) 63.2 Am J Comp L 493.

56 See the literature referred to in Schmalz (n 12).

57 See Section 14.5.

58 See Section 14.6.

59 This is a well-known tenet in comparative corporate law analysis. See R Kraakman and others (n 23) 30ff.

60 D Puchniak, 'The False Hope of Stewardship in the Context of Controlling Shareholders: Making Sense Out of the Global Transplant of a Legal Misfit' (2021) Am J Comp L (forthcoming).

whether controlling shareholders' (industrial families or other institutional owners) interests may occasionally or stably be aligned with those of Indexed Funds towards a collusive objective.[61] But the role of Indexed Funds in these cases could only be marginal. For instance, one *might* think of a potential role of investment funds in relation to information exchanges within the same industry, so to ease up the collective action problems that are normally seen in collusive contexts with many players.[62] But such a hypothesis, unless corroborated with sound empirical research, should be considered as little less than fantasy for the time being.

Another difference between the US and the EU context is that Indexed Funds may not employ the same indexes in the two economic environments. In fact, the equivalent of the S&P index in Europe is the FTS Eurofirst 300. Yet, it does not seem to enjoy much success when it comes to indexing. The EU is rather diversified both from an institutional and industrial perspective – which makes regional areas extremely differentiated from an investment perspective.[63] Therefore, for investors, such as BlackRock, it makes sense to create Indexed Funds based on country-based indexes (e.g. iShares MSCI Germany Index Fund (NYSE: EWG)).[64] Indexed Funds' overall investment techniques may be characterised by more significant fragmentation in the European context, as compared to the US one. Such a fragmentation may reduce the degree of coordination vis-à-vis potential interventions within the governance of the target companies. But, as already mentioned, what represents one of the core obstacles in tackling potential issues deriving from common ownership is the legal variable.

14.5 EU COMPETITION LAW AND THE ABSENCE OF AN ADEQUATE LEGAL FRAMEWORK FOR PARALLEL HOLDINGS

The hypothetical competitive harm scenario depicted by the common ownership industrial organisation literature encompasses two alternative explanations.[65]

According to one of them, the modification of the investees' corporate ownership structure, subsequent to the increase in common ownership, may induce a behavioural change in the members of the target companies' boards of directors. Corporate directors would tend to compete less vigorously in order to please

61 This would require a degree of stability in the product market in question, i.e. at least a low degree of contestability. See R Van den Bergh, *Comparative competition law and economics* (Edward Elgar Publishing 2017) 57ff.

62 *Ibid.* at 194.

63 This is often acknowledged in those EU reports that focus on industry. See, for instance, European Commission, 'Report of Expert Group on removing tax obstacles to cross-border Venture Capital Investments' (2009) https://ec.europa.eu/taxation_customs/sites/taxation/files/resources/documents/taxation/company_tax/initiatives_small_business/venture_capital/tax_obstacles_venture_capital_en.pdf, 1.

64 'iShares MSCI Germany ETF' (Blackrock) www.blackrock.com/us/individual/products/239650/ishares-msci-germany-etf accessed [12/10/22].

65 S Hemphill and M Kahan, 'The Strategies of Anti-Competitive Common Ownership' (2019) 129 Yale LJ 1392.

common owners – without actually being actively encouraged or forced to do so, i.e. consistently with a passive investment scenario. It has been hypothesised that such behaviour may be reinforced by the fact that directors are remunerated on the basis of the performance of the market, instead of on the basis of the performance of the corporation they serve.[66]

A completely different explanation considers an active involvement of Indexed Funds, directed to curb target companies' directors' behaviours towards a collusive approach. As highlighted by Hemphill and Kahan, this would require the generation of the appropriate strategies, a transmission of the information to the targets' directors and a behaviour inducement.[67] Indexed Funds could also act 'behind the scene' and try to influence corporate directors in the course of private meetings – instead of risking to leave evidence of their intentions in their voting preferences.[68]

Hemphill and Kahan have claimed that most of the abovementioned strategies are unlikely to occur – basing their analysis on the relationships between Common Owners (CCOs) and Non-Common Owners (NCOs). According to the authors, the only effect of common ownership on competition could consist of some cases of selective omission vis-à-vis Indexed Funds' stewardship engagement, because '[c]ompared to NCOs, CCOs would tend to push less for aggressive competition where more aggressive competition would increase firm value (because of its effect on the value of competitors in which the CCO has a stake)'.[69]

But let's hypothesise that Hemphill and Kahan got it wrong and Indexed Funds' managers want to engage also in active behaviours in European companies: let's see how this could be tackled by EU competition law. Let's first consider both the active and passive hypothesis within the EU corporate environment characterised by the same features of the US one – i.e. absence of a controlling shareholder – a type of corporate ownership structure which, as already said, is rather uncommon in continental Europe.[70] A legal framing of such behaviour under EU competition law may not be without difficulties. Unlike presumed by US literature,[71] it has been

[66] Antón and others, 'Common ownership, competition, and top management incentives' (2020) Ross School of Business Paper 1328. It is unclear whether such a claim, when proved truthful, could be labelled as a passive investment case, as the authors suggest. In fact, Hemphill & Kahan (n 65) qualify it as an 'active micro mechanism'.

[67] Hemphill & Kahan (n 65).

[68] M Corradi and A Tzanaki, 'Active and Passive Institutional Investors and New Antitrust Challenges: Is EU Competition Law Ready?' (2017) 1 Antitrust Chronicle 1.

[69] Hemphill & Kahan (n 65) 43. In the sense of a general Indexed Funds' lack of interest for monitoring their investments see L Bebchuk, A Cohen, and S Hirst, 'The Agency Problems of Institutional Investors' (2017) 31 J Econ Perspect 89.

[70] See Section 14.4.

[71] E Elhauge, 'New evidence, proofs, and legal theories on horizontal shareholding' (2018) 37ff https://papers.ssrn.com/sol3/papers.cfm?abstract_id=3096812, claiming the applicability of abuse of collective dominance and excessive pricing to common ownership under TFEU art 102; and at 33ff, claiming the applicability of the rules on concerted practices under TFEU art 101.

demonstrated that at least two potentially relevant EU competition law rules may not apply to such cases.

Firstly, rules on collective abuse of a dominant position will not apply because of the lack of the requirements outlined in the *Airtours*[72] and *Impala*[73] cases.[74] So far, there is no evidence of any coordination – and therefore of any shared understanding regarding such (non-existent) coordination. As a consequence, there is not even question of monitoring and sustainability of such coordination – nor of a threat of competitive constraints jeopardising such coordination.[75]

Secondly, rules on concerted practices may also prove to be of extremely difficult application, both at the level of the market for financial investments and at the level of product markets of the target companies.[76] As a matter of fact, none of the requirements identified in the *Anic* case[77] seem to occur in the case of parallel holdings. Not a concertation between undertakings (no evidence of concertation among investment management corporations nor among the investees), nor a specific behaviour of the undertakings pursuant such (non-existent) concertation.

Not even the *Philip Morris*[78] doctrine – had it to be considered living and applicable –[79] would probably be a good point of reference for such cases. In the *Philip Morris* line of cases the CJEU and later the EU Commission assessed the potential competitive harm deriving from an investment of a firm in one of its *competitors*.[80] But in the EU law pre-dating the first EUMR, and in the context of merger reviews under TEU article 86 (now TFEU article 102) the concept of influence emerged as a way to assess concentrations.[81] Such a concept – had it been properly developed and expanded as a standalone concept – might have helped framing the intermediate, nuanced, stages which may emerge in practice as corporate ownership arrangements that lay in between an anticompetitive agreement and a proper merger, both in their active and passive versions.[82] Nonetheless, neither the EU Commission nor

72 Case T-342/99 *Airtours* v *Commission* [2002] ECLI:EU:T:2002:146.

73 Case C-413/06 P *Bertelsmann and Sony Corp of America v Independent Music Publishers and LabelsAssociation* [2008] ECLI:EU:C:2008:392 ('Impala').

74 A Burnside and A Kidane, 'Common ownership: an EU perspective (2020) 8 JAE 456, 494–495.

75 *Ibid.* at 500.

76 *Ibid.* at 495

77 Case C-49/92 P *Commission v Anic Partecipazioni* [1999] ECLI:EU:C:1999:356. See Burnside & Kidane (n 74) 495.

78 *Am Tobacco Co Ltd and RJ Reynolds Indus Inc v Commission of the European Community*, Joined Cases 142/84 & 156/84, [1987] ECR 4487, [1988] 4 CMLR 24.

79 In this sense, see Burnside & Kidane (n 74) 491, who claim that Philip Morris has not been overruled or contradicted.

80 Even in the Gillette case, the disputed equity (and debt) acquisition by Gillette was in the parent company (Eemland) of its competitor (Wilkinson Sword); see Case No IV/33.440, Warner-Lambert/Gillette and Others, and Case No IV/33.486, BIC/Gillette and Others [1993] OJ L 116/21.

81 B Hawk and H Huser, '"Controlling" the Shifting Sands: Minority Shareholdings under EEC Competition Law' (1994) 17 Fordham Intl LJ 294.

82 As a matter of fact, empirical research shows that increasingly substantial equity stake tends to raise the directors' concern towards their holder. See E Gilje, T Gormley, and D Levit, 'Who's Paying

the CJEU ever seemed to give specific relevance to the concept of influence as an independent legal category to be applied beyond the boundaries of EU merger law pre-dating the first EUMR.[83]

The concept of influence could probably be interpreted as a phylogenetic trace of a former theoretical framework (the pre-EUMR merger one), which no longer plays any role in the present EU competition law system. Even if we considered *Philip Morris*' concept of influence as a living and fully applicable one, its adaptation to common ownership cases would require excessive logical stretching and, worse, a possible misreading of the rationale followed by the CJEU. In common ownership cases there is no issue of minority equity investment *in competitors* involved, because Indexed Funds operate in industries that have little or nothing to do with their target companies: hence the underlying facts are different from the *Philip Morris* scenario, which assessed investment in *competitors*.

As a matter of fact, the industrial distance between Indexed Funds and their target companies renders most of the EU competition law targeting influence down the supply chain inapplicable – as such law postulates a degree of industrially functional relationship between upstream and downstream firms.[84] Such functional relationship is found both in horizontal (competitors) and vertical (supplier/producer/distributor) cases. But in the case of common ownership – as the word suggests – we are in presence of mere 'owners' that are rarely operative in industries bordering with their targets.[85]

Perhaps, a possible way to catch hypothetically relevant Indexed Funds' managers behaviours could be framing them within a hub and spoke scheme, where Indexed Funds, the hubs, retrieve and process information, which they distribute down the chain of their investees. But it goes without saying that there is no evidence of a similar behaviour so far – and the likeability that anticompetitive activism is in the interest of Indexed Funds is rather low.[86] Apart for the limited economic incentives of such conducts, given the degree of public attention that Indexed Funds have received so far, it would be very unlikely that they would engage in such activity out in the open – which in turn may render the hub and spoke case law extremely difficult to apply.[87]

Attention? Measuring Common Ownership and Its Impact on Managerial Incentives' (2020) 137 J Financ Econ 152.

83 Burnside & Kidane (n 74).

84 See for instance the archetypical *Imperial Chemical Industries Ltd* v *European Commission* case (Case T-66/01 [2010] ECR II-02631, ECLI:EU:T:2010:255).

85 A potential industrial overlap might occur in the case where common owners own bank, as big institutional investors have been known for their shadow banking activity. But in this case, the obstacle to the application of EU competition law may derive from the fact that such markets are normally national in nature. See Burnside & Kidane (n 74) 464.

86 Hemphill & Kahan (n 65).

87 GL Zampa and P Buccirossi, 'Hub and Spoke Practices: Law and Economics of the New Antitrust Frontier' (2013) 9 *Competition L Intl* 91, 98ff. The seminal cases on hub and spoke schemes is *AC-Treuhand* v *Commission* (Case T-99/04 EU:T:2008:256) and *AC-Treuhand* v *Commission* (C-194/14 P EU:C:2015:717).

But what is even more difficult to catch under present EU law are passive investments by Indexed Funds. The point of reference would be 'quasi-mergers' and that set of extremely vague situations surrounding the acquisition of a degree of influence over other corporations. Such nuanced situations normally become relevant for EU law only under merger reviews by the DG-Comp – hence posing the existence of a notified or notifiable merger as a pre-condition for the scrutiny of such situations.[88] In such a context the DG-Comp has already assessed the anti-competitive potential of common ownership[89] and it may do so in future on a casuistic base.[90]

Beyond the present state of the art, one may wonder whether new rules might be introduced within the EU competition law system in order to address the potential competitive harm deriving from corporate ownership structure modifications brought by common ownership in the rare cases of dispersed ownership found in the continental European context. One might think this will occur soon, because of the recent studies that the EU Commission[91] and the EU Parliament[92] have dedicated to the common ownership debate. Despite the accuracy of the cited studies, the likelihood that such new rules are introduced light-heartedly may be rather low. Or better, it is precisely the accuracy of such studies which may induce us to predict that such likeability is low.

In fact, since the first decade of the twenty-first century, the EU Commission has investigated a connected, although significantly different case – i.e. that of the potential anticompetitive effects of (non-controlling) minority shareholdings.[93] Such an investigation had culminated in a White Paper[94] which has not resulted in any modification to the EU competition law framework. The attempts to innovate the EU merger legislation in order to accommodate an assessment of minority shareholdings were dismissed on grounds of insufficiency of evidence with regard to the competitive harm deriving from minority equity holdings.[95] Such a dismissal confirmed the cautious attitude of the EU Commission when it comes to introduce completely novel competition rules. A similar cautious approach

88 The problem was already present with reference to minority shareholdings. See Corradi (n 21) 254.

89 Dow/DuPont (Case M.7932); Bayer/Monsanto (Case M.8084).

90 As suggested by A Tzanaki and J Azar, 'Common Ownership and Merger Control Enforcement', in I Kokkoris (ed) *Research Handbook in Competition Enforcement* (Edward Elgar Publishing 2021).

91 N Rosati and others (n 14).

92 S Frazzani and others, *Barriers to Competition through Common Ownership by Institutional Investors* (European Parliament 2020) Study for the Committee on Economic and Monetary Affairs, Policy Department for Economic, Scientific and Quality of Life Policies www.europarl.europa.eu/RegData/etudes/STUD/2020/652708/IPOL_STU(2020)652708_EN.pdf.

93 See Section 14.3.

94 Commission, 'Towards More Effective EU Merger Control' COM (White Paper 2014) 449 final.

95 See EU Dg-Comp Commissioner Margaret Vestager's speech, 10 March 2016, unpublished, as reported in Van Bael & Bellis, 'Merger Control: Competition Commissioner Vestager discusses possible changes to EU merger control system' [2016] (3) VBB on Competition 4 www.vbb.com/media/original-attachments/CL_03_16.PDF.

accompanied the last EU Commission's decision on parallel holdings[96] and the subsequent declarations by DG-Comp Commissioner Vestager.[97]

14.6 EU POLICIES ON CORPORATE GOVERNANCE, COMPETITION GOALS AND COMMON OWNERSHIP: IN SEARCH FOR CONSISTENCY

Imagine that, as some of the authors of the seminal papers on common ownership have claimed, none of the criticisms brought to their work is solidly founded;[98] and/or that, in future, more convincing evidence emerges as to the competitive harm brought by common ownership on a wider sets of product markets than those object of the abovementioned papers.[99] One may still wonder whether the most advisable policy reaction would be to dismantle or limit common ownership, as several US academics suggested.[100] A core guideline in policymaking should be that not necessarily a solution to a problem is found at the same level of that problem. This is because what may be perceived as an issue or as a negative externality may actually produce also positive externalities at the same level: therefore, in such a case policy action could be more fruitfully carried out at a different level, in order to preserve the positive externalities.

To exemplify this principle with reference to common ownership, it is undoubtable that – besides the efficiency of indexing as an investment technique per se –[101] evidence is emerging on the biggest funds' managers capability to provide replies to the 'macro legal risks' (i.e. those corresponding especially to ESG) of our times in a far more efficient way than traditional owners.[102] Even Azar, one of the authors of the seminal common ownership papers, has co-authored a paper analysing the role of the 'Big Three' (BlackRock, Vanguard and State Street) in containing carbon emissions.[103]

[96] Bayer & Monsanto (n 89).

[97] M Vestager, 'Competition in Changing Times' (FIW symposium, Innsbruck, 16 February 18) https://ec.europa.eu/commission/commissioners/2014-2019/vestager/announcements/competition-changing-times-0_en. 'The thing is, just because investors might benefit from less competition, doesn't necessarily mean companies will oblige. There's a difference between holding shares in a company and controlling its decisions. Even without control, there are certainly ways for these funds to make their voices heard. But we can't just assume they have the power to change minds. We need to look closely at what actually happens – whether they can really get companies to compete less hard'.

[98] E Elhauge, S Majumdar, and M Schmalz, 'Confronting Horizontal Ownership Concentration' (2021) 66 Antitrust Bull 3.

[99] *Ibid.* at 5 refer to emerging literature that fortifies the original claims of the authors of the seminal papers on common ownership.

[100] Elhauge, Majumdar and Schmalz (n 98).

[101] See Section 14.2.

[102] A Eckstein, 'The Virtue of Common Ownership in an Era of Corporate Compliance' (2019) 105 Iowa L Rev 507.

[103] J Azar and others, 'The Big Three and Corporate Carbon Emissions Around the World' (2021) J Financ Econ (forthcoming).

ESG objectives, such as anything which has to do with the protection of the environment, the fight against climate change, and ultimately an urgently needed adjustment towards a more sustainable way of doing business, are very close to contemporary consumers' preferences (as well as to emerging investors' preferences)[104] – and in recent times strongly endorsed by policymakers.[105] One may argue that positive role played by IF's managers may not concern most European corporations, because they may be unable to act as stewards for such objectives in corporate environments where concentrated ownership structure prevails.[106] But it is equally true that for such European corporations the potential anticompetitive harm brought by IF funds is still unclear and unproven – and it is unlikely to be particularly relevant.[107]

Besides that, possible policy interventions on common ownership should always consider EU competition law general principles. A core concept around which EU competition law has evolved is consumer welfare, which in the present interpretation refers to price effects. Nonetheless, it has been suggested that in future we may become more and more uncomfortable identifying consumer welfare exclusively with low prices – as we tend to do today.[108] This again may bring ESG positive externalities into the domain of consumer welfare, therefore rendering a dismantlement of common ownership controversial.

Regardless of such potential (and probable) interpretative evolution, consumer welfare does not even represent the only goal of EU competition policies. As the recent empirical paper by Iacovides and Stylianou has shown, in practice consumer welfare is one of the many objectives that are at the core of EU competition policies.[109] At that core there seem to be more a kaleidoscope of rather contradictory objectives than one univocal standard. Some of the objectives at the core of EU law

[104] S Yan, F Ferraro, and J Almandoz, 'The Rise of Socially Responsible Investment Funds: The Paradoxical Role of the Financial Logic' (2019) 64 Admin Sci Q 466. And, note that the kind of investor who selects ESG funds is normally actively scrutinizing the funds' ESG engagement. See A Weinberg, 'Demand for ESG means more decisions for investors' (2020) 48 Pensions & Investments 20.

[105] The problem of the relationships between competition policy and ESG is extremely complex and I am not tackling it in this chapter. Academic research has also reached the institutional arena. See recently OECD, *Sustainability and Competition, OECD Competition Committee Discussion Paper* (2020) www.oecd.org/daf/competition/sustainability-and-competition-2020.pdf. The author of the report has also pioneered the exploration of the legal framework surrounding the possibility to give space to ESG issues, such as the environmental ones within, within the EU competition law framework. See J Nowag, *Environmental integration in competition and free-movement laws* (Oxford University Press 2016). And clearly the discussion about ESG has become prevalent in corporate governance. See C Mayer, *Prosperity: Better Business Makes the Greater Good* (Oxford University Press 2018); C Mayer, 'The Future of the Corporation and the Economics of Purpose' (2020) ECGI Finance Working Paper 710/2020. And see implementation proposals as soft law such as The British Academy, 'Principles for Purposeful Business' (2019) www.thebritishacademy.ac.uk/publications/future-of-the-corporation-principles-for-purposeful-business.

[106] D Puchniak (n 60).

[107] See Section 14.4.

[108] OECD (n 105) 26ff.

[109] K Stylianou and M Iacovides, 'The Goals of EU Competition Law-A Comprehensive Empirical Investigation' (2020) https://ssrn.com/abstract=3735795.

may be efficiency, welfare, fairness, entrepreneurial freedom from competitors, market structure, European integration, and the protection of the competitive process.[110]

Hence, when it comes to introduce new EU competition rules capable to tackle potential issues arising from common ownership, it is inevitable that such rules need to be tested in the light of the different goals advanced by the EU in terms of competition policy. On one hand, given the multiplicity of objectives pursued by EU competition policies, it may be easy to find justifications to any potential way forward, i.e. emphasising one of such policy objectives over the other. But it may equally become easy to find reasons for not regulating common ownership – hence leaving any intervention open to an almost infinite set of potential adjustments – also in the light of the evolution of such standards for adapting to the pursuance of ESG objective.[111]

But given the ever-expanding reach of EU policies, an intervention on common ownership would not be exclusively a matter of internal consistency (i.e. with the goals pursued by competition law). A direct intervention against indexing would entail a redesigning of corporate ownership structure of many companies and such a change would reverberate on their corporate governance. Such shift would in turn raise the question of consistency with EU policies that lay beyond the competition law ones – for instance, corporate governance policies – stewardship, at least for those European companies that are characterised by dispersed ownership structure.[112] One may wonder whether a dismantlement of the biggest Indexed Funds would be consistent with requests for enhanced stewardship, when institutional investors, such as Blackrock or Vanguard have been among the most actively engaged investors in pursuance of sustainability.[113] A direct intervention on Indexed Funds' holdings may be similar to one of those unfortunate Mikado picks that make the whole stick-tower crumble. Hence, before dismantling parallel holdings, it would be better to know what financial reality will come next. And a more cautious way forward would entail examining the overall situation from a better viewpoint and putting all the different pieces of the puzzle in their right place – so to create the lesser frictions possible among different EU policies.

14.7 ZOOMING-OUT AND ZOOMING-IN: LOOKING FOR ALTERNATIVE WAYS FORWARD – ECONOMIC AND POLITICAL TRAJECTORIES

If the issue of parallel holdings is so deeply intertwined with several coexisting layers of policy choices, one may wonder what could be the alternative ways forwards that may produce the most positive externalities while reducing negative externalities.

[110] *Ibid.* at 28, shows the uneven distribution of the centrality of such different goals among different EU institutions.

[111] OECD (n 105) 19ff.

[112] See Section 14.5.

[113] See Eckstein (n 102).

A first point concerns the effects of the academic and institutional debate on Indexed Funds' managers. If Indexed Funds' managers had ever thought about actively engaging in restricting competition, the present trend of literature on common ownership may have persuaded them to refrain from doing so – by recalling the public attention on their activity and therefore increasing their chances they get caught.[114] Hence, today the main threat – if there is any – may derive from common owners' passive investment.[115] A possible way to analyse this case from a broader perspective is to consider one by one the different variables surrounding common ownership, as identified in the papers that have fuelled the debate on this topic. Occasionally, one can apply a counterfactual analysis to the potential modifications brought to each variable – hence comparing different policy alternatives.[116]

To exemplify, policies directed to avoid or limit the potential anticompetitive harm deriving from common ownership may attempt to operate on: the structure of the target companies' product markets;[117] the structure of the financial services product market;[118] the investment techniques adopted by companies active in the financial instruments' product market;[119] and the governance activity carried out by the financial firms within their target companies.[120]

Some of the policy ways forward proposed by US academics aimed at banning[121] or limiting indexing.[122] If we apply a counterfactual reasoning to the proposals aimed at banning or limiting indexing, the chances that removing common ownership may improve competition are at least questionable. Big investment management companies own extremely large amounts of stock and that such financial instruments would need to find new owners. One may wonder whom would purchase that stock. First, although the study of strategies for State direct investments in the economy are not unknown within the EU Member States' political arenas, especially in

114 A notable component of deterrence. See R Cooter and B Freedman, 'The Fiduciary Relationship: Its Economic Character and Legal Consequences' (1991) 66 NYU L Rev 1045.

115 Consistently also with what has been found by Hemphill and Kahan (n 65) and L Bebchuk, A Cohen, and S Hirst (n 69).

116 Counterfactual reasoning has become the cornerstone of EU policymaking. For an in-depth analysis of this technique see D Geradin and I Girgenson, 'The counterfactual method in EU competition law: The cornerstone of the effects-based approach' (2011) https://ssrn.com/abstract=1970917.

117 Both economics and legal literature have highlighted the fact that the core problem underlying the present raise in prices for many consumption goods and services in the US may actually be chiefly explained by the increased product market concentration. See T Philippon, *The Great Reversal* (Harvard UP2019); Rock and Rubenfeld in Corradi and Nowag (n 12).

118 This is what was indirectly suggested by Jack Bogle when denouncing the present barriers to entry in those markets. See text corresponding to n 42. And more recently, see also Goshen & Levit (n 16) 51ff – although the paper proposes a split of the biggest investment management corporations mostly as a way to counter the labour monopsony problem supposedly created by common owners.

119 See Section 14.2.

120 That is, types of indexes employed.

121 Elhauge, 'Horizontal Shareholding'(n 12).

122 Posner, Morgan, and Weyl (n 12), suggesting that institutions should not hold more than 1% in more than a single firm in oligopolies.

the midst of the COVID-19 crisis,[123] it is unlikely that this becomes a generalised trend.[124] Hence, in line with the liberal economic model that the EU pursues, one may imagine that the equity holdings dismissed by Indexed Funds would be purchased by other private economic actor on the stock market, accompanied by some mechanisms due to temper the effects of a temporary oversupply of stock. Among potential purchasers, one might think of entrepreneurial families – the typical continental European blockholder – or for instance of other (non-indexed) investment funds. As to entrepreneurial families, this would contradict the present trend of families looking for external equity investors, more than co-investing in third-parties' companies.[125]

Other (non-indexed) investment funds would probably be the best candidates to substitute Indexed Funds in the ownership of such equity holdings. But literature has shown that the majority of institutional investors *not* employing indexing have not been champions in activism so far[126] – with some notable exceptions, such as hedge funds.[127] But hedge funds have traditionally been backed by other institutional investors for their active strategies.[128] Moreover, hedge funds are renowned for not been particularly well aligned with ESG concerns.[129] And this may again reverberate against the quest for internal EU policy consistency.

An alternative way to obtain a better competitive outcome might be to impose corporate governance rules that prompt investors to actively intervene in governance. One way could be promoting regular meetings for discussing pro-competitive issues, such as for example how to make the company more price efficient, how

[123] Agence France-Presse, 'Le coronavirus vaplonger la France dans la récession, des nationalisations envisages' *L'Express* (Paris, 17 March 2020) www.lexpress.fr/actualites/1/societe/le-coronavirus-va-plonger-la-france-dans-la-recession-des-nationalisations-envisagees_2121120.html.

[124] This would bring us back to times when autarchy prevailed in non-democratic regimes and when centralised holding institutions were created. For Fascist and post-WW2 Italy, see the 'Istituto per la Ricostruzione Industriale' (IRI), founded in 1933, as explained by R Petri, *Storia Economica d'Italia* (Il Mulino 2002) 97ff. For a detailed analysis of the economic activities exercised by the Italian State through IRI, see N Acocella,*L'impresa Pubblica Italiana e la Dimensione Internazionale: il Caso dell'IRI* (Einaudi 1983). For Frankist Spain, see the Instituto Nacional de Industria (INI), founded in 1944, and explained by V Binda and A Colli, 'Changing Big Business in Italy and Spain, 1973–2003: Strategic Responses to a New Context' (2011) 53 Business History 14, 16.

[125] J Neckebrouck, M Meuleman, and S Manigart, 'Governance Implications of Attracting External Equity Investors in Private Family Firms' (2021) 35 Acad Manag Perspect 25.

[126] B Black, Bernard and J Coffee Jr, 'Hail Britannia: Institutional Investor Behavior Under Limited Regulation' (1993) 92 Mich L Rev 1997; S Choi and J Fisch, 'On Beyond Calpers: Survey Evidence on the Developing Role of Public Pension Funds in Corporate Governance' (2008) 61 Vand L Rev 315. Such failure recently also hit Hedge Funds; J Heaton, 'The Unfulfilled Promise of Hedge Fund Activism' (2019) 13 Va L & Bus Rev 317.

[127] B Cheffins and J Armour, 'The Past, Present, and Future of Shareholder Activism y Hedge Funds' (2011) 37 J Corp L 51; M Kahan and E Rock, 'Hedge Funds in Corporate Governance and Corporate Control' (2007) U Pa L Rev 1021.

[128] Hamdani and Hannes (n 27).

[129] V Gerde, J Handy, and D Masson, 'Are Hedge Funds the Big, Bad Wolf' (Proceedings of the International Association for Business and Society 2017) vol 28.

to make its products more attractive and ultimately how to reap one's competitors' market shares. An even simpler way could be to impose a duty to actively promote competition. But it is unlikely that an omission could be sanctioned in a reasonable way: as a matter of fact, this would entail intruding in the discretionary choices of investors and especially directors which in modern corporate law have to abide by the business judgement rule.[130] Moreover, such an intrusion would introduce a level of public ordering that would go well beyond its level even in the most State intervention-prone jurisdictions.[131] A possible further intervention in governance could consist of limiting the potential contacts among different companies by way of dismantling interlocking directorships – which still seem to be very common both in Europe and in the US – and which may be the cause of anticompetitive harm beyond what might be causes by common ownership.[132]

Another way forward may consist of intervening on the structure of the target companies' product markets.[133] It goes without saying that such an intervention – at least in the US – would need to be backed by stronger evidence than presently existing.[134] But in Europe, where most product markets are less concentrated, a generalised policy against concentration may at times produce inefficiencies and it may also contrast with the political objective of the EU. For example, further market integration by facilitating cross-border transaction or even the creation of European national champions – an objective that is already pursued less vigorously than needed by present EU policies.[135] Moreover, in certain cases, such interventions would not even be needed, as some industries in Europe are national by nature or as a consequence of the legislation.[136]

Possibly, the most consistent way forward would entail intervening on the structure of financial services' product markets – i.e. trying to promote new entrants by bringing down barriers to entry and/or intervening with structural remedies, i.e. forcing the largest incumbent investment management corporations to split in a higher number of fund management companies. This idea has been proposed by Goshen and Levit, in relation to a parallel problem which seems connected to the emersion of the largest Indexed Funds, i.e. a monopsony in the labour markets. This has progressively caused a transfer of wealth from employees to equity holders,[137] and has also created labour instability, which seems at odds with the corporate

[130] For a general understanding of the business judgment rule, see SM Bainbridge, 'The Business Judgment Rule as Abstention Doctrine' (2004) 57 Vand L Rev 83.

[131] M Moore, *Corporate Governance in the Shadow of the State* (Hart Publishing 2013).

[132] See the Chapter 9 by Y Nil, Chapter 10 by F Thepot, and Chapter 11 by Ghezzi and Picciau in this book.

[133] E Posner, 'Policy Implications of the Common Ownership Debate' (2021) 66 Antitrust Bull 140, 148.

[134] Philippon (n 117); Rock and Rubenfeld (n 117).

[135] M Corradi and J Nowag, 'The relationship between Article 4 (1)(b) of the cross-border Merger Directive and the European Merger Regulation' in T Papadopoulos, Thomas (ed), *Cross-Border Mergers: EU Perspectives and National Experiences* (Springer 2019) 159.

[136] Burnside & Kidane (n 74) 464.

[137] Goshen & Levit (n 16).

governance-based sustainability objectives highlighted above.[138] Nonetheless, there is question as to whether such a modification in the ownership structure of big investment management corporations would grant the pursuance of the sustainability objectives that have been promoted so efficiently also thanks to the present financial services market concentration. And finally, this would be more a matter for US than EU competition authorities, given the limited reach of common ownership in Europe.

Concluding, there seem to be no perfect fix to the potential competitive harm deriving from parallel holdings by Indexed Funds, while, in a world characterised by urgent environmental and social problems, there seem to be a need for consistency among policies in bordering areas.

14.8 EU POLICIES FOR COMMON OWNERSHIP WITHIN THE GLOBAL CONTEXT

As I started this brief excursus by considering the EU policies on common ownership with a glance to the global perspective, it is worth concluding by considering such a wider viewpoint. And so far, at least one crucial player has not been included yet in this analysis: the PRC. To my knowledge, the MOFCOM has not released any statement concerning common ownership yet. Nonetheless, the present silence of Chinese authorities on this subject matter does not mean that the US and EU policy choices in relation to common ownership are not without consequences for the Chinese economic actors.

As a matter of fact, in the Chinese context, common ownership was already a hot topic far before than the whole Indexed Funds 'scandal' broke out. One may recall the fact that the EU – probably misunderstanding the way the PRC and its Communist Party manage their investment in SOEs – has qualified Chinese holdings in EU companies as common ownership.[139] Advancement on the analysis of the concept of common ownership in the context of Indexed Funds may in turn inform also the policies on SOEs' parallel holdings and vice versa. But beyond a potentially interesting comparison between Indexed Funds and SOEs common ownership law rules, a far more important question concerns the global financial implications triggered by a potential request addressed to Indexed Funds to dismiss part of their holdings –[140] or to allow for new entrants in the market for financial services.[141] In fact, earlier we identified other investment funds not employing indexing as potential acquirers of such holdings, or alternatively the entry of new investment management corporations in the financial market. But we have not discussed

[138] R Eccles, K Miller Perkins and G Serafeim, 'How to Become a Sustainable Company' (2012) 53 MIT Sloan Manage Rev 43.

[139] A Zhang, 'The Antitrust Paradox of China, Inc.' (2017) 50 NYUJ Int'l Law & Pol 159.

[140] See Section 14.7.

[141] *Ibid.*

potential acquisitions of dismissed holdings by PRC SOEs, which are renowned for their interest in cross-border acquisitions.[142]

The inability to replace entirely the present common owners with alternative European or US owners might provide far-East investors with unprecedented financial investments opportunities. And especially Chinese FDI may focus more intensively on Europe, given the limitations brought by the FIRRMA legislation approved under the Trump administration to foreign investment in US companies.[143] But if the EU Commission is still persuaded that most PRC holdings tend to be under the control of the Chinese Communist Party, this may well sound to the DG-Comp like throwing such holdings from the frying pan into the fire.[144] Faced with a potential increased demand from Chinese investors, EU policy-makers might be prompted to build even higher walls against PRC purchases in EU Member States' companies. This is turn may generate a spiral of tit-for-tat reactions – as the one we have already seen between PRC and US – which may be hard to contain and certainly not beneficial for the process of economic integration.[145]

As a matter of fact, the problem of common ownership – although seemingly only technical in nature – may have geopolitical implications hard to imagine for those who are mostly concerned with its potential price effects. And this might be another reason why the EU competition authorities are walking on eggshells – on one hand trying to gather as much data as possible on this subject matter and on the other trying to avoid untimely interventions.[146]

Ultimately, what needs to be understood before a final word is spent on common ownership is how the sustainability/growth conundrum will be solved at a corporate governance level and how each of the largest world economic blocks will carve their role in the pursuance of even far wider objectives – among which we must certainly include the protection of Human Rights.[147] If trust among global players and convergence in their progressive policies increases,[148] we may

142 SOE are less likely to complete successfully cross-border acquisitions than private companies. J Zhang, C Zhou, and H Ebbers, 'Completion of Chinese Overseas Acquisitions: Institutional Perspectives and Evidence' (2011) 20 Intl Business Rev 226. Nonetheless, they are renowned for their minority acquisitions. See Zhang, *Chinese Antitrust Exceptionalism* (n 145).

143 P Edelberg, 'Can Chinese Companies Still Invest in the United States: The Impact of FIRRMA' (2019) 16 US-China L Rev 12.

144 Although, as demonstrated by Zhang (n 139), not necessarily the perceived threat is corroborated by a real danger.

145 A Zhang, *Chinese Antitrust Exceptionalism: How the Rise of China Challenges Global Regulation* (Oxford University Press 2021) 214 ff.

146 See Section 14.6.

147 And there is a hope that institutional investors will improve their much-needed role of championing Human Rights protection. See K Buhmann, 'Institutional investors and climate justice: The role of investors in advancing prevention of human rights abuse in investment chains for fossil-free energy' (2021) in V Mauerhofer, *The Role of Law in Governing Sustainability* (Routledge 2021) 222.

148 Zhang (n 145) 242 explains that 'there is a danger that the current Western trend of politicizing antitrust enforcement, if carried too far, can evolve into a double-standard used against Chinese firms', which in turn may trigger tit-for-tat reactions.

see a far larger set of cross-equity holdings of various nature across the globe and in every possible and imaginable direction. But suspicion and localism may put the word end to such cross-border interactions.[149] The hope is that the democratisation brought by investment funds in the financial arena will evolve into something even more positive – helping spreading progressive value beyond what the world is seeing today.

[149] And it is worth reminding that unfortunately suspicion is not only hovering on PRC's investments but also on Blackrock's ones. See, for instance, J Pouille, 'Blackrock: The financial leviathan that bears down on Europe's decisions' (*Investigate Europe*, 17 April 2019) www.investigate-europe.eu/en/2019/blackrock-the-financial-leviathan-that-bears-down-on-europes-decisions/.

15

Common Ownership and Minority Shareholding at the Intersection of Competition and Corporate Law

Looking Through the Past to Return to the Future?

Anna Tzanaki

15.1 INTRODUCTION

Common ownership is the talk of the town in antitrust land. Surrounded by mystery and noise, the competitive implications of rival firms being partially owned and controlled by a small set of overlapping owners are both fascinating and hotly contested. The fascination comes from the fact that the source of potential competition harm may be minority shareholder control in a setting of widely held companies.[1] In fact, the common ownership phenomenon is so pervasive, in particular in the US,[2] that if this new theory of harm is true, most markets could be beset by serious antitrust concerns. At the same time, scepticism among academics and policymakers abounds. Most notably, critics wonder about the likely prospect, quantum and mechanics of common owners' influence driving any pro- or anticompetitive effects.[3] It is often stressed that the antitrust analysis of common ownership is clearly distinguishable from that of cross-shareholding links between competitors.[4] Indeed,

Senior Lecturer at Lund University, Faculty of Law, Sweden; Senior Research Fellow at UCL Centre of Law, Economics & Society, London, UK; anna.tzanaki@jur.lu.se. This project has received funding from the European Union's Horizon 2020 research and innovation programme under the Marie Skłodowska-Curie grant agreement No. 846270. My special thanks to the editors of this volume for inviting me to contribute and for their careful review of my work. This chapter is part of a bigger research project starting with my PhD thesis and continuing under the Marie Curie grant, which is to be condensed in a forthcoming monograph 'Partial Ownership of Competitors in Europe: Economics, Law and Policy' (Cambridge University Press). This project has greatly benefited from various discussions with José Azar and Giorgio Monti, who I wish to thank for the intellectual stimulation and inspiring exchanges. I am also very grateful to Alessandro Romano, Elias Deutscher, Pedro Caro de Sousa and Stefan Thomas for helpful comments and suggestions.

1 A Tzanaki, 'Varieties and Mechanisms of Common Ownership: A Calibration Exercise for Competition Policy' (2022) 18 JCL&E 168; M Backus, C Conlon and M Sinkinson, 'Common Ownership in America: 1980–2017' Am Econ J: *Microecon* (forthcoming); cf A Dyck and L Zingales, 'Private Benefits of Control: An International Comparison' (2004) 59 J Fin 537.

2 J Azar, 'The Common Ownership Trilemma' (2020) 87 U Chi L Rev 263, 267–268 (summarising the empirical literature); cf N Rosati and others, *Common Shareholding in Europe* (JRC121476, Publications Office of the European Union 2020).

3 See chapter 13 by E Rock and D Rubinfeld in this book.

4 A Burnside and A Kidane, 'Common Ownership: An EU Perspective' (2021) 8 JAE 456, 457–458.

the novel concern caused by common shareholdings derives from indirect, and possibly partial, shareholder overlaps across rival firms rather than directly from competitive overlaps in product markets. A comprehensive account of partial ownership, capturing the competition dynamics of both cross- and common shareholding and the incentives of both individual and institutional investors, is notoriously missing.[5] Yet, so far, the spirited debate between antitrust and corporate law and economics scholars centres on whether this 'knowledge gap' is material, set to be filled by better understanding and experience as a matter of course or whether it is a fictional problem and an empty inquiry that is theoretically implausible and empirically unrealistic to unfold.[6]

Against this backdrop, this chapter aims to illuminate some of the latent connecting points in this debate, by looking back into the past and then fast forward to the future. There are two key takeaways from this analysis. The historical split of corporate and antitrust laws and their gradual specialisation in targeting different issues with distinct objectives in mind has unwittingly created regulatory gaps. This is the source of the present-day problem posed by minority and common shareholdings for competition law. With this understanding clear, the analysis moves on to offer a new taxonomy of (partial) shareholdings in light of their partial control characteristics, with distinguishable classifications based on competition and corporate law, as compared to broader economics-focused notions of control. The industrial organisation perspective reveals that commonly thought passive and highly diversified minority holdings are not necessarily innocuous in terms of their competitive implications. Rather, minority common shareholdings may give rise to actual or potential 'competitive influence' under certain circumstances ('influential' shareholdings).

The corollary is that antitrust cannot afford to neglect such corporate ownership structures and for this reason, it is called to look into the actual corporate governance dynamics in the substantive assessment of cases and in designing appropriate remedies. Yet, the historical and economic analyses further suggest that merger control needs to recalibrate its jurisdictional scope and embrace a 'structural' approach, combined with 'case-by-case', fact-specific analysis, also for shareholdings falling below legal thresholds of control. This reorientation would not only fill enforcement gaps and capture new theories of harm relating to common shareholding but also reconnect merger control to its corporate law origins in a way that holistically addresses agency costs and market power concerns linked to such shareholding. At

[5] Institutional common shareholding marks the double movement from 'direct' to 'indirect' ownership holding structures along the different stages of organisational evolution of capitalism. That is, from retail individual investors to professional intermediary investors (investment fund intermediaries), and from direct ownership links between competing firms to indirect shareholding links via non-industrial third parties (common shareholders-investors). See A Tzanaki, 'The Common Ownership Boom – Or: How I Learned to Start Worrying and Love Antitrust' (May 2019) CPI Antitrust Chronicle 'Common Ownership Revisited' 3 https://papers.ssrn.com/sol3/papers.cfm?abstract_id=3401209.

[6] For an overview of the state of the literature see chapter 12 by M Schmalz in this book.

the same time, corporate law and governance should be cognizant of these parallel developments and tread softly when shaping their own regulations so that they do not augment any antitrust concerns.

The structure of the chapter is as follows. Section 15.2 provides relevant background on the two-sided history of regulating shareholding acquisitions under corporate and competition laws. Section 15.3 illustrates antitrust's embeddedness in pre-existing corporate laws and forms, documenting the early unity and progressive quiet disconnect of the two fields in regulating ownership structures and intercorporate links. Section 15.4 presents the contemporary common ownership (hypo)thesis and the distinct challenges and opportunities that it poses for both antitrust and corporate law. Section 15.5 develops a working taxonomy of (minority) shareholding types and their (partial) control characteristics from different perspectives with a particular focus on competition economics. Section 15.6 focuses on the economic attributes and competitive effects of common shareholding seen and analysed through the lens of corporate property rights theory. Section 15.7 concludes with an urge to competition and corporate governance and finance policy-makers for harmonic progression in seeking regulatory solutions to address common ownership and with further implications for competition law following the preceding analysis.

15.2 MERGERS AND MINORITY SHAREHOLDING: A TWO-SIDED HISTORY

Minority shareholding is an old story in the realm of competition or antitrust laws. It takes us back to the origins of antitrust, or even to preceding developments in corporate law that led to its birth.[7]

Ever since its inception, antitrust was designed to tackle a rampant wave of mergers and acquisitions fuelled by technological and industry developments as well as holding structures ('trusts')[8] between competing companies that essentially led to concentrated economic power and monopolistic market outcomes. The antitrust movement was an immediate reaction to evolving corporate laws. The emergence of the trusts and multistate corporate mergers was the result of a 'race to the bottom'[9]

[7] See chapter 1 by M Meagher in this book.

[8] W Cary, 'Federalism and Corporate Law: Reflections upon Delaware' (1974) 83 Yale LJ 663, 664; H Hovenkamp, *Enterprise and American Law, 1836–1937* (Harvard UP 2009) 259. Hovenkamp lucidly explains that the business and legal 'geniuses who invented the trusts' with the intention to evade state corporate law employed different, privately negotiated, trust arrangements but every such 'late nineteenth-century acquisition was organized around one of three legal models: (1) the stock-transfer trust model; (2) the asset-transfer combination; (3) the holding company'.

[9] On the 'race to the top' versus the 'race to the bottom' debate in corporate law scholarship, indicating states with corporate laws favoring shareholders and minimising agency costs versus states with management-friendly corporate laws, see R Romano, *The Genius of American Corporate Law* (American Enterprise Institute 1993). In this chapter, the 'race to the bottom' argument is employed in the broader context of regulatory competition among jurisdictions, which in attempting to

with US states 'competing' for corporate charters and New Jersey being the first to enable 'interstate' holding structures intended to monopolise or cartelise national industries.[10] US federal antitrust law was born in 1890 in an attempt to rein in this 'accommodating' interstate competition in corporate laws among different states. Up to that point, state law treated jointly 'issues of antitrust and corporate authority'.[11] Yet, not all anticompetitive mergers or restraints of trade were captured by those initial antitrust laws. In fact, the Sherman Act originally targeted 'loose' combinations (cartels) rather than 'tight' ones (mergers)[12] but later case law (1904) also applied it to the holding company ('single business firm').[13] Stock acquisitions only became a specific antitrust target of US merger control with the coming into force of the Clayton Act in 1914.[14]

Similarly, the founders of the EU avoided incorporating rules controlling corporate ownership structures in the Treaty of Rome, which included solely behavioural rules on cartels and abuse of dominance. Only in 1990, EU Members States agreed to have a pan-European Merger Regulation ('EUMR') in place to address cross-border mergers and acquisitions. Till then, the available EU antitrust rules were used as a *de facto* merger control regime.[15] Indeed, over time, EU authorities decided to make use of Article 102 TFEU to address mergers and 'majority' acquisitions.[16] While later on, EU case law further applied Article 101 (and 102) TFEU to minority shareholdings

outperform each other and attract business drive and lower standards to a minimum. Critically for our current discussion on minority shareholding acquisitions, these phenomena can play out at the same time: a 'race to the top' in corporate laws that are efficient for shareholders (and possibly firm value) may simultaneously produce 'race to the bottom' effects in terms of product market competition. In other words, what might be privately optimal for shareholders from an agency theory perspective is not necessarily socially optimal from a competition perspective (a classic instance of externalities that US federal antitrust law was enacted to remedy).

10 M Roe, 'Delaware's Competition' (2003) 117 Harv L Rev 588, 607–610.

11 *Ibid*. at 608 (noting that the two categories were severed when the US federal government took away antitrust from the states).

12 Hovenkamp (n 8) 242, 248–249, 266. The logic was that while rigorous antitrust enforcement was considered 'effective against interstate cartels, merger policy was [better] to be left to individual state [corporate laws]'. Yet, this early antitrust choice had its own unintended consequences as 'the Sherman Act actually forced firms to merge than collude.' At the same time, state corporate law lost its grip once anticompetitive mergers and combinations became 'multistate creatures' and thus 'corporate law forced the common law trusts to reorganize as asset acquisitions or holding companies'. Ironically, the resounding success of federal antitrust and state corporate laws against the trusts led to renewed organizational ingenuity by businesses that sought to control markets.

13 *Ibid*. at 264–266.

14 E Posner, F Scott Morton and E Weyl, 'A Proposal to Limit the Anti-Competitive Power of Institutional Investors' (2017) 81 Antitrust LJ 669, 670–671.

15 A Tzanaki, 'The Regulation of Minority Shareholdings and Other Structural Links between Competing Undertakings: A Law & Economics Analysis' (DPhil Thesis, University College London 2017).

16 Memorandum on The Problem of Industrial Concentration in the Common Market, Commission, Competition Series No 3 (1966); and Case 6/72, *Europemballage and Continental Can v Commission* [1973] ECR 215.

linking competitors and giving rise to 'some influence'.[17] In fact, part of the reason for the adoption of the EUMR was the foregoing 'expansive' use of Articles 101 and 102 TFEU by the European Commission to go after 'minority' share acquisitions in competitors.[18] Under pressure, Member States decided to compromise by yielding part of their regulatory powers checking anticompetitive mergers, acquisitions, and joint ventures under national law rather than be *de facto* completely swept away by creeping EU antitrust competence. The end result of this pragmatic political settlement was that the EUMR was designed to jurisdictionally cover only cases of 'concentrations' that give rise to a 'lasting change of control', i.e. multistate corporate combinations that confer upon the acquirer positive or negative 'decisive influence'.[19]

Perhaps counterintuitively and for different reasons, US and EU merger control laws shared a little noticed, common trajectory in their origin. Their absence was conspicuous in the inaugural design of cross-Atlantic antitrust rules. EU antitrust law had a 'top-down' inception inspired by a high-level political commitment towards an internal market integration objective. Coming only later and independently, EU merger control was the political product of Member States agreeing to a 'lesser evil' against pressing supranational antitrust expansion.[20] Initially, however, cross-border mergers were seen as a positive force furthering European integration and the competitiveness of its industry rather than in need of any legal constraint.[21] In contrast, US antitrust law had clear 'bottom-up' origins reflecting populistic sentiments of the time against cartelising business trusts and monopolistic merger combinations. US merger control also came into force later but predominantly to fill the gaps left by state corporate laws. Accordingly, the initial omission of merger law both in the EU and the US from the traditional body of antitrust law was not a random policy choice. US antitrust legislators consciously chose to break free from the 'formalities' of state corporate law and its 'structural model' of dealing with the 'trust problem' while opting for a 'strategic model' merely governing agreements and combinations in restraint of trade 'based on economic theory that purported to distinguish between competitive [and] anticompetitive' ones.[22] The distinct

[17] Joined Cases 142 and 156/84, *BAT and Reynolds v Commission* [1987] ECR 4487 (*'Philip Morris'*); Cases IV/33.440 *Warner-Lambert/Gillette* and IV/33.486 *BIC/Gillette* [1993] OJ L 116/21.

[18] A Burnside, 'Minority Shareholdings: An Overview of EU and National Case Law' (2013) e-Competitions Bulletin No 56676 2.

[19] EU merger rules make a clear reference both to a lasting structural change in corporate control as well as in industry control affecting competition. See Article 3(1) of the EUMR, and Recitals 6 and 20.

[20] To be sure, there had been previous EU proposals for a pan-European Merger Regulation, repeatedly rejected by Member States. However, once the European Commission grew in determination to employ existing antitrust law to scrutinise merger and minority shareholding transactions and use that position of power as a threat point against continuing non-adoption of the EUMR, the soil was ripe for Member States to retreat.

[21] K Banks, 'Mergers and Partial Mergers Under EEC Law' (1987) 11 Fordham Int'l LJ 255, 257.

[22] Hovenkamp (n 8) 244–249. The 'trade restraints model' chosen by the Sherman Act was the 'weaker' of the two 'because of the "rule of reason" inherent in its application', especially as applying to

concern of the antitrust approach when examining a merger or combination was 'its object or effect' on market competition, not 'its form'.[23] In addition, it was initially believed that issues of firm formation, ownership transfer agreements, and the sale and purchase of property or stock acquisitions, either by a corporation as a legal business entity or by its business owners as physical persons, were beyond the regulatory ambit of antitrust rules.[24]

Seen in this light, the noted 'foundational deficit'[25] of EU competition law in reaching to partial ownership structures and share acquisitions has not been a singular EU story. Traces may also be found in US legal history, albeit in subtler forms. Yet, what is noteworthy about US antitrust law is its ability for fast(er) adaptation to emerging business and economic realities, such as the disaggregation of state corporate and antitrust policy and the proliferation of multistate business firms, as well as to the rapidly changing content and scope of state corporate laws towards more liberal and enabling rules favourable to private ordering. Indeed, jurisdiction and substantive review under US merger control now resolutely rely on 'effects-based' tests, whereas EU merger control jurisdiction retains its 'formalistic' reliance on a narrow legal conception of 'control'.[26]

mergers, whereas state corporate law applied across the board (a categorical '*per se*' approach) prohibiting all mergers or combinations of certain form, not merely the anticompetitive ones. The state corporate model was legal or 'noneconomic'; antitrust had 'economic' grounding since the outset.

[23] H Hovenkamp, 'Antitrust Policy, Federalism, and the Theory of the Firm: An Historical Perspective' (1990) 59 Antitrust LJ 75, 87.

[24] *Ibid.* at 88–90; Tzanaki (n 15) 86, 102, 128. In the EU, share purchase agreements were initially presumed to be outside the scope of EU competition rules until the 1966 Memorandum (n 16). Later case law (n 17) abolished this complete immunity rule and established a 'no influence' safe harbour for minority shareholding up to 25% (ie corresponding to control of 25% of the voting rights and no other special contractual or corporate rights), relying on a formalistic presumption existing under national corporate law (eg Germany at the time). See *ibid.* at 113. Similarly, in the US, shareholders used to have an 'absolute' right to transfer their shares, unless restricted by the corporate charter or state law. Such share transfer agreements were only subject to state corporate law as they touched upon an essential feature of the very corporate form (ie the free transferability of shares). Thus, while it was later recognised that 'every corporation is a "combination" of its shareholders', potentially subject to antitrust review to the extent it resulted in 'a merger [giving] the participants effective control of the market', the 'mere formation of such a combination should never be considered illegal'. See Hovenkamp (n 23) 89.

[25] M Corradi and A Tzanaki, 'Active and Passive Institutional Investors and New Antitrust Challenges: Is EU Competition Law Ready?' (June 2017) CPI Antitrust Chronicle 'Index Funds – A New Antitrust Frontier?' 7 https://papers.ssrn.com/sol3/papers.cfm?abstract_id=2996518.

[26] Economic conceptions of 'control' and theories of harm are notably broader than the legal definition of control under the EUMR, while some Member States have more encompassing national merger control statutes based on wider notions of 'influence' ('material', 'significant'). A Tzanaki, 'The Legal Treatment of Minority Shareholdings Under EU Competition Law: Present and Future' in *Essays in Honour of Professor Panayiotis I Kanellopoulos* (Sakkoulas Publications 2015) 861, 863 (fn 10), 878–880. Indeed, the definition of a notifiable merger transaction can be based on different 'objective' or 'economic' criteria focusing on the potential mechanism of competitive harm. See OECD, 'Definition of Transaction for the Purpose of Merger Control Review' (2014) DAF/COMP(2013)25, 6. The Commission had proposed introducing an 'effect-based model', regardless of the applicable

15.3 ANTITRUST EMBEDDEDNESS IN CORPORATE FORMS: THE QUIET DISCONNECT

But the interplay between competition and corporate laws goes one level deeper. Antitrust choices regarding rules or analytical frames had been implicitly premised on pre-existing corporate law and practice in the formative era. Early corporate law in the US till the end of the nineteenth century was much more restrictive and unitary in nature in regulating business entities, their structure and operation, as a legal and social phenomenon. Corporate law not only included far more outright prohibitions (mandatory rules) rather than balancing or enabling rules regarding ownership structure and governance practices within any individual firm but also strictly regulated intercorporate relations. Indeed, in the early days of US corporate law agency problems within the firm were not a major concern as the law and surrounding circumstances at the time ensured there were:[27]

i) no 'separation of ownership and control',[28]
ii) no 'separation of ownership and consumption',[29]
iii) no 'separation of control (voting rights) and investment (financial interests)'.[30]

Or even further, from the perspective of shareholders:

EUMR turnover thresholds establishing an 'EU dimension' of a notifiable 'concentration', which would practically have allowed it to retain an alternative "back door" to pursue non-controlling minority shareholding cases that would be subject to merger review in at least three Member States. See Commission, 'Green Paper on the Review of Council Regulation (EEC) No 4064/89' COM(2001) 745 final, paras 54–63. Recent EU policy has devised new ways to overcome jurisdictional limitations of EU merger control by allowing case referrals to the Commission by Member States of mergers that may not require notification under national law at all. See Commission, 'Guidance on the application of the referral mechanism set out in Article 22 of the Merger Regulation to certain categories of cases' C(2021) 1959 final.

27 The analysis that follows implicitly compares the position of contemporary US law applicable to large public corporations and surrounding market and investment conditions compared to earlier developments in the nineteenth century. The situation however may differ from country to country and for different types of companies, hence a closer look into the corporate law details and relevant context is warranted in such cases.

28 A Berle and G Means, *The Modern Corporation and Private Property* (Macmillan Co 1932); E Fama and M Jensen, 'Separation of Ownership and Control' (1983) 26 JLE 301 (referring to the 'separation of decision and risk-bearing functions observed in large corporations').

29 H Hansmann and M Pargendler, 'The Evolution of Shareholder Voting Rights: Separation of Ownership and Consumption' (2014) 123 *Yale LJ* 948; cf H Demsetz, 'The Structure of Ownership and the Theory of the Firm' (1983) 26 JLE 375. According to Demsetz, the 'agency problem' (or the cost of 'on-the-job consumption') is not a problem of agency – a single owner may similarly engage in corporate 'waste' if unchecked – but due to lack of competitive pressure or diverging objectives of the controlling owner or manager from the assumed pure profit maximisation motive. In essence, this problem distinguishes the 'real modern corporation' facing positive monitoring costs vis-à-vis the ideal 'profit-maximizing firm of economic theory' that is a 'good approximation of precorporate real firms' of the nineteenth century.

30 F Easterbrook and D Fischel, 'Voting in Corporate Law' (1983) 26 JLE 395, 400, 410 ('It is not possible to separate the voting right from the equity interest. [...] Attaching the vote firmly to the residual equity interest ensures that an unnecessary agency cost will not come into being. Separation of shares from

iv) no 'separation of ownership from ownership',[31] and
v) no 'separation of ownership and awareness'.[32]

The first legally organised companies had been novel combinations of 'private investment and state-granted monopoly privileges' to undertake important community projects under special charters.[33] Once chartered companies obtained 'perpetual existence' and 'strong entity shielding', shareholders acquired a legal 'right to sell their shares without the consent of other owners' in exchange for their lost ability to withdraw from the joint venture at will.[34] Such monopoly grants served two

votes introduces a disproportion between expenditure and reward.'); H Manne, 'The Publicly Held Corporation as a Market Creation' (1981) 137 *Zeitschrift für die gesamte Staatswissenschaft / JITE* 689, 690 ('The share can be viewed as a two-part package of the underlying investment value plus the value of the vote. […] If, however, the shareholders did not have the right to sell their vote, they would be left as residual claimants largely in name only, rather like the presumed beneficiaries of a not-for-profit organization. So long as the votes [whether as part of a share package or separately] can be bought and sold then the stock market will constrain managers to work in the shareholders' interest.'); H Manne, 'Some Theoretical Aspects of Share Voting. An Essay in Honor of Adolf A. Berle' (1964) 64 Colum L Rev 1427, 1432, 1436–1437; cf G Rauterberg, 'The Separation of Voting and Control: The Role of Contract in Corporate Governance' (2021) 38 Yale J on Reg 1124. Voting is a proxy for shareholder power and the default mechanism for board control. Decisions are usually made based on a majority voting rule. The default rule for allocating voting rights among shareholders-owners of the corporation is 'one share-one vote', although contractual deviations are possible. As Easterbrook and Fischel, *ibid.* at 408–409, explain, the principle of the 'presumptively equal voting right attached to shares' is justified from economic efficiency perspective given that shareholders are the 'residual claimants' of the firm generated profits; any departure from this principle creates '(unnecessary) agency costs'.

31 U Rodrigues, 'Corporate Governance in an Age of Separation of Ownership from Ownership' (2010) 95 Minn L Rev 1822, 1826–1829 (crediting Leo Strine as the original inventor of the term); L Strine, 'The Delaware Way: How We Do Corporate Law and Some of the New Challenges We (and Europe) Face' (2005) 30(3) Del J Corp L 673, 687 (referring to this as the 'separation of capital from capital'); cf J Fisch, 'Securities Intermediaries and the Separation of Ownership from Control' (2010) 33 Seattle U L Rev 877, 878–882.

32 H Hovenkamp, 'Neoclassicism and the Separation of Ownership and Control' (2009) 4 Va L & Bus Rev 373, 400–402 (noting that 'the result of marginalist finance theory, particularly the efficient capital market hypothesis, was to take Berle and Means' separation of corporate ownership and control one step further, to the separation of ownership and awareness. […] A random selection of stocks produces the same return as the most careful research. […] Shareholders of publicly traded corporations could invest with indifference and indiscrimination – a massive shift away from the nineteenth century vision of the corporation as a device to facilitate investment predominately by groups of active owner-operators who sought to limit their liability.'); cf Rodrigues (n 31) 1826 (noting that long-term investors are 'indifferent as to how that long-term goal is achieved').

33 H Hansmann, R Kraakman and R Squire, 'Law and the Rise of the Firm' (2006) 119 Harv L R 1333, 1376–1377. As the authors point out, the inventor of the joint stock company was fourteenth century Genoa that 'sold shares in state-backed monopolies' engaged in various public-interested ventures. However, these commercial enterprises were small and 'operate[d] under a rule whereby every owner had to consent to any sale of a firm's shares'. England and the Netherlands followed this example in organising their own large-scale chartered companies in the seventeenth century such as their famous East India Companies but allowing shareholders to freely transfer their shares without prior consent from others.

34 *Ibid.* at 1377 (explaining how 'a company's need for fixed capital' was traded off against 'a shareholder's need for liquidity'). It is also implied that, for practical reasons, the unanimity rule for shareholder voting was set aside once shares were freely tradable.

purposes, one balancing against the other. Monopoly rents were the bait to attract self-interested investors against the risk of 'control-person opportunism'.[35] At the same time, the public interest was also served by enabling large-scale ventures that would not have been possible otherwise. With the corporate form becoming widely available under general incorporation statutes,[36] exclusive privileges were no longer *a priori* guaranteed. Democratisation of the corporate form paved the ground for free market competition. Success in the marketplace was now the driver of private profit-seeking venturers and also the only assurance for firm survival. Competition among independently operating companies was the new *modus operandi* for serving the public and consumer welfare.

Thus, although anachronistic today, it is no surprise that in its early days, US corporate law was primarily seen as a response to problems of monopoly and market power rather than concerned over agency problems inside the firm.[37] Prominent examples are rules regarding voting (caps) or purpose restrictions (*ultra vires* doctrine),[38] prohibition of separately allocating cash flow and control rights or splitting shareholders' property interests in the firm (bar on the separation of ownership/investment and control),[39] prohibition of acquisitions of foreign (out-of-state) companies,[40] prohibition of 'intercorporate stock ownership' (interlocking shareholding or 'common stockholders')[41] and 'intercorporate influence' (interlocking directorates

35 *Ibid.* at 1378–1379. It is further argued that the monopolistic scale of business was to facilitate an efficient market for corporate shares and their free transferability while charters were primarily granted for large fixed-asset investment (rather than manufacturing) projects where the risk of opportunism by firm controllers was minimal.

36 *Ibid.* at 1386, 1394.

37 Hansmann and Pargendler (n 29) 950–951 ('In the late eighteenth and early nineteenth century, the main economic evil linked to the corporate form was not managerial or controlling-shareholder opportunism toward small shareholders, but rather Adam Smith's first concern: monopoly. […] early corporate law and practice were frequently designed to minimize the abuse of that market power.').

38 Hansmann and Pargendler (n 29); Hovenkamp (n 23) 77 (the 'rule that stock transfer trusts involved corporations in *ultra vires* partnerships condemned all mergers by stock transfer trust').

39 See n 30 above.

40 Hovenkamp (n 8) 63–64, 258–262 (noting that a mere transfer of shares evaded this rule because in the holding company the shareholders were 'foreign', not the other corporation as in asset-acquisition mergers); cf Roe (n 10) 609.

41 W Roy, *Socializing Capital: The Rise of the Large Industrial Corporation in America* (Princeton UP 1997) 148–155; Hovenkamp (n 23) 77 (the 'rule forbidding one corporation from owning the shares of another corporation forbade all holding companies'). Roy also discusses the progressive relaxation of rules on intercorporate stock ownership and its implications (151: 'The social structure of ownership permitted by intercorporate stock ownership sharply contrasted with that of individually owned businesses [which] were structurally atomistic [and interacted] primarily through the market. […] proprietary relationships made it possible to control the market through two types of networks [of ownership], holding companies and communities of interest. When states began to allow corporations to own stock in other corporations, they gave birth to the holding company, a company that existed solely to own other companies. […] In a community of interest, competitors own a noncontrolling interest in one another, giving each an incentive to maximize their mutual benefit rather than competing by undermining their rivals.'). Interestingly, exceptions to the prohibition of cross-ownership were permissible primarily for firms operating 'in similar lines of business'. Although

or 'shared directors').[42] During this era, it was not obvious that separate corporate entities could acquire or own property or equity interests (shareholding) in others or engage in combinations (mergers) of assets (productive facilities) or stock (capital).[43] The legal and economic environment of the time was in other words quite different to what is observed today.

Progressively, however, most of these restrictions were abandoned as corporate law relaxed and redirected its focus on the 'internal affairs' of firms,[44] aiming to minimise agency costs and conflicts of interest. Companies were gloriously emancipated from early state (corporate) control; at the age of adolescence, the only credible constraint on their market and transactional activities was (federal) antitrust law.[45] Given its liberalisation trends, corporate law was now oriented on developing alternative means of protecting investors, mostly notably minority shareholders,[46] rather than providing any form of consumer protection against them. While antitrust grew to fill in those gaps, it only comprehensively did so with regard to mergers.

surprising to a modern antitrust minded observer, the logic supporting this rule is understood considering that the 'purpose' of the corporate form or practice was the key criterion for assessing its legality under corporate law.

42 Roy (n 41) 155 ('interlocking directorates helped to control competition among the firms in a market, facilitate raising capital from commercial and investment banks, solidify and reduce transaction costs with suppliers and customers, and coordinate the activities among firms with common ownership.').

43 *Ibid.* at 149–151 (explaining that under the 'property' conception of the firm, corporations were essentially 'a contract among individuals to pool their resources [but] not be entities that themselves could hold property other than their physical assets'. Under the 'entity' view of the firm, the corporation was treated 'as an individual [but] it did not necessarily follow that corporations could fully engage in owning any form of property' as natural individuals. 'Although judicial law generally held that corporations could own physical property [...], there was a continuing debate over their right to own the stock of other corporations.'); Hovenkamp (n 23) 81, 85, 88–89 (noting that under corporate law 'the acquisition of property had to be "useful or convenient" for the corporation's operation of the business "for which it was organized." As a result, horizontal acquisitions [of a competitor's assets] were generally lawful.'; and that the holding company legal merger and share transfers among business owners were over time considered 'merely a purchase and sale of property' and generally legal under state corporate law, but case law had observed that 'because a corporation is merely a fictional person and not a natural one, a corporation's acquisition of property could constitute a "combination"' under antitrust law).

44 Hansmann and Pargendler (n 29) 993.

45 It is also instructive that the predecessor of the US Federal Trade Commission, an independent administrative agency with an antitrust enforcement mandate, was the US Bureau of Corporations (1903–1915). The Federal Trade Commission Act came into force the same year as the Clayton Act (1914), including statutory provisions on the control of mergers and acquisitions and a flat prohibition of interlocking directorates between competing corporations. The US Bureau of Corporations, having a mission of transparency reporting and conducting industry studies (also addressing issues of ownership and control), was a curious experiment in 'state-corporate cooperation'. In effect, it operated as an institutionalised 'forum' for informal bargaining between the US government and business corporations and was 'the pragmatic means by which Roosevelt pursued a conservative, yet effective, reigning in of big business power'. See W Murphey, 'Theodore Roosevelt and the Bureau of Corporation: Executive-Corporate Cooperation and the Advancement of the Regulatory State' (2013) 14 *Am Nineteen Century Hist* 73.

46 cf Hansmann, Kraakman and Squire (n 33) 1398.

Minority share transactions have been loosely regulated especially in the EU whose merger control rules imported corporate law norms, conceptions, and formalities to single out controlling acquisitions from presumably harmless 'non-controlling' ones.[47] Thus, the staggering specialisation of corporate and competition laws on firms and markets, respectively, had its own unintended consequences as the regulation of minority shareholding came to 'fall between the cracks'.

15.4 THE COMMON OWNERSHIP (HYPO)THESIS: CORPORATE SENSIBILITY OR ANTITRUST OVERKILL?

Nowadays, concern over potentially anticompetitive minority shareholding has taken novel forms. The buzzword is 'common ownership'[48] or 'horizontal shareholding'.[49] The dramatic growth of large institutional investors[50] and the indirect concentration of (partial) ownership of publicly listed firms it brought with it, not only signalled the promise of improved corporate governance[51] but also created a major 'challenge to market competition'[52] or indeed the 'greatest anticompetitive threat of our times'.[53] More fundamentally, however, common institutional shareholding has both deep and mixed implications for corporate as well as for competition laws.[54] Arguably, parallel horizontal shareholdings by

47 Tzanaki (n 1).

48 J Azar, M Schmalz and I Tecu, 'Anticompetitive Effects of Common Ownership' (2018) 73 J Fin 1513; OECD, 'Common Ownership by Institutional Investors and Its Impact on Competition' (2017) DAF/COMP(2017)10.

49 E Elhauge, 'Horizontal Shareholding' (2016) 129 Harv L Rev 1267; F Scott Morton and H Hovenkamp, 'Horizontal Shareholding and Antitrust Policy' (2018) 127(7) Yale LJ 2026. Note also the different emphasis by economists (on the market structure and competitive impact of common ownership) vis-à-vis lawyers (on the definition of the antitrust problem and the framing of its implications in terms of the (horizontal) nature of the competitive relationship).

50 L Bebchuk and S Hirst, 'The Specter of the Giant Three' (2019) 99 BU L Rev 721.

51 OECD, *The Role of Institutional Investors in Promoting Good Corporate Governance* (OECD Publishing 2011); E Rock, 'The Logic and (Uncertain) Significance of Institutional Shareholder Activism' (1991) 79 Geo LJ 445.

52 E Posner, F Scott Morton and G Weyl, 'A Monopoly Donald Trump Can Pop' *The New York Times* (New York, 7 December 2016) ('the real challenge to competitive markets today does not come from mergers [...]. The great, but mostly unknown, antitrust story of our time is the astonishing rise of the institutional investor – a large [financial intermediary] company [...] that buys stock in substantial quantities for the benefit of clients and customers – and the challenge that it poses to market competition.').

53 E Elhauge, 'How Horizontal Shareholding Harms Our Economy – And Why Antitrust Law Can Fix It' (2020) 10 Harv Bus L Rev 207, 285.

54 In the sense of the above noted (n 9) disconnect between the private welfare of common shareholders and social welfare. Interestingly, the disconnect may simultaneously be evidenced within the context of both corporate law and competition law for different reasons. Specifically, common shareholders' interests and actions may be found in opposition to the fiduciary principle in corporate law (to the extent they are in opposition to the interests of the firm as a whole and any non-diversified group of shareholders) but also be the source of consumer and competitive harm (to the extent they induce suboptimal outcomes in product markets that would not have existed in the absence of common ownership).

institutional investors may be perceived as the 'new trusts': a modern version of horizontal shareholder structures interconnecting competing firms.[55] The interest and curiosity in increasing common ownership by institutional investors arouse not only due to its *a priori* ambiguous welfare effects[56] but also even more because it challenges the fundamentals of antitrust (and organisational) conventional wisdom.

Traditionally, *minority cross-shareholdings* have been a natural object of competition law concern and attention considering the direct *competitive overlaps* between firms operating in a (horizontal or vertical) competitive relationship.[57] Now, a new 'economic blockbuster'[58] has become the epicentre of ground-breaking competition law and economics scholarship: the same group of large, concentrated, and diversified financial intermediaries partially own and control significant parallel shareholdings in the major competing firms within a given industry across the economy. On the one hand, the stakes held by each institutional investor in individual firms are small in absolute terms, thus considered 'non-controlling' on a stand-alone basis from a governance perspective, and often 'passive' given the indexation and portfolio diversification investment strategies employed by institutional investors from a finance perspective. However, empirical and theoretical economic research reveals that they may (and do) nonetheless affect competition outcomes in product markets.[59] Modern finance theory and the evolution of capital markets have transformed the investment landscape towards increasing diversification and institutional investment, with indirect (and unintended) consequences for corporate ownership,

[55] Elhauge (n 53) 269, 271 (noting that 'the reason that the Sherman Act was called an antitrust law was that it aimed to prohibit trusts that in fact were horizontal shareholders' but also that in contrast to 'pre-Sherman Act trusts' that were per se illegal as they involved 'horizontal agreements with no plausible procompetitive justification', horizontal shareholdings by institutional investors should be scrutinised under a rule of reason standard as they 'provide investment capital and diversification benefits').

[56] That is both anti- and pro-competitive effects. See Á López and X Vives, 'Overlapping Ownership, R&D Spillovers, and Antitrust Policy' (2019) 127 J Pol Econ 2394; J Azar and X Vives, 'General Equilibrium Oligopoly and Ownership Structure' (2021) 89 *Econometrica* 999; M Backus, C Conlon and M Sinkinson, 'The Common Ownership Hypothesis: Theory and Evidence' (2019) Brookings Economic Studies Report https://www.brookings.edu/wp-content/uploads/2019/02/ES_20190205_Common-Ownership.pdf; O Shy and R Stenbacka, 'Common Ownership, Institutional Investors, and Welfare' (2020) 29 J Econ & Manage Strat 706; O Shy and R Stenbacka, 'An OLG Model of Common Ownership: Effects on Consumption and Investments' (2019) 62 J Macroecon 103155; A Gibbon and J Schain, 'Rising Markups, Common Ownership, and Technological Capacities' (2022) Int J Ind Organ https://doi.org/10.1016/j.ijindorg.2022.102900.

[57] OECD, 'Antitrust Issues Involving Minority Shareholdings and Interlocking Directorates' (2009) DAF/COMP(2008)30.

[58] Elhauge (n 49) 1267.

[59] Azar, Schmalz and Tecu (n 48); J Azar, S Raina and M Schmalz, 'Ultimate Ownership and Bank Competition' (2016) Working Paper https://papers.ssrn.com/sol3/papers.cfm?abstract_id=2710252; M Newham, J Seldeslachts and A Banal-Estanol, 'Common Ownership and Market Entry: Evidence from Pharmaceutical Industry' (2018) DIW Berlin Discussion Paper 1738.

governance, and industry structure.[60] The intriguing possibility raised by the 'common ownership hypothesis' is that the combination of institutional re-concentration of ownership and portfolio diversification has systemic corporate governance and market competition effects.[61] In the case of *minority common shareholdings*, the (partial) *shareholder overlaps* in the ownership structure of the major competitors in concentrated industries that are said to (indirectly) increase the 'effective' market concentration and also produce competition harm and possibly productive efficiencies.[62] In effect, the common (financial) owners of rival (industrial) firms may have the incentives and ability to affect the operation of firms and markets away from individual profit maximisation leading to increased prices and reduced industry output.[63]

The fundamental antitrust question is: is this 'new wine' that needs to be distilled and fit into 'old (legal) bottles' or would such a fit simply be unnatural – an 'antitrust overkill'? The myriad of new concerns and possibilities common ownership raises in a variety of legal and economic fields may easily let the debate go astray. Yet, the intimate relation between competition and corporate governance and finance lay at its heart, both in terms of theory and practice. What policy-makers decide on either side shall have profound implications on the way firms are organised and governed as well as on how financial and product markets operate.[64] Therefore, the

[60] Azar (n 2) 263; R Gilson and J Gordon, 'The Agency Costs of Agency Capitalism: Activist Investors and the Revaluation of Governance Rights' (2013) 113 Colum L Rev 863; B Braun, 'American Asset Manager Capitalism' 25–26 https://osf.io/preprints/socarxiv/v6gue/ ('the Great Re-Concentration and the growth of asset managers have transformed the U.S. into a concentrated-ownership liberal market economy with strong minority shareholders and a large amount of indexed, and thus patient, capital. […] Two features, however, distinguish the new asset manager capitalism from the Gilded Age money trust [as well as from corporatist "Germany, Inc." prior to the 1990s]. First, unlike their robber baron predecessors, today's dominant owners are fully diversified. Second, asset managers are economically disinterested intermediaries – they lack skin in the corporate game. […] their business model is to compete for capital and management fees from investors. [They] only own the legal title, not the economic interest in the corporations whose stock they hold. […] asset manager capitalism is without historical precedent.').

[61] Azar (n 2); Backus, Conlon and Sinkinson, 'The Common Ownership Hypothesis' (n 56); J Coffee, 'The Future of Disclosure: ESG, Common Ownership, and Systematic Risk' (2020) ECGI Law Working Paper 541/2020.

[62] Azar and Vives (n 56).

[63] M Schmalz, 'Common-Ownership Concentration and Corporate Conduct' (2018) 10 Annu Rev Financ Econ 413; M Condon, 'Externalities and the Common Owner' (2020) 95 Wash L Rev 1.

[64] See for example the recent but opposing policy initiatives for EU merger control reform regarding minority shareholding (2014) vis-à-vis the Capital Markets Union initiative (2015) and the Revised Shareholder Rights Directive (2017). Arguably, more 'active' and 'empowered' common institutional owners may inadvertently exacerbate any competition concerns over minority shareholding that currently fall outside the EUMR to the extent it is deemed 'non-controlling'. Analogously, specialised regulators in the US move to opposing directions: despite the FTC Hearings on the competition implications of common ownership (2018), the SEC is proposing reforms to limit disclosure obligations for institutional investment managers regarding reporting of their equity holdings (2020).

aforementioned functional regulatory schism offers no excuse for overlooking the systemic consequences of the issue in point.[65]

15.5 SHAREHOLDING TYPES AND ANTITRUST: THE CONTROLLING, THE PASSIVE, AND THE INFLUENTIAL

Let us then take a step back and refocus the analysis in order to better appreciate where we stand. From a competition perspective, the interesting cases of minority shareholding have been those involving 'non-controlling' or 'passive' financial stakes acquired in rival firms, which may escape antitrust scrutiny.[66] Despite the gradual updating of antitrust rules to capture new forms of potentially anticompetitive practices, it remains a matter of debate whether their scope or interpretation extends to 'partial' ownership of a competitor[67] when participation in the share capital is limited to a *minority position* (nominal equity holding) and not accompanied by *majority voting* control (corporate legal control),[68] or any other form of *active influence* (by means of governance actions or activist intent) over the commercial activity of the competing company.[69] Complex theoretical and factual issues at the intersection of competition and corporate laws naturally arise in the analysis of those cases. Changes in the ownership structure (shareholder base) of firms may impact corporate governance (managerial and firm behaviour) which in turn affects competition (market concentration and industry performance).

Usually, control is seen as a key determinant of an antitrust theory harm and also part of the mechanism that translates (partial) common ownership into suboptimal

[65] As the popular parable goes: 'In the land of the blind, the one-eyed man is king' (Desiderius Erasmus is credited with first coining the phrase and coding it in his Adagia (1500)). Let us then proceed on the issue of common ownership cautiously with the limited knowledge we possess at hand, rather than hide behind the limited capacity and mandate of specialised regulators to look at a fragmented view of the problem and thus miss the 'big picture'.

[66] The first term is usually employed in the EU context to suggest the absence of 'legal control' that is used as a jurisdictional criterion under EU merger rules; the latter term is most common in US law & economics literature suggesting that the shareholding is 'silent' (non-voting) or a 'purely financial interest' (without any corresponding 'control rights'), thus not directly affecting the partially acquired rival's behaviour. See D O'Brien and S Salop, 'Competitive Effects of Partial Ownership: Financial Interest and Corporate Control' (2000) 67 Antitrust LJ 559. This terminology also fits the open-ended 'economic effects' jurisdictional test and 'passive investment' exception under US merger control rules. See n 19 and 26 and surrounding text.

[67] Ultimately, both 'cross-ownership' and 'common ownership' are distinct forms (direct vs indirect) of partial ownership of firms competing in the same relevant market. See Tzanaki (n 5).

[68] That is holding 'less than 50% of voting rights attached to the equity of the target firm'. See Annex I 'Economic Literature on Non-Controlling Minority Shareholdings ("Structural links")' to Commission Staff Working Document, 'Towards More Effective EU Merger Control' SWD(2013) 239 final, para 19.

[69] Tzanaki (n 1). In other words, the competition law concept of control ('inter-firm') analytically relies on corporate law conceptions of control ('intra-firm'). For a theoretical voting model that formally links the two, see J Azar, 'Portfolio Diversification, Market Power, and the Theory of the Firm' (2016) Working Paper http://papers.ssrn.com/abstract=2811221.

corporate and market outcomes.[70] Yet, 'control' is a complex and multifaceted concept, and 'partial' control arising from minority shareholding is not clear or well established in legal or economic theory.[71] Indeed, it is often a form of 'factual' control situation that may heavily depend on the surrounding context and specifics of the particular case.[72] At this point, it becomes both interesting and instructive that minority shareholding alludes to the 'many faces' of ownership[73] and 'shades' of control, with each combination leading to different kinds and degrees of competition effects. The variety in effect contrasts sharply with our limited word stock that is often misleading or inaccurate given the overlapping use of common terms such as (ownership or) control for different purposes and bodies of law. In order to dissolve some of the unnecessary confusion and elucidate the competitive harm potential of distinct shareholding types, I elaborate on the different layers of control attending a given minority position. Accordingly, minority shareholding can be classified as follows:

i) *controlling* or *non-controlling* – from the perspective of (EU) competition law – depending on whether the acquirer is able to exercise formal (legal) control over the target or not;[74]
ii) *solely* or *jointly (partially) controlling* – from the perspective of (EU) competition law – depending on whether there is a single dominant shareholder with clear (*de jure*) sole control over the target or control is (*de facto*) shared among many individual minority shareholders, in *ex ante* unascertainable ways (e.g. if joint control exists on the basis of 'changing coalitions' and no 'stable' majority can be established even in the presence of equal equity positions and identical rights among the shareholders[75]);

70 For instance, theories of harm on 'unilateral' anticompetitive effects rely on formally modelling 'control weights' corresponding to 'financial interests' arising out of the acquired shareholding. See O'Brien and Salop (n 66); Azar, Schmalz and Tecu (n 48); Backus, Conlon and Sinkinson (n 1).

71 D O'Brien and K Waehrer, 'The Competitive Effects of Common Ownership: We Know Less than We Think' (2017) 81 *Antitrust LJ* 729, 766–767; Tzanaki (n 5) 8 ('common ownership is not associated to either formal legal control or even clear economic control of the firm on a stand-alone basis but rather with situations of indirect, *de facto*, collective control in firm governance and product markets due to the interaction and cumulative effect of small parallel holdings in competitors by diversified investors').

72 Tzanaki (n 1) 177, 184, 189, 222, 233, 242-243.

73 Tzanaki (n 5) 3. The double separation of 'ownership from ownership' and of 'ownership from control' have split property entitlements in the firm between 'ultimate' and 'beneficial' owners, or between 'legal' and 'economic' owners.

74 See n 19 above and surrounding text.

75 Such minority shareholdings, albeit cumulatively as a group may lead to a situation of *factual* joint control (*de facto* voting bloc power), fall outside the scope of the EUMR as it defines 'joint control' on a *legal* basis (majority control by 'stable coalitions' that is *ex ante* verifiable and creates a 'permanent' change in control) and given a 'strong commonality of interests' (that goes beyond any 'symmetric' financial interests and control rights attached to the equity holdings). Tzanaki (n 15) 84. See also O'Brien and Salop (n 66) 570; M Corradi, 'Bridging the Gap in the Shifting Sands of Non-Controlling Financial Holdings?' (2016) 39 W Comp 239, 248–249.

iii) *active* or *passive* – from the perspective of corporate law – depending on the acquirer's ability to exercise some active (economic) influence over the target or not, usually given its shareholder rights or corporate governance actions;[76]

iv) *totally* or *partially controlling*[77] *(actively influential)*[78] – from the perspective of competition economics and corporate governance – depending on whether there is a dominant shareholder with clear total (legal) control, due to either a majority or a minority equity holding, or a formally non-controlling minority shareholder with some (economic) influence over the target, due to a *de facto* 'blocking minority' (veto power) or some other situation of 'informal influence' arising out of statutory corporate law or contractual rights (e.g. voting rights, information rights, disproportionate board representation, board observer seats);[79] and

v) *actively or passively (strategically)*[80] *influential* – from the perspective of competition economics and corporate governance – depending on whether an 'active' shareholding directly affects the behaviour of the acquired firm given the acquirer's ability to exercise active influence over the target, by operating within its corporate governance, or a formally 'non-controlling' or 'passive' shareholding affects the acquirer's own incentives to compete due to the strategic interaction between rival firms in oligopoly even if the competitors are linked by purely financial interests without any apparent influence or control in the target's governance.[81]

The above exposition reveals that the legal and economic views of the different shareholding types are not fully overlapping. That is, some shareholdings that are: a) only 'partially' or not standalone controlling or b) completely 'non-controlling' and 'passive' as a matter of competition or corporate law, and possibly outside the reach of antitrust or merger laws, may still turn out to be 'competitively influential'

76 See n 24 and 26 above and surrounding text.

77 This distinction (total vs partial control) largely corresponds to the one first suggested by O'Brien and Salop (n 66) 577–584 in their seminal analysis of 'partial ownership' (who also propose several analytical sub-categories of 'partial control') and the quantification of its competitive implications in terms of degree of potential harm.

78 As noted above, some countries (Germany, UK) use such a broader jurisdictional criterion (competitively significant or material influence) based on corporate law rules and an analysis of the actual governance dynamics (eg shareholding position equivalent to that of a blockholder of above 25%) to determine the scope of their merger control regime. See n 24 and 26 above.

79 See relatedly Commission, 'Staff Working Document accompanying the White Paper, "Towards More Effective EU Merger Control"' SWD (2014) 221 final, paras 90–93.

80 In my doctoral dissertation I propose the term 'influential' in the economic sense to signify 'intermediate' cases of minority shareholding that may give rise to positive or negative 'strategic influence' and thus affect the competition dynamics, although formally 'non-controlling' in the legal sense. See Tzanaki (n 15). Unlike actively influential shareholding, strategically influential minority shareholdings are not systematically captured by existing competition and merger control rules. See Tzanaki (n 1), section II.B.

81 Tzanaki (n 1) 232.

as a matter of industrial organisational theory. The economics perspective also vividly illustrates that there is a continuum of effects on competition due to the multiple shades of control and non-control that accompany minority shareholdings. Effectively, this economics-informed analysis adds another shareholding type in the traditional legal dichotomy – controlling, *influential*, passive – that may be of competition concern. That said, this continuity in effects does not necessarily suggest that there is a linear progression in terms of the magnitude of potential harm: occasionally a totally controlling shareholding (active sole control) may be quantitatively more detrimental to competition than a full merger,[82] or similarly, partially controlling or mutually influential shareholdings (*de facto* joint control) may be equally harmful to a full merger.[83]

A visual representation of the taxonomy of shareholding types based on their control qualities from the three distinct analytical perspectives employed above is shown in the following table. The cells highlighted in grey illustrate the potentially problematic (competitively influential) minority shareholdings that may escape competition scrutiny in certain jurisdictions such as the EU or others that follow its example and the underlying reasons that trigger this situation, i.e. legal gaps due to formalistic definitions of shareholdings in competition or corporate law. In light of the above, it is also important to realise that both active and passive minority shareholdings may give rise to 'competitive influence', which may flow from either governance influence or strategic influence, respectively.[84] The table thus visually reflects how precisely and what specific types of minority shareholding came to 'fall between the cracks'.

Taxonomy of shareholding types			
Competition law	Non-controlling	*Actively influential*	Controlling
Corporate law	Passive	*De facto controlling*	Active
Competition economics	*Strategically influential (pure financial interest)*	*Partially controlling (jointly controlling)*	Totally controlling (solely controlling)

Seen from the broader economic point of view, competitively 'influential' minority shareholding may be further subcategorised, considering the time horizon, intensity of economic control, and degree or reciprocity of profit internalisation, as follows:

i) *statically* or *dynamically influential* – depending on whether the acquirer is able to exercise current influence over the target, and thus have an observable impact on competition (present effects) or possibly exercise future influence

[82] O'Brien and Salop (n 66) 578–579.
[83] Tzanaki (n 1) 224.
[84] *Ibid.* at 9, 72.

(potential effects), in light of its theoretical shareholder rights that could put into use (e.g. voting or other special contractual rights such as rights of first refusal);[85]

ii) *proportionately* or *disproportionately influential* – depending on whether the acquirer's degree of internalisation of rival profits (the 'profit weight' as a function of financial interest and control[86]) is proportionate to its partial shareholding investment in that rival (the 'control weight' is equal to the nominal percentage of the equity position[87]) or disproportionate (the actual degree of control vis-à-vis the target's management discretion ('agency costs') is more or less than the nominal equity position);[88]

iii) *one-directionally or bi-directionally influential* – depending on whether only the acquirer is induced to internalise its partially acquired rival's profits, due to its financial interest linked to its shareholding investment, or also the target is induced to take into account the acquirer's shareholding,[89] due to the latter's corporate influence exercised in the target firm's governance,[90] or due

85 Tzanaki (n 15) 87, 96. This distinction focuses on the time horizon of the (present or future) manifestation of competition effects, rather than the time horizon of holding the minority investment stake (ie whether an equity holding is temporary or long-lasting). In fact, depending on the circumstances, a long-term shareholding may have both static and dynamic effects on competition, but possibly also only dynamic ones.

86 Backus, Conlon and Sinkinson (n 1) (suggesting that the common owners' 'profit weights' may be mathematically decomposed into two elements: 'overlapping ownership' and 'relative investor concentration').

87 O'Brien and Salop (n 66) 583 (discussing the 'proportional control' scenario flowing from 'partial ownership').

88 For instance, the theoretical 'proportional control' assumption regarding 'voting' shareholding may not be justified and could be revised accordingly in the specific case. See D O'Brien and S Salop, 'The Competitive Effects of Passive Minority Equity Interests: Reply' (2001) 69 Antitrust LJ 611, 622–625 (suggesting applying a 'discount rate' in estimating the competitive effects of shareholding and calculating the MHHI when the acquirer has no ability to exercise control over the target management in practice, thus no influence over the use and distribution of the target's profits); Azar (n 2) 286–293 (analysing common ownership with managerial entrenchment ('agency costs') within a context of oligopoly theory with (and without) shareholder voting, in which case the theoretical anticompetitive incentives of common owners towards monopoly (under a proportional control assumption) are attenuated).

89 M Hunold and F Schlütter, 'Vertical Financial Interest and Corporate Influence' (2019) DICE Discussion Paper 309, Düsseldorf University Press. Importantly, it is noted that also a unilateral shareholding *may* be able to produce reciprocal influence, ie 'bi-directional internalisation' for the acquirer and the target in case the partial shareholding is accompanied both by cash flow (profit) and control rights. Partial control over the target, even if 'unilateral', matters in estimating both the acquirer's own internalisation function but also that of the partially acquired rival as it affects the incentives of both. That is, the acquirer's 'control rights in one direction' (corporate influence) are said to potentially have the same effect *as if* the target had 'profit rights in the other direction' (financial interest), which is functionally equivalent to a 'reciprocal' shareholding (pure financial interest) by the acquirer and the target in each other.

90 The corporate influence exercised by means of the acquirer's minority shareholding in the target need not be positive ('incentive' to internalise acquirer's profits) but may also be negative ('constraint' on the target's competitive choices or actions). Partial control or influence over the target may lead to a

to target's own parallel shareholding and financial interest in the acquirer.[91] Importantly, a 'bi-directionally influential' minority shareholding (mutual internalisation) need not be harmful to competition (softening of competition or collusion) due to the internalisation of competitive externalities but may also be welfare enhancing (pro-competitive or efficiency creating) due to internalisation of productive or innovation spillovers.[92]

15.6 COMMON SHAREHOLDING IN ANTITRUST AND CORPORATE GOVERNANCE: FROM COMPETITION EFFECTS TO PROPERTY RIGHTS

It follows from the above analysis that minority shareholding that is considered 'non-controlling' or 'passive' in the legal sense may well be *de facto* competitively 'influential' in the economic sense given its present or potential impact on the corporate control and competition dynamics. Further, from a corporate perspective, so long as the shareholding is 'voting' stock it is not really a passive one but rather *dynamically* influential in that the power of the vote may always be exercised later in the future,[93] or in fact, the implicit threat stemming from its mere existence may produce *current* results and change equilibrium outcomes given its deterrent disciplining effect.[94] In addition, so long as stock is voting and 'freely

situation of 'mutual internalisation' or to a 'competitive disadvantage' imposed on the target (and an 'artificial advantage' secured by the acquirer). See M Hunold and K Stahl, 'Passive Vertical Integration and Strategic Delegation' (2016) 47 Rand J Econ 891; I Lianos and others, 'Financialisation of the Food Value Chain, Common Ownership and Competition Law' (2019) 16 ECJ 149; Tzanaki (n 15).

91 A 'bi-directionally influential' minority shareholding may thus also arise because of purely financial interests among competitors that are parallel and induce an alignment of interests of rival firms and their managers to their shareholders' interests under a unilateral theory of harm. This situation may emerge only due to a 'passive' form of economic control that implicitly relies on the assumption that shareholders are interested in the internalisation of competitive externalities of the rival firms' conduct and managers are interested in the maximisation of shareholder profits. See Tzanaki (n 1) (elaborating on plausible passive influence mechanisms); R Inderst and S Thomas, 'Common Ownership and Mergers between Portfolio Companies' (2019) 42 W Comp 551 (outlining the unilateral theory of harm based on common ownership); J Azar and A Tzanaki, 'Common Ownership and Merger Control Enforcement' in Ioannis Kokkoris and Claudia Lemus (eds), *Research Handbook on the Law and Economics of Competition Enforcement* (Edward Elgar Publishing, 2022) (similarly).

92 López and Vives (n 56); Azar and Vives (n 56).

93 Although potentially in combination with other voting shareholders in order to reach the requisite majority under corporate law (majority voting bloc), if not possible by means of the *de jure* or *de facto* vote share corresponding to any individual minority shareholding. The *possibility* of a majority voting position or coalition is critical to make the shareholders' threat to vote against management 'credible'. See A Shleifer and R Vishny, 'A Survey of Corporate Governance' (1997) 52 J Fin 737, 764–765. Thus, while (a group of) concentrated shareholder(s) may be relied upon to solve the 'free rider problem' among shareholders in corporate governance and as a result, the vertical agency problem; if the coalition is solid albeit changing, they may potentially create a horizontal agency problem between the shareholders who are in control versus others.

94 In equilibrium the vote need not be exercised to impact outcomes and behaviour. Its potential use may discipline management and change behaviour as long as the threat of its use is 'credible' and the

tradable' (either as a package of share plus vote or simply the vote), there is no real 'separation of ownership and control'[95] in the sense that corporate control is *contestable*.[96] Management is disciplined by both the stock market and the market for corporate control, while shareholders remain 'residual claimants'[97] with the power to hold/exercise and buy/sell their votes. The latter bear both the residual risk and the corresponding residual rights to control of the corporate property (due to their equity share in the corporation's profits). Thus, the 'atom of property',[98] albeit diffused among many shareholders and partially split between principals-passive owners and agents-actual managers in large public corporations,[99] is remarkably solid: out of all corporate constituents, only shareholders as a class generally bear the marginal gains and losses of corporate actions or omissions and thus have the right incentives at the margin to check and redirect management towards improved

possession of voting rights is 'known' (conditions easily met since voting rights typically attend shareholding by statute, unless otherwise provided, and majority voting control is possible absent a dominant blockholder) in order to be anticipated, internalised and be able to *ex ante* deter undesirable behaviour. For the realistic nature of such potential, see Coffee (n 61) discussing two fundamental changes occurring in US securities markets: '(1) institutionalization (with the result that institutional investors now dominate both trading and stock ownership); (2) extraordinary ownership concentration (with the consequence that the three largest U.S. institutional investors now hold 20% and vote 25% of the shares in S&P 500 companies)'.

95 G Stigler and C Friedland, 'The Literature of Economics: The Case of Berle and Means' (1983) 26 JLE 237, 248 ('The majority of the voting stock is the ultimate control over a corporation even if that stock is diffused among many owners. The stock may be acquired by a small group by stock purchases if the shares become an attractive speculation, so in an ultimate sense ownership and control cannot be separated. […] In the absence of a struggle for control, one cannot know whether a given management or set of stockholders controls the selection of the board, or indeed whether they are a single coalition. We suggest a test of *de facto* control').

96 Given the threat of takeover against inefficient firm managers, ultimate control remains with shareholders even in large corporations. See n 30 above, especially Manne (1981) regarding the dynamics of the market for corporate control and the significance of the free transferability of votes; K Kastiel and Y Nili, 'Competing for Votes' (2020) 10 Harv Bus L Rev 287 (suggesting that the free 'float' of votes, the distribution of control/ voting power among shareholders and the fluctuation in voting patterns matter for the intensity of competition for votes [the 'liquidity' of this voting market] to reach majority control).

97 From a financial point of view, all common stock shareholders of large corporations – regardless of the distribution of power within a given corporation – are considered 'residual risk bearers' that 'contract for the rights to the net cash flows' and thus have a residual claim in the firm's profits. See E Fama and M Jensen, 'Agency Problems and Residual Claims' (1983) 26 JLE 327, 428. From a corporate law perspective, however, one also needs to consider any relevant statutes and bylaws to see whether there are multiple classes of equity and whether some of them may not be qualified as having a residual claim.

98 L Ryan, 'Shareholders and the Atom of Property: Fission or Fusion?' (2000) 39(1) Bus & Soc 49 ('if the atom did split, it may now be fused' given the recent re-concentration of corporate ownership and control, in light of the growth and governance role of institutional investors).

99 Although shareholders are 'passive' property owners in the sense that they have delegated day-to-day management and operational decisions of the corporation to 'specialised agents', they retain (latent) 'ultimate control' as principals and can shift the strategic direction of the organisation by possessing the residual control rights (voting) or by operation of the market for corporate control (takeover). This specialisation of functions, including the shareholder-investor 'passivity', is an inherent feature of the

corporate performance by the (actual) use or (deterrent effect of) possession of voting rights.[100] Consequently, shareholders' private profit motive remains the (valid) driver for financial investment in corporations and management discipline as well as for more efficient use of an industrial property. Private property, free markets, and competition reassuringly remain the 'holy triad' upon which modern corporate and industrial organisation solidly relies.[101]

The above analysis also makes clear that investor 'passivity' does not necessarily translate into permanent corporate 'silence' or would justify an *a priori* antitrust immunity.[102] If the minority shareholding is accompanied by voting rights and the shares or votes can be exchanged, potential control persists. Yet it is difficult to tell *ex ante* if and how such shareholder power may be exercised.[103] Considering this *ex ante* uncertainty and the importance of the surrounding factual circumstances (shareholder control dynamics, market and legal constraints) to assess the competitive significance and effects of any minority shareholding, it is unlikely that a purely *ex ante* merger control regime will be effective in distinguishing and addressing potentially harmful cases of minority cross- or common shareholding. This is so even if such prophylactic regimes were not structural (corporate law model) or formalistic (as in EU merger control) but effects-based (as in US merger control).

modern corporate form and does not upset *per se* the allocation of property *rights* in the firm. Thus, although shareholders may occasionally *de facto* lose (part of) their corporate power vis-à-vis management, they always hold the *legal* right to control (as a group). See J Coates, 'The Future of Corporate Governance Part I: The Problem of Twelve' (2018) Harvard Public Law Working Paper No 19-07. Managerial entrenchment and fiduciary duties towards shareholders-principals are factual matters. See M Isaksson and S Çelik, 'Who Cares? Corporate Governance in Today's Equity Markets' (2013) 8 OECD Corporate Governance Working Papers No 8 50 (discussing the fiduciary duty of institutional investors to their ultimate beneficiaries, whose interpretation they suggest is an 'empirical matter').

100 Easterbrook and Fischel (n 30) 403–406 ('shareholders are the residual claimants to the firm's income. [...] The right to vote [that is, the right to exercise discretion] follows the residual claim.').

101 A Alchian, 'Corporate Management and Property Rights' in Henry G Manne (ed), *Economic Policy and the Regulation of Corporate Securities* (American Enterprise Institute 1969) 339, 342, 350.

102 O'Brien and Salop (n 88) 625 (suggesting that even a conservative economic 'analysis would not justify an exemption from Section 7 or a dramatic increase in antitrust permissiveness towards passive minority financial interests'); Elhauge (n 49) 1305–1312 (cogently explaining that even institutional investors with passive financial investment strategies do not usually qualify for either the substantive [liability] or the filing [notification] passive investment exemption under US merger control given that: i) 'antitrust passivity' requires lack of any (even legitimate) influence (voice, voting) by large institutional investors as 'active owners' that may affect corporate management and, in any event, is negated in case of actual anticompetitive effects, and ii) the filing exemption narrowly applies to investors with 'no intention to participate in or influence management' who acquire less than 10% of the target's voting securities (15% for the special case of institutional investors); while US antitrust authorities consider 'merely voting' as not *a priori* inconsistent with 'passive investment intent', it is suggested that in light of the latest common ownership scholarship, this interpretation of the statute is 'unwisely overbroad because horizontal investors who individually have less than 10–15% of corporate stock can nonetheless significantly alter the competitive incentives of corporate management by simply voting their shares, especially because collectively their share of corporate stock may be far higher than 10–15%').

103 That is, when and how a *dynamically* influential shareholding may turn into a *statically* influential one.

Nonetheless, the US merger regime has a resolutely sound economic structure: its open-ended scope for liability (no safe harbour for any actual 'lessening of competition') combined with its 'passive investment' exemption from filing a notification provide both flexibility and reduced regulatory burden yet leave the door open for 'residual *ex post* enforcement' in case a 'passive' investor's initial intent changes later and becomes 'active'. Furthermore, the 'solely for investment' exemption explicitly does not apply in case of cross-shareholding (the acquirer is a competitor) or interlocking directorates (a controlling shareholder, director, officer, or employee simultaneously serves as an officer or director of the issuer), and more generally if the holder of voting securities (1) nominates a board candidate or is represented in the corporate board; (2) submits a shareholder proposal for approval; or (3) solicits proxies.[104] Therefore, US merger law is fit to capture a range of potentially problematic minority acquisitions by applying: i) an *ex ante* licensing regime (transaction filing and regulatory approval) when the potential of harm is most likely to materialise (active financial investments) and foreseeable (present corporate influence) and ii) an *ex post* safety valve (potential future liability and enforcement) when passive intent is negated by the acquirer's subsequent corporate governance actions (*ex post* opportunism) or actual competition harm is evidenced (passive financial investments, individually or collectively). Seen in this light, 'passive' minority shareholding merely indicates cases where a full fact-specific antitrust analysis is required. If needed, such analysis will become relevant after the actual acquisition.

While *investor passivity* and the *vertical agency problem* are an inherent part of the modern corporation model and no obstacle to antitrust enforcement, the real challenge for both corporate and antitrust law is *investor diversification*. Common shareholding that is not only 'passive' but also 'diversified' changes the analysis completely: it surely can be 'influential' in the antitrust sense (in terms of its competition impact) but in counterintuitive ways (in terms of its mechanics). The 'separation of ownership from ownership'[105] and the ensuing *horizontal agency problem* (potential conflicts between diversified versus undiversified shareholders) challenge long-standing foundations and analytical frames in corporate finance and governance (shareholder unanimity[106] or homogeneity as a class[107]) and competition

[104] Elhauge (n 49) 1311–1312 (discussing the statutory requirements and the related guidance by US antitrust agencies).

[105] See n 31 above.

[106] H DeAngelo, 'Competition and Unanimity' (1981) 71 Am Econ Rev 18; Azar (n 2) 272.

[107] On the 'Fisher Separation Theorem' which shows that under perfect competition all shareholders agree on a 'single firm objective' (own firm profit maximisation) that may hold 'despite the heterogeneity of shareholders' preferences' under certain conditions, and on the heterogeneity (and complexity) of institutional investors and the shareholdings in their portfolios, see A Romano, 'Horizontal Shareholding and Network Theory' (2021) 38 Yale J on Reg 363, 366 ('The problem with diffuse institutional ownership is not so much that it reduces the incentives of horizontal competitors to engage in aggressive competition, but that it results in institutional investors having a different objective function from that of other shareholders.'; and quoting 'Hansmann [who] argued that one of the advantages of

law (control-based and entity-centric antitrust analysis[108]). The 'democratisation of investment'[109] brought about by the 'index investing revolution'[110] has triumphantly enabled access to low-cost, widely diversified portfolios via a single investment product for a wider part of the population. However, this paradigmatic shift towards passive portfolio investment strategies has transformed not only the investment landscape but also it has created far beyond ripple effects yet to be fully appreciated. For one, the resultant widely diversified ownership structures (shareholder overlaps in many competing firms across industries) may well make firm-specific or market structure irrelevant, signalling a fundamental change not from firm 'independence' to inter-firm 'control' (the focal point of traditional antitrust analysis), but from shareholder 'focus' to investor 'indifference' (the new corporate reality brought about by financial innovation).[111] Diversified investors are rationally interested in the aggregate return gained from their portfolio investments,[112] following a portfolio-wide investment and governance strategy,[113] and less so in the individual

investor-owned firms is that "investors generally share a single well-defined objective: to maximize the net present value of the firm's earnings per dollar invested."'); E Rock and D Rubinfeld, 'Antitrust for Institutional Investors' (2017) NYU Law and Economics Research Paper 17-23 10–16 (noting that the common ownership thesis explicitly challenges 'the basic assumption in finance research that a firm's objective is to maximize its own value and that firm and investor optimization are separable' and also, it 'assumes implicitly that individual firms maximize the weighted average of the profits enjoyed by the shareholders of the firms, accounting for the shareholders' ownership of horizontal competitors.').

108 Under EU competition law, 'positive' control (actual) is key to determine whether firms form part of a 'single economic entity' (for purposes of vicariously attributing parental liability for subsidiary companies' antitrust violations under Article 101 TFEU) and 'negative' control (potential) is the criterion used to decide whether there is a 'merger or acquisition' (for purposes of assessing jurisdiction in case of a possible permanent change of control between previously independent companies, and increased market concentration, under the EUMR).

109 B Novick, 'How Index Funds Democratize Investing' *Wall Street Journal* (New York, 10 January 2017) A.11; J Duca, 'The Democratization of America's Capital Markets' (2001) Federal Reserve Bank of Dallas – Economic and Financial Review 10 (noting the 'dramatic' decline in transaction costs of mutual funds and ETFs, that induced rising household investing in 'a diversified stock portfolio by buying mutual fund shares rather than by directly buying stocks').

110 R Wigglesworth, 'Passive Attack: The Story of a Wall Street Revolution' (*Financial Times*, 20 December 2018). Critics had called 'the greatest invention in the history of finance', the 'index-tracking mutual fund' for mass investors, as 'un-American', 'devouring capitalism' and 'worse than Marxism' as it aimed at mimicking the market and achieving 'average returns' for investors.

111 See L Boller and F Scott Morton, 'Testing the Theory of Common Stock Ownership' (2019) NBER Working Paper 27515, 6 (distinguishing between 'common ownership' by diversified, overlapping shareholders and 'focused ownership' by undiversified shareholders that have more incentives to compete in product markets as they internalise only profits from their own firm); and n 35 above (where Hovenkamp and Rodrigues describe the model of the 'indifferent investor' propelled by modern finance advances). To be sure, common ownership induced by passive index investment can be an extreme example of financial diversification that exacerbates its effects such as the 'indifference' of diversified investors.

112 That is both diversified institutional investors and the part of retail or individual investors that are indirectly diversified through them.

113 Coffee (n 61) 2–5, 36 ('Not since Berle and Means announced the separation of ownership and control have shareholders as a group perceived themselves to possess the power to behave as "true owners." But, unlike the "true owners" of the 19th Century [the railroad, oil and bank barons], the

performance of portfolio companies[114] or spurring atomistic competition in product markets.[115] Common diversified shareholding takes the 'depersonalisation of ownership' of the public corporation[116] one step further: private property interests have become not only 'split' as in the age of managerial capitalism (specialisation of ownership and management functions) but also 'parallel' and 'concurrent' in the current capitalism era of professional portfolio managers and savings planners[117] (many small shareholders are partial 'co-owners' not only of a single but also several competing corporate enterprises at the same time). Corporate ownership is rendered both diffuse and collectivised at the same time: the concern now is not the 'objectification of the corporate enterprise'[118] (with business management separate and independent of its own shareholders – 'owners') but rather the 'institutionalisation'[119] of investment and savings (with institutional intermediaries separate and independent from any individual business corporation, and its undiversified shareholders). Consequently, the cherished image of a (homogeneous) shareholder as a corporate 'property owner' is shattered, and we may no longer speak of individual

focus of institutional investors as owners will logically shift to maximizing portfolio value, not the value of individual stocks. […] The era in which retail investors "owned" companies or moved the trading markets is long gone […] with high common ownership across a broad portfolio, it becomes rational and predictable that these institutional investors will make both investment and voting decisions on a portfolio-wide basis […]. This, in turn, permits the netting of gains and losses across the portfolio, and the implications of this transition are sweeping.').

114 Isaksson and Çelik (n 99) 38, 42 ('the fundamental economic rationale for providing shareholders with the means to monitor and engage' and '[a]ll of these rights are given to shareholders under the assumption that they, as residual claimants, have a unique incentive to care and inform themselves about the long-term success of the enterprise. It is assumed that there is a direct link between the performance of the corporation and the shareholder's income. […] this direct link is broken by an increasingly complex universe of intermediaries whose business is to manage other people's money. […] Has the fundamental incentive for active and informed ownership – on which so much of the corporate governance doctrine rests – simply disappeared for large or dominant groups of shareholders?'). It is also stressed that the different categories of shareholders, the 'lengthened and ever complex chain of intermediaries between savers and companies' and the great heterogeneity of institutional investors complicate general corporate governance policy, in particular given the possibility that 'regulatory initiatives to increase shareholder engagement may have unintended consequences'.

115 Azar (n 69) 17–20 (discussing the inapplicability of the Fischer separation theorem and the profit maximisation assumption of 'atomistic' firms if there is 'imperfect competition' in product markets and firms are not 'separately owned').

116 Berle and Means (n 28) 352 (quoting Walther Rathenau); Fisch (n 31) 886 (discussing the shareholder-centric model of corporate law on the basis of property rights theory and the implications given contemporary trends in institutional stock ownership).

117 R Clark, 'The Four Stages of Capitalism: Reflections on Investment Management Treatises' (1981) 94 Harv L Rev 561. The main figures and stage roles of investors along the evolutionary path of capitalism are said to be: (1) the entrepreneur, (2) the owner, (3) the capital supplier, and (4) the beneficiary.

118 Berle and Means (n 28) 352 (quoting Walther Rathenau); Fisch (n 31) 887.

119 D Langevoort, 'The SEC, Retail Investors, and the Institutionalization of the Securities Markets' (2009) 95 Va L Rev 1025, 1025–1026, 1081 (noting that the US securities regulator 'thinks of itself as the [retail] investors' advocate […] The last thirty years or so have brought a rapid shift toward institutionalization in the financial markets in the United States […] to repeat what now should be almost self-evident, the SEC is the retail investor's champion only in a bounded way.').

shareholders (even if passive investors) as 'residual risk bearers' identifiable with a distinct corporate organisation[120] as they may not fully bear any firm-specific risk or be concerned about targeted governance actions.[121]

The horizontal 'separation of capital from capital'[122] creates a 'double split' in the 'atom' of corporate property, both with regard to the unity and identity of its key *actors* (shareholders) and *components* (shares). On the one hand, institutionalisation has produced two sets of 'owners': 'ultimate' owners, who retain investment authority (but not necessarily voting control authority) and the associated risk for their investment choices, and 'beneficial' owners, who are only entitled to a future stream of profits from the invested funds (a claim that is more of a fixed contractual than residual nature).[123] It will depend on the circumstances to decide whether and who of any institutional or individual investors have in fact residual or beneficial ownership status. On the other hand, diversification introduces another form of 'decoupling'[124] financial interests (risk) from corporate control

[120] S Martin and F Partnoy, 'Encumbered Shares' (2005) 3 Ill L Rev 775, 778, 813 (speaking of 'financial innovation' and analogous derivates cases and their implications for the allocation of corporate voting [residual control] rights, 'it is far too simplistic to assume that shareholders uniformly hold the residual claims to a corporation's assets or cash flows.' [...] 'assumptions central to the paradigmatic position on corporate voting [homogeneity of shareholder preferences, residual claimant position of shareholders] are no longer valid.').

[121] Diversification acts as *de facto* insurance against such 'unsystematic' risk. See Coffee (n 61) 10, 35 (noting the divergence of interests between diversified institutional and undiversified individual investors as regards risk, the first being more exposed and sensitive to 'systematic' risk, which cannot be diversified away, while the latter are more interested in 'unsystematic' or firm-specific risk); Fisch (n 31) 882.

[122] See n 34 above.

[123] It may be that institutional investors bear the investment authority and associated risk, in which case they are the ones, perhaps counterintuitively, to be considered 'ultimate owners'. If retail investors retain investment risk and authority, they may still delegate any voting authority with regard to their shares to fund management agents. Thus, the identity of investors who have 'ultimate' or 'beneficial' status will depend on the details of the particular investments involved. See Tzanaki (n 5) 3–5 (pointing out the differences between index funds and ETFs regarding this distinction); Ryan (n 98) 68–69 (distinguishing between 'defined benefit' and 'defined contribution' retirement plans and analysing their respective property rights implications as to who, between institutional and retail investors, retains 'ultimate' versus 'beneficial' ownership status); cf Braun (n 60) 18 (analysing the position of 'disinterested' shareholders that hold 'the legal title (shares and the attached voting rights) but not the economic interest' vis-à-vis the 'ultimate "asset owners" (retail or institutional investors)').

[124] WG Ringe, 'Hedge Funds and Risk-Decoupling – The Empty Voting Problem in the European Union' (2013) 36 *Seattle U L Rev* 1027, 1030 ('while a normal shareholder would always bear a certain economic risk that corresponds to the size of their stake in the company, hedge [and analogously index] funds, by contrast, try to disconnect the relationship between equity and risk'). Risk-decoupling may be: i) 'negative' – 'a shareholder with reduced risk exposure retains its voting power and its influence in the company, but it does not bear the risk of negative returns'; or ii) 'positive' – 'activist investors acquire an economic stake in a company without gaining voting power', in which case no disclosure is required during a takeover. Risk-decoupling may create distorted incentives for the exercise of voting rights assigned to shareholdings and also 'private benefits of control' for the risk-decoupled shareholder (conflicts of interest with other shareholders). In essence, 'a risk-decoupled shareholder creates new agency costs'. See *ibid.* at 1059, 1062.

(influence).[125] That is, diversification of investment may render (legal) ownership 'empty'[126] and (voting) control 'hidden':[127] the legal title is not congruent with economic interest and voting power need not follow the residual claim. As the economic link between cash flow and control rights is broken, economic and voting ownership is no longer proportionate to the nominal equity holding of a shareholder.[128] Thus, the nominal level of the shareholding does not automatically reflect the level of economic risk and governance power a 'shareholder' may have.

This 'double split of ownership' in equity shareholding – i.e. 'two faces of ownership' and the 'risk-bearing dilution' brought about by passive, diversified investment[129] – has important implications for corporate governance. First, it significantly complicates the analysis as to who and to what extent is a residual claimant and thus raises questions as to the actual allocation of property rights in firms (real versus nominal owners). Second, it may lead to *ex ante* unforeseeable or *de facto* 'morphable' control situations. Given the fragmentation of shareholding in large public corporations and in the absence of a large dominant block holder or special asymmetric governance structures, control is likely shared among several shareholders and not *ex ante* ascertainable or fixed.[130] Control is 'morphable' in that although no single shareholder has standalone control, some of them have the *de facto* ability to form control coalitions as a group.[131] Third, it raises the possibility that the

125 Fisch (n 31) 882–883, 878 ('Diversification, however, decouples economic interest from ownership in the same way as complex financial products. […] the decoupling effected by intermediation offers the potential to alter corporate decision making. The extent to which this decoupling affects corporate operations depends on the extent to which intermediaries can exercise governance power. […] decoupling may create incentives for some market participants to exercise control rights in a manner that is inconsistent with the interests of other shareholders and the corporate enterprise and that, most problematically, these actions can be undertaken in secret.'); Ringe (n 124) 1066–1067 (noting that in case of 'risk-decoupling' by index funds as opposed to activist hedge funds, diversified institutional investors may come to 'hold the shares of two direct competitors' unintentionally or randomly whereas hedge funds' strategy is 'intentional').

126 Tzanaki (n 5) 4–5 (referring to this phenomenon as 'nominal ownership', 'bare ownership', 'ownership by proxy', 'ownership via intermediation'); cf Ryan (n 98) 49, 68–69 (speaking of 'ownership representation').

127 Or indeed, control becomes *de facto* 'morphable'. By reverse analogy to the terminology used by Hu and Black, who first analysed these 'decoupling' phenomena. See H Hu and B Black, 'The New Vote Buying: Empty Voting and Hidden (Morphable) Ownership' (2006) 79 South Calif Law Rev 811.

128 *Ibid.* at 908 ('existing legal and economic theories of the public corporation presume a [proportional] link between voting rights and economic ownership that can no longer be relied on.'); Ringe (n 124) 1073 ('Economically, […] a risk-decoupled share is more akin to debt than equity, but legally speaking, a risk decoupler remains a shareholder [of an empty shell] and retains the voting right. […] If this risk is eliminated, the justification for the assignment of voting rights disappears. […] A risk-free shareholder cannot fulfill the function of the vote – to express the best possible decision for the strategic direction of the company [and thus promote firm value, directly, and societal value, indirectly]').

129 Tzanaki (n 5) 3, 5.

130 Tzanaki (n 1) 184, 222, 243.

131 cf Hu and Black (n 127) 812.

individual self-interest may become 'destructive' both for the corporation and society as the pursuit of private profit and the exercise of voting rights may produce externalities on third parties (e.g. undiversified shareholders, other stakeholders, consumers) under certain circumstances.[132] Put differently, the concern is not only that individual investors may not be the 'real' owners and institutional investors are but also that no one is a truly responsible and concerned 'owner' in the traditional sense (sole proprietor).[133] With the (partial) separation between financial risk and control due to diversification, it is not that self-interest is extinguished but rather that the very diversified investors' self-interest is oriented towards the maximisation of their collective interests flowing from the pool of their portfolio invested firms' profits (portfolio value maximisation). In addition, there are actors (institutional investors and business managers) that could potentially implement such altered preferences – to the extent they come to benefit themselves from any strategic shift away from individual firm profit maximisation and atomistic market competition. Indirectly, this complex and opaque constellation of agency relationships and fragmentation of property rights may further raise concern as to the robustness of market forces (capital market, market for corporate control, product markets) to efficiently allocate financial or investment capital, to drive corporate management towards improved performance and to move economic resources to their most productive uses and users across society.

The implications for competition law are equally significant as diversification and common ownership by large institutional investors induce corporate shareholders to be both rationally 'apathetic' and 'indifferent'[134] – a mutation of the archetype.[135] At this point, it is worth revisiting the potential competitive effects of common shareholding in light of the above taxonomy on the various 'shades' of partial control related to partial ownership. Accordingly, common diversified shareholding, although individually a minority one with no standalone control, may be *dynamically* influential (potential effects on competition)[136] as it may affect both

[132] Of course, it is also possible that large, diversified investors' self-interest operates in 'beneficial' for society ways in that they may create positive externalities (innovation) or internalise negative ones (climate change). In fact, they have been called to act as 'stewards for the commons', see G Serafeim, 'Investors as Stewards of the Commons?' (2018) 30 *J App Corp Fin* 8. Importantly, however, the extent to which the self-interested activity of diversified investors produces net harm or benefit from a societal point of view always depends on whether this 'will benefit their portfolio on a net basis'. See Coffee (n 61). This is a factual matter.

[133] cf Coates (n 99) 2; Tzanaki (n 1) 217.

[134] Fully diversified investors become 'passive' (no control) and 'indifferent' (no ownership) given the devaluation or decoupling of the vote and the diluting of firm-specific risk that attends index funds and passive financial investment strategies, as noted above. This is not an aberration, but they should rationally be so, as per modern finance theory. Yet, in such novel universe, established notions and common language terms, such as (partial) ownership and control, start to lose meaning.

[135] See Hovenkamp (n 32) noting this evolutionary transformation in shareholder character.

[136] See n 85 above and surrounding text.

the commonly held firms' incentives to compete and their corporate governance.[137] Such common shareholding may further qualify as *disproportionately* influential (given the potential concentrated influence and financial interest of the common owners linked to the shareholding)[138] and also as *bi-directionally* influential (due to the potential mutual influence such shareholding may induce among the commonly held rival firms).[139] Thus, depending on the circumstances, minority common shareholding that is considered passive and diversified may lead to situations of either 'hidden control' (shareholder concentration) or 'hidden reciprocity' (internalisation of externalities) in terms of effects despite its form (direction or symmetry of equity holding). Potential aggregation of individually small passive shareholdings and their parallelism in interest may give rise to cumulative *de facto* control and interactive, compound or network-like, competitive effects.[140]

The transformed quality of risk-diluted shareholding as closer to a debt holding in nature may add to such possibility. Interestingly, in this sense, 'negative' financial decoupling (disproportionate influence compared to the risk and size of a shareholding)[141] may indirectly lead to 'positive' linking of profits between competing firms (*de facto* profit correlation due to the rivals' competitive relationship and their common ownership links).[142] Mutual internalisation of rivals' profits may thus arise either due to common owners' asymmetric corporate influence or their (symmetric) parallel financial interests, given their *de facto* control in portfolio firms' governance and their aligned incentives to compete, or the induced financial dependence linked to their potential *de facto* position as largest shareholders and creditors of portfolio companies.[143] Besides, when 'exit' is excluded for index funds,[144]

[137] See n 74–81 and 84 above and surrounding text.

[138] See n 86–88 above and surrounding text.

[139] See n 89–92 above and surrounding text.

[140] Romano (n 107); L Enriques and A Romano, 'Institutional Investor Voting Behavior: A Network Theory Perspective' (2019) 1 Ill L Rev 223; Lianos and others (n 90).

[141] cf Ringe (n 124) 1073.

[142] R Reynolds and B Snapp, 'The Competitive Effects of Partial Equity Interests and Joint Ventures' (1986) 4 Intl J Industrial Org 141, 141–142. The profit internalisation may be reciprocal, but the mechanism and competitive effects are unilateral to begin with. See Azar and Tzanaki (n 91) 258–259; Tzanaki (n 1) section III.A and 235-236.

[143] Indeed, there is limited authority in EU case law suggesting that even a nonvoting, totally passive minority shareholding, originating from a loan, may lead to mutual internalisation of competitive externalities, with the same effect *as if* acquirer and target held cross-shareholdings in each other. See Cases IV/33.440 *Warner-Lambert/Gillette* and IV/33.486 *BIC/Gillette* [1993] OJ L 116/21. See also n 93 and 95 above and surrounding text, and Tzanaki (n 1).

[144] Unlike traditional index funds, ETFs may be freely traded (and may also be actively managed), which may impact and further complicate the competition analysis while tracking complex agency relationships and property rights allocations. See W Birdthistle, 'The Fortunes and Foibles of Exchange-Traded Funds: A Positive Market Response to the Problems of Mutual Funds' (2008) 33 *Del J Corp L* 69, 110 (suggesting that ETFs 'create a market – rather than a regulatory or litigated – solution to much of the mutual fund difficulties'; however, they have their own possible conflicts of interest, eg arising from stock lending plans).

the 'voice'[145] of diversified institutional investors is amplified, thus potentially having a greater weight in managerial and firm governance decisions and indirectly in competition outcomes in product markets.[146] Indeed, the voice of large 'long-term' institutional investors is actively encouraged by regulators and has become quasi-permanent (although *ad hoc* in its manifestation) and systemic (reaching their whole portfolio of invested companies).[147] It follows that there might be several ways through which passive diversified investors may be *competitively influential*, either at present or in the future, and not only in one direction but potentially bidirectionally.

15.7 IMPLICATIONS AND CONCLUSIONS

Coming full circle and looking back to press forward, history teaches us that it repeats itself. New forms of minority shareholding pop up as new ways of aggregating capital and savings and linking businesses are devised. Common shareholding by institutional investors brings to the fore the early unity and much-needed congruence between competition and corporate laws. The lesson for their continued interaction is for each discipline to assume a measure of modesty rather than 'going all the way' – alone – in solving the 'common ownership trilemma'.[148] 'New finance' with all the good that it brings for firms, markets, and people and the 'new trusts' with all their potential implications and distortions for the competition are one and the same problem: despite their modern functional split and specialisation, antitrust and corporate governance cannot bypass their deep interdependence both in terms of theoretical foundations and balanced regulatory solutions.

Yet, in this novel and unwieldy setting, a new role encounters antitrust: competition law enforcement may help rebalance and restore the initial allocation of property rights within firms (shareholders' residual claim) and thus indirectly protect undiversified shareholders, to the extent corporate law control mechanisms (fiduciary duties) are ineffectual. Antitrust could therefore be used to protect non-common shareholders who may be harmed – along with consumers – by suboptimal outcomes in the performance of individual corporate entities and industries.

[145] A Hirschman, *Exit, Voice, and Loyalty: Responses to Decline in Firms, Organizations, and States* (Harvard UP 1970).

[146] E Elhauge, 'The Causal Mechanisms of Horizontal Shareholding' (2021) 82 Ohio St LJ 1, 66; I Appel, T Gormley and D Keim, 'Passive Investors, Not Passive Owners' (2016) 121 J Financ Econ 111, 133 (suggesting that passive institutional investors have an 'influential voice in decisions pertaining to firms' governance structures'); J Fisch, A Hamdani and S Solomon, 'The New Titans of Wall Street: A Theoretical Framework for Passive Investors' (2020) 168 U Pa L Rev 17, 37, 71.

[147] Fisch, Hamdani and Solomon (n 146) 27, 54; J Fichtner, E Heemskerk and J Garcia-Bernardo, 'Hidden Power of the Big Three? Passive Index Funds, Re-Concentration of Corporate Ownership, and New Financial Risk' (2017) 19 *Business and Politics* 298, 309, 321, 323; cf WG Ringe, 'Stewardship and Shareholder Engagement in Germany' (2021) 22 EBOR 87.

[148] Azar (n 2).

Developing an antitrust policy to tackle common ownership by large diversified institutional investors (*shareholder concentration and diversification*) and to supplement existing merger policy (*market concentration*) may unexpectedly return antitrust to its corporate law origins. Increasing diversification in financial investment and concentration and parallelism in corporate ownership calls antitrust to shift its operation from a pure conduct-oriented ('strategic model') to a structure-oriented approach: acting as a *de facto* early corporate law-like 'structural model' of checking the corporate structure and shareholder property rights exchange, internalising portfolio investment and governance externalities, and ensuring ongoing private versus public interest balancing.[149]

While antitrust is to retain its focus on economic effects, the source of potential competitive effects from minority shareholding and common ownership originates in changed corporate ownership structures well below any formal competition law threshold of 'control' (as in EU merger control). The foundations of competition and merger control when designing their scope and aims may be challenged, however, considering: i) the liberalisation of corporate law lifting intercorporate ownership and influence restrictions and ii) recent organisational and financial market developments undermining early corporate law assumptions (no separations of ownership or investment from control or consumption) that antitrust inherited. By turning its look inside corporate governance and shareholder structures, antitrust could provide an effective alternative tool to holistically capture problematic minority shareholdings that create both agency problems or conflicts of interest and market power concerns (just as early corporate law regulation of mergers and shareholding acquisitions did). Such a solution would not only rebalance disperse shareholders' private interests (property rights) inside the firm but in view of the historical split between corporate and competition law, it would also aim to safeguard and prioritise the public interest (consumer welfare). Against this backdrop, antitrust can simply not afford to not look closer at minority shareholding structures that 'came to fall between the cracks'. Essentially, and unlike the main antitrust rules that target behaviour (Sherman Act Sections 1 and 2; Articles 101 and 102 TFEU), merger control rules within modern competition law regimes have inherited and preserved to a certain extent corporate law's 'structural' regulatory approach. The question now is that merger control adjusts its jurisdictional ambit and tools below and beyond

[149] cf Hovenkamp cited in n 22 above and surrounding text, distinguishing the 'structural model' of early corporate law and the 'strategic model' adopted by antitrust law; cf also D Crane, 'The Dissociation of Incorporation and Regulation in the Progressive Era and the New Deal' in Naomi R Lamoreaux and William J Novak (eds), *Corporations and American Democracy* (Harvard UP 2017) 110 (noting that in the twentieth century the US federal government, having failed to introduce a federal chartering or licensing regime, 'found itself in the position of regulating *conduct* by "corporate persons" rather than creating, structuring and regulating *corporations themselves*'). Under the former model, antitrust would obtain a more discretionary character and a quasi-regulatory function.

obsolete legal thresholds and economic assumptions. The concentration of corporate ownership through novel shareholding structures and intermediaries may produce competitive influence, in significant although unfamiliar ways, which impels antitrust to be alert in shifting its attention and finetuning its enforcement tools. Curiously, as the new reality of the such evolved capitalist environment and organisational structure sets in, 'anti-trust' may be found anew to be well worth its name.[150]

At the same time, on a substantive level, common institutional shareholding calls antitrust to be not merely future proof but 'future perfect': new intriguing possibilities, both with regard to novel theories of harm and efficiencies, will have to be acknowledged and incorporated into competition law enforcement if it is to remain relevant. In light of its mixed effects, competition law should go past imposing hard limits or any *per se* prohibition against common ownership, even if a 'structural' approach is systematically employed to assess *ad hoc* their competitive significance and effects in the specific case. In such case, antitrust will have to enrich, refine, or complement its merger law-based measurement tools (HHI and MHHI), depending on the circumstances. In other words, the 'structural' approach will need to be combined with case-by-case analysis based on the specific factual context. In this connection and as illustrated above, it is important to realise that the combination of concentration and diversification related to common institutional ownership lends corporate property rights 'dual' or 'quantum' qualities: 1) minority shareholding may be both 'passive' and 'dynamically influential' at the same time, so long as there is some competitive relationship between the interlinked firms that may be undermined;[151] 2) diversified shareholders may be both 'owners' of the firm but 'empty' of any economic interest in its performance, challenging their residual claim status; 3) control may be 'hidden', concentrated and disproportionate in its actual *ex post* manifestations compared to its *ex ante* hypothetical properties considering the size and risk attached to a stand-alone shareholding; 4) in the presence of common ownership, the quantum 'atom' of corporate property may be composed of not only 'solid particles' (control rights) but also 'invisible waves' (parallel interests), the latter fundamentally changing the traditional identity of an equity share and a shareholder.[152] Yet, the existence and impact of these parameters are hard to pin down in the abstract; better observation and empirical evidence are needed and also bold theoretical leaps forward to fill gaps in our understanding of the emerging reality. While by no means easy, 'the only way out is through'.[153]

150 See Elhauge cited in n 55 above and surrounding text.

151 See Section 15.5 above.

152 See Section 15.6 above.

153 This is a sentiment common to laborers of all sorts, eloquently crystallised in Robert Frost's poem 'Servant to Servants'.

Generations of law and economic scholars will no doubt devote lifetimes to unravel the 'gordian knot' presented by common ownership. As Minority Report[154] reminds us one may not be able to predict the future from the past or credibly form a single-minded assessment of the likelihood of harm materialising or not. Still, it is possible to change the future once one is aware of its prospect. For the sake of a sustainable capitalist future and society, may both public officials and economic agents be mindful of the power they possess and use it with wise restraint and prudent foresight.

[154] A science fiction film (2002) directed by Steven Spielberg. By analogy to a pre-merger control regime, a futuristic, all-prescient government aims to completely prevent crime before it happens ('pre-crime' enforcement) by use of 'pre-cognition'. Yet, besides its theoretical perfection and immaculate prediction record, the system does present flaws and inaccuracies that were kept secret until exposed in a 'minority report': a dissenting prediction of the future that 'might' tell a different story and questions some of the predicted 'reality'. Tom Cruise, 'falsely' targeted as a future crime perpetrator, ultimately reveals the system's main flaw: 'people can change their future once they become aware of it'.

16

Competition Law, Big Tech, and Financialisation

The Dark Side of the Moon

Ioannis Lianos and Andrew P. McLean

16.1 INTRODUCTION

In recent years, the competition law community has become absorbed in discussions around the role of competition law in the digital economy. Debate typically centres on the largest digital platform companies: Google, Apple, Facebook, Amazon, and Microsoft ('GAFAM').[1] Such studies have helped to shift competition law beyond the neoclassical price theory framework that underpins the consumer welfare standard, raising significant issues including what is the most appropriate unit of analysis for understanding competitive interactions in the digital economy and how to define power in the digital age.[2] These are pertinent questions that will rightly continue to attract the attention of scholars and regulators.[3] Still, in this brief chapter, we wish to highlight important shortcomings of the existing literature and therefore promote a different perspective on the digital economy than the 'monopoly power' narrative that has dominated competition law discourse regarding digital platforms in recent years.

The current dominant narrative on the power of digital platforms stays silent on the *cui bono* question: Who benefits from this digital transformation? To answer this, one needs to address the inner logic of modern financial capitalism, the prevalence

[1] For a range of views, see the articles in the special issue in Industrial and Corporate Change and the introduction to the special issue by M Jacobides and I Lianos, 'Regulating Platforms and Ecosystems: An Introduction' (2021) 30(5) Industrial and Corporate Change; T Wu, *The Curse of Bigness: Antitrust in the New Gilded Age* (Columbia Global Reports 2018); L Khan and S Vaheesan, 'Market Power and Inequality: The Antitrust Counterrevolution and Its Discontents' (2017) 11 *Harv L Policy Rev* 235; M Meagher, *Competition Is Killing Us: How Big Business Is Harming Our Society and Planet and What to Do About It* (Penguin 2020).

[2] For a discussion, see I Lianos and B Carballa Smichowski, 'Economic Power and New Business Models in Competition Law and Economics: Ontology and New Metrics' (2021) UCL Centre for Law, Economics and Society Research Paper 3/2021 https://ssrn.com/abstract=3818943 accessed 22 November 2021.

[3] For a systematic critique, see I Lianos, *Competition Law and the Intangible Economy* (Oxford University Press 2022, forthcoming).

of the shareholder value principle,[4] the transformation of the 'shareholder' concept with the emergence of institutional investors as primary holders of global capital as an important episode in the trend towards financialisation,[5] and the way this impacts on the competitive strategies of Big Tech.

Financialisation is a broad, and somewhat contested, term. Economist Gerald Epstein offers a frequently cited definition of financialisation as 'the increasing role of financial motives, financial markets, financial actors, and financial institutions in the operation of the domestic and international economies'.[6] This study focuses on the corporate aspects of financialisation, namely the growth of the financial dimension of value generation in the digital economy and the reorientation of corporate governance around the principle of shareholder value maximisation. Following Hyman Minsky, we also highlight the increasingly speculative nature of economic behaviour under financialisation.[7]

Subject to a few exceptions, the extant literature fails to acknowledge the importance of financialisation in driving the growth of GAFAM.[8] While the majority of scholarship on the digital platforms focuses on network effects and market tipping in promoting their growth, financialisation is also key to understanding value capture in the digital economy and in particular the competitive strategies employed by the same platforms. As noted, here we understand financialisation to mean the growth of the financial dimension of value generation and the reorientation of corporate governance around the principle of shareholder

4 See, for a similar perspective, G Davis, 'Taming Corporate Power in the Twenty-First Century' in Subhramanian Rangan (ed), *Performance and Progress: Essays on Capitalism, Business, and Society* (Oxford University Press 2015).

5 See, R Eccles, 'Concentration in the Asset Management Industry: Implications for Corporate Engagement' *Forbes* (Jersey City, 17 April 2019), www.forbes.com/sites/bobeccles/2019/04/17/concentration-in-the-asset-management-industry-implications-for-corporate-engagement/?sh=69109b55402f accessed 22 November 2021; F Franzoni, 'The effects of concentration in the asset management industry on stock prices' (*VOX CEPR*, 3 June 2019) https://voxeu.org/article/concentration-asset-management-industry-and-stock-prices accessed 22 November 2021 (noting that (s)ince 1980, the top ten institutional investors have quadrupled their holdings in US stocks. As of December 2016, the largest institutional investor oversaw 6.3% of total equity assets, and the top ten investors managed 26.5% of these assets). A more concentrated picture emerges if one looks to the concentration of asset management in the digital economy, in particular, for certain kind of management for well advanced digital economy projects.

6 G Epstein, 'Introduction: Financialization and the World Economy' in Gerald A Epstein (ed) *Financialization and the World Economy* (Edward Elgar 2005) 3.

7 See H Minsky, *Can 'It' Happen Again?: Essays on Instability and Finance* (Routledge 1982).

8 See I Lianos, A Ivanov and D Davis, *Global Food Value Chains and Competition Law* (Cambridge University Press) ch 4 (forthcoming); I Lianos, 'Competition Law for the Digital Era: A Complex Systems' Perspective' (30 August 2019) http://dx.doi.org/10.2139/ssrn.3492730 accessed 22 November 2021; I Lianos and others, 'Financialization of the Food Value Chain, Common Ownership and Competition Law' (2020) 16 *ECJ* 149; A McLean, 'A Financial Capitalism Perspective on Start-up Acquisitions: Introducing the Economic Goodwill Test' (2021) 17 *JCL & E* 141; *Ioannis* Lianos, 'Law and Capital Accumulation in the 21st Century Digital and Financial Capitalism' (2021) CLES Research Paper 6/2021 (forthcoming).

value maximisation.[9] Significantly, it is also associated with an increasingly speculative approach to investment.[10] Nowhere is this more apparent than in the digital economy. Expectations around the future profits of technology firms are extremely buoyant, and often quite distinct from the reality of markets as they presently exist.[11] By achieving central positions within digital ecosystems, GAFAM are beneficiaries of such financial speculation. They enjoy enormous financial clout that then enables them to further entrench their power, primarily through intensive merger and acquisitions ('M&A') activity. This has allowed them to expand outside of their core business activity into adjacent and/or overlapping fields of activity. That is, financialisation plays a vital role in intensifying the accumulation of power, and therefore rents, in the digital economy. Too much focus has been placed on digitisation without comprehending that the shift may not have had such dramatic economic and social consequences if it was not paired with the emergence of financial capitalism.[12]

This financial capitalism perspective invites us to consider who really benefits from GAFAM's dominance. Competition law typically considers participants in the economy in the binary terms of consumer welfare and producer welfare, with the terms 'consumer' and 'producer' stylised concepts that mask the variety of positions an economic actor may hold within an economy. Under financialisation, people are not simply consumers but may also be investors. It is therefore worth considering the extent and distribution of equity ownership in digital platforms. Given that equity ownership is heavily skewed towards the wealthiest and most privileged in society, we consider that the role of competition law may be to represent those who do not share in the power of GAFAM through their involvement in capital markets.

The further limitation we highlight is a failure to consider GAFAM's dominant position in the global economy from an organisational perspective. As in the field of competition law more broadly, scholarship on competition in the digital economy pays little attention to corporate governance. While many commentators observing GAFAM's M&A strategy draw a comparison with the conglomerates that dominated the American economy following World War II, there has been insufficient work to

9 For a discussion, see G Davis and S Kim, 'Financialization of the Economy' (2015) 41(1) Ann Rev of Socio 203.

10 See H Minsky, 'The Financial Instability Hypothesis' in Philip Arestis and Malcolm Sawyer (eds), *Handbook of Radical Political Economy* (Edward Elgar 1993).

11 See R Foroohar, 'Another tech bubble could be about to burst' *Financial Times* (London, 27 January 2019).

12 None of the reports issued to discuss digital competition incorporated a financial capitalism dimension and any mention of institutional investors, despite them holding significant shares in digital platforms, see J Furman and others, 'Unlocking digital competition: Report of the digital competition expert panel' (Government of the United Kingdom 2019) https://assets.publishing.service.gov.uk/government/uploads/system/uploads/attachment_data/file/785547/unlocking_digital_competition_furman_review_web.pdf accessed 22 November 2021; For an inclusion of the financial capitalism dimension, see ILianos and A Ivanov (ed), Digital Era Competition BRICS Report (September 2019) https://papers.ssrn.com/sol3/papers.cfm?abstract_id=3901413 accessed 22 November 2021.

uncover the accuracy of this analogy. The post-war conglomerates were run by and for a managerial class, largely free from interference by shareholders.[13] This may be contrasted with the corporate governance of firms following financialisation, in which the interests of shareholders are paramount. We undertake empirical work to uncover whether GAFAM truly do resemble historical conglomerates rather than the financialised firms typical of the post-1980 period. We find that GAFAM's corporate governance regimes, to varying degrees, exhibit a hybrid blend of characteristics and resist easy categorisation.

The chapter is split into three substantive sections. Section 16.2 uncovers the interaction between financialisation and growth of the digital platforms. Section 16.3 addresses the question of who benefits from their dominance and the implications of this for competition law. Section 16.4 presents empirical evidence on the corporate governance regimes of the GAFAM firms, comparing and contrasting them with the managerial primacy of the post-war conglomerates and the shareholder-led approach that typifies financial capitalism. Section 16.5 concludes.

16.2 THE CHANGING COMPETITIVE GAME: FINANCIALISATION, FUTURITY, AND THE DOMINANCE OF DIGITAL PLATFORMS

Work on competition in the digital economy has helped to move competition law beyond its traditional focus on output restriction by product market monopolists.[14] This is apparent, for example, in the literature on digital ecosystems, which have emerged as a new structure of economic relationships.[15] Such work helps us to understand the centrality of GAFAM in the digital space; they have attained 'architectural power', positioning themselves so that they influence the way that ecosystems are structured and shaping the allocation of value between ecosystem participants.[16] Undoubtedly, this governance architecture may generate value and

[13] On the dispersal of share ownership, see G Means, 'The Separation of Ownership and Control in American Industry' (1931) 46(1) Q J Econ 68; A Berle and G Means, *The Modern Corporation and Private Property* (Transaction Publishers 1932).

[14] I Lianos, 'Competition law for a Complex Economy' (2019) 50 IIC 643.

[15] Ecosystems are regarded as communities of collaborating firms that collectively produce a good, service, or solution with an aligned vision – ecosystems thus do not merely denote 'theory of the firm' alternatives to vertical integration or supply-chain arrangements, rather the concept reflects the emergence of business environments marked by modularity in production, co-evolution, and decisional complexity; R Adner, 'Ecosystem as Structure' (2017) 43 J Manag 39; R Kapoor, 'Ecosystems broadening the locus of value creation' (2018) 7 J Organ Des, art 12; E Autio and T Llewellyn, 'Tilting the Playing Field: Towards an Endogenous Strategic Action Theory of Ecosystem Creation' in S Nambisan (ed), *Open Innovation, Innovation Ecosystems, and Enterpreneurship: Multidisiplinary Perspectives* (Word Scientific 2018) ch 5; see also M Jacobides, C Cennamo, and A Gawer, 'Towards a theory of ecosystems' (2018) 39 Strateg Manag J 2255; J Moore, 'Predators and Prey: A New Ecology of Competition' (1993) 71(3) Harv Bus Rev 75.

[16] Ecosystem orchestrators set the activity and value architectures of ecosystems with the purpose to maximize its resilience and capacity to generate value. For instance, ecosystem orchestrators controlling

promote innovation. However, competition law scholarship still does not fully grasp the dynamics driving GAFAM's dominance of the digital economy and its long-term impact on social and consumer welfare.

Arguably, the most important factor is the consolidating effect of financialisation. Modern competition law holds that if a firm engages in some type of conduct, or wishes to merge with another, this is more than likely because it would enhance efficiency.[17] Yet, under financial capitalism, competitive behaviour is not only about improving efficiency to succeed in product markets in the present, as assumed by the competition orthodoxy. Rather, they engage in 'futurity-led' competition, in which firms seek capital asset appreciation by convincing investors of their expected dominance in the future – futurity denoting the reorientation of economic activity towards the future and firm valuation coming to rest on expected future profits.[18]

In a 1925 manuscript, the institutional economist John Commons explained futurity in the following manner:

> [Present values rest] not on account of what has happened in the past, nor even on account of what is happening at the present point of time, but on account of what I and others hope, expect, or fear will happen in the future. The extent to which this human ability of forecasting has its influence on present behavior and values may be given the name, Futurity.[19]

Thus, futurity is 'a factor that indicates anticipation'.[20] Writing a century ago, Commons identified the emergence of futurity by analysing a series of cases heard by the US Supreme Court at the end of the nineteenth century. Prior to this time, firm valuation was based solely on the estimated market price of tangible assets. That is, firms were treated as if they had ceased to trade and were simply a collection of illiquid assets awaiting liquidation. Commons' analysis of futurity centres on the replacement of this practice by the treatment of firms as living entities, as 'going concerns', that are expected to earn profits in the future.[21] By the turn of the twentieth century, the US Supreme Court had come to recognise that firms can

an operating system make a strategic use of their application programming interfaces (APIs), which enable external apps to connect with the operating system, hardware or web-based system, algorithms based on Big data analytics, or contractual restrictions, among other forms of ecosystem 'glue', in order to ensure interconnectivity and interoperability for final consumers, but by the same also offer profitable points of control for the dominant firm in the ecosystem and the resources to build a strategic competitive advantage. This leads to a new set of dynamics, whereby those who control ecosystems can generate profit through a fresh set of dynamics. See E Autio, 'Orchestrating ecosystems: a multi-layered framework' (2021) Innovation: Organization and Management.

17 See F Easterbrook, 'The Limits of Antitrust' (1984) 63 *Tex L Rev* 1.

18 R Palan, 'Futurity, Pro-cyclicality and Financial Crises' (2015) 20 *New Political Economy* 367.

19 *Reasonable Value* (1925) 2 (as cited in G Atkinson and C Whalen, 'Futurity: cornerstone of Post-Keynsian Institutionalism' in Charles J Whalen (ed) *Financial Instability and Economic Security after the Great Recession* (Edward Elgar 2011) 53–54).

20 J Commons, *Institutional Economics: Its Place in Political Economy* (Macmillan 1934).

21 *Ibid.*

own something that they do not actually possess, expected future profits, the value of which began to be incorporated into firms' value.[22]

Futurity is inherently tied to the financial system because it is finance that provides 'the necessary link between the present and the future'.[23] Under financial capitalism, unfettered financial markets are driving an intensification in futurity. With their 'animal spirits' unleashed, investors in the modern economy care less and less about the profits and cashflow firms achieve in the present day and instead aspire speculatively towards realising tremendous profits many years in the future.[24] In this configuration, where futurity is key, value is not determined and generated by the present market exchange but by an expected succession of events. Consequently, we see a 'subtle shift of mindset from profit (and isolating mechanisms) to wealth creation (and the potential for asset appreciation)'.[25]

Nowhere is futurity-led competition more apparent than in the digital economy, in which economic decision-making is driven by speculative visions of extraordinary profits in the future that is seemingly detached from present-day reality. Consider, for example, the extraordinary valuations of companies like Uber and Tesla that are yet to record meaningful, sustained profits.[26] As noted by economist Ronen Palan:

> The theory of futurity implies that not only financial system is vulnerable to sentiments about the future, but the entire economy in the age of futurity also has lost its anchoring in any objective measures of value as such (if there ever were any in the first place).[27]

The major digital platforms have benefitted immensely from this trend, with their market capitalisations skyrocketing in the last decade. At the time of writing, GAFAM are five of the six most valuable companies by market capitalisation globally (their hegemony broken only by Saudi Armco): Apple is valued at $2.6 trillion, Microsoft is valued at $2.5 trillion, Amazon is valued at $1.8 trillion, Alphabet is valued at

[22] J Commons, *Industrial Goodwill* (McGrew-Hill 1919); S Kemper, *The Capitalization of Goodwill* (John Hopkins Press 1921); R Palan, 'The Financial Crisis and Intangible Value' (2013) 37 *Capital & Class* 65; Palan (n 18).

[23] W Peterson, 'Institutionalism, Keynes, and the Real World' (1977) 11(2) J Econ Issues 201, 217.

[24] See H Minsky, 'The Financial Instability Hypothesis' in Philip Arestis and Malcolm Sawyer (eds), *Handbook of Radical Political Economy* (Edward Elgar 1993); S Banner, *Speculation: A History of the Fine Line between Gambling and Investing* (Oxford University Press 2017) 307–330; S Leins, *Stories of Capitalism: Inside the Role of Financial Analysts* (University of Chicago Press 2018); E Chiapello, 'Financialisation of Valuation' (2015) 38 *Human Studies* 13.

[25] M Jacobides, T Knudsen and M Augier, 'Benefiting from Innovation: Value Creation, Value Appropriation and the Role of Industry Architectures' (2006) 35 *Research Policy* 1201, 1212.

[26] See, for example, J Schumpeter, 'Are technology firms madly overvalued? Three financial sanity tests for whether there is a bubble' (*The Economist*, 23 February 2017); H Horan, 'The Uber Bubble: Why Is a Company That Lost $20 Billion Claimed to Be Successful?' (*ProMarket*, 20 November 2019); N Aschoff, 'No Rational System Would Value Tesla at $100 billion' *Jacobin* (New York, 26 January 2020).

[27] Palan (n 18).

$1.9 trillion, and Facebook (Meta) is valued at $0.9 trillion.[28] Together, they constitute 24.7% of the Standard and Poor's (S&P) 500's total market capitalisation.[29] Such valuations are principally motivated by high expectations for phenomenal profits in the not-so-immediate future because of their position as gatekeepers controlling important bottlenecks in digital ecosystems (for example, operating systems, search engines, app stores, and the cloud). To the extent that, in view of its essential characteristic of futurity, the main source of value in the digital economy emanates from financial markets valuing expected returns, ecosystem orchestrators attract important investments, in particular, if they command control over an essential bottleneck for complementors (gatekeepers).

In turn, the futurity-driven market capitalisations enjoyed by GAFAM provide them with immense financial firepower, which enables them to further shape the digital economy in their own favour.[30] There appears to be a 'growth-funding' feedback loop, 'by which the future supply of effective funding increases as a result of the conditions created by a speculative expansion, and ends up lowering the cost of capital'.[31] Moreover, digital platforms directly benefit from financialisation as they own large stocks of financial assets (bonds, cash, or other financial instruments).[32] Rodrigo Fernandez and his co-authors note that the seven largest Big Tech companies (Apple, Microsoft, Alphabet, Facebook, Amazon, Alibaba, and Tencent) own more than $700 billion financial assets, including cash, government bonds, corporate debt securities, mortgage-backed securities, investments in money market funds, and equity securities, among others,[33] which represent a much higher percentage of their total assets than traditional S&P 500 companies.[34]

Significantly, GAFAM are able to use their enormous financial clout to further entrench their power through engaging in intensive M&A activity. In the period from their founding to 2018, Alphabet has acquired 214 companies, Amazon 77

[28] Data sourced from YCharts: see 'Apple Inc (AAPL) chart' (*Ycharts*) https://ycharts.com/companies/beta/AAPL/market_cap accessed 22 November 2021; 'Microsoft Corp (MSFT) chart' (*Ycharts*) https://ycharts.com/companies/beta/MSFT/market_cap accessed 22 November 2021; 'Amazon.com Inc (AMZN) chart' (*Ycharts*) https://ycharts.com/companies/beta/AMZN/market_cap accessed 22 November 2021; 'Alphabet Inc (GOOG) chart' (*Ycharts*) https://ycharts.com/companies/beta/GOOG/market_cap accessed 22 November 2021; 'Facebook Inc (FB) chart' (*Ycharts*) https://ycharts.com/companies/beta/FB/market_cap accessed 22 November 2021.

[29] The total market capitalisation of the S&P 500 at the time of writing is $39 trillion. The combined market capitalisation of the five Big Tech companies is $9.7 trillion. 'S&P 500 Market Cap chart' (*Ycharts*) https://ycharts.com/indicators/sp_500_market_cap accessed 22 November 2021.

[30] See, R Fernandez and others, 'The financialisation of Big Tech' (SOMO, December 2020) www.somo.nl/the-financialisation-of-big-tech/.

[31] R Caballero, Emmanuel Farhi and Mohamad L Hammour, 'Speculative Growth: Hints from the U.S. Economy' (2006) 96 *Am Econ Rev* 1159.

[32] *Ibid.* at 23.

[33] *Ibid.* at 30 (Figures 3.1 and 3.2).

[34] *Ibid.* at 32 (Figure 3.4). Their total debt has also grown from US$94 billion in 2014 to US$295 billion in 2019 (Figure 3.6).

companies, and Facebook 65 companies.[35] Similarly, between 1991 and 2018, Microsoft has acquired 189 companies and Apple 89 companies.[36] Through such transactions, GAFAM have been able to further develop digital ecosystems and cement their critical positions within them. Amazon, for instance, started off as an online retailer of books before being vertically and horizontally integrated with other entities which enabled it to become a vendor of various products and a media and entertainment company that competes with other media and entertainment companies the products of which it also sells on its platform. Amazon has also expanded its activities into Internet cloud business and storage and the transmission of content to consumers.

Financialisation and futurity, therefore, create a virtuous feedback loop for these firms in which power in the digital economy precipitates financial power, which in turn enables them to deepen their power in the digital economy. In this manner, the speculation that characterises the wider digital economy prompts the development of a more 'rational bubble' in GAFAM stock valuations.[37] The perception that they (could) control a valuable bottleneck that may provide them with a sustainable competitive advantage and abnormal profits in the long term is a crucial driver for strategic action by the management of the relevant firm. This relatively new phenomenon is reinforced by the learning-by-doing effects engendered by the use of data accumulation, advanced artificial intelligence capabilities, and the central positioning of digital platforms as gatekeepers in various economic sectors in the digital economy, which enable them to draw on their significant predictive power and to potentially leverage that to a central positioning in the financial anchorages of the global economy.[38]

This financial capitalism account sheds light on the dynamics driving the expansion of digital platforms, moving the discussion beyond efficiency-based explanations and inviting us to view their growth with a greater degree of scepticism.

16.3 WHO BENEFITS FROM THE DOMINANCE OF THE DIGITAL PLATFORMS? DISTRIBUTIONAL IMPLICATIONS AND AGENT-BASED MODELLING

Beyond highlighting the role of financialisation and futurity-led competition in driving the growth of the digital platforms, the financial capitalism perspective invoked here also invites us to consider who actually benefits from GAFAM's dominance of

[35] M Doucette, 'Visualising Major Tech Acquisitions', (visualcapitalist.com, 24 July 2018), www.visualcapitalist.com/interactive-major-tech-acquisitions/.

[36] *Ibid.*

[37] Caballero and others (n 31)

[38] See, for an interesting discussion, M Iansiti and K R Lakhani, *Competing in the Age of AI* (Harvard Business Review Press 2020).

the digital economy. The current market-based competition law framework does not attempt to provide a holistic answer to this vital question, focusing narrowly on consumer welfare. Yet, following financialisation, people are not only consumers but also may be investors who share in the benefits of GAFAM's power through stock ownership.

Notably, despite a widespread myth about the 'democratisation of finance', shareholding remains highly concentrated among the wealthiest and most privileged in society.[39] In the US, for example, the vast majority of people own very little or no corporate equity: at the end of the first quarter of 2021, the wealthiest top 1% of Americans owned 20% of corporate equities and mutual fund shares, with the top 10% holding 13% and the entire bottom 50% just 0.2%.[40] As highlighted in the following section, institutional investors, who invest on behalf of this wealthy minority, own significant stakes in each of the GAFAM firms. Clearly, then, it is the most well-off who benefit from GAFAM's dominance via stock ownership.

This distributional impact of competition law enforcement has not yet been adequately examined, although there have been some efforts, still uncomplete, to move towards this direction.[41] To the extent that competition law only focuses on consumer welfare, defined as the behaviour of a representative agent, the consumer, it is agnostic as to distributional effects to other sociological categories of agents, such as workers, investors, and other categories of individuals that may be delineated according to their average income or wealth.[42] Such analysis, if it is to be complete, needs to be performed at the level of each jurisdiction, taking into account all the affected stakeholders.[43] One can imagine that such analysis is performed at least intuitively when deciding about the stance of a specific jurisdiction with regard to the social costs (and benefits) of the economic power of Big Tech

39 See L Palladino, 'Democratizing Investment' (2019) 47(4) *Pol & Soc'y* 573; I Erturk and others, 'The democratization of finance? Promises, outcomes and conditions' (2007) 14(4) *Rev Int'l Pol Econ* 553; Edward Wolff, 'The Decline of African-American and Hispanic Wealth since the Great Recession' (2018) NBER Working Paper No 25198 www.nber.org/papers/w25198 accessed 22 November 2021.

40 The Federal Reserve, 'Distribution of Household Wealth in the US since 1989' (21 June 2021) www.federalreserve.gov/releases/z1/dataviz/dfa/distribute/table/#quarter:126;series:Corporate%20equities%20and%20mutual%20fund%20shares;demographic:networth;population:all;units:levels. See also D Greenwald, M Lettau and S Ludvigson, 'How the Wealth Was Won: Factors Shares as Market Fundamentals' (2021) NBER Working Paper No 25769 www.nber.org/papers/w25769 accessed 22 November 2021.

41 See, S Vaheesan, 'Accomodating Capital and Policing Labor: Antitrust in the Two Gilded Ages' (2019) 78(4) *Mary L Rev* 766.

42 For a discussion of the importance of assessing the distributional impact of competition law enforcement and policy see, I Lianos, 'Competition Law as a Form of Social Regulation' (2020) 65 *Antitrust Bull* 3.

43 At least this would be what would require a polycentric competition law model: see, I Lianos, 'Polycentric Competition Law' (2018) 71 *Current Legal Problems* 161.

in order to design their specific regulatory response, in view of their institutional capabilities and resources.[44] A more systematic analysis would require the use of different tools than those traditionally employed by competition authorities, in order to map the power of these digital platforms and assess their incentive and capacity to produce effects in each jurisdiction and determine the social 'geography' of such direct or spill-over effects.

An important tool that has not been adequately explored so far by competition law literature[45] is agent-based modelling.[46] This tool provides a bottom-up approach to simulate a system of heterogeneous autonomous agents, thus accounting for different attributes, such as the size, the business model, as well as the specific ownership structure and corporate governance of undertakings, and could also integrate a dynamic perspective by designing these agents to be adaptive through learning. A similar modelling can be done for various sociological categories of individuals, such as 'investors', 'labour', and 'consumers', accounting for their income, education or wealth level, varying degrees of rationality, thus not relying on the average behaviour of individuals defined *in abstracto* but on the basis of their real attributes and those the theory/hypothesis to be tested considered important. The model may not only focus on price-system intermediated interactions but also centre on or combine non-price ones. It may be possible to also develop a typology of realistic rule sets to be applied to all or categories of agents, as well as different agent environments (taking into account the different spheres of competition – markets, ecosystems, sectors) that more comprehensively account for the complexity of these interactions and relationships (for example, competition, cooperation, co-opetition, ownership, control, influence) and open up to various behavioural frameworks that fit the research question asked (this will be different, for instance, if the research focuses on the impact on privacy, prices and output, quality, innovation, democracy, among other dimensions). The interactions to take into account may be financial flows, unique

44 The literature so far has focused on geopolitics, but these are of course related to some form of assessment of the broader social impact of Big Tech conduct and how this affects the stakeholders situated in the specific jurisdiction, if one of course makes the assumptions of the public interest theory of regulation. See see, for instance, M Jacobides, M Bruncko, and R Langen, 'Regulating Big Tech in Europe: Why, so What, and How Understanding Their Business Models and Ecosystems Can Make a Difference' (*Evolution*, 20 December 2020) https://papers.ssrn.com/sol3/papers.cfm?abstract_id=3765324 accessed 22 November 2021.

45 See, however, I Lianos, 'Competition Law for the Digital Era: A Complex Systems' Perspective' (n 8) 12–13, 15.

46 There is a significant literature on agent-based modelling. For its use in economics and industrial organization theory, see, among others, R Axelrod, *The Complexity of Cooperation: Agent-Based Models of Competition and Collaboration* (Princeton UP 1997); L Tesfatsion, 'Agent-based computational economics: A constructive approach to economic theory' in Leigh Tesfatsion and Kenneth L Judd (eds), *Handbook of computational economics: Agent-based computational economics*, vol 2 (North-Holland 2006) 831; L Hamill and Nl Gilbert, *Agent-Based Modelling in Economics* (Wiley 2016); J Sanchez-Cartas, 'Agent-based models and industrial organization theory. A price-competition algorithm for agent-based models based on Game Theory' (2018) 6 *Complex Adaptive Systems Modelling* 2.

visitors metrics and time spent on a website, information exchange/data flows, and the expression of emotions ('likes', 'dislikes', 'friends', 'followers') in order to determine the 'ties' between the various agents and the topography of the network.

Calibrating such models may take significant resources, and naturally, their degree of validity may depend on the way the model matches with the available data and on the initial conditions chosen to design the model. Although such tools also require significant sources of data, it is easier than it has ever before to gather in view of digitisation and the expansion of the digital economy. The agent-based model will run on various simulations and other computations and will eventually provide important insights through the visualisation of the interactions between agents, and the predicted evolution and outcomes of such interactions in different virtual worlds. The economic process would thus be modelled as a dynamic system of interacting agents. The topology of such interactions between agents is complex as the scale of the system/environment the agent-based model aims to explain is driven by the specific social phenomenon of interest. The tool may thus enable competition authorities to better capture emerging phenomena and to improve their understanding of the broader social impact of the examined behaviour in the context of a specific jurisdiction, not only at a purely abstract level but also taking into account a more realistic depiction of the status and motives of the agents. However, one should note the limitations of such tools, in view of the important complexity of adaptive systems, and the evidential value of simulation methods in legal processes. Notwithstanding, the tool may be employed more safely for case selection and prioritisation.

16.4 ARE DIGITAL PLATFORMS TYPICAL CONGLOMERATES?

The intensive M&A activity undertaken by GAFAM is a well-documented feature of the digital economy. In light of their merger-induced diversification, commentators frequently invoke a conglomerate analogy to describe the GAFAM firms.[47] However, analyses have so far stopped short of testing this analogy by evaluating their corporate governance regimes. Most work has so far focused on the governance of the Big Tech ecosystems, which is of course important and crucial if one is to superpose some form of public governance to the private governance structures that have been put in place by Big Tech platforms, through technology, the use of contract law or even what some have named the 'uncontract',[48] but little has been

[47] M Bourreau and A de Streel, 'Conglomerates and EU Competition Policy' (28 March 2019) available at https://papers.ssrn.com/sol3/papers.cfm?abstract_id=3350512 accessed 22 November 2021; Andrew Ross Sorkin, 'Conglomerates Didn't Die. They Look Like Amazon' *The New York Times* (New York City, 19 June 2019); P Olson, 'How Zuckerberg Is Feeding His Facebook Conglomerate' *Forbes* (Jersey City, 27 March 2015).

[48] For analysis, see I Lianos, K Eller and T Kleinschmitt, 'The Limits of Private Governance of Ecosystems' (2021) CLES Research Paper Series 07/2021 (forthcoming).

done to explore from a competition law perspective their corporate governance. As a discipline, competition law treats firms' internal dimensions as a 'black box' that left to corporate law.[49] Here, we open this black box and interrogate the validity of the conglomerate hypothesis, assessing whether GAFAM resemble the conglomerates that were a prominent feature of the post-war economy or if they are closer to the financialised firm typical of the post-1980 period.

In the decades following World War II, a combination of strict financial regulation and atomised shareholding left managers as the predominant force in US corporate governance.[50] Unlike under financial capitalism, shareholders were paid little mind.[51] Managers sought growth through conglomeration. These large conglomerates dominated large chunks of commerce and emerged as multinational corporations organised as an M-form business organisation that expanded their reach in different parts of the globe with the view to develop 'synergies'. Conglomeration and the concept of synergies were however increasingly subject to extensive criticism in business literature in the 1980s: Michael Porter criticised the relevance of portfolio management, at least for advanced economies, and explained in his work 'how diversified companies do not compete; only their business units do' and that 'diversification inevitably adds costs and constraints to business units'.[52] These conglomerates also relied on the central role of important 'industry captains', such as Harold Geneen of the ITT Corporation or James Ling, of the now defunct Ling-Temco-Vought conglomerate, that built the acquisitive conglomerate model through a succession of M&As in the 1960s and early 1970s.[53]

Notably, conglomerates pioneered the strategy of corporate growth through capitalising on financial markets – a strategy now being taken up by the digital platforms.[54] Many conglomerates acquired more than 50 firms during the decade

[49] F Thépot, *The Interaction between Competition Law and Corporate Governance* (Cambridge University Press 2019); S Weber Waller, 'Corporate Governance and Competition Policy' (2011) 18 *Geo Mas L Rev* 833.

[50] A Chandler Jr, *The Visible Hand: The Managerial Revolution in American Business* (first published 1977, Belknap Press 1999).

[51] S Deakin, 'Corporate governance and financial crisis in the long run' in Cynthia A Williams and Peer Zumbansen (eds) *The Embedded Firm: Corporate Governance, Labor, and Finance Capitalism* (Cambridge University Press 2011).

[52] M Porter, 'From Competitive Advantage to Corporate Strategy' *Harvard Business Review* (May 1987) https://hbr.org/1987/05/from-competitive-advantage-to-corporate-strategy (arguing that that 'a company will create shareholder value through diversification to a greater and greater extent as its strategy moves from portfolio management toward sharing activities' and that 'a corporate theme is a good way to ensure that the corporation will create shareholder value').

[53] A Schleifer and R Vishny, 'Takeovers in the '60s and the '80s: Evidence and Implications' (1991) 12 *Strategic Management Journal* 51; T Hurley, 'The Urge To Merge: Contemporary Theories on The Rise of Conglomerate Mergers in the 1960s' (2006) 1 *J Bus & Tech L* 185.

[54] S Knafo and S Dutto, 'Patient capital in the age of financialized managerialism' (2016) 14 *Socio-Economic Review* 771; N Fligstein, *The Transformation of Corporate Control* (Harvard UP 1990); N Fligstein, 'The Theory of Fields and Its Application to Corporate Governance' (2016) 39 *Seattle U*

up to 1968,[55] with the very largest, including ITT, making more than 20 acquisitions in 1968 alone.[56]

One of the reasons and possible advantages of conglomerate mergers during this period was the need to develop internal capital markets at the level of the conglomerate, as the managers of the firm were thought to have information advantages over the external capital markets that were not that developed in the 1960s in order to allocate capital for projects with higher rates of return. Conglomeration enabled cross-subsidisation between different divisions within the same diversified company.[57] Some firms were perceived to have information advantages over the external capital markets, for instance in the allocation process of capital and the operational aspects of each business division. However, as external capital markets develop, 'many firms can provide company-specific information to the capital markets directly' and thus 'more easily bypass firm internal capital markets for investment funds'.[58]

Crucially, conglomerates were a key driver of technological progress. Profits were retained and reinvested into the corporation. Economist John Kenneth Galbraith noted how managerialism entailed a 'shift of power in the industrial enterprise [...] from capital to organised intelligence', allowing for the significant commitment of time and resources necessary to produce technical innovation.[59] Yet, the concept of conglomeration came under attack in the context of the structural crisis of the 1970s.[60] Furthermore, the development of external capital markets in the 1970s, in particular with the development of technology enabling external (to the firm) capital markets to work around the clock and provide immense amounts of information and data for analysis, reduced the importance of the information advantages of internal capital markets.[61] This has led to the emergence of different organisational structures.

Following financialisation and the onset of shareholder primacy, the corporation was mostly seen as a portfolio of activities, managed according to their financial performance (in terms of rate of return on investment), rather than defined in terms of synergetic productive capabilities at a conglomerate level. To raise share prices, managers divested large swathes of their firms. By 1995, the average large firm that

L Rev 237; A Schleifer and R Vishny 'Takeovers in the '60s and the '80s: Evidence and Implications' (1991) 12 Strategic Management Journal 51.

55 N Berg, 'What is Different about Conglomerate Management' (1969) 47 Harv Bus Rev 112, 113.

56 R Sobel, *The Rise and Fall of the Conglomerate Kings* (Beard Books 1984) 118.

57 See, R Glenn Hubbard and D Palia, 'A Reexamination of the Conglomerate Merger Wave in the 1960s: An Internal Capital Markets View' (1999) 54(3) *J Fin* 1131.

58 *Ibid.* at 1150.

59 J Galbraith, *The New Industrial State* (Princeton UP 1967) 70.

60 For a critical perspective on this view, see Peter G Klein, 'Were Acquisitive Conglomerates Inefficient?' (2001) 32(4) The RAND Journal of Economics 745.

61 S Sassen, 'The locational and institutional embeddedness of electronic markets: the case of the global capital markets' in Mark Bevir and Frank Trentmann (eds), *Markets in Historical Contexts* (Cambridge University Press 2004).

had started the 1980s operating in dozens of industries operated in only one.[62] In parallel, the adoption of open-system standards by major players in the computer industry led to the weakening or abandonment of internal research and development within major corporations in favour of patenting, cross-licensing, outsourcing, and the takeover of start-ups. Technically, this was accompanied by the design and development of modular components that were manufactured by offshore companies and vertically integrated into niche markets. Financially, the shift was made possible through the rise of organised venture capital, cushioned by large investments from large retirement and pension funds.

This technological and economic transformation was built around a new mantra: shareholder value maximisation, which forms a key tenet of financial capitalism. The shareholder primacy principle changed managerial priorities from that of maximising growth by re-investing corporate savings in the long-term productive potential of the corporation (the 'principle of retain and re-invest') to that of maximising stock value through extensive buybacks of corporate stocks (share repurchase) in order to inflate stock prices as the resulting artificial scarcity of shares boosts their value.[63] Disciplined by a corporate market for control dominated by financial interests, in particular institutional investors, corporate managers became increasingly aligned with the interests of shareholders, and adopted strategies aiming to increase the price of their corporate stocks. They downsized their corporations (in particular cutting labour costs) in order to create short-term shareholder value and distributed the freed-up corporate revenues to financial interests, particularly shareholders, instead of re-investing them in the corporation (the principle of 'downsize and distribute').[64]

Literature on financialisation tells us that there are various characteristics of a 'financialised' firm: 1) pronounced institutional investor shareholding; 2) extensive influence of such institutional investors, including through voting rights; stock-based corporate remuneration; and 3) the distribution of cash to shareholders through dividend issues and share buybacks, typically at the expense of productive investment (for example, in research and development).[65] Put together, we may imagine a 'financialised firm' index, composed of these three elements, that indicates the extent to which a firm's corporate governance is guided by shareholder primacy. By examining GAFAM through the lens of these factors, we may determine whether their corporate governance resembles that of the post-war conglomerate or that of the post-1980 firm.

[62] G Davis, K Diekmann and Catherine H Tinsley, 'The Decline and Fall of the Conglomerate Firm in the 1980s: The Deinstitutionalization of an Organizational Form' (1994) 59(4) *American Sociological Review* 547.

[63] W Lazonick, 'Profits without Prosperity' *Harvard Business Review* (September 2014) https//hbr.org/2014/09/profits-without-prosperity; L Palladino, 'Stock Buybacks, Driving a High-Profit, Low Wage Economy' (*Roosevelt Institute*, March 20, 2018) http://rooseveltinstitute.org/stock-buybacks-high-profit-low-wage/.

[64] Lazonick (n 66)

[65] The presence of institutional investor shareholdings is a necessary (but insufficient) precondition for the financialisation of a firm. Institutional investors, through concentrating the stock ownership of dispersed asset holders, strengthen the voice of shareholders.

TABLE 16.1 *Institutional and non-institutional shareholdings in Big Tech*

Firm	Institutional investor shareholding (%)	Non-institutional investor shareholding (%)
Alphabet	80.4	19.6
Amazon	59.4	40.6
Apple	59.1	40.9
Facebook	81.4	18.6
Microsoft	72.2	27.8

Source: Yahoo Finance, as of 16 August 2021

Current accounts of the development of digital conglomerates do not take into consideration these internal (ownership structure and corporate governance-related) drives for the behaviour of Big Tech platforms. Nicolas Petit builds an argument for a competition law immunity of Big Tech platforms (which he calls 'moligopolies') distinguishing them from monopolies, as moligopolies 'channel sizeable amounts of resources into R&D' and invest in human resources, particularly entrepreneurship, thus indirectly referring to the fact that moligopolies retain their earnings and do not distribute.[66] However, this assertion is not factually supported. Marc Bourreau and Alexandre de Streel make the analogy with conglomerates, but they arrive at different conclusions than Petit, noting the gatekeeping role of Big Tech platforms and their ability to pre-empt competition by, from the outset, killing any opportunity for a potential competitor to emerge.[67] Similarly, Jean Tirole raises concerns as to the adoption of possible bundling practices that may exclude new entrants from the markets in which are active these conglomerates.[68] What is crucially missing from these analyses, however, is the consideration of the internal dynamics of each of these firms, as this is determined by their ownership structure and corporate governance, this time not in order to assess the broader social costs of digital platforms, but in order to gather elements that would help policy-makers to predict their behaviour.

We examine the ownership structure of Microsoft, Apple, Amazon, Alphabet, and Facebook. We observe that each firm is predominantly owned by institutional investors. Table 16.1 illustrates the proportion of GAFAM shares held by institutional investors versus non-institutional investors. Evidentially, institutional investors are major shareholders in GAFAM, cumulatively holding between three-fifths and four-fifths of their shares. However, these figures overstate the importance of institutional investors within the digital economy, especially within Google, Facebook,

[66] N Petit, 'Technology Giants, the Moligopoly Hypothesis and Holistic Competition: A Primer' (2016) https://papers.ssrn.com/sol3/papers.cfm?abstract_id=2856502, 65–66.

[67] M Bourreau and A de Streel, 'Conglomerates and EU Competition Policy', *Report of CERRE/CRIDS* (2019).

[68] J Tirole, 'Regulating the Disrupters', (livemint.com, 1 January 2019), www.livemint.com/Technology/XsgWUgy9tR4uaoME7xtITI/Regulating-the-disrupters-Jean-Tirole.html.

TABLE 16.2 *Investor voting rights in Big Tech*

Firm	Investor	Voting rights (%)
Google	Larry Page*	26.3
	Sergey Brin*	25.3
	Eric Schmidt*	4.5
	Vanguard	3.0
	BlackRock	2.7
	John Doerr*	1.5
Facebook	Mark Zuckerberg*	57.7
	Eduardo Saverin*	6.9
	Dustin Moskovitz*	3.8
	Vanguard	2.7
	BlackRock	2.3
	Fidelity	1.8
Amazon	Jeffrey Bezos	14.0
	Vanguard	6.4
	BlackRock	5.5
Apple	Vanguard	7.8
	BlackRock	6.6
	Berkshire Hathaway	6.0
Microsoft	Vanguard	8.2
	BlackRock	6.8

Note: * indicates individual investor holding disproportionately weighted voting shares.
Source: Securities and Exchange Commission 2020 10-K filings.

and Amazon. Google and Facebook offer dual-class shareholdings. Share class differentiation reduces the strength of the link between observed shareholding and voting rights, skewing voting rights heavily towards firm insiders. Although Amazon's share structure is more traditional, with one vote per share, Jeff Bezos owns a clear majority of shares.[69] Microsoft and Apple also adhere to a traditional share structure, with institutional investors dominating share ownership and therefore voting rights. This is illustrated in Table 16.2, which shows the investors with notable voting rights in Google, Facebook, Amazon, Apple, and Microsoft, respectively. Although institutional investors hold a majority of stock in GAFAM, they are not necessarily endowed with the greatest voting rights. Rather, individuals,

[69] Alphabet has three classes of shares: Class A shares, which confer one vote per share; Class B shares, which confer 10 votes per share; and Class C shares, which do not confer any voting rights. Only Class A and Class C are available to purchase on public equity markets, with Class B owned only by insiders and not publicly traded. Similarly, Facebook has a dual class share structure: Class A shares conferring one vote per share and Class B shares conferring 10 votes per share. Class A can be publicly traded, while Class B is reserved for insiders. On dual class shareholding more broadly, see M Moore, 'Designing Dual-Class Sunsets: The Case for a Transfer-Centered Approach' (2020) 12(1) *Wm & Mary Bus L Rev* 93.

typically founders, retain the most significant voting power in Alphabet, Facebook, and Amazon.

After institutional investor share ownership and voting power, the next aspect of firm financialisation to consider is how corporate executives are remunerated. In this regard, GAFAM companies may be viewed as more conventionally financialised. Although the chief executive officers of Alphabet, Amazon, Apple, and Facebook did not receive stock-based compensation in 2020, the other C-suite level executives at these firms did. All C-suite executives at Microsoft, including its chief executive officer, Satya Nadella, received stock-based compensation in 2020.

The final component of the hypothesised financialised firm index is to consider how much cash each of the GAFAM firms distributes to shareholders through dividend issuances and share buybacks. Ordinarily, there is a view that financialised firms distribute their cash to shareholders at the expense of making longer-term productive investments. Again, the situation with GAFAM is complex and does not fit neatly into this narrative. While both Microsoft and Apple buy back shares and issue dividends, Amazon does not buy back its own shares or issue dividends, and Alphabet and Facebook, although they buy their own stock, do not issue dividends. Furthermore, as is frequently pointed out, these companies also invest heavily in research and development. Digital platforms seem to constitute a hybrid of the old managerial 'retain and reinvest' and the financialisation 'downsize and distribute' models.

Based on the above observations, we find an interesting paradox – despite the tremendous goodwill that GAFAM enjoy in capital markets, they are not uniformly financialised in accordance with the three parameters noted above. Rather, we find a mixed picture, with the corporate governance regimes of Amazon, Facebook, and Google closer to the managerialism of the post-war conglomerates and Apple and Microsoft closer to the shareholder-centric firm that characterises financial capitalism. We hope that the exercise undertaken here, opening the black box of corporate governance, may promote a more nuanced understanding of GAFAM going forward.[70]

16.5 CONCLUSIONS

In this chapter, we explore a missing dimension of the discussion over Big Tech platforms in competition law: financialisation and its impact on competitive strategies and the social impact of Big Tech's economic power. We draw on insights from economics and corporate governance to offer a broader analysis of the five major digital platforms. We offer three contributions. First, we argue that financialisation and futurity have played a prominent role in GAFAM's expansion. Second, taking

70 See McLean (n 8); P Regibeau and I Lianos, 'Digital Mergers: A Primer' (5 May 2021) available at https://papers.ssrn.com/sol3/papers.cfm?abstract_id=3837281 accessed 21 November 2021.

into account the social dimension of financialisation and the heavily skewed distribution of stock ownership in society, we argue that the distributional implications of Big Tech Power and of competition law enforcement, respectively, need to be assessed more systematically. We examine that the tool of agent-based modelling may contribute to this analysis and help us move beyond the traditional focus on consumer welfare. Third, we explore as an additional dimension of financialisation the role of ownership structure and corporate governance in influencing the broader economic model of behaviour followed by Big Tech platforms and we offer an empirical examination of GAFAM's corporate governance regimes, interrogating the conglomerate analogy frequently invoked in the digital economy,

For EU product safety concerns, contact us at Calle de José Abascal, 56–1°, 28003 Madrid, Spain or eugpsr@cambridge.org.

www.ingramcontent.com/pod-product-compliance
Lightning Source LLC
LaVergne TN
LVHW011704200926
848484LV00004B/1063
9781108841870